Strategic Pervasive Computing Applications: Emerging Trends

Varuna Godara
Sydney College of Management, Australia

INFORMATION SCIENCE REFERENCE

Hershey · New York

Director of Editorial Content:	Kristin Klinger
Director of Book Publications:	Julia Mosemann
Acquisitions Editor:	Lindsay Johnston
Development Editor:	Christine Bufton
Publishing Assistant:	Deanna Zombro
Typesetter:	Devvin Earnest
Quality control:	Jamie Snavely
Cover Design:	Lisa Tosheff
Printed at:	Yurchak Printing Inc.

Published in the United States of America by
Information Science Reference (an imprint of IGI Global)
701 E. Chocolate Avenue
Hershey PA 17033
Tel: 717-533-8845
Fax: 717-533-8661
E-mail: cust@igi-global.com
Web site: http://www.igi-global.com/reference

Library of Congress Cataloging-in-Publication Data

Strategic pervasive computing applications : emerging trends / Varuna Godara, editor.
    p. cm.
  Includes bibliographical references and index.
  Summary: "The focus of this book is on the ever increasing capacity of
Pervasive context-aware applications that are aiming to develop into context-
responsive applications in different application areas"--Provided by
publisher.
  ISBN 978-1-61520-753-4 (hardcover) -- ISBN 978-1-61520-754-1 (ebook) 1.
Ubiquitous computing. 2. Context-aware computing. 3. Application software.
I. Godara, Varuna.
  QA76.5915.S873 2010
  005.3--dc22
                          2009050069

British Cataloguing in Publication Data
A Cataloguing in Publication record for this book is available from the British Library.

All work contributed to this book is new, previously-unpublished material. The views expressed in this book are those of the authors, but not necessarily of the publisher.

Dedicated to Subhash my Husband and Siddharth my son

Sudhir kumar, *CCS Haryana Agricultural University, India*
Usha Manjunath, *Birla Institute of Technology and Science, India*
Deo Prakash Vidyarthi, *Jawaharlal Nehru University, India*
Jambhika Godara, *Leica Microsystems, Australia*
Ramesh Kumari Mehta, *CCS Haryana Agricultural University, India*
Petr Tucnik, *University of Hradec Kralove, Czech Republic*
Sayel Ramadhan, *Ahlia University, Kingdom of Bahrain*

Table of Contents

Section 1
Foundation, Software and Technology of Pervasive Computing

Section 2
Securing Pervasive Computing Environment

Section 3
Applications of Pervasive Computing

Section 4
Pervasive Healthcare

Section 5
Pervasive Education

Detailed Table of Contents

Section 1
Foundation, Software and Technology of Pervasive Computing

This chapter gives introduction of Pervasive computing including pervasive devices, middleware, and applications and proposes a Pervasive computing system that is unobtrusively embedded in the environment, is completely connected, intuitive, effortlessly portable, and constantly available. This chapter explains concepts of Gaze tracking, magic pointing, geometry sensitive devices, etc and discusses future trends of Pervasive computing including wearable computers, smart homes and smart buildings, etc. It details the pervasive computing tools such as application-specific integrated circuitry (ASIC); speech recognition; gesture recognition; system on a chip (SoC); perceptive interfaces; smart matter; flexible transistors; reconfigurable processors; field programmable logic gates (FPLG); and micro electromechanical systems (MEMS), etc.

Chapter 2

This chapter emphasises that the choice of kernel function and its parameter is very important for better performance of support vector machine. It proposes few new kernel functions which satisfy the Mercer's conditions and a robust algorithm to automatically determine the suitable kernel function and its parameters based on AdaBoost to improve the performance of support vector machine. Based on experiments this chapter suggest that for different data sets, the Gaussian kernel is not always the best choice to achieve high generalization of support vector machine classifier.

This chapter presents the application of periodic wave concepts in management of software Parallel processing projects or processes. This chapter proposes a new and dynamic way to control the software project estimation activity of Runaway project/processes, thereby reducing their future occurrences. This chapter also explains how the equations of unidirectional periodic Waves can be applied in software Parallel processing to measure quality and project execution in a dynamic way at any point in time. The concepts proposed here are dynamic unlike PERT/CPM and other metrics, which fail in worst-case scenarios.

Chapter 4

This chapter discusses Pervasive computing and requirements to develop software components that are reusable across the pervasive computing applications. It emphasises the requirement of considering the variations and properties (mobility, adaptability, composability, context awareness etc.) that may be required for different pervasive computing applications (application types). It describes Component based software engineering and proposes a model of "Generic Component" with 'Component Generator' that generates components according to the requirements of a specific pervasive computing application. Based on research this chapter starts a discussion and calls for more extensive research oriented studies by professionals and academicians for perfection of the model

Section 2
Securing Pervasive Computing Environment

Chapter 5

Security is the primary concern of the users of pervasive computing and so is of the service providers. Cryptography is used for safe message transmission in Pervasive environment also which requires a secret key. This chapter explains the key management service that includes initializing the end users of the key, generating the key, distributing the key to each user, installing the key at each user, controlling the usage of the key, updating the key, revoking the old key and destroying the old key. This chapter discusses the key establishment issues for securing pervasive wireless sensor networks. It describes key establishment schemes and various issues in establishing a secret key.

This chapter recognises the importance of security in Mobile Ad hoc Network (MANET)/ Wireless Sensor Network (WSN) and discusses the functioning of Route Falsification Attack and explains how it is easy to launch Route Falsification Attack in MANETs or wireless ad hoc network. It further explains the how a Secure Hybrid Routing Information Protocol (SRIP) can be implemented to prevent route falsification attack in MANETs. This chapter further evaluates performance of SRIP in Qualnet Simulator with and without route falsification attack and suggest suitability of SRIP to stop this attack.

This chapter discusses the dynamic property of pervasive computing that hinders users to have complete knowledge of the relationship among services, service providers, and credentials. In this chapter a progressive approach to solve the problem of secure service discovery is explained in which users and service providers expose partial information in turn and avoid unnecessary exposure if there is any mismatch. On the basis of experiments this chapter proposes that this approach protects sensitive information with little overhead.

Chapter 8

This chapter addresses the security problems in Pervasive computing that has lots of applications in military, medical and smart home domain. It discusses Pervasive networks, ad hoc networks and a prominent on-demand reactive routing protocol for mobile ad hoc networks known as AODV (Ad Hoc On demand Distance Vector). It explains that in existing AODV, there is no security provision against well-known attack known as "Black hole attack". This chapter further presents the watchdog mechanism for the AODV routing protocol to detect misbehaviour based on promiscuous listening. The proposed method first detects a black hole node and then gives a new route bypassing this node.

Section 3
Applications of Pervasive Computing

Chapter 9

Mei-Chih Hu, National Tsing Hua Univeristy, Taiwan
Chien-Hung Liu, Feng Chia University, Taiwan
Ching-Yan Wu, Macquarie University, Australia

This chapter details the causes of developing a wireless city especially the wireless city cases of Singapore and Taipei. It discusses in context the Diffusion of Innovations theory and Technology acceptance model. The chapter then explores the impact of factors influencing consumer usage behavior on the development of wireless cities with diverse resource bases. The chapter describes three variables including service quality and extended applications, price of usage and government policy and business strategy that influence the two internalized innovation and technology acceptance beliefs of perceived usefulness and perceived ease of use in the emerging wireless city. The chapter concludes that the internal and external influencing factors are related to each other and to the innovation adoption intentions during the development of a wireless city. It also suggests that the factors influencing innovation adoption intentions have varying impacts on the development of a wireless city given the diverse resource bases available.

Chapter 10

Chun Kwong Han, Universiti Putra Malaysia, Malaysia

This chapter addresses the fact that in developing countries of Asia, various new knowledge and ICT mega-projects aimed at pervasive computing are being designed and executed at the international, national, state and industry levels to sustain competitiveness. These countries are in the process of transitioning from a production economy to a knowledge-based economy (k-economy). This chapter gives introduction to a new world of knowledge economy, innovation and dream economies followed by a section on limits to knowledge and ways of seeing and doing. It discusses the structuration theory that initially had nothing to do with pervasive computing but given the pervasiveness of technology in organizations' everyday operations, especially in reality construction; various attempts have been made to extend Giddens's ideas by including an explicit IT dimension in social analysis. The chapter further clarifies that the structures and processes by which these "knowledge super corridors" are developed and implemented are complex economic-social-political decisions. Therefore with help of two case studies concerned with formulating and implementing a k-economy, this chapter illustrates and assesses an in-depth understanding of the knowledge super corridors. It draws various success strategies for the implementation of pervasive computing from analyses based on the structurational framework.

Chapter 11

Joydip Dhar, Indian Institute of Information Technology and Management, India
Abhishek Vaid, Indian Institute of Information Technology and Management, India
Manyata Goyal, Indian Institute of Information Technology and Management, India
Shilp Gupta, Indian Institute of Information Technology and Management, India

Shilp Gupta, ABV – Indian Institute of Information Technology and Management, Gwalior, M.P., India
This chapter recognises the need for Online Test Management Systems and gives example of various examinations conducted online. It identifies automated question selection as an emerging problem in the industry of Online Test Management and details the features of the existing systems. This chapter presents a novel technique for administering question sets in an intelligent and automated approach. It further explains how Artificial Intelligence, in the form of Self Organizing Feature Maps is utilized for question selection process.

Section 4
Pervasive Healthcare

Chapter 12

Ankur Choubey, Institute of Technology & Management, India
Ramesh Singh, National Informatics Centre, India

This chapter emphasises the importance of non-verbal behaviour as a major factor in the efficient human-computer interaction. It describes the evolution of Neuro-Linguistic Programming and proposes a hypothetical model to study the use of Neuro-Linguistic Programming and computing system as an aid to cognizance and perception of human interactions. It suggests that by successful modelling the interaction between humans and the computers, including robots can be made more natural. It discusses various uses of NLP including Psychotherapy, Interpersonal Communication Skills, Artificial intelligence, B.P.O., entertainment etc.

Chapter 13

Anubhav Kumar Singh, National Institute of Technology, India
Ramesh Singh, National Informatics Centre, India

This chapter gives the reference of researches that explain that the mental and psychological disorders are rising today among the general population. It describes Tele-immersive technology as one of the various advanced methods and techniques that have been developed to combat these disorders. It explains Tele-Immersion as a technology which uses immersive cooperative environments over long distances. It has an immediate application in psychotherapy where psychologists can control and monitor their patients and their immersive treatments over long distances. This chapter presents one such application model based in a tele-immersive environment and is based on the ongoing research on Tele-immersive systems and their applications at National Informatics Centre, New Delhi, India.

Chapter 14

Lutfi Mohammed Omer Khanbary, University of Aden, Yemen
Deo Prakash Vidyarthi, Jawaharlal Nehru University, India

This chapter discusses the Genetic Algorithm in detail and presents the mobility management model for healthcare services developed for the efficient utilization of the network infrastructure. The chapter also explains a framework to describe the relations between types of hospitals and specialists with the use of Hospital Information Systems (HIS). The model for pervasive healthcare is to manage the specialists' movements between the hospital nodes with the objective to serve the maximum number of patients in minimum amount of time and the experiments show that this model performs better in servicing the patients in the service area.

Section 5
Pervasive Education

Chapter 15

This chapter comprehensively examines the differences in learning approaches in e-learning environment. It starts with the discussion on the importance of reviewing the educational courses and the delivery approaches when class-sizes are increasing, expectations of international students are differing, student's mobility is increasing and computer technology is penetrating all the interaction points and processes of students and educational institutes especially teaching. It explains the vital strategy of understanding how students learn to enhance learning outcomes and provide more satisfying learning experience to students. This chapter is based on an exploratory study which focused on a group of students in a second year business marketing module in an Australian university, when e-learning system was considered as the primary communication and the learning resource for them. It further looks at the relationship between various demographic factors and various learning outcomes including deep and surface learning.

Chapter 16

This chapter focuses on the importance of teaching AmI tools and methods to the students who are potential Managers or IT professionals so that when they enter workforce they have the abilities to define requirements for the structure and behaviour of AmI from various angles including from final users' perspective. It discusses the background of Ubiquitous Computing and Ambient intelligence including AmI networks, and goals and actors of AmI scenarios. It recognises that the AmI systems are of very high level of complexity and describes a holistic approach to Ambient Intelligence. It finally briefs the situation in the selected Czech university relevant to teaching Ambient Intelligence to the students.

Chapter 17

This chapter addresses the fact that University System is confronted with a changed environment which necessitates re-engineering of the higher education. It proposes framework of a new Pedagogic System that can be embedded in the Knowledge Management System, in seamless manner, through pervasive computing. This chapter suggests that the University system should deliver graduates who can be directly absorbed into industry and therefore proposes a complete change in the University *philosophy* and *methods. The re-engineering proposal includes*: e-learning and blended learning, pervasive computing, distance and open learning and an outcomes approach to pedagogy.

Chapter 18 explains the future of Pervasive computing environment followed by introduction of the concept of Virtual Vidyalaya as one of the applications of Pervasive computing. It describes the increasing use of pervasive computing enabled e-learning not only in corporate training world but also in the different sections of society. It further discusses the pervasive devices used in elearning and recommends some strategies for a successful, effective and efficient implementation of Virtual Vidyalaya system.

Chapter 19

Starting with the transition of various economies and societies from hunting and gathering economy to the information economy this chapter explores the impact of instructional design elements and discipline area on the quantity of learner-learner interactions. It reviews the literature on student's interaction, student's perceptions in various contexts including online environment and different aspects of distance education. This chapter is based on the study in which data was collected from the online courses offered at one of the major Rocky Mountain University. The chapter concludes with the result of a negative relationship between group size and overall interaction and that the interactivity in an online class depends on group size, grade weight for discussion, use of web 2.0 technologies and multimedia and the discipline it belongs to.

Foreword

Pervasive computing, ubiquitous computing and ambient intelligence. These are just three phrases which describe a rapidly growing area of research and, especially in recent times, the phrases also describe numerous innovative applications of computing. Novel combinations of hardware and software are required to realize applications embedded in our daily life and work. A key aspect of pervasive computing involves embedding sensing, networking and computation into everyday objects and everyday life processes. To do this is non-trivial and involves innovations that will continue many years from now. Innovations include new concept systems that previously are not feasible but now feasible due to fundamental advances in hardware and networking.

This book provides an exciting overview of developments in pervasive computing technology, security concerns in pervasive computing and innovative applications and strategic trends. While in recent years, numerous authored and edited books have emerged in the area of pervasive computing, this book provides an important "brick" towards building the pervasive computing "high tower", with diverse perspectives. I trust you will enjoy the range and diversity of, not only technology, but also applications this book offers, while capturing the spirit of making computing ubiquitous and pervasive.

The pervasive computing vision has reached across the globe so that work on the area is being carried out in numerous groups worldwide, in developed and developing economies and nations. Recent conferences in pervasive computing suggest extensive work done in different continents, and this book includes contributions from India, USA, Australia and Taiwan.

Pervasive computing is multifaceted; it is not only technological issues of software development or hardware design that are concerns, but also user acceptance and adoption of the technologies, touching on policy and management issues, be it company-wide or city-wide, as also noted in this book. Since pervasive computing applications affects daily life and influences aspects of our life, including health care and simply interacting with computers, specific applications in healthcare or general human-computer interaction are also considered in this book.

Indeed strategic applications of pervasive computing to maximise benefit and acceptance is still fairly unexplored ground even as new technologies continue to emerge without necessarily immediate uptake. For example, if I could track the locations of employees, as a manager, should I do so, and what benefits would there be in doing so? If a hospital could track where its equipment goes, how would that be helpful versus the cost and maintenance required – would that help in resource allocation? If I could interact by voice with a system or with the machines in the office, is that beneficial? If I could add wireless access to materials for the company or restaurant, is that beneficial? How would mobile services and location-based systems impact on healthcare and the environment? How could sensor networks be used in healthcare, business process, manufacturing or environment monitoring effectively? The question of strategically applying such technology for business or individuals, or for a city or nation, remains an interesting one, and this book is aptly titled.

Seng W. Loke, PhD
July 2009
Reader and Associate Professor
Department of Computer Science and Computer Engineering,
La Trobe University, Australia

Seng W. Loke *is a Reader and Associate Professor at the Department of Computer Science and Computer Engineering in La Trobe University. He leads pervasive computing research at La Trobe, and has authored 'Context-Aware Pervasive Systems: Architectures for a New Breed of Applications' published by Auerbach (CRC Press), Dec 2006. He has (co-) authored more than 180 research publications including work on context-aware computing, and mobile and pervasive computing. He research has been published in journals such as IEEE Pervasive, Knowledge Engineering Review, Elsevier'sPervasive and Mobile Computing Journal, and Theory and Practice of Logic Programming.*

Preface

There is no question about the ability of computing to offer unlimited solutions, although complexity has been a very big problem for not only the application developers and the maintenance teams, but also for the users. Intention of the developers of Pervasive computing applications is to reduce the complexity, extend ad-hoc process based programming, limit innovation and maintenance costs, increase portability and offer absolutely networked sensor nodes to empower the users without them realizing their presence. Pervasive computing, Ubiquitous computing or transparent computing they all are proving to be incredible technology that have the capacity to empower individuals by equipping them with the small or little tools to look after their health and wellness, work, enjoy, communicate and stay in touch, while they are mobile. Pervasive computing can initiate and allow communities to develop and communicate their mission, culture and agendas and grow across the physical location or time. For business as well as non-business organizations it is aiming to be a receiver of real-time corporate data, a creator of an up-to-date knowledge base and a link connecting business intelligence, business processes and business rules engines.

The focus of this book is on the ever increasing capacity of Pervasive context-aware applications that are aiming to develop into context-responsive applications in different application areas. The real value to the users and effective ubiquity do not come from just the embedded sensors, mobile and portable devices, middleware or end user applications, and networks, it also needs support of different other technological components such as perpetual user interfaces, Power line Carrier Systems (PCS), gesture and motion readers, emotion processors, tracking- marking- visualisation terminals, Neuro Linguistic Programming, Genetic Algorithms, high performance computing involving micro electromechanical systems (MEMS), etc, multicore parallel computing, field programmable logic gates (FPLG), Software Parallel Processing, symmetric multiprocessing (SMP), Data warehousing (DW), ad hoc sensor networks, flexible transistors, application-specific integrated circuitry (ASIC), system on a chip (SoC), reconfigurable processors and much more. This book includes the trends in Pervasive computing applications and discusses in details various applications of Pervasive computing such as Gaze tracking, knowledge super corridors, magic pointing, Automatic Question Set Generation, geometry sensitive devices, Tele- Immersive Psychotherapy, wearable computers, smart homes and smart buildings, smart matter, wireless cities, etc.

In continuation to various tools and technologies involved in Pervasive computing this book discusses the types of multi-class classification algorithms and identifies Support Vector Machine (SVM) as most accepted classification technique in literature. It recognizes choice of kernel function and its parameter as very important for better performance of support vector machine. To improve the performance of support vector machine the author proposes the use of AdaBoost approach and presents new kernel functions and a robust algorithm to automatically determine the suitable kernel function and its parameters.

Project management is an important yet controversial management discipline. Projects drive businesses irrespective of the industry sector. They ruin the businesses as well with the cost, time and pain unless they are carefully planned, rolled out and implemented. Sometimes these projects can't start on time, sometimes project managers can't work within limits and sometimes they don't identify problems in the project stages in time. Pervasive computing projects are no exceptions. This book discusses the application of periodic wave concepts in the management of Parallel execution of projects or software. It proposes new and dynamic way of using periodic wave equations to estimate the flow of execution of the critical or run-away project that scores over the PERT/CPM due to its dynamic nature.

In order to provide dynamic and ad hoc services in Pervasive computing environment it is important to consider developing reusable software components. Different architectures such as Product-line architectures are being used to assist in reusing the software components across Pervasive computing settings. These reusable software components are small in size and are designed to be adaptive to heterogeneous hardware platforms and are capable of being delivered by air. This book discusses variations and properties that may be required for different pervasive computing applications and describes Component based software engineering. It proposes a "Generic Component" model with 'Component Generator' that generates pervasive computing application-based components.

Security and privacy provision is one of the major focuses of Pervasive service providers, applications developer and the users. It is worth discussing various security mechanisms in Pervasive networks including Mobile Ad hoc Networks (MANETs) and wireless sensor networks, which use different protocols and algorithms, and ensure integrity of data, access control and authentication. Cryptographic algorithms, that require secret key, are used in transmitting information safely. This book covers the explanation of the key management service and key establishment schemes in the context of pervasive computing environment. It contains the explanations on the processes including key generation, key distribution to each user, key installation at each user's end, key usage control, key updating process, revoking the old key and destroying the old key.

Pervasive computing applications involve sensors, controls, adaptive software, portable hardware and networks, and are facing increasing number of security attacks aimed at some or all of the components of the applications these days. This book describes various security attacks in pervasive computing and identifies the need for high assurance security and defence mechanisms. It discusses the functioning of Route Falsification Attacks in MANETs and how a Secure Hybrid Routing Information Protocol (SRIP) can avoid route falsification attack. It further explains that in on-demand reactive routing protocol for mobile ad hoc networks known as AODV (Ad Hoc On demand Distance Vector), there is no security provision against Black hole attack. Then it gives explanation of how the watchdog mechanism for the AODV routing protocol can be used to detect misbehavior based on promiscuous listening.

In order to obtain maximum benefit of the technologies and serve the residents, all the cities and remote areas must get completely wirelessly networked. Seamless wireless and pervasive technology enabled cities will make the lives much safer, secure and easier by capturing and delivering real-time information of the events and accidents, and directing the residents in case of emergencies. The wireless cities will benefit students, businesses, police, traffic controllers, hospitals, travelers, neighbors and other entities by keeping them informed. These projects are valuable for the cities and yet expensive and face many challenges such as user behaviors and capacity to pay, government policies and alignment of wireless city projects with their strategies, the business model for wireless city development, business innovations and their network usage plans, operational issues of the pervasive technology, lack of infrastructure for installation of pervasive equipment and sensors. This book includes the discussion on wireless city applications and explores the causes of developing a wireless city and the impact of consumer usage behavior on the development of wireless cities with diverse resource bases. It talks about the knowledge economy and knowledge super corridors, and draws various success strategies for the implementation of pervasive computing from analyses based on the structurational framework.

Seamless wireless networks and the portable mobile devices help students access the learning material in an interactive mode and benefit from the blended E-learning applications. PDAs, ipods and other little devices are being used for elearning and off campus distance learning. Students download the study material on their devices and study wherever they like and whenever they like in a given time period. Many researches are being conducted on prospects and consequences of such a use. Behavioral scientists and education specialists are taking interest in studying the change in learning behavior and positive or negative impact of this technology on different age groups. Part of interactive pervasive elearning is testing the learning outcomes. We, therefore, need to develop interactive examination Systems. This book discusses the application area Online Test Management Systems, details the features and identifies automated question selection as an emerging problem. It also proposes a technique for administering question sets in an intelligent and automated approach.

Human computer interaction is an area that has broadened its scope from fixed desktops to every day pervasive computing devices which are wireless, embedded, mobile and portable. It is important to study the impact of the human interaction with these devices and minimise the negative impact. This book includes a chapter on the significance of non-verbal behaviour on the efficient human-computer interaction and the description of hypothetical model to study the use of Neuro-Linguistic Programming and computing system as an aid to cognizance and perception of human interactions. It looks into the importance of successful modelling in making interaction between humans and the computers including robots more natural. It also discusses various uses of NLP including Psychotherapy, Interpersonal Communication Skills, Artificial intelligence, B.P.O., entertainment etc.

Tele-immersion is one of the collaborative technologies that create a simulated environment for geographically scattered group members to cooperate with each other in real-time. Many Psychotherapists and doctors are using this technology to treat an increasing number of patients suffering from mental and psychological disorders from long distances. This book explains Tele-immersive technology as an advanced method to combat these disorders and describes how its applications in psychotherapy help psychologists control and monitor their patients and their immersive treatments over long distances. The objective of pervasive computing applications is to optimize the efficiency and effectiveness of the doctors and minimize the location constraints to serve maximum number of patients. This book further explains the application of Genetic Algorithm in the mobility management model for healthcare services developed for the efficient utilization of the network infrastructure. It further uses a framework to describe the relations between types of hospitals and specialists with the use of Hospital Information Systems (HIS). It proposes a model for pervasive healthcare to manage the specialists' movements between the hospital nodes to serve the maximum number of patients in minimum amount of time.

Another primary feature of this book is its focus on pervasive education environment that can be used to enhance student learning by incorporating both formal and informal learning interactions without fixed time constraints. Pervasive simulation games can be used to make the learning environment more adaptive, reduce extensive cognitive load, and learner's need based. Chapter 15 focuses on learning approaches in e-learning environment when class sizes and student mobility are increasing. It discusses the penetration of computer technology into different interaction points and processes of students and educational institutes especially teaching. It explains the issues of surface and deep learning and discusses how students learn to enhance learning outcomes and how to provide more satisfying learning experience to students. Chapter 16 identifies and discusses in detail the significance of teaching Ambient Intelligence (AmI) tools and methods to the students who are potential Managers or IT professionals. It describes AmI systems as having very high level of complexity. It also describes a holistic approach to

Ambient Intelligence. Chapter 17 reinforces the fact that educational organizations are facing challenges of dynamic environment which requires re-engineering of the higher education that includes e-learning, blended learning, pervasive computing, and distance and open learning. It presents a framework of a new Pedagogic System that can be embedded in the Knowledge Management System, in seamless manner, through pervasive computing. Chapter 18 gives introduction of Virtual Vidyalaya that uses Pervasive computing environment for e-learning. This chapter recommends some strategies for successful, effective and efficient implementation of Virtual Vidyalaya system. Chapter 19 discusses the transition of various economies and societies from hunting and gathering economy to the information economy. It further describes various aspects of instructional design elements, learner-learner interactions, student's perceptions, online and distance education.

Success of Pervasive computing lies in the appropriate use of theories of human psychology and behavior in development of applications. Cognitive theories on attention and memory can be used in developing advertising applications, whereas theories on intelligence, problem solving and decision-making can be used in developing BI applications. Due to high returns on investment Game industry is one of the first industries to attract application developers of pervasive technology. Children spend hours on pervasive devices to play games and if developmental theories related to parental styles, attachment theories, moral development and role playing are properly used while developing these applications, it can reduce the worry of parents to some extent. Latest researches depict that toddlers and preschool kids are spending much time on computer games and mobile phone games rather spending time on playing in grounds or listening to stories. Pervasive computing has by and large the capacity to empower parents, individuals, students, doctors, patients and society if the applications being developed are carefully designed and used.

Varuna Godara

CEO
Sydney College of Management, Australia
3 September 2009

Acknowledgment

I express my gratitude to all the authors of different chapters in this book who conceived and detailed the chapters and helped shaping the book. This book is the result of joint efforts, patience and commitment of everybody who contributed to this book.

I would like to thank Seng Loke, La Trobe University, Australia, for writing a foreword for this book and am grateful to all the colleagues at different universities and organizations who reviewed this edition.

I am indebted to all my colleagues at University of Western Sydney especially Graydon Davison (Head of School), Stephen Waters (Associate head of School) and Rakesh Agrawal for their continuous support and valuable insights. I must thank the team at IGI Global in compilation of this book. I benefited from the excellent advice and directions from my acquisition editor.

My overriding debt to my husband, Subhash Bishnoi, who provided me with the time and support needed to prepare this book. I acknowledge the love, affection and blessings of my mother in-law Maya Devi and father in-law Manohar Lal Bishnoi, which inspired me. I express my loving thanks towards my elder sister Smriti and her husband Pradeep Poonia, younger sister Jambhika and her husband Nipun Sagar and brother Chaitanya for never ending love and encouragement.

Feelings from core of my heart could not be expressed in words for the vision, real encouragement, love and affection by my mother Chander Kala and father Nathu Ram Godara. Many thanks to my son Siddharth who sacrificed the fun we could have together while I was working on this book project. In fact it is our book.

Varuna Godara

CEO
Sydney College of Management, Australia
September 2009

Section 1
Foundation, Software and Technology of Pervasive Computing

Chapter 1
Recent Trends in Pervasive and Ubiquitous Computing:
A Survey

Ramesh Singh
National Informatics Centre, India

ABSTRACT

Pervasive computing is the trend towards increasingly ubiquitous connected computing devices in the environment, a trend being brought about by a convergence of advanced electronic – and particularly, wireless - technologies and the Internet. Pervasive computing devices are not personal computers but very tiny - even invisible - devices, either mobile or embedded in almost any type of object imaginable, including cars, tools, appliances, clothing and various consumer goods – all communicating through increasingly interconnected networks. In the future these smart devices will maintain current information about their locations, the contexts in which they are being used, and relevant data about the users. The goal of researchers is to create a system that is pervasively and unobtrusively embedded in the environment, completely connected, intuitive, effortlessly portable, and constantly available. Among the emerging technologies expected to prevail in the pervasive computing environment of the future are wearable computers, smart homes and smart buildings. Among the myriad of tools expected to support these are: application-specific integrated circuitry (ASIC); speech recognition; gesture recognition; system on a chip (SoC); perceptive interfaces; smart matter; flexible transistors; reconfigurable processors; field programmable logic gates (FPLG); and micro electromechanical systems (MEMS).

DOI: 10.4018/978-1-61520-741-1.ch001

PERVASIVE COMPUTING MODEL

The technological advances necessary to build a pervasive computing environment fall into four broad areas: devices, networking, middleware, and applications.

Devices

An intelligent environment is likely to contain many different device types:

- Traditional input devices, such as mice or keyboards, and output devices, such as speakers or light-emitting diodes;
- wireless mobile devices, such as pagers, personal digital assistants, cell phones, palmtops, and so on;
- Smart devices, such as intelligent appliances, floor tiles with embedded sensors, and biosensors.

Ideally, pervasive computing should encompass every device worldwide that has built-in active and passive intelligence.

Pervasive Networking

The number of pervasive devices is expected to multiply rapidly over the next few years. There will be more than 300 million PDAs; two billion consumer electronic devices, such as wireless phones, pagers, and set-top boxes; and five billion additional everyday devices, such as vending machines, refrigerators, and washing machines embedded with chips and connected to a pervasive network. As a consequence of this proliferation, many current technologies must be revamped. In addition to extending the backbone infrastructure to meet the anticipated demand, global networks like the Internet also must modify existing applications to completely integrate these pervasive computing devices into existing social systems.

Pervasive Middleware

Like distributed computing and mobile computing, pervasive computing requires a middleware "shell" to interface between the networking kernel and the end-user applications running on pervasive devices. This pervasive middleware will mediate interactions with the networking kernel on the user's behalf and will keep users immersed in the pervasive computing space. The middleware will consist mostly of firmware and software bundles executing in either client-server or peer-to-peer mode. User interfaces are another aspect of middleware. Standard Web browsers represent the high end of interface sophistication. They use more color, graphics, and controls than users typically expect on pervasive devices. Mobile computing has already introduced micro-browsers.

Pervasive Applications

Pervasive computing is more environment-centric than either Web-based or mobile computing. This means that applications will guide the middleware and networking issues to a large extent. Consider a heart patient wearing an implanted monitor that communicates wirelessly with computers trained to detect and report abnormalities. The monitor should know when to raise the alarm, based on its knowledge about the environment. So this is much more than simple wireless communication.

PERVASIVE COMPUTING TECHNOLOGIES

Perceptual Interfaces

Gaze Tracking

Attentive user interfaces are related to perceptual user interfaces (PUI), which incorporate Multimodal input, multimedia output, and human-like perceptual capabilities to create systems with natural human-computer interactions. Whereas the emphasis of PUI is on coordinating perception in human and machine, the emphasis of AUI is on directing attention in human and machine. For a system to attend to a user it must not only perceive the user but it must also anticipate the user. The key lies not in how it picks up information from the user or how it displays information to the user; rather, the key lies in how the user is modeled and what inferences are made about the user. Critical to AUI is multimodal input: speech, gesture, eye gaze, and so on. Eye gaze plays an important role in human-human communication; for instance, a speaker normally focuses attention on the listener by looking, and looking away or avoiding eye-contact may reflect hesitation, embarrassment, or shyness (Campbell, et. al., 2000). SUITOR (Simple User Interest Tracker) it fills a scrolling ticker on a computer screen with information related to the user's current task. SUITOR knows where you are looking, what applications you are running, and what Web pages you may be browsing. If a person is reading a Web page about IBM, for instance, the system presents the latest stock price or business news stories that could affect IBM. If he reads the headline off the ticker, it pops up the story in a browser window. Thus it is an attentive system—one that attends to what people are doing, typing, reading, so that it can attend to the information they need.

Magic Pointing

It allows humans' eyes to affect the movement of the cursor. Having the eyes wholly determine cursor movement turns out to be impractical because many eye movements are Involuntary. If we try to control the cursor with our eyes, we'll quickly find ourselves exhausted and confused. The gaze-tracking cameras follow our eyes, but your fingers have to be involved as well. As soon as we touch the pointing device, the cursor jumps precisely to the point of our gaze.

Within five years, eye-tracking technology will be common, if not ubiquitous, as people find themselves living and working in "attentive environments," places that contain a multiplicity of computing devices. In an attentive environment, gaze tracking simplifies the task of speech recognition. If a device knows it's being looked at, it can, in effect, pay attention. That way, every device in a room won't be struggling, for instance, to make sense of the 'play' command that we've given to our VCR.

Geometry Sensitive Devices

Capability 1: Casual Access to Computing
Users should not be required to go to a special place (i.e., the desktop) to interact with the computer. Nor should they be required to wear special devices or markers to have the computer know where they are. This goal of "casual access to computing" means that the computer should always be available anywhere in a suitably equipped space. Through cameras, microphones, and other input devices, the user will always be able to signal the computer. Conversely, through displays, speakers, and specialized output devices, the computer will always be able to signal the user. With appropriate sensors, (cameras, pressure sensors, active badges), the computer will know the location and identity of users as well as the context in a given space, thus allowing devices to signal the users in a suitable, unobtrusive way. Signaling requires knowledge of the physical space beyond merely the proximity of the user to appropriate devices. There are several ways in which the simple task of notifying the user of a phone call or e-mail could fail without a suitably rich geometric model:

- The screen used for display (though inches away) is behind the user, so the displayed message cannot be seen.
- The speaker used for sounding a ringing signal is on the other side of a wall from the user, muffling the sound.
- Two people are in a room, and one is typing on a keyboard. Which application receives the keystrokes?

With a geometric model, appropriate decisions can be made to select one device over another, based on their physical locations, e.g., a large display far away might be more appropriate than a small display close up. It further enables the user interface designer to properly select and optimize an interaction based on the dynamic configuration of the I/O devices. While geometric knowledge alone is insufficient to select the best device for a given interaction (context and other world knowledge are helpful), it is a necessary component for reaching the ideal decision. Currently, computing and home electronic systems have an extremely impoverished world model. They lack significant knowledge about the layout of the physical space, the presence of other devices, or the current physical context. The addition of basic geometric knowledge to the ubiquitous computing system greatly increases the shared understanding between user and system. If the user requests "light," he can reasonably expect that a light nearby will come on. Without this shared knowledge, the user would need to specify precisely which light (e.g., by name, ID number, network address, etc.), rather than being able to assume the system will interpret his request correctly. For computing to move off the desktop and be accepted, it must have a comprehension of physical space that is related to that of the user, or else the proliferation of smart devices will only increase the complexity of the user's experience instead of simplifying it.

Capability 2: Extensible Computing

Similar to the concept of "plug and play," the capabilities of an intelligent environment should grow automatically as more hardware is added. One aspect of such extensibility is "resource extensibility," by which new devices become new resources that the system can use at will. If, for instance, a CRT is added to the kitchen, it becomes a new way of presenting information in that space, and the system should automatically take advantage of it. Another aspect is "physical

extensibility." If a new camera is added, it not only extends the system's resources as a new device, but also extends the system's physical coverage. The complexity introduced by physical extensibility can be simplified through the use of geometry. When trying to marshal an interaction, investigating the physical relationship of every possible combination of devices to the target user (or users) is a computationally expensive proposition, which grows combinatorially with the number of devices. If that lookup can be bounded by requesting only devices in the region surrounding the user, every device on the network need not be independently examined. Similarly, when one device is trying to communicate location-sensitive context, geometry gives a mechanism to avoid system-wide broadcast. For example, if the system wants to notify someone in a space via an acoustic signal, it need only check nearby audio-related devices to determine if that signal is likely to be heard. In other words, by utilizing information about the physical world, device lookups can be reliably and accurately scoped. Resource extensibility is greatly eased by the abstraction layer that a geometric model provides. Consider a phone system that routes incoming calls to the physical phone nearest the intended recipient. Such a system could obtain person location information directly from an active badge system. However, what if different parts of the building utilize different localization technologies? The routing system would have to know explicitly about all different perception methodologies, and be able to speak to and understand them all. If, instead, a geometric model is used, the sensing components can provide information to this model, and the telephone system can query the model. Neither information provider nor information consumer need know about each other. Additionally, this abstraction layer simplifies sensor fusion. Sensed geometric information will always have uncertainty associated with it. Worse yet, multiple sensors may perceive the world in inconsistent ways. A geometric model can hide this complexity, allowing applications that use geometric knowledge to be independent from a particular perception technology.

Existing Approaches

Many intelligent environment systems have avoided using an explicit geometric model by manually entering the physical configuration of devices, assuming network-presence translates to co-location, hand-coding the available inter-actions, or otherwise implicitly representing the requisite geometric information.

Fixed Configuration

While adequate for demonstration purposes, it is unreasonable to expect that future ubiquitous computing systems will be comprised only of static elements. Obviously, PDA's, cell phones and laptops will change locations frequently, and will be expected to work appropriately with an understanding of their locale. Another type of dynamism occurs when a consumer purchases a new device for their home, car or office. To integrate this new device into the system, it is preferable to avoid requiring the user to take any action beyond merely plugging the device in, or otherwise giving it power and data connectivity.

Implicit Geometry

Beyond assuming a fixed configuration of devices, a straightforward next approach is to use implicit geometry, assuming that network or data connec-tivity is equivalent to co-location. One might as-sume that if two devices can communicate directly (by RF, IR or other "local" transmission method), they are co-located. However, RF transmission (not to mention physical network protocols) can easily span rooms, floors, or even buildings. With-out a more precise model of geometry, making this type of assumption will result in an excessively large set of potentially available devices, many of which may not actually be available or usable for any particular task. For single-room demonstration systems, again, this assumption is reasonable; it stops being viable when the system must scale to larger spaces.

Dedicated Devices

Another alternative to having a geometric model is to directly couple particular devices to par-ticular tasks. However, this scales poorly, both in terms of system complexity and extensibility. For example, an IR motion sensor can be tied to the lights in the room. To make the Called an nTag, each delegate's device was pre-programmed with the conference schedule, which could be displayed on a small screen on the front of the tag, as well as with personal information supplied earlier to the organizers. This included the wearer's contact details, employment history, their professional interests and personal hobbies. The tags com-municate with each other via an infrared link to find out whether their owners have much in com-mon. When an nTag finds a good match, it does what any good party host would do and alerts its owner to the other person. Figure 1 and Figure 2 respectively. The relatively simple machines run on four AAA batteries and have 128 kilobytes of RAM, and 64 kilobytes of flash memory- about enough to store 60 pages of text as an electronic file. As well as communicating with each other via infrared links, nTags also use an RFID (radiof-requency identity) chip to talk to a central server. This allows delegates to download other people's details to an email address of their choice.

Wearable Computers

Currently, several companies sell wearable's and there is a considerable literature on the subject. Some wearable computers are basically desktop or notebook computers that have been scaled down for body-wear. Others employ brand new technology. Both general and special purposes

Figure 1. (http://www.toshiba.com/news/980715.htm)

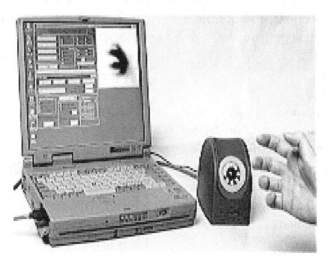

Figure 2. (http://www.csl.sony.co.jp/person/rekimoto/papers/iswc01.pdf)

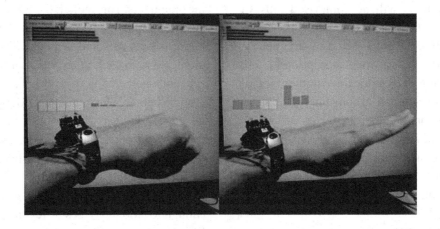

are envisioned. A number of wearable have been designed for the disabled. Among the challenges of wearable computers are: how to minimize their weight and bulkiness, how and where to locate the display, and what kind of data entry device to provide. Some of the applications envisioned for wearable computers include:

- Augmented memory (Rhodes B J, 1997), a concept originated by Thad Starner and being developed by Bradley Rhodes at the MIT Media Lab, in which as a person

enters a room, his/her wearable computer could sense the people present and remind him/her of their names or personal history, or a scheduler could whisper the time of an important meeting in a person's ear, or a "remembrance agent" could look for related documents by observing the words he/she were typing

- Immediate access to important data for anyone whose occupation requires mobility, such as real estate agents, rural doctors, fire and police professionals, lawyers in courtrooms, horse bettors, military personnel, stock brokers, and many others

- The ability to take notes immediately. For example, for reporters, geologists, botanists, vendor show representatives, field service repair personnel.

Smart Spaces

A smart home or building is a home or building, usually a new one that is equipped with special structured wiring to enable occupants to remotely control or program an array of automated home electronic devices by entering a single command. For example, a homeowner on vacation can use a Touchtone phone to arm a home security system, control temperature gauges, switch appliances on or off, control lighting, program a home theater or entertainment system, and perform many other tasks. The field of home automation is expanding rapidly as electronic technologies converge. The home network encompasses communications, entertainment, security, convenience, and information systems. Smart Spaces:

- Identify and perceive users and their actions and goals
- Have speech, natural language, computer vision input
- Interact with information-rich sources
- Enable devices worn in space to be integrated with devices present in space
- Provide extensive information-presentation capabilities
- Understand and anticipate user needs during task performance
- Provide improved memory and summaries of activities for later use

A technology known as Power line Carrier Systems (PCS) (Ishchenko D, et. el., 2005) is used to send coded signals along a home's existing electric wiring to programmable switches, or outlets. These signals convey commands that correspond to "addresses" or locations of specific devices, and that control how and when those devices operate. A PCS transmitter, for instance, can send a signal along a home's wiring, and a receiver plugged into any electric outlet in the home could receive that signal and operate the appliance to which it is attached. One common protocol for PCS is known as X10, a signaling technique for remotely controlling any device plugged into an electrical power line. X10 signals, which involve short radio frequency (RF) bursts that represent digital information, enable communication between transmitters and receivers. In Europe, technology to equip homes with smart devices centers on development of the European Installation Bus, or Instabus* .This embedded control protocol for digital communication between smart devices consists of a two-wire bus line that is installed along with normal electrical wiring. The Instabus line links all appliances to a decentralized communication system and functions like a telephone line over which appliances can be controlled. The European Installation Bus Association is part of Konnex, an association that aims to standardize home and building networks in Europe.

Network technology for residential wiring. EIB is designed for two-wire cable only. EIB versions for electrical cables as well as wireless systems for radio and infrared - as a functional prototype - have recently become available. The Siemens "Instabus" complies with the guidelines of the EIB standard as well as Domotik developed by Bosch. The version EIB.net can also use normal data networks in accordance with IEEE 802.2 with transfer rates of up to Ethernet 10 Mbit/s. The extension EIB.net allows forwarding, for example via the normal IP router and thus the EIB connection via the Internet. Maximum EIB data transfer rate is 9.6 Kbit/s.

Mobility and Networking

In an ideal pervasive computing environment, a large number of connected smart devices are deployed to collaboratively provision seamless services to users. Pervasive computing is enabled by various advanced technologies, particularly wireless technologies and the Internet. It has become a trend for our future lives. A pervasive computing environment can be extremely heterogeneous. We can imagine how many different devices are involved in a smart home: TVs, phones, cameras, coffee makers, or even books and bookshelves. Mobile computing emerged from the integration of cellular technology with the Web. Both the size and price of mobile devices are falling everyday and could eventually support Weiser's vision of pervasive inch-scale computing devices readily available to users in any human environment. Cellular phone systems that separate the handset from the subscriber identity module (SIM) card approximate this model of operation. Subscribers can insert their SIM card and automatically use any handset, placing and receiving calls as if it were their own phone. Users can already access the same point in the Web from several different devices—office or home PC, cell phone, personal digital assistant, and so forth. In this sense, for most users, what matters is the view a particular machine provides of the digital world. SIM cards also demonstrate that the end system is becoming less important than the access to the digital world. In this sense, we are well on the way to computers "disappearing," freeing users to focus beyond them.

The "anytime anywhere" goal of mobile computing is essentially a reactive approach to information access, but it prepares the way for pervasive computing is proactive "all the time everywhere" goal. Pervasive computing is a superset of mobile computing. In addition to mobility, pervasive systems require support for interoperability, scalability, smartness, and invisibility to ensure that users have seamless access to computing whenever they need it. Tiny computers that blend into the fabric of our daily lives are starting to help us live healthier lives, predict the breakdown of our machines—and may potentially invade our privacy. MIT, researchers are studying how dime-sized sensors located in light switches, medicine cabinet doors, chairs, and other invisible locations throughout the house can help with biometric health monitoring (http://hbswk.hbs.edu/YouAreWhatYouCompute HBS Working Knowledge.htm). The goal: Keep the elderly living at home as long as possible, reducing healthcare costs and providing peace of mind to families. Unlocking the data stored in sensors and other chips is the business of Axeda (http://www.primidi.com/2003/11/13.html#a645), which sells devices that track real-time performance of medical, office, and industrial equipment, and reports back to owners using the Internet.

The devices can be used to help predict failures, aid remote maintenance, and allow manufacturers to see how customers use their products, said Richard Barnwell, vice president of services. While there are some 150 million CPUs, or central processing units, in computers worldwide, there are 7.5 billion micro controllers—chips that act as sensing and control devices. For the most part, these chips are deaf and blind, not in touch with their environment. Ember (http://www.primidi.com/2003/11/13.html#a645) is developing wireless networks that connect micro controllers, such as the chips that control the heating, ventilation, and air conditioning systems in buildings. The networks can automatically hand off and reroute signals, ensuring a "self-healing" network with no single point of failure.

Practical and Industrial Applications of Pervasive Computing

Motion Processor (Toshiba)

A prototype motion processor developed by Toshiba allows a computer to recognize hand motions and to display them in real-time on the computer's display. Proposed applications include word processing using input with hand sign language, games, and other entertainment and educational approaches in which hand motion could result in multimedia effects.

Toshiba's motion processor (http://www. toshiba.com/news/980715.htm) works by emitting an infrared transmission light near the hand area and "reading" the light reflected back from the hand. Reflections from areas beyond the hand don't occur because the light is quickly dissipated over distance. The reflected light allows the computer to continuously build a 3-D motion image of the hand, which can be displayed or not. The prototype motion processor consists of eight light emitting diodes (LED), a lens, a CMOS image sensor, and a dedicated LSI that synchronizes transmission and reception of the light signal. It delivers a seven-bit, 64 x 64 pixel image to the PC, at a rate of 30 or 50 frames a second. The processor has an object range from 30 to 90 cm, and covers an area 40 centimeters square. The interactive potential of the motion processor can be seen in two successful test applications: playing the traditional Japanese game of rock, paper, scissors against a computer, and a virtual conductor game, in which different hand movements generate various sounds. The commercialized image processor will provide support for computers that recognize sign language and advanced interactive applications in multimedia and edutainment.

Geology-Smart Space Suit Developed (www.physorg.com/ Geologysmartspacesuitdeveloped.htm)

European researchers have developed a device that analyzes geological features for astronauts as they move around on extraterrestrial bodies. The computer-enhanced astro-biological scanner was developed by German and Spanish researchers at the Center for Astrobiology in Madrid, led by Patrick McGuire (McGuire P., 2005). The prototype

consists of a hand-held video camera connected to a wearable computer, but later versions may link the camera to a head-up display within an astronaut's visor. U.S. astronauts who visited the moon were trained in geology, enabling them to identify ancient rocks that might reveal signs of water or life. The prototype flags anything a geologist might find interesting, based on its unusual or distinctive appearance. 4.3 Gesture Wrist and Gesture Pad: Unobtrusive Wearable Interaction Devices (Sony) (http://www.csl.sony.co.jp/person/rekimoto/papers/iswc01.pdf). This project is developing two input devices for wearable computers, called Gesture Wrist and Gesture Pad. Both devices allow users to interact with wearable or nearby computers by using gesture-based commands. Both are designed to be as unobtrusive as possible, so they can be used under various social contexts. The first device, called Gesture Wrist, is a wrist band type input device that recognizes hand gestures and forearm movements. Unlike Data Gloves or other hand gesture-input devices, all sensing elements are embedded in a normal wristband. The second device, called Gesture Pad, is a sensing module that can be attached on the inside of clothes, and users can interact with this module from the outside. It transforms conventional clothes into an interactive device without changing their appearance.

Gesture Wrist and Gesture Pad: Unobtrusive Wearable Interaction Devices (Sony) (http:// www.csl.sony.co.jp/person/ rekimoto/papers/iswc01.pdf)

This project is developing two input devices for wearable computers, called Gesture Wrist and Gesture Pad. Both devices allow users to interact with wearable or nearby computers by using gesture-based commands. Both are designed to be as unobtrusive as possible, so they can be used under various social contexts. The first device, called Gesture Wrist, is a wrist band type input device that recognizes hand gestures and forearm movements. Unlike Data Gloves or other hand gesture-input devices, all sensing elements are embedded in a normal wristband. The second device, called Gesture Pad, is a sensing module that can be attached on the inside of clothes, and users can interact with this module from the outside. It transforms conventional clothes into an interactive device without changing their appearance.

Ounces Prototype Portable Computer (IBM) (www.ibm.com)

IBM Research has invented a prototype 9-ounce portable computing device that could pave the way for a new set of functionality in the handheld space. Codenamed "Meta Pad", the device is about the size of a ¾ inch thick stack of 3-by-5 index cards, and is part of IBM's research to explore how humans interact with computers and define the technologies needed for future pervasive devices. To make Meta Pad so small, IBM researchers pulled the power supply, display and I/O connectors out of the computer core -- leaving processor, memory, data and applications. The components pulled from the machine become accessories, and the individual users decide how they want to use their portable device. For example they could:

- Attach it to a small touch screen and carry it like a handheld personal digital assistant, but with all the power and functionality of a desktop
- Place it into a cradle which is attached to a keyboard and display at home, work or in a hotel
- Place it into a laptop-like shell and use it like an IBM ThinkPad
- Attach it to a wearable harness with a small head-mounted display for use in certain work environments that require hands-free computing
- Place it into a connector in an airplane seat that is linked to a touch screen display

It is unique from today's handhelds because all of a user's data and applications remain inside the core, eliminating the need for "synching"

Figure 3. (http://www.csl.sony.co.jp/person/rekimoto/papers/iswc01.pdf)

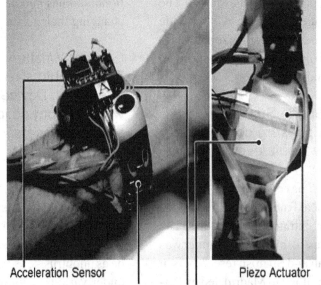

Acceleration Sensor   Piezo Actuator

Receiver Electrodes   Transmitter Electrode

among multiple devices. In addition, it can run multiple operating systems that share the same data, allowing users to run any application they want. IBM has also incorporated its advanced speech technologies and ink recognition software to further improve the interface to the Meta Pad. Another potential application of Meta Pad is in the super dense server space, offering an alternate way to build servers. By plugging many of these small devices into a rack system, you can get high-performance in a very small form factor, making it easier and more affordable for individuals to have their own personal server.

Linux Watch Enhanced Shell with Bluetooth (IBM) (www.whatis.com)

Linux Watch is designed to communicate wirelessly with PCs, cell phones and other wireless-enabled devices using Bluetooth. It has a touch panel and a roller wheel as user interfaces. It also has small microphone and speaker in it. At present it might not be possible for have a voice capability by itself due to its tiny CPU power. But in combination with a powerful host system, it can acquire voice capabilities by simply sending and receiving digitized voice data to and from the host system using the Bluetooth communication. Changing the internal battery and exchanging data with PC can be done via a cradle. TRL has demonstrated some watch applications using Bluetooth as a front-end user interface device of PCs and servers at the conference and the Expo all over the world, e.g. controlling the PC presentation using Freelance and PowerPoint and the server applications like Interacted Ad- Board and Trans-coding from the watch.

Linux Watch Basic Shell with OLED Display

The OLED display is capable of rendering very high resolution images with a pixel density of 740 pixels per inch, in a VGA 640 by 480 formats. In addition to text and graphic images, pictures containing gray scale images may also be shown

Figure 4. (www.whatis.com)

Meta Pad computer core specifications (www.ibm.com)

- 9 ounces,
- 3x5 inch, 3/4 inch thick,
- 800 MHz processor,
- 128 MB SDRAM,
- 10 GB hard disk drive,
- 3D Graphics chip with 8 MB RAM

Figure 5. (www.whatis.com)

using dot density methods producing photographic like images.

Philips - No Kidding (www.phillips.com)

Garments use mobile phone and camera technology to help parents pin point their kids' position, but also fabric antennas, radio tagging and miniature remote cameras to allow children to play exciting games outdoors. Physical characters with identity chips can be attached to the respective garments. The child sees the character that represents another child on his screen and as children move around their characters also move on the screens, allowing them to create their own stories or hide and seek situations.

Smart Clothes (www.taipeitimes.com/ news/2001/12/10/story/0000115251)

A US$484,000 project involving an industrial designer, a clothing designer and Pioneer Corp will allow consumers to wear a computer on their sleeve Kayoko Tanaka of Japanese electronics maker Pioneer wears a jacket which features an electronic luminescence display. The technology to do so in the form of screen known as Yuki EL is already a reality with limitations. It is an organic electroluminescent display that can be operated with a low voltage and can easily be applied on clothes. It is not very difficult to produce, but the battery does not last very long, only 4 hours. For now, the screen fitted in one of Sone's coats only has the memory to show a video lasting about three minutes on the screen integrated into the garment. There will be a day when entire computers will no longer need to be carried around, but accessed remotely from the technology embedded in the garments.

Telematics - Intelligent Filtering and Abstraction of Heterogeneous Pervasive Data (www.research. ibm.com/people/a/archan/ mcommerce2002.pdf)

Vehicle telematics systems may be used for a number of purposes, including collecting road tolls, managing road usage, tracking fleet vehicle locations, recovering stolen vehicles, providing automatic collision notification, and providing location-driven driver information services. Vehicle telematics systems are also increasingly being used to provide remote diagnostics; a vehicle's in-built systems will identify a mechanical or electronic problem, and the telematics package will automatically make this information known to the vehicle manufacturer and service organisation. Other forthcoming applications include on-demand navigation, audio and audio-visual entertainment content. The telematics platform on the car is likely to be closely controlled by the vehicle manufacturer and could differ across different manufacturers and brands. Each brand may be associated with a specific Telematics Service Provider (TSP), who determines the application suite and services installed on the vehicular computer and the type and format of vehicular data that can be exposed to external (Internet-based) applications. Retaining control over the application suite is important to ensure that user interfaces do not lead to dangerous forms of driver distraction (e.g., all Web applications may be constrained to be voice-based while a car is in motion). Providing configuration control over vehicular data exported to external applications is important to satisfy many critical concerns associated with data privacy and confidentiality.

The communication infrastructure between the vehicular platform and the backbone TSP infrastructure is likely to utilize commercial wireless packet-networking technologies. Many telematics applications are based on the retrieval and correlation of diagnostic, location and other information from the vehicle and the eventual composition of compound events from the raw data. The telematics applications space is, however, characterized by significant variation in the rate, frequency and quality of the vehicular data that is required by any specific application. For example, an insurance application offering rebates to drivers who drive less than 500 miles a week needs to retrieve odometer data only once a week. On the other hand, an application using vehicular speeds to detect highway congestion must monitor speedometer readings with much greater frequency (e.g., once every 30 seconds). To compound this diversity in application requirements, the actual rate of data dissemination from different cars may also

exhibit significant variation, depending both on the manufacturer's chosen platform and the type of data. For example, our current telematics applications utilize GPS data from a moving vehicle that is streamed to the central gateway once every 8 seconds. Diagnostic data, such as tire pressure and emission readings, in contrast, are reported only once every few minutes. A middleware platform is needed to shield the individual applications from the platform-dependent variations in data sources and data rates and intelligently filter, transform, and format the platform-dependent data into a device-independent format that conforms to the specific needs of an individual application. An insurance application can then be written without an explicit knowledge of the different rates and precise formats in which different cars export their odometer information; the middleware is responsible for collecting and filtering the raw data to conform to the granularity, frequency and quality needed by a specific application.

Pervasive Initiatives

Both academia and industry have recently advanced pervasive computing projects:

Disappearing Computer Initiative Projects (http://www.disappearing-computer.net/index.html)

The Disappearing Computer (DC) is a EU-funded proactive initiative of the Future and Emerging Technologies (FET) activity of the Information Society Technologies (IST) research program. The mission of the initiative is to see how information technology can be diffused into everyday objects and settings, and to see how this can lead to new ways of supporting and enhancing people's lives that go above and beyond what is possible with the computer today.

Specifically, the initiative focuses on three-interlinked objectives:

Figure 6. (http://2wear.ics.forth.gr/)

1. Create information artifacts based on new software and hardware architectures that are integrated into everyday objects.
2. Look at how collections of artifacts can act together, so as to produce new behavior and new functionality.
3. Investigate the new approaches for designing for collections of artifacts in everyday settings, and how to ensure that people's experience in these new environments is coherent and engaging.

The initiative addresses these three objectives with a number of independent research projects and a number of support activities run by a network made up of a representation of all project partners.

2WEAR (http://2wear.ics.forth.gr/)

The 2WEAR project explores the concept of a personal system that is formed by putting together computing elements in an ad-hoc fashion using short-range radio. Certain elements are embedded into wearable objects, such as a wristwatch and small general-purpose compute/storage modules that can be attached to clothes or placed inside a wallet. Others have the form of more conventional portable computers, like PDAs and mobile phones. Also, there are stationary elements as part of the environment, some of which are visible, such as big screens and home appliances, while others are not directly perceivable by the user, such as network gateways and backend servers.

This setting deviates from the conventional computing paradigm in significant ways. What is usually referred to as the personal computer is a collection of physically separate and possibly autonomous elements that co-operate with each other without relying on external infrastructure or a pre-arranged setup. Various functions and applications are distributed on different platforms that can be widely heterogeneous in terms of computing resources and user interaction capability. In addition, the system configuration changes dynamically and several times during application execution due to devices being switched on and off, or moved into and out of range. The 2WEAR project (http://2wear.ics.forth.gr/deliverables/2wear_FinalReport_draft.pdf) was started at January 2001 and was successfully ended December 2003.

ATELIER - Architecture and Technologies for Inspirational Learning Environments (http://atelier.k3.mah.se/home/)

The aim of the ATELIER project (Architecture and Technology for Inspirational Learning Environments) is to contribute to inspirational learning environments, which are grounded in an understanding of creative practices within design, architecture and art. The project starts out from interactions between people and material artifacts in physical places and asks how we should enhance such an environment with digital technologies to turn it into a resource for inspiration and creative learning by an integrated design of learning materials, interactive technologies and architectural space.

The project will:

- Develop, experiment with, and evaluate a design-oriented approach to inspirational learning, based on ethnographic research on creative design work in an architectural master class and an interaction design studio,
- Design, assemble and test architecture and technical components for such mixed media environments, based on ethnographic work on how learners interact with space, artifacts (tangible and digital, present and distant) and materials of mixed media origin and with co-present and distant people. ATELIER (http://atelier.k3.mah.se/publications/final_report.pdf) is a EU-project within the programs for Future and Emerging Technologies and the Disappearing Computer.

The project, that started on 1 December 2001, lasting for 30 months, is carried out in close cooperation with partners in Sweden, Austria, Finland and Italy.

Inter Living (http://interliving.kth.se/)

The goal of the Inter Living project is to, together with families, study and develop technologies and artifacts for communication between generations.

Coordination and Partners

Inter Living is coordinated by CID (Centre for User Oriented IT-Design), at the Royal Institute of Technology in Stockholm. Partners are INRIA (Institut Nationale de Recherche en Informatique et Automatique), LRI (Laboratoire de Recherche en Informatique Université de Paris-Sud) in France and the Human-Computer Interaction Lab at the University of Maryland in the USA. InterLiving is funded for three years by EU's program "Disappearing Computer".

Aim

The aim of the Inter Living project is to develop technology that can contribute to bringing family members together. In order to do so we need to know what keeps families together. We do not only need to know what an artifact that the families are willing to place in their different homes should do, how it should work. We need to get the whole picture also including the products' appearance and expression. We need to be able to design the artifacts in such a way that the families will accept to have them in their homes. This can of course include all kinds of aspects like status, exclusiveness, etc. The results could even involve "invisible" design. Since we only have to consider the situation when the artifact is in the home we can really focus on the "needs and desires" that the families express. We do not have to consider other aspects such as: marketing, branding, manufacturing, distribution, disposal, recycling, price, etc.

Methods

Inter Living is a cooperative project between researchers from different scientific disciplines; ethnology, psychology, industrial design and computer science, and six families, three in Sweden and three in France. The cooperation with the families will in its first stage create understanding for the complexity for their geographic and communicative situation. In the second stage the researchers and the family members will together design useful and adaptable technology. We will mix reliable scientific methods and exploratory development. Examples of methods are ethnographic studies, interviews, video diaries, and "work-and-play"-workshops.

MiME (http://www.mimeproject.org/)

Intimate Media describes the stuff that people create and collect to store and share their personal memories, interests and loves. Typical examples of intimate media include photo albums, souvenirs and diaries - although anything could be intimate media depending on the meaning and value that has been attributed to it. That meaning can relate to a person's past, their present or potential futures. The MiME project focuses on the relationship between computer technology and people's experience of their intimate media collections around the home.

As computers steadily move into every aspect of personal life, MiME proposes that instead of allowing intimate media to disappear into the computer, artifacts and systems should be designed to better promote human experiences around the collection, storage and sharing of intimate media.

ORESTEIA -MODULAR HYBRID ARTIFACTS WITH ADAPTIVE FUNCTIONALITY (HTTP://WWW. IMAGE.NTUA.GR/ORESTEIA/)

The main objective of ORESTEIA IST (http://www.image.ntua.gr/oresteia/deliverables/ORESTEIA-IST-2000-26091-ND4.1.pdf) project is to define, design and validate the internal architecture and the collaborative functionality of artifacts with embedded hybrid intelligence. The targeted artifacts will possess encapsulated local decision capabilities, as well as on-line adaptability of their behavior, while being able to communicate to each other producing new more complex functionalities. Micro-power sources will enable artifacts to "live" in an autonomous mode. The proposal focuses on the creation of artifacts responsible for interaction with humans, possessing modularity, hybrid architecture composed of sub symbolic and symbolic components which continuously interact with each other, adaptable functionality and ability to communicate with each other and with information sites based on common structure of the information they possess, extract and exchange. Of particular importance to the project is the design of collections of artifacts providing health status analysis and hazard avoidance.

SHAPE - Situating Hybrid Assemblies in Public Environments (http://www.shape-dc.org/)

SHAPE is devoted to understanding, developing and evaluating room-sized assemblies of hybrid, mixed reality artifacts in public places. Hybrid artifacts exhibit physical and digital features and can exist in both physical and digital worlds. They combine interactive visual (computer graphical and video) and sonic (music, recordings and live sound) material with physically present manipulable devices. Hybrid artifacts can communicate with one another as part of room-sized assemblies that provide groups of people with a coherent, yet rich, sensory experience of a large-scale mixed reality. These assemblies can be deployed in public spaces such as museums and Exploratorium's to establish new kinds of engaging and educational social experience.

Project Objectives

- to explore hybrid, mixed reality artifacts and the various relationships that are possible between physical and digital manifestations, and create prototype demonstrators to examine and construct organized assemblies of hybrid artifacts within room-sized environments as a means for delivering a thematically integrated, yet rich, social experience using social scientific research methods.
- to study and develop a detailed understanding of the activities of members of the public as they engage with exhibited artifacts in public places such as museums and Exploratorium's.
- to deploy such an understanding, combined with techniques of participatory design,
- to develop actual public exhibitions demonstrating the project's technologies, 'living exhibitions'
- to reflect on the project's design methods and evaluate its technical products.

The consortium combines computer scientific and social scientific expertise and is concerned to develop a methodical approach which integrates design, empirical study and user participation. Exciting innovative technologies need to be developed but in ways which can be grounded and evaluated in terms of people's practical experience and capabilities. To this end, the consortium has secured collaborations with a number of institutions for whom the design of interactive experiences is important including a variety of European museums and Exploratorium's. These will provide field sites for study as well as settings where, from a very early stage in the project, members of the general public as well as museum professionals (curators, exhibit-designers) can be involved in participating in the design of our prototypes which can, in turn, be presented direct to the public. To realize this aim, the project will adopt a number of novel research management strategies, including working on-site within collaborating institutions for extended periods of time as part of 'living exhibitions'.

This will allow the monitoring of the use of these spaces on an ongoing basis, and to provide on-site practical advice and support to the site staff concerning the hybrid spaces. It will also ensure that the experimental technology underlying the hybrid artifacts is maintained during implementation and trials with members of the public, and that useful empirical data on the way in which participants interact with, and report on, the experience can be captured for later analysis.

The project subscribes to an evolutionary and iterative design methodology that will ensure that later prototypes build on the experience gained in engineering the early prototypes, and in the evaluation of the prototypes by consulting with members of the public directly as well as through studying their interactions. The explicit recognition, within the project, of the need to work with several collaborating institutions, varying in their objectives and scale, allows exploration of issues concerning cost, scale and focus of the planned exhibitions.

Description of Work

SHAPE is a three year project with four partners adding complementary skills and roles. The project will map out different ways of linking physical objects with digital representations so as to develop a typology of hybrid, mixed reality artifacts. Assemblies of hybrid artifacts shall be constructed at different levels of scale and explore means for managing inter-artifact communication in ways which link low-level protocols with applications. The project will establish an archive of empirical materials collected at a variety of public places such as museums and Exploratorium's. Methods employed by visitors as they interact with exhibited artifacts and each other, will be analyzed. On the basis of empirical analysis, a design framework for informing the development of hybrid digital-physical artifacts will be produced. The project intends to create, through participatory design with personnel from collaborating museums, two public exhibitions demonstrating technologies developed in the project as a means of integrating project results across partners and evaluating emerging technologies in practical, public settings. A series of workshops is proposed to reflect on the progress and methods of the project and to consolidate its results for dissemination. The project involves a number of innovative management strategies, designed to increase the involvement of 'grass roots' researchers in project planning, while promoting the internal mobility of researchers within the consortium, thereby instantiating some of the wider features of the Disappearing Computer programme within the project (e.g. 'research troubadours').

Smart-Its Artifacts (http://www.smart-its.org/)

The Smart-Its Project

"Ubiquitous Computing is fundamentally characterized by the connection of things in the world with computation" (Brown J, Weiser M.). The Smart-Its project is interested in a far-reaching vision of computation embedded in the world. In this vision, mundane everyday artifacts become augmented as soft media, able to enter into dynamic digital relationships. In our project, we approach this vision with development of "Smart-Its" - small-scale embedded devices that can be attached to everyday objects to augment them with sensing, perception, computation, and communication. We

think of these "Smart-Its" as enabling technology for building and testing ubiquitous computing scenarios, and we will use them to study emerging functionality and collective context-awareness of information artifacts.

Smart-Its (Alahuhta P, et.al., 2001) is a collaboration of Lancaster University, ETH Zurich, University of Karlsruhe, Interactive Institute and VTT. The project is part of the European initiative The Disappearing Computer, and funded in part by the Commission of the European Union and by the Swiss Federal Office for Education and Science. The Smart-Its project is based on a philosophy of building and trying fully functional prototypes, and from day one the partners have begun to implement hardware/software artifacts that enable us to study issues in augmentation and networking of everyday objects. The device development is based on experience from the partner's previous research, for example conducted in the European project TEA, in TecO's Mediacup work, and in VTT's Soap Box development.

The Smart-Its Vision

The project envisions small-scale smart devices - "Smart-Its" - that can be attached to mundane everyday artifacts to augment these with a "digital self". These devices will be as cheap, as unobtrusive and as generic as state-of-the-art smart labels (i.e., RFID tags). In addition these devices will be enabled with perception of their environment, with peer-to-peer communication, and with customizable behaviour. Collections of such devices will be used to augment and interconnect entire families of artifacts, such as scattered personal belongings, toys in the playroom, and objects in collaborative interactive experiences.

Project Objectives

- to develop a range of Smart-Its devices, varying in processing power, sensory capabilities, and energy consumption

Figure 7. (http://www.sics.se/accord/index.html)

This Smart-It is based on Atmel's
ATmega103L microcontroller with 128 kB
of in-system programmable flash memory
and only 4 kB of SRAM. Ericsson's
Bluetooth modules allow communication
between different devices.

This device is integrates a PIC 16F876 20
MHz for processing, RFM 868 MHz for
communication (128kbit/s), on board
sensors and an I2C interface for
sensor/actor boards. Power is supplied by

RS232 Add-On (AR 0.0-0)
Interfaces to Smart-Its
RS232 level
IrDA physical layer
Power supply through main board (e.g.
Smart-It)

I/O add: Temperature, Display, Sound
(TDS 0.0-0)
Interface: I2C
8 char x 2 line display
High-Resolution temperature sensor
Piezo sound
Power supply through main board (e.g.
Smart-It)

Test I/O (IO-TS 0.0-0)
I/O Test board for input and output
Power supply through main board (e.g.
Smart-It)

- to investigate perceptual computing methods for ad hoc connected sensor devices
- to develop service infrastructure for interconnected embedded technologies
- to develop an open architecture for collective context-awareness
- to explore novel applications and use experiences enabled by Smart-Its technology.

The first device prototypes are based on two different microcontroller platforms, Atmel and PIC. The Atmel platform enables us to look into Bluetooth integration, while the PIC-based platform is used in conjunction with RFM communication.

The overall device architecture is modular so that different sensor boards can be connected to either microcontroller platform.

ACCORD (HTTP://WWW. SOUNDOBJECT.ORG/)

Background

The ACCORD project is funded under the Disappearing Computer proactive initiative of the Future and Emerging Technologies (FET) key action of the Information Society Technologies Programme (IST) of the European Commission's community research.

The goals of this initiative can be summarized as follows:

To explore how everyday life can be supported and enhanced through the use of collections of interacting artifacts. Together, these artifacts will form new people-friendly environments in which the computer-as-we-know-it has no role. The aim is to arrive at new concepts and techniques out of which future applications can be developed.

Specifically, the initiative focuses on three inter-linked objectives:

1. Developing new tools and methods for the embedding of computation in everyday objects so as to create artifacts.
2. Research on how new functionality and new use can emerge from collections of interacting artifacts.
3. Ensuring that people's experience of these environments is both coherent and engaging in space and time.

Objectives

The main aim of the ACCORD (http://www. sics.se/accord/plan/del/D51a.doc) project is to develop facilities to construct, administer and manage future interactive home environments. It sees the arrangement of interactive devices as the principle means of controlling the complexity inherent in domestic environments. It wishes to realize dynamic and adaptive methods, techniques and facilities to allow inhabitants to evolve their own Tangible Interactive Environment (TIE).

In particular, it wishes to empower future household inhabitants by developing a Tangible Toolkit that they can use to meet their local demands. In order to realize this Tangible Toolkit we need to undertake fundamental research focusing on:

1. How inhabitants understand and alter their domestic environments. What current and new forms of application are likely to emerge

within the home and what activities need to be supported?
2. How inhabitants might relate to future interactive environments. How do we develop and refine for new uses of information and new forms of applications?
3. What are the core elements needed to realize a Tangible Interactive Environment? How do we identify the core elements with an environment and how do we characterize these so they are readily understood by users?
4. How might inhabitants construct domestic interactive environments from set of components? What mechanisms are needed to support the rapid construction of a TIE from a set of components?

GROCER - GROCERY STORE (HTTP://WWW. DISAPPEARING-COMPUTER.NET/ PROJECTS/GROCER.HTML)

The main aim of GROCER is to place new technologies (Bluetooth, WAP, RFID, etc.) at the level of the practical user by allowing users to use these technologies to perform everyday activities (in the case of this project grocery shopping). The idea will also be to eventually allow users to access the same set of services (searching the Internet, making phone calls, buying items through the Internet, checking the weather, etc.) wherever they are, not just in their own homes.

The focus on the GROCER project will be on building two main technical products: 1) embedded location-based artifacts in real-world objects such as cereal boxes in grocery stores; and 2) a wireless architecture and application server system integrating these artifacts with handheld devices and distributed software agents.

The GROCER project is based on the notion that computing can be performed by any object supporting wireless communication through the Internet, if it is located appropriately. The GRO-

CER pilot will, using the two technical products described above, test the ability of users to purchase items and access/receive information on items within the setting of a grocery store. The GROCER project will thus work toward taking e-commerce (electronic commerce) a step further to m-commerce (mobile commerce). Using the technologies mentioned above, consumers would be able to purchase products, receive advertisements for products, and perform other Internet related activities through mobile phones, PDAs (Personal Digital Assistants) and other handheld portable devices.

SOB - SOUNDING OBJECT PROJECT (HTTP://WWW. SOUNDOBJECT.ORG/)

The SOb project is part of the Disappearing Computer proactive initiative of the IST Future and Emerging Technologies. The Sob (Bresin R.,et. al.,2003) project aims at developing sound models that are responsive to physical interactions and are easily matched to physical objects. The sound models, being specified by physical descriptions and actions, will be ready to be integrated into artifacts that interact with each other and that accessed by direct manipulation. Control models are developed in order to reproduce parametric variations that are natural according to the dynamics of human gestures and expressive intentions. Sound and control models are developed after the phenomenological and psychophysical characterization of a restricted class of sound events. The results of research are demonstrated by means of a dynamic sound library and an application that will allow users to interact with objects using only gestures and auditory display.

The project is innovative in several ways:

- It takes a physics-based approach to sound modeling, as opposed to signal based approaches that are more conventional in sonification, auditory display and multimedia;
- It brings together researchers from diverse fields, such as experimental psychology, signal processing, human-computer interaction and acoustics;
- It aims at developing models and algorithms that have a solid physical basis while being accessible in a human-oriented fashion;
- It aims at developing a phenomenology and a psychophysics of sound events that are relevant for interaction with and among artifacts;
- A continuous evaluation process of sound and control models is run throughout the project using the methods of experimental psychology.

WORKSPACE - DISTRIBUTED WORK SUPPORT THROUGH COMPONENT BASED SPATIAL

Computing Environments (http://www.daimi.au.dk/ workspace/index.htm)

People's activities at work often generate dynamic configurations of spaces, information, and people - within the office, but also beyond. Increasingly, both digital and physical materials are part of such configurations; and much of people's work centers on making sense of one piece of information in relation to many others. For many professionals information comes in many different formats and often also needs to be made sense of in relation to features in the real world. These practices pose great challenges to the computer as-we-know-it today and open up a range of opportunities for innovative design. Spatial computing environments respond to these challenges. They exploit technical possibilities to support the social and spatial organization of work. WorkSPACE takes

Figure 8. (http://www.daimi.au.dk/workspace/index.htm)

aesthetic design – in 88architecture, landscape architecture, and product design – as an inspirational test case. Through ethnographic studies, participatory design collaboration with professionals and aesthetic design strategies the project seeks to develop software components and hardware artifacts that may be combined and integrated into hybrid spatial computing environments in the office, on the move, and on site.

Objectives

The main objective for WorkSPACE is to augment the work environment – whether it be the office, places encountered whilst on the move, or site locations – through spatial computing components, initially for members of the design professions, but with applicability to a wide range of work domains. Spatial computing refers to technical possibilities as well as the social and spatial organization of people's activities and defines five specific objectives for WorkSPACE.

To enable documents and working materials to be represented, displayed, organized and worked on in a collaborative hybrid environment.

1. To go beyond the WIMP screen and keyboard to realize this environment in a range of forms and media – some small and portable, others large and immersive.

2. To enable people and their working materials to combine together in more fluid and transparent ways than through conventional electronic networks and interfaces.

3. To embed computation in physical environments, materials and tools through augmentation and hypermedia linking and to introduce materiality and opportunities for embodied engagement into electronic spaces and materials.

4. To take initial steps, using spatial positioning technologies, towards connecting physical spaces in the outside world, such as (landscape) architecture sites, and their digital representations, allowing users to act in one through the other and to represent, display, organize and work on information in relation to physical locations. To achieve these objectives and enable support for a diversity of work situations ranging from individual work, through local collaboration,

to distributed collaboration, WorkSPACE brings together collaborative virtual environments, computational augmentation, hyper medial relationships, connectivity between devices, sensors, actuators, projection and display technologies, new interaction devices and metaphors.

Examples of Work

WorkSPACE focuses on the working environment (including the field and mobile working environments) rather than, for example, domestic or leisure environments. In particular, we have chosen aesthetic design in architecture, landscape architecture and product design; not least because:

1. The work of design professionals is highly varied, involving aesthetic, technical and administrative components.
2. It is collaborative, flexible, and information intensive, drawing upon diverse, digital and physical work materials.
3. Aesthetic design is a particularly clearly embodied, situated, and material activity.

4. Real spaces form part of the information landscape.

Complex relationships connecting diverse people, materials, objects and spaces mean that aesthetic design provides a strong test and strong opportunities, for technical support. To gain a closer understanding of practices in aesthetic design, we undertake ethno methodological studies of work. Yet, it is not enough to study existing work practices to inform the design of technologies that aim to support and enrich future working cultures. Workplace studies must seek to understand evolving new ways of working as well as existing working practices. To address this demand, the WorkSPACE team has opted for an approach that combines ethnographic studies in real world work settings with experiments and attempts to promote the development of new work practices through 'bricolage' within the workplace and 'future laboratory workshops'.

The figure shows a screen shot of a Linux Topos client. It shows an open workspace containing a set of document objects. Double clicking any of the document objects will launch the document in its application, and changes to it will be reflected within Topos in near real time. The objects can be

Figure 9. (http://www.daimi.au.dk/workspace/index.htm)

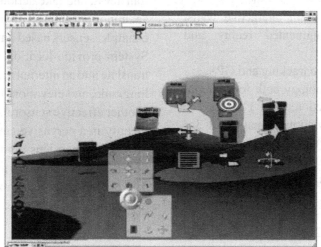

Topos(Gronbaek K , et.,al.2001)

sized, moved, rotated, etc; light effects may be applied; documents can be made (semi-) transparent; organized into groups; and much more. The screen shot also shows the use of an (abstract) textured, light mapped and shadowed terrain, floating semi-transparent toolbars, a multi-selection "blob" and a halo of manipulation tools around the selected objects. Topos is the name of both the software infrastructure to support all the demonstrators of WorkSPACE project, as well as the 3D interface client to the infrastructure. The Topos client is a multiple-document-interface (MDI) windowed application presenting a 3D spatial hypermedia interface to document and material organization. A central concept in Topos is the *workspace* which is the primary means of grouping and organizing materials and documents in 3D space. The workspaces themselves can be grouped, mixed and connected in a variety of ways.

The Topos system originally was a complete re-implementation of the Manufaktur system developed within the Esprit LTR Desarte project. It has, however, developed into much more. Topos now allows for manipulation and maintenance of relationships among materials in a 3D spatial environment. It also:

- integrates with standard applications (Word, Excel, AutoCAD,),
- supports real-time collaboration among clients on an intranet or the Internet,
- is geared towards both interactive walls, tables, mobile augmented reality and desktops,
- integrates with video tracking and GPS,
- utilises RFID technology both for material tracking and interaction,
- can act as a 3D window manager for 3rd party applications (under Linux),
- can work inside a web server to provide limited integration via an un augmented web browser,
- and it is running cross platform between Linux, Windows 2000, XP (and MacOS X).

The Topos infrastructure consists of all these elements:

- SQL databases to keep the persistent state of shared collaborative workspaces;
- a collaboration server to support real time interactive collaboration;
- an awareness agent to better support also off-line collaboration;
- a location-based service discovery framework to better support pervasive, configuration-less networked services, and
- the Topos client itself.

ACADEMIA PROJECTS

Media Cup (http://www.teco. uni-karlsruhe.de/~michael/ publication/mediacup/)

The University of Karlsruhe's Media Cup (Beigl M,et.al.,2001) project is an experimental deployment of everyday objects activated in this sense. The project's guiding principle is to augment objects with a digital presence while preserving their original appearance, purpose, and use. Sensors that automatically gather information, transfer it, and take actions based on it represent an important subset of pervasive devices. For example, sensors based on the Global Positioning System provide location data that a device can translate into an internal representation of latitude, longitude, and elevation. Stereo camera vision is another effective sensor for tracking location and identity in a pervasive environment. These fast-processing, two-lens digital cameras can record both background images and background shapes. The results are much more robust for tracking motion such as gestures.

Figure 10. (http://www.daimi.au.dk/workspace/index.htm)

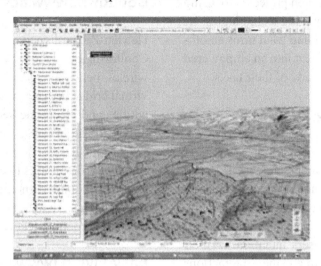

Aura (www.cs.cmu.edu/~aura/)

Carnegie Mellon University characterizes its Aura (Garlan D, et.,al.) project as "distraction free ubiquitous computing." The project aims to design, implement, deploy, and evaluate a large scale computing system demonstrating a "personal information aura" that spans wearable, handheld, desktop, and infrastructure computers. Aura is a large umbrella project with many individual research thrusts. Darwin is an intelligent network at Aura's core. Coda is a distributed file management system that supports nomadic file access, and Odyssey provides operating system support for resource adaptation. These products and others are evolving within the Aura project, which emphasizes pervasive middleware and application design.

Endeavor (www.endeavour. cs.berkeley.edu/)

The University of California at Berkeley's Endeavor project is an academic effort that focuses on the specification, design, and prototype implementation of planet scale, self organizing, and adaptive "information utility". This smart environment is pervasive everywhere and always there with components that flow through the infrastructure, shape them selves to adapt to their usage, and cooperate on tasks. Endeavour's key innovative technological capabilities its pervasive support for fluid software. It includes processing, storage, and data management functionality to arbitrarily and automatically distribute itself among pervasive devices and along paths through scalable computing platforms that are integrated with the pervasive networking infrastructure. The system can compose itself from preexisting hardware and software components to satisfy a service request while advertising the services it can provide to others.

Oxygen (www.oxygen.lcs.mit.edu/)

The Oxygen project, and perceive an MIT initiative, envisions a future in which computation will be freely available everywhere, like oxygen in the air we breathe. The project rests on an infrastructure of mobile and stationary devices connected by a self configuring network. This infrastructure supplies abundant computation and communication, which are harnessed through system, perceptual, and software technologies to meet user needs. The Oxygen project is focusing on eight environment-enabling technologies. Its emphasis is on understanding what turns an otherwise dormant environment into an empowered one to which users shift parts of their tasks.

Portolano (www.portolano. cs.washington.edu/)

In its Portolano project (Anderson T, et.,al.,1999), the University of Washington seeks to create a test bed for investigating pervasive computing. The project emphasizes invisible, intent-based computing, which infers users' intentions via their actions in the environment and their interactions with everyday objects. Project devices are highly optimized to particular tasks so that they blend into the world and require little technical knowledge on the user's part. In short, Portolano proposes an infrastructure based on mobile agents that interact with applications and users. Data-centric routing automatically migrates data among applications on the user's behalf. Data thus becomes "smart," and serves as an interaction mechanism within the environment.

Sentient Computing (www. uk.research.att.com/spirit/)

AT&T Laboratories, Cambridge, UK, is collaborating with the Cambridge University Engineering Department on the Sentient Computing project. The project explores user interfaces that employ sensors and resource status data to maintain a world model shared by users and applications. The world model for the Sentient Computing project covers an entire building. Interfaces to programs extend seamlessly throughout the building. Computer desktops follow their owners and reflect real-time updates for object locations. This project has led to some new kinds of applications, like context-aware filing systems and smart posters.

Cooltown (www.cooltown.com)

Hewlett-Packard's pervasive computing initiative, Cooltown, focuses on extending Web technology, wireless networks, and portable devices to create a virtual bridge between mobile users and physical entities and electronic services. Cooltown uses URLs for addressing, physical beaconing and sensing of URLs for discovery, and localized Web servers for directories to create a location-aware system that supports nomadic users. It leverages Internet connectivity on top of this infrastructure to support communications services.

Easy Living (www.research. microsoft.com/easyliving/)

The Easy Living project of Microsoft Research's Vision Group is developing architecture and related technologies for intelligent environments. The project supports research addressing middleware, geometric world modeling, perception, and service description. Key system features include computer vision, multiple sensor modalities, automatic and semiautomatic sensor calibration, and device-independent communication and data protocols.

Web Sphere (www-3.ibm. com/software/pervasive/)

Everyplace IBM's pervasive computing work focuses on applications and middleware that extends Web Sphere software platform. The company is spearheading consortia and initiatives for open standards to support pervasive computing applications. It is also working with hardware vendors such as Palm (www.palm.com), Symbol Technologies (www.symbol.com), and Handspring (www.handspring.com) to develop a new generation of devices.

Pervasive Computing and Communications – University of Texas Arlington (http://crewman.uta.edu/psi)

For efficient and real-time tracking of objects, a generic, distributed, scalable architecture based on Radio Frequency Identification (RFID) tags (Basu K, et.,al.,2004),(Das S, et.,al.,2003) that could be globally deployed for implementing inter organizational transactions of physical tagged objects, is being developed. Based on their architecture, the team has defined location tracking and update protocol for the real-time tracking of the mobile objects. In this project, they are working on a theoretical framework to get a stochastic estimate of the average spread of object distributions and the amount of messaging necessary for a Product Recall based on the concepts of Scale Free Networks and Epidemic Theory. Fusion of information arriving from disparate sources and making appropriate decisions is a challenging and laborious task. As part of the PSI project, they are in the process of creating communities of delegents (software agents) to aid in the information fusion aspects of the PSI project. We have identified and are developing delegents to play four different types of roles - perception, comprehension, projection and resolution. A Bayesian based network approach is being used to generate rules for delegent reactions to events. Integration of these rules into communities is expected to address issues of sufficiency and efficiency in identifying particular situations when certain events take place in the environment.

IPCRES (http://www.indiana. edu/~uits/cpo/ipcres/overview.html)

The Indiana Pervasive Computing Research (IPCRES) Initiative is a partnership between Indiana University and the Lilly Endowment to develop a world-class research capability in Indiana to advance research in some of the fundamental technologies that will drive the 21st century in-formation economy and to use this capability to help grow the information economy in Indiana. IPCRES seeks to leverage what is clearly emerging as one of the major macro phenomena in information technology (IT) in the next century pervasive computing.

The overall strategy of IPCRES will be to:

- Significantly expand IT research in Indiana, specifically in pervasive computing, and
- leverage this research to expand the information economy in Indiana.

Key to this Initiative will be the establishment of six world-class research laboratories in areas that will be fundamental to building the pervasive computing environment of the future. These IPCRES Laboratories will be headed by researchers of the highest international standing, Distinguished Scientists who are recognized as leaders in their respective fields and who will attract highly talented young faculty and graduate students to join them. The Laboratories will be of substantial size and well-equipped, and will provide an outstanding environment that will help attract researchers of the highest quality to Indiana.

The focus of the work of the IPCRES Laboratories will be on research that is fundamental to pervasive computing. This will be carried out in two broad field's software technologies and advanced telecommunications. In each of these two fields five major research areas have been identified from which the areas for the final IPCRES Laboratories will be established.

In the field of software technologies these five areas are:

- **Information Grids and Portals.** A laboratory in this area would investigate the next generation of Internet application protocols and their evolution into pervasive information services and knowledge tools.
- **Human-Computer Interaction.** An HCI laboratory within IPCRES would focus on the exploration of tele-immersion,

augmented reality, user interfaces, and the design of usable information systems.

- **Smart Devices.** A laboratory in this area would investigate the problem of bringing thousands of small sensors, remote instruments, intelligent appliances and hand-held personal digital assistants onto the information grid.

- **Network Agents.** Pervasive computing is causing a rethinking of the way software is designed. A laboratory in this area would investigate the design and architecture of software components and software agents (components that move through the network doing work on a user's behalf).

- **Open Software.** Software interoperability is the key to pervasive computing. The most important way that interoperability is created is to allow a community of experts to share the standard protocols and "community-supported" utilities and tools and incrementally improve it in the public domain. The Internet is based on open-source software standards and tools. An IPCRES laboratory in this area will support open-source projects and establish new ones that enable pervasive computing technologies.

Whereabouts Project (http://whereabouts.eecs.umich.edu/)

Whereabouts(CPOL:,2005),(Gifford S.,2005),(Gifford S, et.,al.,2005) is a project at the University of Michigan to build a location sensing network using widely available off-the-shelf components, such as RFID sensors and 802.11 stations. Their goal is to build a network of sensors that will allow users and computers to share their location information, and provide an interface to query and monitor that information. This network and query interface will serve as infrastructure for research in areas such as ubiquitous computing, privacy, large and rapidly changing databases, and whatever else we come up with.

University of Bath (http://www.bath.ac.uk/comp-sci/pervasive/)

The members of the Mobile and Pervasive computing group are interested in designing truly pervasive systems that would flood a whole city or country with pervasive services. They are developing the fundamental understanding of how this can by done by taking into account social issues and factors. They are also interested in making such systems context-aware. To this extent, they are developing the fundamental theory for context-aware systems by using activity theory as a starting point. They would also like this greater pervasive environment to enhance the creativity of its users. They are currently studying creativity and the processes that go on during creative activities, and they are trying to understand how these new mobile and pervasive technologies can assist in creative activities. Some of the projects are:

- **Context Awareness:** Recently, in a mobile and ubiquitous computing environment, the users are able to do their everyday life activities and at the same time access information or use computing services across multiple places and times. As a result, the user's attention may be divided between several simultaneous activities. Moreover, computing devices are becoming smaller to disappearing, resulting in usability issues. Context awareness is a concept of exploiting information relating to users, devices and environments to improve user interaction in mobile and ubiquitous computing. This is so by using the information about user, devices and environment to reduce the explicit input from user. As the context awareness is still at its infant, the main objective is to provide operational context model and use it as a design tool for developing a context aware system that it is easy to use by reducing explicit input from user. This context model should be a simple model that takes into account the important elements that have influence on human activity. As we human do not need to understand everything in others' mind but they still can make sense of each other.

• **Cityware:** Urban Design and Pervasive Systems

The goal of Cityware (Fatah S A, et., al.,2006)) is to develop theory, principles, tools and techniques for the design, implementation and evaluation of city-scale pervasive systems as integral facets of the urban landscape. While architecture has shaped the built environment to satisfy urban dwellers aesthetically and to accommodate their functional needs such as face-to-face interactions and travel, pervasive systems shape electronically mediated interactions in urban space, including use of both fixed and mobile displays and wireless communication. A major issue is space and its relationship with behavior: how do we design the space created by fusing electronically created interaction space with architecturally created physical space? Another major issue is infrastructure: how do we provide interaction and interoperability that scales up to city-scale pervasive systems, while ensuring that they function appropriately and merge aesthetically with urban spaces, materials, forms and uses? Cityware is a multidisciplinary research project, integrating the disciplines of architecture and urban design, human-computer interaction and distributed systems.

University of Florida (http://www.icta.ufl.edu/projects_B.htm)

Programmable Pervasive Spaces

The University of Florida's Mobile and Pervasive Computing Laboratory (Abdulrazak B, et.,al.,2005), (Elzabadani H, et.,al.,2005), and (Helal A.,2005) is developing programmable pervasive spaces in which a smart space exists as both a runtime environment and a software library. Service discovery and gateway protocols automatically integrate system components using generic middleware that maintains a service definition for each sensor and actuator in the space. Programmers assemble services into composite services and applications, which third parties can easily implement or extend.

The Sensor Platform Project - Self-Integrative Sensor Network (Ali M, et. al., 2005). Their goal is to create a sensor network platform (hardware) and associated software architecture that will allow for sensors to be utilizable (programmed) within a highly programmable pervasive space framework. Once a sensor or an actuator is powered on, it should be immediately made visible to other services and applications and can be utilized by a programmer in a new application. Self Sensing Spaces (Abudlrazak B, 2005), (El-abadani H, et.,al.,2006). In this project they will explore (1) emerging sensor network technology, (2) real world modeling techniques, (3) Computer Vision, and (4) self-organizing system principles, to realize the vision of self sensing spaces. Their vision is to create new capabilities in which smart spaces such as homes sense themselves and their residents; create their respective real world models; and enact an accurate mapping between the real world model elements and the physical world. If realized, this vision will enable many applications that rely on remote monitoring/intervention such as for the elderly and the disabled. Location Tracking Sensors/Systems in Pervasive Spaces (Giraldo C.,et.,al.,2003),(Helal A, Kaddourah Y, King,et. al,2005). The goal of the project is to investigate location tracking technologies and to create passive and active sensors that would enable application level development of location based services in a pervasive space. The goal is to achieve a high precision location and tracking of presence, position and orientation. Another goal of the project is to achieve cost-effectiveness, reliability, and to shield sensor technology developments or changes from the application development process.

SmartWave: Meal Preparation System for the Elders (Davenport R, Helal S, et.al.2004)

The goal of this project is to help elderly people cook independently despite visual or cognitive impairments. The goal is to create a pervasive microwave based cooking system which makes it easier for elderly people to enjoy a hot meal without having to read cooking instructions or interact with the microwave buttons. Additionally, SmartWave provides memory and coordination assistance to aid elderly with minor cognitive impairment.

Elder Cognitive Assistant (Giraldo C, Helal A, Kaddoura Y, et.,al.,2003), (Giraldo C, Helal S, Mann W.,2002)

The goal of this project is to design, and implement and extensively test an indoor/outdoor elder digital assistance and a number of associated applications and services and to overcome the challenging task of designing a powerful and capable platform that can be utilized by a simple voice based interface, that can work autonomously outdoors but that can exploit the pervasive space and its sensor networks indoor. Another challenge is to use as much commercial off the shelf components (COTS) and produce a replicable Elder Assistant platform that can be used in extensive clinical and usability studies.

AMADEUS – The University of York (http://www.cs.york.ac.uk/amadeus/)

The chief aim of AMADEUS (Ariyaeeinia A,et.,al.,2005), (Bailey C, Freeman M.,2005), (Bailey C, Meng H, Pears,2005), (Jayasooriya T G, Manandhar S., 2005) is to develop component technologies for future pervasive computing environments. Such components will typically be hardware IP cores, but will occasionally include modular software technologies. AMADEUS seeks to develop particular component technologies in the following areas:-

- Video Processing Subsystems
- Audio Processing Subsystems
- 'Intelligent' data processing architectures
- Embedded human-machine interactivity
- Biometric awareness components
- Home networking elements

Ultimately, AMADEUS aims to develop and exploit component technologies that will facilitate the rapid development of sophisticated ubiquitous computing systems, and to develop demonstrators and systems which exemplify these technologies.

CHALLENGES

Technical Challenges

Security (www.doc.ic.ac.uk/~mss)

- Interactions cross multiple organizational boundaries
- Specification, analysis and integration for heterogeneous OS, databases, firewalls and routers
- Vulnerability to hacking
- Small communicators with confidential data are easily lost or stolen – biometric authentication.

Privacy (www.doc.ic.ac.uk/~mss)

- Privacy of Location (Weiser M, 1993)

Cellular systems inherently need to know the location of devices and their use in order to properly route information. For instance, the traveling pattern of a frequent cellular phone user can be deduced from the roaming data of cellular service

Figure 11. Technical research problems in pervasive computing. M. Satyanarayanan, "Pervasive Computing: Vision and Challenges," IEEE Personal Communications, August 2001. (Satyanarayanan M.,2001)

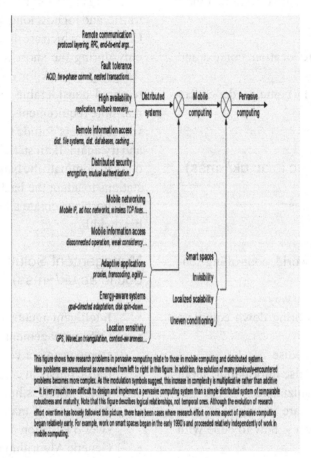

providers. This problem could be much worse in ubiquitous computing with its more extensive use of cellular wireless. So a key problem with ubiquitous computing is preserving privacy of location. One solution, a central database of location information, means the privacy controls can be centralized and perhaps done well—on the other hand one break-in there reveals all, and centrality is unlikely to scale worldwide. A second source of insecurity is the transmission of the location information to a central site. This site is the obvious place to try to snoop packets, or even to use traffic analysis on source addresses.

One preferred design avoids a central repository, instead storing information about each person at that person's PC or workstation. programs that need to know a person's location must query the PC, and proceed through whatever security measures the user has chosen to install. Accumulating information about individuals over long periods is one of the more useful things to do, but quickly raises hackles. A key problem for location is how to provide occasional location information for clients who need it, while somehow preventing the reliable accumulation of long-term trends about an individual. It is important to realize there can never be a purely technological solution to privacy, and social issues must be considered in their own right. Only society can cause the right system to be used. To help prevent future oppressive employers or governments from taking this power away, we are also encouraging the wide dissemination of information about location systems and their potential for harm.

- System can correlate location, context and behaviour patterns
- Constant spam of context dependent advertising.

Management (www.doc.ic.ac.uk/~mss)

- Huge complex systems
- billions of processors
- multiple organizations
- managing physical world, controlling sensors, actuators
- Humans will be in the way
- Errors propagate to bring down complete regions
- Hacker and virus paradise
- System propagates false information about individuals and organizations
- Complexity of software installations on a work station or server – how to cope with billions?

A "media access" protocol provides access to a physical medium. Common media access methods in wired domains are collision detection and token-passing. These do not work unchanged in a wireless domain because not every device is assured of being able to hear every other device (this is called the "hidden terminal" problem). Furthermore, earlier wireless work used assumptions of complete autonomy, or a statically configured network, while ubiquitous computing requires a cellular topology, with mobile devices frequently coming on- and off-line. A media access protocol called MACA (Weiser M.,1993) has been developed. The key idea of MACA is for the two stations desiring to communicate to first do a short handshake of Request-To-Send-N-bytes followed by Clear-To-Send-N-bytes. This exchange allows all other stations to hear that there is going to be traffic, and for how long they should remain quiet. Collisions, which are detected by timeouts, occur only during the short Request-To-Send packet. Adapting MACA for ubiquitous computing use required considerable attention to fairness and real-time requirements. MACA requires stations whose packets collide to back off a random time and try again. If all stations but one back-off, that one can dominate the bandwidth. By requiring all stations to adapt the back-off parameter of their neighbors, we create a much fairer allocation of bandwidth.

Management Solutions (www. doc.ic.ac.uk/~mss)

- Intelligent agents, mobile agent's policy
- QoS management - Fat pipes and large storage can convert media streams to short traffic bursts in core network but still needed for wireless links
- Adaptive self management is the only answer o Partition domains of responsibility
- Genetic Algorithm may be suitable for long term strategy but need more deterministic solution for short term decision making
- Remove human from the loop

Research Challenges (Brumitt B, Krumm J, 2000)

Ubiquitous computing is a very difficult integration of human factors, computer science, engineering, and social sciences. Current researches try to address the new technological issues raised, analyzing the impact on the people and how to bridge the social-technical gap. A set of research challenges:

- **Semantic Modeling:** Use of ontologies to describe users' task environments, as well as their goals, to enable reasoning about a user's needs and therefore to adapt to changes. It is a challenge to develop on a high-level model language to express the complex nature of ontologies.

- **Building the Software Infrastructure:** The application must determine the user's context, must provide reasonable functionalities with bad connectivity, must recover from failover, and must be scalable.

- **Developing and Configuring Applications:** There is a need of a shift in the developers' mindset while building pervasive application. There is a need to describe on a high-level the task a user needs to perform. The challenge is to be able to specify the interaction logic at an "intent-level" and the application's requirements on data and computation.

- **Validating the User Experience:** The utility of some computing advancements cannot be evaluated without performing significant user studies and in some cases, widely deploying it. Consequently, the development of effective methods for testing and evaluating the usage scenarios enabled by pervasive applications is an important area that needs more attention from researchers.

CONCLUSION

Pervasive computing is about making our lives simpler through digital environments that are sensitive, adaptive, and responsive to human needs. Far more than mobile computing, this technology will fundamentally change the nature of computing, allowing most objects we encounter in daily life to be "aware," interacting with users in both the physical and virtual worlds. While research challenges remain in all areas of pervasive computing, all the basic component technologies exist today. In hardware, we have mobile devices, sensors, and even smart appliances. Supporting software

technologies include digital signal processing and object-oriented programming. Advances in networking support mobility management, ad hoc routing, and global reach ability. Hence, in the near future, we can expect our homes to network intelligent devices that transparently support our information and communication needs.

REFERENCES

Abdulrazak, B., Helal, A., Jansen, E., King, J., & Yang, H. (2005). *A Programming Model for Pervasive Spaces*. Submitted to the 3rd International Conference on Service Oriented Computing, Amsterdam, The Netherlands, December 12-15.

Abudlrazak, B., El-Zabadani, H., Helal, A., & Jansen, E. (2005). Self-Sensing Spaces: Smart Plugs for Smart Environments. In *Proceedings of the third International Conference on Smart homes and health Telematic (ICOST)*, Sherbrooke, Québec, Canada.

Alahuhta, P., Beigl, M., Gellersen, H., Holmquist, L., Mattern, F., & Schiele, B. (2001, September). Smart-Its Friends: A Technique for Users to Easily Establish Connections between Smart Artifacts. In *Proc. of UBICOMP 2001*, Atlanta, GA.

Ali, M., Aref, W., Bose, R., Elmagarmid, A., Helal, A., Kamel, I., & Mokbel, M. (2005). NILE-PDT: A Phenomenon Detection and Tracking Framework for Data Stream Management Systems. In *Proceedings of the Very Large Databases Conference (VLDB)*, Trondheim, Norway.

Anderson, T., Borriello, G., Esler, M., & Hightower, J. (1999). Next Century Challenges: Data-Centric Networking for Invisible Computing (The Portolano Project at the University of Washington). In the proceedings of Mobicom 99, Seattle, Washington.

Ariyaeeinia, A., Sotudeh, R., & Xu, J. (2005). User Voice Identification On FPGA. In Perspectives in Pervasive Computing. London: IEE.

Bailey, C., & Freeman, M. (2005). Designing an ubiquitous computing development kit. In Perspectives in Pervasive Computing. London: IEE.

Bailey, C., Meng, H., & Pears, N. E. (2005). FPGA Based Video Processing System for Ubiquitous Applications. In Perspectives in Pervasive Computing. London: IEE.

Basu, K., Das, S., & De, P. (2004). An Ubiquitous Architectural Framework and Protocol for Object Tracking using RFID Tags. In *Proceedings of ACM Mobi Quitous Networking Conference*, Boston.

Beigl, M., Gellersen, H., & Schmidt, A. (2001). MediaCups: Experience with Design and Use of Computer-Augmented Everyday Artifacts. *Computer Networks . Special Issue on Pervasive Computing, 35*(4), 401–409.

Borriello, G., Farkas, K.I., Pering, T. & Want, R. (2002). Disappearing hardware. *Pervasive Computing, 1*(1).

Bresin, R., Fernström, M., & Rocchesso, D. (2003, April). Sounding Objects. *IEEE MultiMedia, 10*(2), 42–52. doi:10.1109/MMUL.2003.1195160

Brown, J., & Weiser, M. (1997). Beyond Calculation: The Next Fifty Years of Computing. New York: Springer-Verlag.

Brumitt, B., Krumm, J., Meyers, B., & Shafer, S. (2000). Ubiquitous Computing & The Role of Geometry. IEEE Personal Communications.

Campbell, C., Maglio, P., Matlock, T., Smith, B., & Zhai, S. (2000). In *Proceedings of The third International Conference on Multimodal Interfaces*, Beijing, China (LNCS Vol. 1948, pp. 1-7). Berlin: Springer.

Cohen, P., & Oviatt, S. (2000). Multimodal interfaces that process what comes naturally. *Communications of the ACM, 43*(3), 45–53. doi:10.1145/330534.330538

CPOL. *High-Performance Policy Evaluation.* (2005). Presented at the 12th ACM conference on Computer and communications security.

Das, S., Kumar, M., & Shirazi, B. (2003, April). Pervasively Secure Infrastructures (PSI) through Communitys Computing. In *Proc of the Texas Workshop on Security of Information Systems*, College Station, USA, (pp. 5-10).

Davenport, R., Helal, S., Mann, W., Russo, J., & Sukojo, A. (2004). SmartWave Intelligent Meal Preparation System to Help Older People Live Independently. In *Proceedings of the Second International Conference on Smart homes and health Telematic (ICOST2004)*, Singapore.

El-Zabadani, H., Helal, A., Mann, W., & Schmaltz, M. (2006). *PerVision: An integrated Pervasive Computing/Computer Vision Approach to Tracking Objects in a Self-Sensing Space.* Submitted to the 4th IEEE International Conference on Pervasive Computing and Communications (PerCom), Pisa, Italy.

Elzabadani, H., Helal, A., Jansen, E., Kaddourah, Y., King, J. & Mann, W. (2005). Gator Tech Smart House: A Programmable Pervasive Space. *IEEE Computer magazine*, 64-74.

Fatah, S. A., Fraser, D. S., Jones, T., Kindberg, T., Kostakos, V., O'Neill, E., & Penn, A. (2006). Design Tools for Pervasive Computing in Urban Environment. In *proceedings 8th International Conference on Design & Decision Support Systems in Architecture and Urban Planning*, Eindhoven, The Netherlands, Springer.

Garlan, D., & Sousa, J. (2002). Aura: an Architectural Framework for User Mobility. In Ubiquitous Computing Environments. In *the Proceedings of the 3rd Working IEEE/IFIP Conference on Software Architecture*, (pp. 29-43).

Gifford, S. (2005). Experiences with Location Sensing Systems. Presented at the *2005 NSF CISE/CNS Pervasive Computing Infrastructure Experience Workshop*, at the University of Michigan.

Gifford, S., & Sharma, S. (2005). Using RFID to Evaluate Evacuation Behavior Models. Presented at the *2005 North American Fuzzy Information Processing Society conference*.

Giraldo, C., Helal, A., Kaddoura, Y., Lee, C., Mann, W., & Zabbadani, H. (2003). Smart Phone Based Cognitive Assistant. In *Proceedings of the The 2nd International Workshop on Ubiquitous Computing for Pervasive Healthcare Applications*, Seattle, WA.

Giraldo, C., Helal, S., Kaddourah, Y., Lee, C., Mann, W., Ran, L., & Winkler, B. (2003). Enabling Location- Aware Pervasive Computing Applications for the Elderly. In *Proceedings of the First IEEE Pervasive Computing Conference*, Fort Worth, TX.

Giraldo, C., Helal, S., & Mann, W. (2002). mPCA - A Mobile Patient Care-Giving Assistant for Alzheimer Patients. In *First International Workshop on Ubiquitous Computing for Cognitive Aids (UbiCog'02), in conjunction with The Fourth International Conference on Ubiquitous Computing (UbiComp'02)*, Göteborg, Sweden.

Gronbaek, K., Mogensen, P., & Orbaek, P. (2001). Interaction techniques for spatial organization of digital and Physical materials – The Topos Approach. In *the Proceedings of First Danish Human-Computer Interaction Research Symposium*, (pp. 51-52).

Hazen, T. J., & Park, A. (2002). ASR dependent techniques for speaker identification. In *Proc. of ICSLP*, Denver, CO, (pp. 1337– 1340).

Helal, A. (2005). Programming Pervasive Spaces. *IEEE Pervasive Computing magazine, 4*(1).

Helal, A., Kaddourah, Y., & King, J. (July 2005). Cost- Precision Tradeoffs in Unencumbered Floor-Based Indoor Location Tracking. In *Proceedings of the third International Conference On Smart homes and health Telematic (ICOST)*, Sherbrooke, Québec, Canada.

Ishchenko, D., Kinne, C. P., Mork, B. A., Quest, R. P., Wang, X., & Yerrabelli, A. D. (2005). *Power Line Carrier Communications Systems Modeling*. Presented at the International Conference on Power Systems Transients (IPST'05) in Montreal, Canada on June 19-23, Paper No. IPST05 – 247.

Jayasooriya, T. G., & Manandhar, S. (2005). Networking In A Smart Home - Providing Lightweight Networking Services for Heterogeneous Devices. In Perspectives in Pervasive Computing. London: IEE.

McGuire, P. (2005). The Cyborg Astrobiologist: Scouting Red Beds for Uncommon Features with Geological Significance. *International Journal of Astrobiology, 4*(2). doi:10.1017/S1473550405002533

Rhodes, B. J. (1997). The wearable remembrance agent: a system for augmented memory. In *Proc. of First International Symposium on Wearable Computers (ISWC '97)*, (pp.123).

Robertson, G., & Turk, M. (2000). Perceptual user interfaces. *Communications of the ACM, 43*(3), 33–34.

Satyanarayanan, M. (2001). Pervasive Computing: Vision and Challenges. IEEE Personal Communications.

Weiser, M. (1993). Some Computer Science Issues in Ubiquitous Computing. *Communications of the ACM, 36*(7). doi:10.1145/159544.159617

ADDITIONAL READING IN PERVASIVE COMPUTING

Adjie-Winoto, W., Schwartz, E., Balakrishnan, H., & Lilley, J. The design and implementation of an intentional naming system *Proc. 17th ACM SOSP*, Kiawah Island, SC, December 1999.

(2001). Anind k. Dey, Understanding and Using Context. *Personal and Ubiquitous Computing, 5*(Issue 1).

Czerwinski, S. Ben Y. Zhao, Todd Hodes, Anthony Joseph, and Randy Katz. An Architecture for a Secure Service Discovery Service. In Proceedings of MobiCom '99

Energy-aware adaptation for mobile applications, Jason Flinn, M. Satyanarayanan, SOSP 1999.

Investigating Upper Bounds on Network Lifetime Extension for Cell-Based Energy Conservation Techniques in Stationary Ad Hoc Networks Douglas Blough. Georgia Institute of Technology, USA, Paolo Santi, Istituto di Informatica e Telematica, Italy. MobiCom 2002.

Krashinsky, R., & Balakrishnan, H. Minimizing Energy for Wireless Web Access with Bounded Slowdown, MobiCom 2002.

Kravets, R., and Krishnan, P. Application-driven power management for mobile communication. ACM Wireless Networks 6, 4 (2000), 263{277.

(2001, August). Location systems for ubiquitous computing. By J. Hightower and G. Borriello. *IEEE Computer, 34*(8), 57–66.

Magdalena Balazinska, Hari Balakrishnan, and David Karger INS/Twine: A Scalable Peer-to-Peer Architecture for Intentional Resource Discovery, Pervasive 2002.

Minimum-Energy Broadcast in All-Wireless Networks. NP-Completeness and Distribution Issues Mario Cagalj, Jean-Pierre Hubaux, Swiss Federal Institute of Technology, Christian Enz, Swiss Center for Electronics and Microtechnology, Switzerland. MobiCom 2002.

Next century challenges: data-centric networking for invisible computing. By M. Esler, J. Hightower, T. Anderson, G. Borriello. In *Proceedings of the 5th ACM/IEEE International Conference on Mobile Computing and Networking*, pages 24-35, Seattle, Washington, August 1999.

Pervasive computing: vision and challenges. By M. Satyanarayanan *IEEE Personal Communications*, 8(4):10-17, August 2001.

Power management for energy-aware communication systems . ACM Transactions on Embedded Computing Systems, Auguest 2003.

PowerScope. A Tool for Profiling the Energy Usage of Mobile Applications, Jason Flinn, M. Satyanarayanan, IEEE WMSCA, 1999.

(2002, April-June). Project Aura: toward distraction-free pervasive computing. By D. Garlan, D. Siewiorek, A. Smailagic, and P. Steenkiste. *IEEE Pervasive Computing / IEEE Computer Society [and] IEEE Communications Society, 1*(2), 22–31. doi:10.1109/MPRV.2002.1012334

"Real-Time Dynamic Voltage Scaling for Low-Power Embedded Operating Systems," Padmanabhan Pillai and Kang G. Shin, in Proc. of SOSP 2001.

Self-Tuning Wireless Network Power Management. Manish Anand, Edmund B. Nightingale, and Jason Flinn, MobiCom 2003.

Stoica, I., Morris, R., & Karger, D. M. Frans Kaashoek, and Hari Balakrishnan, Chord: A Scalable Peer-to-peer Lookup Service for Internet Applications, ACM SIGCOMM 2001.

(2002, January-March). System software for ubiquitous computing. By T. Kindberg and A. Fox. *IEEE Pervasive Computing / IEEE Computer Society [and] IEEE Communications Society, 1*(1), 70–81. doi:10.1109/MPRV.2002.993146

System support for pervasive applications. By R. Grimm and B. Bershad. In A. Schiper, A. A. Shvartsman, H. Weatherspoon, and B. Y. Zhao, editors, *Future Directions in Distributed Computing*, pages 212-217, volume 2584 of *Lecture Notes in Computer Science*. Springer-Verlag, Heidelberg, April 2003.

System support for pervasive applications. By R. Grimm, J. Davis, E.. Lemar, A.. MacBeth, S. Swanson, T. Anderson, B. Bershad, G. Borriello, S. Gribble, and D. Wetherall. Submitted for publication.

(1991, Sept.). The computer for the twenty-first century. By M. Weiser. *Scientific American, 265*(3), 94–104.

(2002, April-June). The interactive workspaces project: experiences with ubiquitous computing rooms. By B. Johanson, A. Fox, and T. Winograd. *IEEE Pervasive Computing / IEEE Computer Society [and] IEEE Communications Society, 1*(2), 67–74. doi:10.1109/MPRV.2002.1012339

The location stack: a layered model for location in ubiquitous computing. By J. Hightower, B. Brumitt, and G. Borriello. In *Proceedings of the 4th IEEE Workshop on Mobile Computing Systems and Applications*, pages 22-28, June 2002.

Wake on Wireless: An Event Driven Energy Saving Strategy for Battery Operated Devices Eugene Shih, *Massachusetts Institute of Technology*, USA, Paramvir Bahl, Michael Sinclair, *Microsoft Research*, USA. MobiCom 2002.

XenoSearch: Distributed Resource Discovery in the XenoServer Open Platform, HPDC 2003

KEY TERMS AND DEFINITIONS

ASIC: An ASIC (application-specific integrated circuit) is a microchip designed for a special application, such as a particular kind of transmission protocol or a hand-held computer. You might contrast it with general integrated circuits, such as the microprocessor and the random access memory chips in your PC. ASICs are used in a wide-range of applications, including auto emission control, environmental monitoring, and personal digital assistants (PDAs). An ASIC can be pre-manufactured for a special application or it can be custom manufactured (typically using components from a "building block" library of components) for a particular customer application.

Ambient Intelligence: Ambient Intelligence is a step beyond Ubiquitous Computing. There is an explicit focus on individuals in an environment. As we look across Wearable Computers and this event there is a shift taking place. Tom Rodden, University of Nottingham, UK, put it bluntly - for 40 years our thoughts have been dominated by the PC, keyboard and mouse. This has actually been a diversion away from finding out what "will be our every day relationship with computing." One of the most important changes is the social context and awareness that permeates the use of computers in every day life. The shift is profound: So far the individual has had to adapt to what the computer could do for the person; now with ambient intelligence the computer must adapt to the individual. These are implications that are only becoming evident

Autonomic Computing: A type of computing model, in which the system is self-healing, self-configured, self-protected and self-managed. Designed to mimic the human body's nervous system—in that the autonomic nervous system acts and reacts to stimuli independent of the individual's conscious input—an autonomic computing environment functions with a high level of artificial intelligence while remaining invisible to the users. Just as the human body acts and responds without the individual controlling functions (e.g., internal temperature rises and falls, breathing rate fluctuates, glands secrete hormones in response to stimulus), the autonomic computing environment operates organically in response to the input it collects.

Mobile and Nomadic Computing: Nomadicity is the tendency of a person, or group of people, to move with relative frequency. Leonard Kleinrock and others have written of the need to support today's increasingly mobile workers with nomadic computing, the use of portable computing devices and, ideally, constant access to the Internet and data on other computers. Standards such as the IETF's Mobile IPv6 standards and Dynamic Host Configuration Protocol (DHCP) can be said to support nomadic computing. According to Kleinrock, the goal of nomadic computing is to enable a consistent experience for users anywhere in the world, including as they travel from one place to another. A nomadic environment is said to be one that is transparent to the user, regardless of location, the device and platform they're using, the available bandwidth, and whether or not they are in motion at any given time

Location-Aware Computing: Refers to computing that takes into account a particular context (mainly position). Location-aware computing relies on location-based services. In a narrow sense, such services are tied to mobile networks. Services based on other information like IP numbers probably rather use the more "geo-location" term. (1) Location Based Services (LBS) are information and entertainment services accessible with mobile devices through the mobile network and utilizing the ability to make use of the geographical position of the mobile device. ([http://en.wikipedia. org/wiki/Location-based_service Wikipedia], retrieved 13:37, 3 June 2008 (UTC).). (2)Location-based services can deliver location-aware content to subscribers on the basis of the positioning capability of the wireless infrastructure.

Context-Aware Computing: Context awareness originated as a term from ubiquitous computing or as so-called pervasive computing which sought to deal with linking changes in the environment with computer systems, which are otherwise static. Although it originated as a computer science term, it has also been applied to business theory in relation to business process management issues

Ubiquitous or Pervasive Computing: Pervasive computing is the trend towards increasingly ubiquitous (another name for the movement is *ubiquitous computing*), connected computing devices in the environment, a trend being brought about by a convergence of advanced electronic - and particularly, wireless - technologies and the Internet. Pervasive computing devices are not personal computers as we tend to think of them, but very tiny - even invisible - devices, either mobile or embedded in almost any type of object imaginable, including cars, tools, appliances, clothing and various consumer goods - all communicating through increasingly interconnected networks.

Gesture Recognition: Gesture recognition is human interaction with a computer in which human gestures, usually hand motions, are recognized by the computer. Recognizing gestures as input might make computers more accessible for the physically-impaired and make interaction more natural for young children. It could also provide a more expressive and nuanced communication with a computer. Several companies have developed prototype products. Gesture recognition is already being used for interaction with a 3-D immersion environment.

Micro Electromechanical Systems: Microelectromechanical systems (MEMS) is a technology that combines computers with tiny mechanical devices such as sensors, valves, gears, mirrors, and actuators embedded in semiconductor chips. Paul Saffo of the Institute for the Future in Palo Alto, California, believes MEMS or what he calls analog computing will be "the foundational technology of the next decade." MEMS is also sometimes called *smart matter*.

Smart Matter: Smart matter is another term for micro-electromechanical systems (MEMS), a technology that combines computers with tiny mechanical devices such as sensors, valves, gears, mirrors, and actuators imbedded in semiconductor chips. Paul Saffo of the Institute for the Future in Palo Alto, California, believes MEMS or what he calls analog computing will be "the foundational technology of the next decade."

Virtual Reality: An artificial environment created with computer hardware and software and presented to the user in such a way that it appears and feels like a real environment. To "enter" a virtual reality, a user dons special gloves, earphones, and goggles, all of which receive their input from the computer system. In this way, at least three of the five senses are controlled by the computer. In addition to feeding sensory input to the user, the devices also monitor the user's actions. The goggles, for example, track how the eyes move and respond accordingly by sending new video input. To date, virtual reality systems require extremely expensive hardware and software and are confined mostly to research laboratories.

Smart Spaces: Smart spaces are synonymous with concepts such as ubiquitous and pervasive computing, and the disappearing computer. The concept behind this paradigm are environments saturated with embedded computational devices that enables the environment to learn about their occupants, connect to the work they are doing, or their goals, and possible enable social exchanges. When coupled with mobile devices, the power of smart spaces is that they can adapt to specific needs and characteristics of inhabitants as well as consider the context of the interaction in order to improve the user's experience in that environment. However, the sensing functionality does not have

to interface exclusively to mobile devices. In fact, the use of biometrics is becoming increasingly popular as it relies solely on the individual. These sensing systems may include face-tracking and facial-expression analysis system, and an audio-based expression and speech analysis system, gesture analysis and tracking.

Wearable Computing: Some inventors and other theorists not only believe you could wear a computer; they believe there's no reason why you shouldn't. Assuming you remembered to wear it, a wearable computer is always available. Currently, several companies sell wearables and there is a considerable literature on the subject. Some wearable computers are basically desktop or notebook computers that have been scaled down for body-wear. Others employ brand new technology. Both general and special purposes are envisioned. A number of wearables have been designed for the disabled.

Ad Hoc Networks: Ad Hoc" is actually a Latin phrase that means "for this purpose." It is often used to describe solutions that are developed on-the-fly for a specific purpose. In computer networking, an ad hoc network refers to a network connection established for a single session and does not require a router or a wireless base station. For example, if you need to transfer a file to your friend's laptop, you might create an ad hoc network between your computer and his laptop to transfer the file. This may be done using an Ethernet crossover cable, or the computers' wireless cards to communicate with each other. If you need to share files with more than one computer, you could set up a mutli-hop ad hoc network, which can transfer data over multiple nodes.

Telematics: Originally coined to mean the convergence of telecommunications and information processing, the term later evolved to refer to automation in automobiles. GPS navigation, integrated hands-free cellphones, wireless communications and automatic driving assistance systems all come under the telematics umbrella. General Motor's OnStar was the first to combine

GPS with roadside assistance and remote diagnostics (see GPS).Bluetooth wireless is used to interface a driver's cellphone and PDA into the vehicle's audio system, and a wireless standard for all vehicles is expected.

Perceptual Interfaces: One common definition of perceptual interfaces is they describe features that increase perceptual bandwidth. Perceptual interfaces can interact with users via more and different sensory channels than are possible with traditional interfaces. If a traditional interface has only typing and mousing in response to pictures and words, a perceptual one adds speaking, touching, gesturing, emoting, and gazing. This notion of perceptual interfaces illustrates the enthusiasm for more elaborate sensory exchanges between humans and computers. But other elements of a definition must be added to go beyond a simple notion that the number of senses involved in the exchanges is greater. First, definitions need to specify whose perceptions and of what. Second, definitions should provide categories that help organize the different elements of perception. We'll try to answer the first issue with a model of communication exchanges, and the second with a brief review of the domains of perception research.

WEB SITE REFERENCES

http://www.doc.ic.ac.uk/~mss (n.d.).

http://www.domino.watson.ibm.com/comm/wwwr_thinkresearch.nsf/pages/coverstory100.html (n.d.).

http://www.comsoc.org/pci/private/2000/oct/pdf/brummit.pdf (n.d.).

http://www.cmc.cs.dartmouth.edu/cmc/papers/chen:thesis-tr.pdf (n.d.).

http://www.voicerecognition.com/dragtool.html (n.d.).

http://www.sls.lcs.mit.edu/sls/ publications/2003/ICMI_Hazen.pdf (n.d.).

http://www.primidi.com/2003/11/13.html#a645 (n.d.).

http://www.cs.uiuc.edu/events/ expwork-2005/Jun_Wang_Abstract.pdf (n.d.).

http://hbswk.hbs.edu/You Are What You Compute HBS Working Knowledge.htm (n.d.).

http://www.toshiba.com/news/980715.htm (n.d.).

http://www.physorg.com/Geologysmart space suit developed.htm (n.d.).

http://www.csl.sony.co.jp/person/rekimoto/papers/iswc01.pdf (n.d.).

http://www.ibm.com (n.d.).

http://www.whatis.com (n.d.).

http://www.ece.rutgers.edu/~parashar/Classes/02-03/ece572/perv-reading/pc-overview.pdf (n.d.).

http://www.research.ibm.com/people/a/archan/mcommerce2002.pdf (n.d.).

http://www.taipeitimes.com/news/2001/12/10/story/0000115251 (n.d.).

http://www.phillips.com (n.d.).

http://www.cs.cmu.edu (n.d.).

http://www.disappearing-computer.net/index.html (n.d.).

http://2wear.ics.forth.gr/ (n.d.).

http://atelier.k3.mah.se/home/ (n.d.).

http://interliving.kth.se/ (n.d.).

http://www.mimeproject.org/ (n.d.).

http://www.image.ntua.gr/oresteia/ (n.d.).

http://www.shape-dc.org/ (n.d.).

http://www.smart-its.org/ (n.d.).

http://www.sics.se/accord/index.html (n.d.).

http://www.soundobject.org/ (n.d.).

http://www.daimi.au.dk/workspace/index.htm (n.d.).

http://www.teco.uni-karlsruhe.de/~michael/publication/mediacup/ (n.d.).

http://www.cs.cmu.edu/~aura/ (n.d.).

http://www.endeavour.cs.berkeley.edu/ (n.d.).

http://www.oxygen.lcs.mit.edu/ (n.d.).

http://www.portolano.cs.washington.edu/ (n.d.).

http://www.uk.research.att.com/spirit/ (n.d.).

http://www.cooltown.com (n.d.).

http://www.research.microsoft.com/easyliving/ (n.d.).

http://www-3.ibm.com/software/pervasive/ (n.d.).

http://crewman.uta.edu/psi (n.d.).

http://www.indiana.edu/~uits/cpo/ipcres/overview.html (n.d.).

http://whereabouts.eecs.umich.edu/ (n.d.).

http://www.bath.ac.uk/comp-sci/pervasive/ (n.d.).

http://www.icta.ufl.edu/projects_B.htm (n.d.).

http://www.cs.york.ac.uk/amadeus/ (n.d.).

http://2wear.ics.forth.gr/deliverables/2wear_FinalReport_draft.pdf (n.d.).

http://atelier.k3.mah.se/publications/final_report.pdf (n.d.).

http://www.image.ntua.gr/oresteia/deliverables/ORESTEIA-IST-2000-26091-ND4.1.pdf (n.d.).

http://www.sics.se/accord/plan/del/D51a.doc (n.d.).

http://www.disappearing-computer.net/projects/GROCER.html (n.d.).

Chapter 2
Kernel Parameter Selection for SVM Classification:
Adaboost Approach

Manju Bala
Jawaharlal Nehru University, India

R. K. Agrawal
Jawaharlal Nehru University, India

ABSTRACT

The choice of kernel function and its parameter is very important for better performance of support vector machine. In this chapter, the authors proposed few new kernel functions which satisfy the Mercer's conditions and a robust algorithm to automatically determine the suitable kernel function and its parameters based on AdaBoost to improve the performance of support vector machine. The performance of proposed algorithm is evaluated on several benchmark datasets from UCI repository. The experimental results for different datasets show that the Gaussian kernel is not always the best choice to achieve high generalization of support vector machine classifier. However, with the proper choice of kernel function and its parameters using proposed algorithm, it is possible to achieve maximum classification accuracy for all datasets.

INTRODUCTION

In the past two decades valuable work has been carried out in the area of text categorization (Joachims, Thorsten, 1998; Thorsten et al., 2001), optical character recognition (Mori et al., 1992), intrusion detection (Mukkamala et al., 2002), speech recognition (Schmidt, 1996), handwritten digit recognition (Weston & Watkins, 1999) etc. All such real-world applications are essentially multi-class

DOI: 10.4018/978-1-61520-741-1.ch002

classification problems. Multi-class classification is intrinsically harder than binary classification problem because the classification has to learn to construct a greater number of separation boundaries or relations. Classification error rate is greater in multi-class problem than that of binary as there can be error in determination of any one of the decision boundaries or relations.

There are basically two types of multi-class classification algorithms. The first type deals directly with multiple values in the target field *i.e.* K- Nearest Neighbor, Naive Bayes, classification trees in the class etc. Intuitively, these methods can be interpreted as trying to construct a conditional probability density for each class, then classifying by selecting the class with maximum a posteriori probability. For data with high dimensional input space and very few samples per class, it is very difficult to construct accurate densities. While the other approaches decompose the multi-class problem into a set of binary problems and then combining them to make a final multi-class classifier. This group contains support vector machines, boosting and more generally, any binary classifier. In certain settings the later approach results in better performance then the multiple target approaches.

Support Vector Machine (SVM) is most commonly and popular classification technique used in literature. Support Vector Machines (SVMs) are based on statistical learning theory developed by Vapnik (Vapnik, 1998; Corts & Vapnik, 1995; Corts & Vapnik, 1995; Burges, 1998). It transforms the training vectors into a high-dimensional feature space, labeling each vector by its class. It classifies data by determining a set of support vectors, which are members of the set of training inputs that outline a hyperplane in feature space (Kittler & Hojjatoleslami, 1998). It is based on the idea of Structural risk minimization, which minimizes the generalization error. The number of free parameters used in the SVM depends on the margin that separates the data points and not on the number of input features. SVM provides a generic technique to fit the surface of the hyperplane to the data by employing an appropriate kernel function. Use of a kernel function enables the curse of dimensionality to be addressed, and the solution implicitly contains support vectors that provide a description of the significant data for classification (Scholkopf & smola, 2002).

In literature, the most commonly used kernel functions are linear, polynomial and Gaussian. However, it has been suggested that the choice of these kernels may not be appropriate for many real time datasets. It is shown in literature (Corts & Vapnik, 1995) that the classifier accuracy of

SVM is being improved upon with the use of new kernels other than using linear, polynomial and Gaussian. In training a SVM, we need to select an appropriate kernel with its parameter and suitable choice of the margin parameter C for achieving better classification accuracy. The suitable kernel function can be used in SVM provided the distribution of the data is known. However, finding a suitable kernel function and its parameter becomes more challenging when the underlying distribution is unknown. In such situation, there is need to identify kernel function and its parameters for which the classifier provides maximum classification accuracy. Since for multi-class data, the classification is carried out by constructing and combining several binary SVM classifiers, it is possible that single choice of kernel function and its parameter may not provide better classification accuracy. To improve the performance of SVM classifier, there is need to select appropriate kernel function and its parameters for each individual classifier involved in a multi-class classification problem.

We have proposed few new kernel functions which satisfy Mercer's condition and may be more suitable for classification. Also, based on previous work (Tian et al., 2004; Amores et al., 2006; Yu et al., 2006), we propose a new boosted kernel parameters selection framework to automatically learn the best kernel function and its parameters to achieve maximum classification accuracy for a given multi-class classification problem.

SUPPORT VECTOR MACHINE CLASSIFIER

Theory of SVM

This section briefly introduces the theory of SVM. Let $\{(x_1,\ y_1),...,(x_m,\ y_m)\} \in R^n \times \{+1,-1\}$ be a training set. The SVM classifier finds a canonical hyperplane $\{x \in R^n: w^T x + b = 0, w \in \mathcal{R}^n, b \in \mathcal{R}\}$

which maximally separates given two classes of training samples in R^n. The corresponding decision function $f : \mathcal{R}^n \rightarrow \{+1, -1\}$ is then given by $f(x)$ = sgn$(w^T x + b)$. For many practical applications, the training set may not be linearly separable. In such cases, the optimal decision function is found by solving the following quadratic optimization problem:

$$\text{Minimize } J(w, \xi) = \frac{1}{2} w^T w + C \sum_{i=1}^{l} \xi_i$$

$$\text{Subject to } y_i(w^T x_i + b) \geq 1 - \xi_i, \geq 1 - \xi_i,$$
$$\xi_i \geq 0, i = 1,2,...,m \; \xi_i \geq 0, i = 1,2,...,m \quad (1)$$

Where ξ_i is a slack variable introduced to relax the hard-margin constraints and the regularization constant $C > 0$ determines the trade-off between the empirical error and the complexity term. The generalized optimization is based on a theorem about the VC dimension of canonical hyperplanes. It was shown that if the hyperplane is constructed under the constraint $\|w\| \leq A$ then the VC- dimension of the class H is bounded by $h \leq \min(R^2 A^2, n) + 1$ (Vapnik, 1995), where R is the radius of the smallest sphere around the data. Thus, if we bound the margin of a function class from below, say by $2/A$, we can control its VC dimension and hence apply the SRM principle.

Applying the Karush-Kuhn Tucker complimentarily condition (Fletcher, 1987) which gives optimal solution of a non-linear programming problem, we can write $w = \sum_{i=1}^{m} y_i \alpha_i x_i$ after minimizing (1). This is called the dual representation of w. A x_i with nonzero α_i is called a support vector. The coefficients α_i can be found by solving the dual problem of (1):

$$\text{Maximize } L(\pm) = \sum_{i=1}^{l} \alpha_i - \frac{1}{2} \pm \sum_{i=1}^{l} \alpha_i - \frac{1}{2}$$

$$\sum_{i,j=1}^{l} \alpha_i \alpha_j) = \sum_{i=1}^{l} \alpha_i - \frac{1}{2} \sum_{i,j=1}^{l} \alpha_i \alpha_j y_i y_j x_i x_j$$

Subject to $0 \leq \alpha_i \leq C, i = 1,2,...,l$ and

$$0 \leq \alpha_i \leq C, i = 1,2,...,l \sum_{i=1}^{m} \alpha_i y_i = 0 \text{ and}$$

$$\sum_{i=1}^{m} \alpha_i y_i = 0 \quad (2)$$

Let S be the index set of support vectors, then the optimal decision function becomes

$$f(x) = \text{sgn} \left(\sum_{i \in S} y_i \alpha_i x^T x_i + b \right) \quad (3)$$

The above equation gives an optimal hyperplane in R^n. However, more complex decision surfaces can be generated by employing a nonlinear mapping $\Phi : \mathcal{R}^n \rightarrow F$ while at the same time controlling their complexity and solving the same optimization problem in F. It can be seen from (2) that x_i always appears in the form of inner product $x_i^T x_j$. This implies that there is no need to evaluate the nonlinear mapping Φ as long as we know the inner product in F for a given $x_i, x_j \in \mathcal{R}^n$. so, instead of defining $\Phi : \mathcal{R}^n \rightarrow F$ explicitly; a function $K : \mathcal{R}^n \times \mathcal{R}^n \rightarrow \mathcal{R}$ is introduced to define an inner product in F. The only requirement on the kernel $K(x, y)$ is to satisfy Mercer's condition which states: There exists a mapping Φ and an expansion

$$K(x, y) = \sum_i \Phi(x)_i \cdot \Phi(y)_i$$

if and only if, for any $g(x)$ such that $\int g(x)^2 dx$ is finite then $\int K(x, y) g(x) g(y) dx dy \geq 0$.

Substituting K(x_i, x_j) for $x_i^T x_j$ in (3) produces a new optimization problem:

Maximize $L(\pm) = \pm \sum\limits_{i=1}^{m} \alpha_i - \frac{1}{2} \sum\limits_{i,j=1} \alpha_i \alpha_j) =$
$\sum\limits_{i=1}^{m} \alpha_i - \frac{1}{2} \sum\limits_{i,j=1} \alpha_i \alpha_j y_i y_j K(x_i, x_j)$

Subject to $0 \leq \alpha_i \leq C, i = 1, \ldots, m$ and

$0 \leq \alpha_i \leq C, i = 1, \ldots, m$ $\sum\limits_{i=1}^{m} \alpha_i y_i = 0$ and
$\sum\limits_{i=1}^{m} \alpha_i y_i = 0$ (4)

Solving it for $\pm$ gives a decision function of the form

$f(x) = \text{sgn} \left(\sum\limits_{i=1}^{m} y_i \alpha_i K(x_i, x_j) + b \right)$ (5)

Whose decision boundary is a hyperplane in F, and translates to nonlinear boundaries in the original space.

Multi-Class Support Vector Machines

All real world classification problems often involve more than two classes. Therefore, binary SVMs' are usually not enough to solve the whole problem. The most common way to build a k-class SVM is by constructing and combining several binary classifiers. To solve multi-class classification problems, we divide the whole pattern into a number of binary classification problems. The two representative ensemble schemes are One against All (1-vs-many) and One against One (1-vs-1) (Knerr et al., 1990). One against All is also known as "one against others." It trains k binary classifiers, each of which separates one class from the other $(k-1)$ classes. **Given a point** X to classify, the binary classifier with the largest output determines the class of X. One against One constructs $k(k-1)/2$ binary classifiers. The outputs of the classifiers are aggregated to make the final decision. Decision tree formulation is a variant of One against All formulation based on decision tree. Error correcting output code is general representation of One against All or One vs. One formulation, which uses error correcting

codes for encoding outputs. The One against All approach provides better classification accuracy in comparison to others (Rifkin & Klautau, 2004). Consequently, we have applied One against All approach in our experiments.

KERNEL PARAMETER SELECTION ADABOOST ALGORITHM

Kernel Function

It is reasonable to assume that there may be other kernel functions that map the unknown dataset better in high dimensional space. Recently, a new kernel function, Cauchy (Chen & Wang, 2002) is defined:

$K(\mathbf{x}, \mathbf{y}) = \left(1 \middle/ \left(1 + \gamma \mid x - x_i \mid^2 \right) \right)$ (6)

It satisfies Mercer's condition. Similarly, one can also define a new kernel function which satisfies Mercer's condition and can enhance classifier accuracy by appropriate transformation in high dimensional space. We can define the new kernel functions with the knowledge of the following two theorems (Abe, 2005):

Theorem 1: If $K(\mathbf{x}, \mathbf{y}) = a$ where a > 0 then, $K(\mathbf{x}, \mathbf{y})$ is a positive semidefinite.
Theorem 2: If $K_1(\mathbf{x}, \mathbf{y})$ and $K_2(\mathbf{x}, \mathbf{y})$ are positive semidefinite then,

$K(\mathbf{x}, \mathbf{y}) = K_1(\mathbf{x}, \mathbf{y}) K_2(\mathbf{x}, \mathbf{y})$ is also positive semidefinite.

Since, polynomial function, $K_1(\mathbf{x}, \mathbf{y}) = (1 + xy^T)^d$ and

Gaussian function, $K_2(\mathbf{x}, \mathbf{y}) = \exp(-\gamma \mid x - x_i \mid^2)$ are positive semidefinite.

Hence, $K(\mathbf{x}, \mathbf{y}) = (1 + xy^T)^d \exp(-\gamma \mid x - x_i \mid^2)$ is also positive semidefinite according to

Table 1. Kernel functions

Kernel Function	$K(x, x_i)$ for $\gamma > 0$
Polynomial	$(1 + xx_i^T)^d$
Gaussian	$\exp(-\gamma \mid x - x_i \mid^2)$
Cauchy	$1 \big/ (1 + \gamma \mid x - x_i \mid^2)$
Gauss cum Poly	$\exp(-\gamma \mid x - x_i \mid^2) * (1 + xx_i^T)^d$
Cauchy cum poly	$(1 \big/ (1 + \gamma \mid x - x_i \mid^2)) * (1 + xx_i^T)^d$
Laplace	$\exp(-\gamma \mid x - x_i \mid)$
Hypersecant	$2 \big/ (\exp(\gamma \mid x - x_i \mid) + \exp(-\gamma \mid x - x_i \mid))$
Square sync	$\sin^2 (\gamma \mid x - x_i \mid) \big/ (\gamma \mid x - x_i \mid)^2$
Symmetric triangle	$\max(1 - \gamma \mid x - x_i \mid, 0)$

Theorem 2 (Abe, 2005). We called this new kernel function as Gaussian cum polynomial.

Similarly, $K(\mathbf{x}, \mathbf{y}) = (1 \big/ (1 + \gamma \mid x - x_i \mid^2)) * (1 + xx_i^T)^d$ is also positive semidefinite. We called this new kernel function as Cauchy cum polynomial.

Table 1 above shows Kernel functions used in our experiment.

Kernel Parameter Selection with AdaBoost

Boosting (Fletcher, 1987) is a machine learning algorithm that can be used in combination with many other learning algorithms to improve its performance. The basic principle involved in boosting algorithms is to combine many simple and moderately accurate classifiers (called weak classifiers)

$$E_k = \min_{Ker\_ch, C, \gamma} Error\_rate_{Ker\_ch, C, \gamma}$$

- Let $g_k = g_{Ker\_ch, C, \lambda}$ with ker_ch, C, γ minimizing the error rate
- Compute the weights of the classifier α_k based on its classification error rate:

$$\text{Let } \alpha_k = 0.5 \log\left(\frac{(1 - E_k)}{E_k}\right);$$

- Update and normalize the weights for each sample of D.

Table 2. Description of dataset

dataset	#training data	#testing data	#class	#attributes
Bupa	345	0	2	6
Mammographic_masses(1)	961	0	2	5
Pima-indians-diabetes	768	0	2	8
Haberman	306	0	2	3
Iris	150	0	3	4
Wine	178	0	3	13
Glass	214	0	6	9
Vowel	528	0	11	10
Vehicle	846	0	4	18
Satimage	4435	2000	6	36

$$W_{k+1}(i) = W_k(i) *$$

$$\begin{cases} \exp(-\alpha_k) & \text{if } g_k(\mathbf{x}^i) = y_i \text{ (correctly classified)} \\ \exp(\alpha_k) & \text{if } g_k(\mathbf{x}^i) \neq y_i \text{ (incorrectly classified)} \end{cases}$$

End for k

Final prediction $G(\mathbf{x}) = \sum_{k=1}^{k_{max}} \alpha_k g_k(\mathbf{x})$

EXPERIMENTAL RESULTS

For each SVM, the hyperparameters space is explored on a two dimensional grid with the following values:

$\gamma = [2^{-8}, 2^{-6} \dots, 2^2]$ and $C = [2^0, 2^2 \dots, 2^{10}]$. All kernel functions given in Table 1 are considered in our experiments. All the experiments are performed on a computer having Pentium 4 processor with 512 MB RAM.

Dependence of Performance on Choice of Kernel Function and its Parameters

The experimental results on few datasets of UCI repository of Machine Learning (Blake & Merz, 1998) given in Table 2 show that the performance of SVM depends upon the choice of kernel function and its parameters.

Figure 1 shows the average cross-validation accuracy of the multi-class SVM classifier for the glass dataset using Gaussian kernel as a function of the two parameters C and γ. Figure 1 shows the variation in accuracy for 121 combinations of C and γ only. The optimal values of parameters can be chosen by visualizing the maximum value of average accuracy attained on the grid.

Similarly, the experiments were performed on different datasets using other kernel functions. We observed that multi-class SVM demonstrates better accuracy for certain value of C and γ. The significance of choosing appropriate values of C and γ can be realized from above 3D plot. However, we have analyzed the cross sectional view of the same in 2D. Due to the scarcity of space, we are presenting only the graphs for the kernel function having wider variation in classifier accuracy. Figure 2(a) shows the variation of classifier accuracy of iris dataset with C for different values of γ using Gauss kernel function. Similarly, Figure 2(b) shows the variation of classifier accuracy of glass dataset with C for different values of γ using Laplace kernel function. The variation of classifier accuracy of wine dataset with γ for different values of C using Squared Sinc kernel function is shown

Figure 1. Average classifier accuracy for Glass dataset using Gauss Kernel

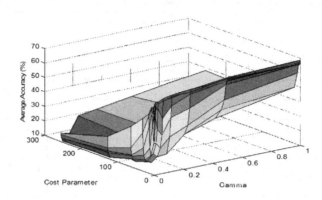

Figure 2. Average classification accuracy for different values of cost parameter and gamma. (a) Iris data using gauss kernel. (b) Glass data using laplace kernel. (c) Wine data using squared sinc kernel. (d) Glass data using squared sinc kernel

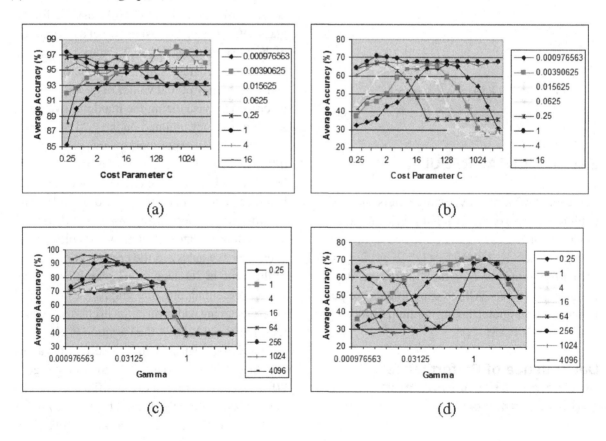

Figure 3. Average classification accuracy of (a) wine dataset with γ for different kernel functions for C = 4096. (b) wine dataset with C for all kernel function for γ = 0.5

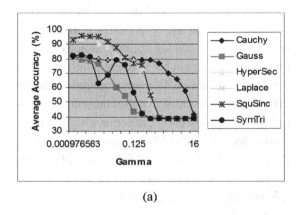

(a)

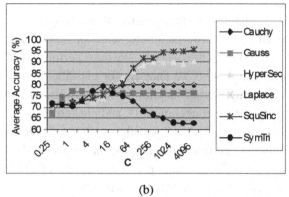

(b)

in Figure 2(c). Similarly, Figure 2(d) shows the variation of classifier accuracy of glass dataset with γ for different values of C using Laplace kernel function. We have observed from Figure 2(a)-2(d) that the accuracy of multi-class SVM classifier for a given kernel function depends on the choice of C and γ.

Figure 3(a) shows the variation of classifier accuracy of wine dataset with γ for different kernel functions for C = 4096. Similarly, Figure 3(b) shows the variation of classifier accuracy

of wine data with C for all kernel function for γ = 0.5. It can be seen that for certain values of C, variation in certain range of γ does not affect the cross-validation accuracy much, whereas large variation was observed in few cases. We found similar variation in results for all datasets by varying C and keeping γ being constant. We observed from above figures that accuracy of the classifier for a given dataset depends on the choice of kernel function and its parameters.

Table 3. Comparison of classification accuracy

Dataset	Case 1	Case 2 Kernel parameter selection AdaBoost algorithm
Bupa	69.71	**69.86**
Mammographic_masses(1)	80.02	**81.69**
Pima_diabetes	67.188	**77.35**
Haberman	76.144	**78.76**
Iris	97.333	**98.667**
Wine	81.46	**92.22**
Glass	75.2336	**84.1121**
Vowel	75	**75.7576**
Vehicle	53.4279	**76.4775**
Satimage	67.7339	**91.5671**

Performance of Kernel Parameter Selection with AdaBoost

We evaluated the performance of our proposed algorithm for kernel parameter selection based on AdaBoost on same datasets. We have performed experiments with all datasets for classification considering Kernel function to be Gaussian and exploring the better choice of C and γ in kernel parameter selection AdaBoost algorithm to achieve minimum classification error for each individual weak classifier for final prediction of classifier. We have also performed experiments for classification exploring the better choice of kernel function, C and γ in kernel parameter selection AdaBoost algorithm to achieve minimum classification error for each individual weak classifier for final prediction. The number of weak classifier in our experiment is considered to be 5. Table 3 shows the comparison of classification accuracy of various data with Kernel parameter selection AdaBoost algorithm for two different cases: Case 1: Only Gaussian kernel is considered and explored better choice of C and γ for each individual weak classifier and Case 2: Explored better choice of kernel function, C and γ with Kernel parameter selection AdaBoost algorithm.The best result for each dataset is indicated in bold. It can be observed from Table 3 that the performance of SVM is better in case 2 for all datasets.

Case 1: Considering only Gaussian kernel function and all values of C and γ in kernel parameter selection AdaBoost algorithm

Case 2: Considering all kernel functions, C and γ in Kernel parameter selection AdaBoost algorithm

CONCLUSION

In this chapter, we have proposed few new kernel functions which satisfy the Mercer's conditions and a robust algorithm to automatically determine the suitable kernel function and its parameters

based on AdaBoost to improve the performance of support vector machine. This is essential as the performance of SVM depends on the choice of kernel function and its parameters and there is no way to determine the optimal choice of kernel and its parameters in SVM to gain high accuracy for any given dataset. The experimental results for different datasets show that the Gaussian kernel is not always the best choice to achieve high generalization accuracy of SVM classifier. However, with the proper choice of kernel function and optimal choice of its parameters using proposed algorithm, it is possible to achieve maximum classification accuracy for all datasets.

FUTURE TRENDS

It will be both interesting and challenging to determine the association between the kernel function and the underlying distribution of data to achieve better performance of SVM. SVM are basically designed for solving binary class classification problems. If SVM is used for solving multiclass problem then there is need to design ensemble classifier using *One against One* and *One Against One* approach. But in both of these multiclass SVM methods there is a problem of unclassifiable region. So there is need to develop ensemble methods for designing multiclass SVM to reduce unclassifiable region.

REFERENCES

Abe, S. (2005). Support Vector Machines for Pattern Classification. Kobe, Japan: Springer.

Amores, J., Sebe, N., & Radeva, P. (2006). Boosting the Distance Estimation Application to the K-Nearest Neighbor Classifier. *Pattern Recognition Letters*, *27*(3), 201–209. doi:10.1016/j.patrec.2005.08.019

Blake, C. L., & Merz, C. J. (1998). *UCI Repository of Machine Learning Databases*. Univ. California, Dept. Inform. Computer Science, Irvine, CA. [Online]. From http://www.ics.uci.edu/~mlearn/ML-Repository.html

Burges, C. J. C. (1998). A tutorial on support vector machines for pattern recognition. *Data Mining and Knowledge Discovery, 2*(2), 121–167. doi:10.1023/A:1009715923555

Chen, Y., & Wang, A. J. (2002). Learning with kernels. Cambridge, MA: MIT Press.

Corts, C., & Vapnik, V. N. (1995). Support Vector Networks . *Machine Learning, 20*, 273–297.

Corts, C., & Vapnik, V. N. (1995). The Nature of Statistical Learning Theory. Berlin: Springer.

Fletcher, R. (1987). Practical Methods of Optimization, (2nd ed.). New York: John Wiley & Sons, Inc.

Freund, Y. (1997). A decision-theoretic generalization of online learning and an application to boosting. *Journal of Computer and System Sciences, 55*, 119–139. doi:10.1006/jcss.1997.1504

Freund, Y., & Schapire, R. E. (1999). A short introduction to boosting. *Journal of Japanese Society for Artificial Intelligence, 14*(5), 771–780.

Gutschoven, B., & Verlinde, P. (2000), Multimodal identity verification using support vector machines (SVM). In *Proc. 3rd Int. Conf. Information Fusion*, (vol. 2, pp. 3-8).

Joachims, T. (1998). Text categorization with support vector machines: Learning with many relevant features. In Proc. of the European Conf. on Machine Learning. Berlin: Springer.

Joachims, T., Cristianini, N., & Shawe Taylor, J. (2001). Composite Kernels for Hypertext categorization. In proc. of Int'l Conf. on Machine Learning.

Kittler, J., & Hojjatoleslami, A. A. (1998). Weighted combination of classifiers employing shared and distinct representations. In *IEEE Proc. Computer Vision and Pattern Recognition*, (pp 924-929). Retrieved from http://www.idiap.ch/~norman/fusion

Knerr, S., Personnaz, L., & Dreyfus, G. (1990). Single-layer learning revisited: A stepwise procedure for building and training a neural network. Neurocomputing: algorithms, architectures and applications. Berlin: Springer.

Mori, S., Suen, C. Y., & Yamamota, K. (1992). Historical review of OCR research and development. *IEEE Proc., 80*, 1029–1058. doi:10.1109/5.156468

Mukkamala, S., Janoski, G., & Sung, A. H. (2002). Intrusion Detection using neural networks and support vector machines. In IEEE Proc. of Int'l Joint Conf. on Neural Networks, (pp. 1702-07).

Rifkin, R., & Klautau, A. (2004). In Defense of One-Vs.-All Classification. *Journal of Machine Learning, 5*, 101–141.

Schmidt, M. (1996). Identifying speaker with support vector networks. In Interface '96 Proc., Sydney.

Scholkopf, B., & smola, A. J. (2002). *Learning with kernels*. Cambridge, MA: MIT Press.

Tian, Q., Xie, Q., Yu, J., Sebe, N., & Huang, T. S. (2004). Towards an Improved Error Metric. In *Proc. IEEE Int'l Conf. Image Processing*.

Weston, J., & Watkins, C. (1999). *Multi-class Support Vector Machines*. Paper presented at M. Verleysen, (Ed.), the Proc. ESANN99, Brussels, Belgium.

Yu, J. Amores, Sebe, N., & Tian, Q. (2006). Toward Robust Distance Metric analysis for Similarity Estimation. In IEEE Proc. Int'l Conf. of Computer Vision and Pattern Recognition.

ADDITIONAL READING

Bennett, K. P., & Campbell, C. (2000). Support Vector Machines: Hype or Hallelujah? *SIGKDD Explorations, 2*(2), 1–13. doi:10.1145/380995.380999

Boosting.org: a site on boosting and related ensemble learning methods.

Catanzaro, Sundaram, & Keutzer (2008). Fast Support Vector Machine Training and Classification on Graphics Processors. In: International Conference on Machine Learning.

Cristianini, N., & Shawe-Taylor, J. (2000). An Introduction to Support Vector Machines and other kernel-based learning methods. Cambridge University Press, ISBN 0-521-78019-5.

Fradkin, D., & Muchnik, I. (2006). Support Vector Machines for Classification. in J. Abello and G. Carmode (Eds), Discrete Methods in Epidemiology (pp. 13-20), DIMACS Series in Discrete Mathematics and Theoretical Computer Science, Vol. 70.

Huang, T.-M., Kecman, V., & Kopriva, I. (2006). Kernel Based Algorithms for Mining Huge Data Sets, Supervised, Semi-supervised, and Unsupervised Learning, Springer-Verlag, Berlin, Heidelberg, 260 pp. 96 illus., Hardcover, ISBN 3-540-31681-7.

Ivanciuc, O. (2007). Applications of Support Vector Machines in Chemistry. *Reviews in Computational Chemistry, 23*, 291–400. doi:10.1002/9780470116449.ch6

JBoost, a site offering a classification and visualization package, implementing AdaBoost among other boosting algorithms.

Polikar, R. (2006). Ensemble Based Systems in Decision Making [A tutorial article on ensemble systems including pseudocode, block diagrams and implementation issues for AdaBoost and other ensemble learning algorithms.]. *IEEE Circuits and Systems Magazine, 6*(3), 21–45. doi:10.1109/MCAS.2006.1688199

Shawe-Taylor, J., & Cristianini, N. (2004). Kernel Methods for Pattern Analysis. Cambridge University Press, ISBN 0-521-81397-2.

Steinwart, I., & Christmann, A. (2008). Support Vector Machines. Springer-Verlag, New York, ISBN 978-0-387-77241-7.

Tan, P. J., & Dowe, D. L. (2004). MML Inference of Oblique Decision Trees, Lecture Notes in Artificial Intelligence (LNAI) 3339, Springer-Verlag, pp. 1082-1088.

Vapnik, Vladimir & Kotz, S. (2006). Estimation of Dependences Based on Empirical Data. Springer, ISBN 0387308652, 510 pages [this is a reprint of Vapnik's early book describing philosophy behind SVM approach. The 2006 Appendix describes recent development].

Vojislav, K. (2001). Learning and Soft Computing - Support Vector Machines, Neural Networks, Fuzzy Logic Systems. The MIT Press, Cambridge, MA.

KEY TERMS AND DEFINITIONS

AdaBoost: It is an algorithm for building a strong classifier as linear combination of weak classifiers.

Recognition: It is process of identifying objects, events or samples that have been seen earlier.

Classification: It is process of grouping information into different labeled categories.

Binary Classification: Separating a set of data sample in two categories based upon some constraint is called binary classification.

Multi-Class Classification: Dividing given data samples into more than two categories is called multi-class classification.

Support Vector Machine: Support Vector Machines (SVMs) is pattern classifier based on statistical learning theory developed by Vapnik. It transforms the training vectors into a high-dimensional feature space, labeling each vector by its class. It classifies data by determining a set of support vectors, which are members of the set of training inputs that outline a hyperplane in feature space.

Kernel Function: Kernel function is a function of two variables that defines an integral transform or technique to write a nonlinear operator as a linear one in a space of higher dimension.

Mercer's Conditions: A real valued kernel function $K(x, y)$ is said to satisfy Mercer's condition: If there exists a mapping and an expansion $K(x, y) =$ if and only if, for any $g(x)$ such that $g(x)^2\, dx$ is finite then $K(x, y)\, g(x)\, g(y)\, dx\, dy$.

VC-Dimension: VC dimension for a set of functions F (where *that maps points from* R^n into set $\{0, 1\}$ or $\{-1, 1\}$) is defined as the largest number of points that can be shattered by F

Classification Accuracy: The classification accuracy of a classifier depends on the number of samples correctly classified and is given by the formula: where *m* is the number of sample tuples correctly classified, and *n* is the total number of sample tuples.

Chapter 3

Software Parallel Processing in Pervasive Computing

Jitesh Dundas
Edencore Technologies, USA

ABTRACT

This chapter proposes the application of periodic wave concepts in management of software Parallel processing projects or processes. This chapter lays special emphasis on Runaway project, which create a lot of problems in Project Management for the stakeholders. This chapter proposes a new and dynamic way to control the software project estimation activity of Runaway project/processes, thereby reducing their future occurrences. This chapter also explains how the equations of unidirectional periodic Waves can be applied in software Parallel processing to measure quality and project execution in a dynamic way at any point in time. The concepts proposed here are dynamic unlike PERT/CPM and other metrics, which fail in worst-case scenarios. The Propagation Speed 'C' at any point in time of a stage or part of a software system executing in Parallel can be given by: C = H/ k (1). Where, H = length of the Wave (i.e. highest point), k = time taken in completing the stage.

INTRODUCTION

As the environment in which we use technology becomes more and more pervasive (Mark .W., 1999), the efficient execution of software has become very important for us. Thus, Parallel processing of software is one step forward in this direction. It is very well known that Parallel processing can help us reduce time of execution.

Any software function running in Parallel can be divided into stages, with each stage running with varying degrees of freedom, without controlling or affecting the other stages or pieces during execution. We can use equations of periodic Waves to control, monitor and predict the flow of the Parallel execution of software /project. If we arrange these pieces in their order of execution, we will find that they all work in Parallel. Any software that is to be run in Parallel needs to be connected by some link,

DOI: 10.4018/978-1-61520-741-1.ch003

if being run for the first time. For the first time scenario, the pieces will run one after another, provided the second piece's input is dependent on the first's output. Thus, it will create a staircase like figure.

As the process is repeated again and again, this software will be able to reduce the time-lag in running the pieces in Parallel. This is because the same process is repeated frequently and thus the processing becomes predictable with each execution. Thus, all those pieces or stages of software that are not dependent on the other can be started. As the number of executions increases, the logic of the software for execution becomes more and more familiar and thus it can be executed faster and faster. Thus, the effort for the perfect Parallel execution would be that all the stages are running in Parallel, without any dependency and thus achieving faster execution. However, care must be taken to prevent any loss of quality or Efficiency. In short, the processing cycle expands horizontally and contracts vertically. This is called "The Sandwich Effect".

For e.g.) Assume that there is a software 'S' made up of pieces A,B,C,D,E,F. Thus, the sum of efficiencies of all runs of software pieces or stages should be greater than the Efficiency of the entire software run as a whole.

Thus, we get,

$$\sum St_i >_\Sigma S, \text{ where} \qquad (1)$$

i=0 to n
St = Stages of project's SDLC cycle or pieces of software
n = Number of stages or pieces of the software

Parallel software development/processing will be useful and efficient only if the above inequality holds true. This research paper employs the dynamics of Wave functions and their attributes in Parallel software development.

Any two stages are separated by a separation line. This line is important as it shows the end of one stage and the start of another. It also explains the point that any two stages may be related or dependent but they need to be executed independently. The vertical line shows the execution time for the Wave and thus decides its Amplitude. Also, any stage execution starts from the starting point of the separation line for that stage and ends with the end-point for that stage. As time is always positive and moving forward, the Wave will be unidirectional and periodic. The starting point "i" and ending point "j" will give the Wave representation of any stage S by:

$$_{i=0}{}^{j}\!\int S_{ij},$$

where i moves from 0 to j

The imaginary line that separates two consecutive stages is always constant. Thus, the vertical line (that depicts the execution time) decides the height or Amplitude of the periodic Wave. In order to include the imaginary separation line that separates two stages, we need to create a Wave like representation.

BACKGROUND

Here, we can use the Wave sine equation (Raymond D, 2007) here to find the displacement of the Wave at any point in time as:-

$$y(t) = A*\sin(\omega t + \Theta) \qquad (2)$$

Which describes a Wavelike function of time (*t*) with:

1) peak deviation from center = *A* (aka *Amplitude*)
2) angular frequency ω, (radians per second)
3) phase = θ

When the phase is non-zero, the entire Waveform appears to be shifted in time by the amount

θ/ω seconds. A negative value represents a delay, and a positive value represents a "head-start".

Efficiency of the software piece or project stage execution in any Execution Cycle can be given by the velocity v of the Wave. It determines how efficiently the Wave is moving in the graph.

The speed of a Wave "v" (Crowell B., 2005 pp. 62-75) is related to the frequency, period, and Wavelength by the following simple equations:

$$v = \lambda T \tag{3}$$

$$v = \lambda f \tag{4}$$

Where v is the Wave speed, λ is the Wavelength, T is the period, and f is the frequency.

DISCUSSION

PERT/CPM is used widely for project management. However, it is not dynamic. If we represent carefully, the stages of any software project (Pressman, 2005) or software pieces that are running in Parallel can be represented in a two-dimensional graph plotted between time and stage-units (it means the unit measure of any stage. This graph is similar to the one having showing the vibrations of a string (Enns, 2005 pp. 71). Let us say for e.g.) 1 kg for weight, 1 cm for length. In the same way 1 stage-unit for stages)

If we observe properly, any software or project, if represented on a graph, can show a Wave-like motion for each stage. Each new stage starts from

1)   The origin if it is the first point. Else it is
2)   The end-point of the previous stage.

Thus, the graph will always go in the upwards direction, without any hindrance from the stages movement. The stages can go in either direction:-

1)   Towards the right if the stages are executing correctly and efficiently, one after another.
2)   Towards the left if the stages are going back in execution due to some change or error in functions or execution of the software.

Thus, in an ideal or perfect execution, any software or project, being executed in Parallel, will show a staircase-like graph, with no bars or interrupts in them. If the graph shows any bar (See figure -3), then we can deduce that at least one stage (all the stages that are a part of the bar-like figure) had a rerun or inefficient run. A Wave (Firk, 2000) can be plotted (See Figure 2) from the start point of the stage to the end-point of the stage, creating a half Wave-like figure. The Amplitude shows the duration taken for the completion of the stage. In this case, the Wavelength will be given by $\lambda/2$, since the Wave is half of the polarized Wave (Beranek, 1996). The shorter the Wave, the faster will be the displacement (Schaorghofer, 2005).

Figure 1. The stages in **software** *executed in* **Parallel***, when information is new*

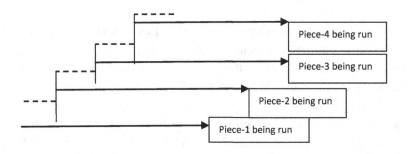

Figure 2. Graphical representation for measuring parallel processes

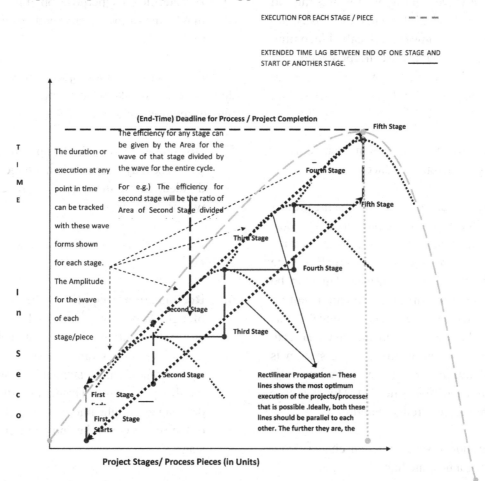

Thus, we can imply that the execution of the stage will be faster if the Wave is shorter. The longer the Wave, the slower will be the execution.

Also, if any stage just keeps executing in a straight line vertically infinitely or crossing the stage completion deadline, then it will imply that the software or project has become a runaway project (See Figure 3). This is the worst-case scenario for any software or project that cannot be completed in time. It is strongly recommended that we closely monitor or pay diligent attention to the execution process, if at least one or more bars have been created in the graph. This graph can also show the execution at any point of time,

using the sine-function for any Wave (See Figure 3). This graph is called the "Runaway Control Graph".

The Wave created for each stage or piece can be used to measure the Efficiency or relative execution speed for each stage. There are several characteristics of Waves that can be employed here to manage the Parallel software development process (Jalote, 2000). It can be deduced that the Wave properties like refraction, reflection, polarization hold true in the case of Parallel execution of software.

We know the properties of any Wave (Ashby & Miller, 1970) like reflection, refraction, diffraction, etc. The Wave that is going towards the end of the cycle are called the outgoing Waves and the ones that move inwards are called incoming Waves. This is similar to the concept of incoming and outgoing Waves shown by in Mathematical Waves (Masujima, 2005). They can be associated here such that:-

1) **Reflection**(Wave direction change from hitting a reflective surface)

Here the reflective surface will be the project deadline. If the stages of the project do not complete in the deadline, then the line that represents the progress of the stages in the graph will be reflected by the deadline surface. This can be implied as the case when the software is not up to the required levels of expectations and thus has been rejected or the requirements have changed. In any such case, an overhaul of the system is needed and thus, rework or new start of the project/software execution is needed. This is a case of Software Project/Product Failure.

2) **Refraction** (Wave direction change from entering a new medium)

This is the same case as the above case of reflection, except for the condition that there is no overhaul of the execution process needed. There will be a change in the requirements and a major repair work will be needed in this case. There will be a stretching of the deadline in this case and thus there will be delay in the execution process (and thus deliverable outputs).

3) **Diffraction** (bending of Waves as they interact with obstacles in their path, most pronounced for Wavelengths on the order of the diffracting object size). This is the same as the refraction case except that minor delays or changes in execution may be needed. The execution may be affected a little or may even complete on time.

4) **Interference** - superposition of two Waves that come into contact with each other (collide).

This happens when a project stops execution due to exceptions like resource problems, scrapping of requirements, etc.

5) **Dispersion** - Wave splitting up by frequency. This case may happen when a stage may be divided, during the execution process, into two or more stages.

This is a risky situation and should be avoided.

6) **Rectilinear propagation** - the movement of light Waves in a straight line. This is an ideal condition which we should strive to achieve, but is rarely possible. This is the optimum quality standard for software Parallel processing. This can be shown by drawing a straight line from the end point of the first stage to the end point of the last stage.

However, we also need to look at it in terms of the type of project or software that is being executed. If being executed for the first time, then the project will be a staircase-like figure, without any bars (Figure 1). However, in the second run or in the case of any routine or known software run, the number of steps in the stair-case line will reduce. As the number of runs or the familiarity and control over the process of the software execution increases, the execution process evolves into a more horizontal rather than vertical process.

MAIN FOCUS OF THE CHAPTER

Let us consider the example below to understand the above concept. Consider the Figure 3 shown in the pages below. The software execution pro-

Figure 3. Graphical representation For **Runaway project**/*Processes*

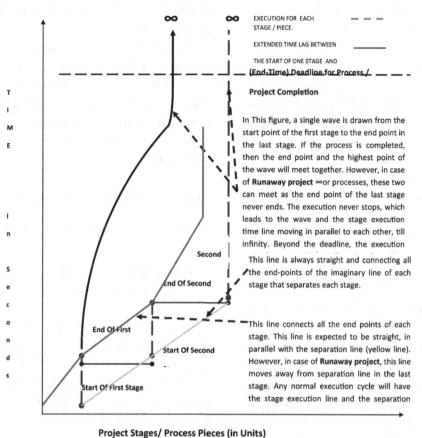

Project Stages/ Process Pieces (in Units)

cess/project has been divided into 5 stages. The first stage executes normally as per the project schedule. However, in the second phase, the execution takes a lot of time and soon crosses the project execution deadline. If we draw one full Wave from the starting point of the project/ process to the end point of the project, we will see that the line showing the stage's Amplitude of the last executed stage (here it is stage-2) will be Parallel to the Wave created till that point. This is because the stage has not ended and is still pending completion. This leads to very high Amplitude for the Wave, which is not a good sign for the project. As shown to happen in the case of Waves (Caulson, 1977), here the scenarios of Reflection, Refraction, Diffraction and Interference are created. However, consider the Figure 2)

in the pages below, where all the stages have been completed well in time and on schedule. Thus, if a Wave from the start point of the project to the end-point of the graph is created, we will see that the line showing the Amplitude of the last executed stage (here it is stage-2) will be intersecting at a point below the project completion deadline. Such Parallel processing scenarios can lead to Rectilinear Propagation, or the optimum project/ process execution. The lines that represent them will always be Parallel to each other throughout the cycle in such an ideal scenario. Figure 2) shown in the pages below shows several unidirectional periodic Waves (half Waves). These Waves prove two points if they intersect with the Amplitude line of that stage:-

a) The stage has been completed and will start a new stage. Moreover, there is Amplitude for each Wave that is created.

b) It gives a clear idea of the resources consumed, specially time, at the end of the execution of the stage. This practice gives a better estimation of the project becoming runaway to the stakeholders. This can help them to take corrective actions, like increasing resource allocation or extending the completion deadline.

c) With reference to the ideal case of Rectilinear Propagation lines, both the lines should be Parallel to each other. The further they are, the more will be the deviation from the optimum

Execution. This will also show the extent of resource wastage in Parallel processing The lines that represent they will always be Parallel to each other throughout the cycle.

In Figure 2), we can see that the each stage/piece has a Wave associated with itself. The execution time associated this stage/piece will be the Amplitude of that Wave.

Also, we can find the execution time for the entire Execution Cycle by plotting a Wave from the starting point of the first stage and the end-point of the last stage. This Wave will have Amplitude that represents the total execution time for this cycle till that last stage. Thus, we can find the Efficiency of the execution for any stage (in %age) by:

Execution Efficiency Factor for Stage S_{ij} = ((Area of Curve (Wave S_{ij}))/ (Area of Curve (S_{om})) * 100)

Where, i = starting point of stage S_{ij}

$_{j=}$ ending point of the separation line of stage S_{ij}

o = Origin point of the curve $S_{om\,i.e.}$ the starting point of the first stage

k = Ending point of the separation line for the curve $S_{om\,i.e.}$ the end point of the last stage

The Area can be measured using the normal distribution curve method for any curve that is used in statistics.

We can also find if the stage execution is on the verge of becoming runaway by comparison between the stage Areas with the Average Area. Thus, we need to find the Average Area for the cycle. This is done by finding the average of all the individual stages in the Execution Cycle. It is given by:-

Average Area for the Curve $Avg(S_{on}) = \sum S_{ij} / n$

where n = total number of stages in the cycle

i = starting point of stage S_{ij}

$_{j=}$ ending point of the separation line of stage S_{ij}

The lower the execution Efficiency factor or EEF, the higher will be the Efficiency of the stage execution process. To find if the stage is on the verge of making the project runaway, a comparison of its Area with the Average Area for the cycle is done. We can safely imply from the comparison that:

1) Generally if the stage is on the verge of becoming a runaway, the Area of that stage will be double or greater than the Average Area i.e. if Area (S_{ij}) >= ($Avg(S_{on})$ * 2)

2) If the stage execution is efficient, the Area of that stage will be lesser than the Average Area i.e. if Area (S_{ij}) < ($Avg(S_{on})$)

3) If the stage execution is inefficient but not runaway, the Area of that stage will be almost equal to the Average Area i.e. if Area (S_{ij}) ~ ($Avg(S_{on})$)

For e.g.) Consider the stage 2 in the Figure 2). Here we find that the Wave for this entire Execution Cycle (yellow line) has an Area (say) 50 square units and the Wave for the second stage has an Area (say) 5 square units. Thus the Execution Efficiency Factor for the second stage will be (5/50) * 100 = 10%. The lower the Factor, higher will be the Efficiency for that stage. This is because the Area of the Wave has to be smaller for smaller Amplitude (stage execution time) length. This means that the stage was executed very fast and consumed fewer resources. The Area for each curve is given by the formula for normal distribution curve that is used in probability distribution curve methods (Collins, 2003).

Consider the Figure 3).There is an imaginary line (yellow color in the figure) that connects all the start points of the stages in the cycle. This line is always straight as this line connects all the end-points of the imaginary line for each stage that separates each stage. This line connects all the end points of each stage. This line is expected to be straight, in Parallel with the separation line (yellow line). However, in case of Runaway project, this line moves away from separation line in the last stage. Any normal Execution Cycle will have the stage execution line and the separation line move in Parallel or move closer towards each (or/and intersect). This shows us how to detect when the execution getting out of control.

There are several points in support for the methods mentioned in this paper:

a) This method scores over the PERT/CPM due to its dynamic nature. This method is very useful when there is a need to control or manage critical or Runaway project.

b) Runaway project or stages or points that are critical in any software process/project can be controlled and managed at any point in time.

c) This method is easier to use and learn than the PERT/CPM method of software project management. It uses the elementary knowledge of graphs and periodic Waves (Waves that oscillate in one direction) as opposed to PERT/CPM (that needs advanced mathematical skills).

d) This method is useful to track and control the execution of Runaway project/processes,

which is one Area where PERT/CPM has not been very useful (or viable). PERT/CPM and other techniques of project Management do not apply to Parallel processing methods of execution of software projects/processes. This is a big issue in the management of project management techniques. This paper fills the void that was initially present.

There are several advantages that can be cited for this method:

a) This method gives the position of the software or project execution process at any point of time, this method is dynamic in nature.

b) This method gives a more accurate picture of the execution as it shows any anomalies at any stage dynamically. This is not the case in methods like PERT/CPM.

c) This paper lets you find out if the project/process at any stage has become a runaway project or not. Once we have this information, it becomes easier to handle the project/process.

The scope of this paper is limited to the following points:

a) In this paper, periodic Waves are those Waves that oscillate in one direction only. Since time always moves upwards and is non-negative, we have considered only the positive direction only.

b) This method is useful for Runaway project and those projects that are not easy to manage. PERT/CPM will be useful for those processing tasks that have novel requirements(being executed for the first time) and which are not runaway in their execution. However, if such tasks become runaway, then this new method can be employed.

c) The Waves that have considered here are only the periodic Waves that oscillate in one direction only. Since time is always going in the positive direction, the upward oscillation of the periodic Waves has been considered.

d)   There are several ways of executing a project or process like linear, Parallel, etc. However, we have considered only the Parallel mode of execution in this paper.

FUTURE TRENDS

Parallel Processing of Software is an Area with a lot of potential for research. A lot of work is being done in this Area. In future, we can expect that the process of Parallel execution of software to become faster and better. As pervasive computing becomes more and more important day by day, the use of Parallel processing of software in pervasive computing will definitely become important. This work can be extended by further including the use of other mathematical concepts to measure the Efficiency of any stage in Parallel processing. Further, it would be a good option to evaluate the use of square Wave equation in software Parallel processing (Riley & Hobson, 2002).

Also, it would be interesting to extend the application of Waves in software Parallel processing by studying how to reduce the impact of Runaway project. This can be done by studying the effects of reflection, refraction and other Wave properties to study their impact. Also, we can look for ways to bring the Runaway project under control.

CONCLUSION

The processing of software in Parallel is a very hot Area of research in the present times. As time passes by, the need for pieces/project stages to execute faster in Parallel increases day by day. The software pieces/project stages can be made to execute faster by automating their activities and giving them as much freedom as possible. Thus, with each Execution Cycle, the vertical length of the Execution Cycle will decrease. This is known as the "Sandwich Effect". Each stage can be represented by a Wave that spans over the imaginary line for that stage. Each stage can thus be represented by the Wave equations for Waves, including their properties like refraction, reflection, diffraction, rectilinear propagation etc. The Efficiency for each stage can be obtained by measuring as a percentage, the Area bound by that stage as a proportion to the Area of the Wave for the entire cycle. Also, by comparing the average Area for the cycle with any stage of the same cycle, we can obtain a clear idea of whether the stage is being executed efficiently or not. The uses of methods like PERT/CPM in Parallel processing of software does not ensure the expected dynamic control over the Execution Cycle. This method fills in the void in the management of Parallel processing of software.

The level of software quality that is expected from the software depends on the developers and the users of the software system. Thus, it is in the hands of these system stakeholders that the quality of the system rests. This paper helps us to manage the software execution in a much better way. However, it still needs the sincere effort and belief of the software stakeholders to work towards achieving the best from the process.

REFERENCES

Ashby, N., & Miller, S. (Eds.). (1970). *Principles Of Modern Physics*. New York: Holden-Day, Inc.

Beranek, L. L. (Ed.). (1996). *Acoustics*. New York, USA: Acoustical Society Of America.

Caulson, C. A., & Jeffrey, A. (Eds.). (1977). *Waves: A mathematical approach to the common types of Wave motion*. London: Longman.

Collins, G. W. (Ed.). (2003). Fundamental Numerical Methods and Data Analysis.

Crowell, B. (Ed.). (2005). *Vibrations And Waves*. Fullerton, CA: Light And Matter.

Enns, H. R. (Ed.). (2005). *Computer Algebra Recipes for Mathematical Physics*. Boston: Birkhauser.

Firk, K. F. (Ed.). (2000). *Essential Physics Part-1*. CT: Guilford.

Mark, W. (1999). Turning pervasive computing into mediated spaces. Armonk, NY: IBM. Jalote, P. (Ed.), (2004). Software Engineering. Mumbai.

Masujima, M. (Ed.). (2005). Applied Mathematical Methods in Theoretical Physics. Weinheim, Germany: WILEY-VCH Verlag GmbH & Co. KGaA

Pressman, R. (Ed.). (2005). *Software Engineering –A Practioner's Approach*. Mumbai: McGraw Hill Publications.

Raymond, D. (2007). *Waves*. Retrieved Jan 17, 2009 from http://physics.nmt.edu/~raymond/classes/ph13xbook/node5.html

Riley, K., & Hobson, M. (Eds.). (2002). *Mathematical methods for physics and engineering*. Cambridge, UK: Cambridge University Press.

Schaorghofer, N. (Ed.). (2005). *The Third Branch Of Physics: Essays On Scientific Computing*. Author.

Serway & Jewett (Ed.). (2003). *Physics for Scientists and Engineers*. College Text.

Tarantola, A. (Ed.). (2005). *Elements for Physics: Quantities*. Qualities, and Intrinsic Theories.

ADDITIONAL READING

Ames, K., & Brenner, A. (Ed.).(1994), Frontiers of Supercomputing-II: A National Reassessment, University Of California Press, USA.

Ashby, N., & Miller, S. (Ed.). (1970), Principles Of Modern Physics, Holden-Day, Inc.

Barney, B. "Introduction to Parallel Computing",(2009). Retrieved on 2007-11-09 from http://www.llnl.gov/computing/tutorials/parallel_comp/.

Blandford, R. D., & Thorne, K. S. (Eds.). (2002). *Applications of Classical Physics*. California Insitute of Technology.

Blazek, J. (Ed.).(2001), Computational Fluid Dynamics - Principles and Applications, Elsevier Science Ltd, UK

Cahn, S., & Nadgorny, B. (Ed.).(2004), A Guide to Physics Problems Part 1 - Mechanics, Relativity, and Electrodynamics, Kluwer Academic Publishers, New York

Cahn, S., & Nadgorny, B. (Ed.).(2004), A Guide to Physics Problems Part 2. Thermodynamics, Statistical Physics and Quantum Mechanics, Kluwer Academic Publishers, New York

Einstein, A. (Ed.). (1920), Relativity: The Special and General Theory.

Fox. G., Roy. W. & Messina. P.,(1994), Parallel Computing Works, Morgan Kaufmann Publishers, Inc, Retrieved On 4-03-2009 from http://www.new-npac.org/projects/cdroms/cewes-1998-05/copywrite/pcw/book.html

Gibilisco, S. (Ed.). (2002). *Physics Demystified*. USA: McGraw Hill.

Greenfield, A. (Ed.). (2006). *Everyware: The Dawning Age of Ubiquitous Computing*. USA: New Riders.

Hooft, G. (Ed.).(1998), Introduction To General Relativity, Institute For Theoretical Physics, Netherlands

Jensen, M. (Ed.).(2003), Computational Physics, Department of Physics, University of Oslo

Lomax, H., Pulliam, T., & Zingg, D. (Ed.). (1999), Fundamentals of Computational Fluid Dynamics, EULER EQUATIONS265.

Mason, G. Merrill & Thorne.(Ed.).(1997), Physical Science Concepts, Grant W Mason, USA.

Orwat, C., Graefe, A., & Faulwasser, T. (2008). Towards pervasive computing in health care – A literature review . *BMC Medical Informatics and Decision Making*, *8*(26), 1–18.

Schiller, C. (Ed.).(1997), The Adventure of Physics, Motion Mountain

Schlager, N. (Ed.). (2002). *Science of Everyday Things* (*Vol. 2*). Michigan, USA: Physics, Gale Group.

Sommerville, I. (Ed.). (2001). *Software Engineering, Pearson Education*. Addison Wesley.

Weiser, M., Gold, R., & Brown, J. (1997). The origins of ubiquitous computing research at PARC in the late 1980s . *IBM Systems Journal*, *38*(4), 693–696.

Wevers, J. (Ed.). (2001). *Physics Formulary, J. C.A. Wevers*.

KEY TERMS AND DEFINITIONS

Waves: Vibrations moving in a direction that are caused along a medium due to some ripples caused by anything having force.

Parallel Processing: This refers to the execution or processing of the project stages or pieces of the software in Parallel to each other. This can happen when each piece has some degree of freedom in its execution.

PERT/CPM: Program Evaluation and Review Technique/Critical Path Method are techniques in software project management to manage software projects in the most optimum path.

Software Development: This refers to the development of software. It involves a cycle called the software development life cycle (SDLC) which is followed for developing any software.

Software Pieces: This refers to the units or parts of software. The complete software is divided in several pieces to aid the process of software Parallel processing.

Periodic Waves: These are the Waves that move in a periodic fashion along a path.

Refraction: When a Wave moves through a semi-transparent medium, it causes a deviation in its path by a certain angle. This is called Refraction.

Reflection: When a Wave moves through an opaque medium, it causes the Wave to be thrown back. This is called Reflection.

Efficiency: It is the measure to ensure that a process is executed with good quality and in the most optimum form.

Rectilinear Propagation: This is nothing but the movement of Wave in a straight line.

Chapter 4
A Software Component Generation Model for Pervasive Computing Environment

Ratneshwer
Banaras Hindu University, India

ABSTRACT

*In order to develop software components that are reusable across the pervasive computing applications it would be required to consider the variations and properties (**mobility**, adaptability, composability, context awareness etc.) that may be required for different pervasive computing applications (application types). It should go without saying that various requirements and variations may not always be known a priori and hence developing all the multiple variants may not always be possible or feasible. It is quite unlikely that all the pervasive computing applications would be able to reuse a component 'as-is' always. One idea is to use lightweight components such that the overheads (those that are not required in a particular pervasive computing application) do not get transported with the body of the component. Based on this idea, a model of "**Generic Component**" with 'Component Generator' has been proposed that will generate components according to the requirements of a specific pervasive computing application. This work starts a discussion and calls for more extensive research oriented studies by professionals and academicians for perfection of the model.*

INTRODUCTION

The world of software development and the contexts in which software is being used are changing in significant ways. One of the emerging trends that promise to have a major impact on software development is that of pervasive computing. Pervasive computing comprises a computing universe populated by a rich variety of heterogeneous computing devices [Garlan & Schmerl, 2001]. Apart from the device heterogeneity, the hardware and software resources, devices and services, available to an application are highly dynamic, due to factors like user mobility, fluctuating network connectivity or

DOI: 10.4018/978-1-61520-741-1.ch004

changing physical context [Becker et. al., 2004]. Developing and executing applications in pervasive computing environments is a non-trivial task. Pervasive computing demands applications that are capable of operating in highly environments and of placing minimal demands on user attention [Henricksen & Indulska, 2004]. Pervasive computing is maturing from its origins as an academic research area to a commercial reality. This transition has not been a smooth one and the term itself, pervasive computing, still means different things to different people [Becker et. al., 2004]. Currently there is no well established approach to design, implement, deploy, execute and manage pervasive computing [Endres & Butz, 2005]. An approach towards pervasive application development preferably should have a modular structure as it is feasible to make small context aware modules such that a module can be easily modified, replaced and enhanced without affecting the other modules. What is required at this stage is that to move from traditional software development to reuse based development. **Component-Based Development (CBD)**, an approach to develop a software system with help of reusable **software components**, may help to reduce development time and cost and will increase reliability and maintainability of such systems. Component development is considered as a separate activity in **CBD**. In **CBD**, components developed once, can be reused many times in various applications. **Software components** for a pervasive computing environment can be developed and stored in a **repository** and later they can be used in a pervasive computing software development (using component based approach). The idea is to design pervasive computing related **software components** with attributes and functionalities that will always be essential in its any deployment with some scope for addition of, or modification in, functionalities as per requirements of specific pervasive computing applications.

The normal practice in **CBD** is to develop components once and use them 'as-is' in various applications. It should be noted that the component technology has come into being on the line of usage of components in the hardware and consequently promotes *as-is* reuse of non-modifiable units knows as components. Such an assumption makes it necessary to keep multiple variants of a component so as to be able to provide the most suitable components whenever there is a request for such a component. It should go without saying that various requirements of a pervasive application may not always be known a priori and hence developing all the multiple variants may not always be possible or feasible. It is quite unlikely that all the pervasive applications would be able to reuse a component 'as-is' always. In order to make components that are reusable across the pervasive applications it would be required to consider the variations that may be required for different pervasive applications (application types). It may not always be possible to visualize all possible variations during development of a component. Further newer types of characteristics that may not have been considered when the component was developed may emerge at later times. For example, if a component is developed for desktop computer environment and after some time a need arise to implement the same functionality in mobile computing environment. It is the question that how a component that meant for a desktop application can work efficiently with mobile computing environment. Such a situation may demand possibly redesigning (or may be re-engineering) the component for the newer requirements. A component developer has to develop different versions of a component for different pervasive applications (that may have slight variations in their functionalities). In order to make components composable in various pervasive applications, one goes for incorporation of properties that form a superset of requirements of all possible pervasive application types and consequently such a component becomes heavy as, when deployed in an pervasive application, it carries with it attributes and operations that may not be of any use in the given application. As we know **mobility** and adaptability are essential characteristics of a pervasive application, so such a component will contribute a good deal of problems in terms of **mobility** & adaptation and possibly the performance may also be affected. One can say that the component in this situation does have a lot of unused code and data structures. Presence of the unnecessary code in the component sometimes may degrade the performance of the component or may create some negative effects in a pervasive application where this component is going to get plugged into. This factually is the real reason behind the composition service failure, apart from other deficiencies. This idea would not be feasible because inclusion of all possible variations into the internal code would make the component heavy and the component has to carry unnecessary code that may not be required in that particular pervasive application.

It would be quite desirable to have a possibility of making available a component that is exact fit for a pervasive application that the component is being requested for. One approach may be to write different components for different pervasive application requirements. For example a component, of the STACK data structure, may be used in a stand alone system/networking system/distributed system/mobile system or with other handheld devices. Different environments may have different stack size requirements as a mobile computing system may have some memory limitations and a real time system may have some response time limitations etc. The basic functionality of this component will be the same but the internal code for the component would be different for various pervasive environments and hence separate components can be developed for each pervasive environment like one component for laptop environment, one for palmtop environment, and one for mobile computing environment and so on. The other possible approach may be, to write a '**generic component**' and a function that can generate components according to the requirements of

the particular pervasive computing environment. The idea of "**lightweight components**" has been proposed here such that the overheads (those that are not required in a particular pervasive computing application) do not get transported with the body of the component. Based on this idea, we propose the model of "Component Generation Framework along with a Component Generator" for a pervasive computing environment that will help to generate the components according to the requirements of the specific pervasive computing application. It is this approach that has been discussed here.

BACKGROUND

Researchers and practitioners have been considering various aspects of pervasive computing and related issues. It is required to consider these efforts for the purpose of identification of issues, challenges and problems in the field so as to be able to ascertain some important considerations that need urgent, and possibly immediate attention. This section attempts to present, in a concise manner, the research efforts related to the topic of discussion i.e. pervasive computing in the context of **Component Based Software Engineering**. Practical realization of pervasive computing will require us to solve many different design and implementation problems. Pervasive computing influences the way of software development and so concepts of software engineering. Software engineering community heretofore has given little attention regarding the design and development methodology of pervasive applications. The conventional development methodologies, proposed in software engineering literature, focus on non-pervasive computing development of software. The issues related to the pervasive applications are important because the slow rate of practices of pervasive computing may be a result of the use of software engineering principles and practices meant for non-pervasive computing applications.

Researchers and practitioners have been considering various issues related to the pervasive computing like **mobility**, adaptability, context-awareness, resource optimization, location transparency, deployment, **composability** etc.

Pervasive computing represents a major evolutionary step in a line of work dating back to the mid 1970's. Two distinct earlier steps in this evolution are distributed systems and mobile systems [Satyanarayanan, 2001]. In [Schmidt et. al., 2006], various real world issues and challenges of pervasive computing have been discussed. Garlen & Schmerl [Garlen & Schmerl, 2001] have discussed the research issues in pervasive computing in context of **CBSE** and described their work in Aura Group at Carnegie Mellon University. Pervasive computing requires different deployment strategies. Anderson has asserted [Anderson, 2000] that a deployment model for pervasive computing must support the **component based development**, different delivery models, and installation and activation strategies. Flissi et. al. [Flissi, Gransart & Merle, 2005] have proposed a component based model and a software infrastructure to design, discover, deploy and execute pervasive contextual services on mobile end user devices. Beckar et. al. have presented PCOM [Beckar, 2004], a component system for pervasive computing that offers application programmers a high level programming abstraction which captures the dependencies between components using contracts. Kalasapur and Shirazi have proposed composition mechanism for pervasive computing by employing the service oriented middleware platform to represent resources as services [Kalasapur & Shirazi, 2007]. Chakraborty et al. have presented a distributed, de-centralized and fault tolerant design architecture for reactive service composition in pervasive environment [Chakraborty, et. al., 2002]. A case study of component based pervasive computing system is given in [PECOS]. Esler et. al. have discussed the Communication issues in pervasive computing [Esler, 1999]. Users in pervasive

computing environments will demand ubiquitous access to their computing applications, which will create a requirement for universally available user interfaces. Early efforts in this area are already emerging, such as MoDAL [Eustice et, al., 1999] which enables graphical user interfaces to be specified independently of platform and instantiated with regard for the context (including user preferences) at execution time. User interfaces should be designed for ordinary people, rather than just for technologists [Normam, 1998]. Many context models [Henricksen & Indulska, 2004; Kulkarni & Tripathi, 2008] have been developed to support context-aware and adaptive systems and applications by providing context representation, interpretation and dissemination. Some ongoing projects in area of pervasive computing are PIMA [Banavar, et. al., 2000], Aura and Portolano [Want & Garlan, 2000]. **Composability** is a property of a software component meaning that it may easily and systematically be combined with other components [Barbier, 2002]. **Composability** of **software components** in a pervasive environment is an important issue and has been given little attention. This work attempts to put light on the **composability** issue in pervasive environment by proposition of light weight components that can efficiently be composed in various pervasive applications.

COMPONENT BASED SOFTWARE ENGINEERING

Component Based Software Engineering (CBSE) is a process that emphasizes the design and construction of software systems using reusable **software components**. CBSE encompasses two parallel engineering activities [Pressman, 2001]: **domain engineering** and Component-Based development. **Domain engineering** explores an application domain with the specific intent of finding functional, behavioral and data components that are candidates for reuse. Component-Based development elicits requirements from the customer, selects an appropriate architectural style to meet the objective of the system to be built and then selects, qualifies, adapts and integrates the components to form a subsystem and the application as a whole. The *domain engineering* explores resources and develops reusable components whereas *application engineering* reuses such reusable components to assemble products. The new paradigm [Panfilis and Berre, 2004] of assembling components and writing code to make these components work together has a name, and of course an acronym, *Component-Based Development (CBD)*, while the whole discipline including components identification, development, adoption and integration in larger software systems is called *Component-Based Software Engineering (CBSE)*. Consumers of conventional software products will be end-users whereas CBS products would have two types of consumers: end-users and Component-Based software developers [Tripathi et. al., 2008]. **CBD** includes parallel development activities i.e. development of **software components** and development of software with readymade components. Component development is considered as an important activity. The two processes (one for creation of components and other for creation of Component Based Software development) can be performed independently of each other. Some standard definitions of **software components** are given below.

"A software component is a unit of composition with contractually specified interfaces and explicit context dependencies only. A software component can be deployed independently and is subject to composition by third party" [Szyperski, 1999].

"A software component is a software element that conforms to a component model and can be independently deployed and composed without modification according to a component standard" [Councill & Heineman, 2001, p. 7].

SOFTWARE COMPONENT DEVELOPMENT IN CONTEXT OF PERVASIVE COMPUTING

CBSE should bring a number of advantages to the pervasive systems world such as fast development time, the ability to secure investments through reuse of existing components, and the ability for domain experts to interactively compose sophisticated **embedded systems** software. Unfortunately **CBSE** can not yet be easily applied to pervasive systems development today for a number of reasons [Muller et. al., 2001]. Today, mainstream IT players have not paid much attention to the relatively small but quickly growing, embedded system market and consequently have not provided it with suitable technologies or off-the-shelf components. All of this requires that the embedded system software be modular and composed of loosely coupled largely self sufficient and independently deployable **software components**. For pervasive software, nonfunctional specifications such as memory consumption of a component, worst case execution time of a component, and expected power consumption of a component under a certain execution schedule are an equally important part of the component contract. Component interfaces are equally implemented as object interfaces supporting polymorphism by late binding. Whereas late binding allows us to connect contracts that are completely unaware of each other beside the contracting interface, this flexibility comes with a performance penalty. A component model for pervasive devices should allow for procedural interfaces and object interfaces with and without polymorphism. Semantic specifications, like pre and post conditions, are of great value for the software quality especially if they are checked during run time. However, for pervasive devices these additional run time checks may turn out not to be feasible if microcontroller resources are limited. Pervasive computing involves increased demands for application interconnectivity between, for example, mobile phones, personal digital assistants, home devices or industrial automation devices. In a pervasive environment, functionality of **software components** must be accurate and deterministic because they have to react in same way always for the same input [Muller et. al., 2001]. Many a times, similar software applications are developed by different groups and there is no possibility of interaction between functions that have some commonality within the organization. It is possible to develop these functions as sharable across systems by developing them as reusable components. A scalable supporting infrastructure will be required, in order to enable the dynamic discovery of **software components** and information; the dynamic interconnection of components; the sensing, interpretation and dissemination of context; the **mobility** and adaptation of components; and the rapid development and deployment of large numbers of **software components** and user interfaces [Henricksen et. al., 2001]. For **CBSE** has to be succeed and be accepted in pervasive computing environment, **software components** have to be developed with minimal support from user.

To be successful in pervasive environment, components need to exhibit the following characteristic:

- Components should be adaptable in various pervasive environments.
- Components should make optimal use of available resources to perform user tasks.
- Components should be able to work in different computing power, memory and battery consumption
- A component needs some contextual requirements, in which it is going to get composed. This information should be kept as minimum as possible.
- Components should have small interface(s).
- Components must provide information regarding exceptions that may be raised during its functioning

- Run time checking should kept as minimum as possible.
- As users can be mobile and able to exploit the capabilities of several devices simultaneously, mechanisms will be required to enable the **mobility** and distribution of software. These mechanisms should be largely transparent to component developers, who should not be concerned with program and data migration or synchronization and coordination of distributed components [Henricksen et al., 2001].

THE PROPOSED 'COMPONENT GENERATION' MODEL

It is an important issue in **CBSE** that, if a component is written for a desktop application then how can it be made pluggable into a new setup such as client/server, distributed or **embedded systems**. To make a component to be able to compose in various environments, there is a need to add some sort of programmability in creation and delivery of a component. A component should have an ability to generate/modify itself according to the specific pervasive application requirements. Components should be developed to be delivered in such a manner so that problems in integration and composition, in various pervasive applications, do not arise and overheads (those that are not required in a particular pervasive application) do not get transported with the body of the component. Now **composability** would not be an afterthought, if an exact fit component is always delivered on demand.

Our idea is to develop a component in semi-code form (the component will have attributes and functionalities, some of them possibly in abstract form, common in all the pervasive applications) and store it in a **repository**. A component may have different variations in functionality for different pervasive applications. In another part of the **repository**, all the possible variations in functionality of a component will be stored. For example, consider the case of a component 'Student Grade Sheet'. The functionality of the component may have some variations like there may be statistical grading or absolute grading; there may be a semester system or a year system etc. First a "**generic component** of Student Grade Sheet" (having common attributes and functionalities) will be developed and will be stored in a **repository**. In another part of the **repository** there would be the possible functional/ non-functional variants (like one variant for statistical grading, one variant for absolute marking, one variant for semester system, one variant for yearly system etc) corresponding to this '**generic component**'. A numeric binding scheme can be used to show the relation between the **generic component** and its corresponding functional/non-functional properties. For example a **generic component**, in one **repository**, is coded a 'C' then the corresponding properties, in another part of the **repository**, can be termed as C1.1, C1.2, C1.3 etc. If a component user requires a specific component for his application, then the component developer will use some sort of generation function that will choose the **generic component** and the desired functionality (as required by the component user) and by combining both (with help of some mechanism), the final component will be delivered as per requirements of the user. The '**generic component**' can be transformed into a lightweight component as per requirements of the application and it carries in itself only those functionalities and attributes that are required only in this application. The idea is to define and implement a '**generic component**' that will be used by the 'Component Generator' function to deliver the appropriate most component as demanded.

The basic idea is that:

1. A component be designed with attributes and functionalities that will always be essential in its any deployment, and

2. It should have scope for addition of, or modification in, other functionalities as per requirements of the specific application.

The example shown above is very simple in nature. Some complex type of components can also be designed and developed by this approach. For example, if a software component is written for stand alone system then requirements (or expectations) of the application in hand, in which component is going to get plugged, would be simple. If same software component is written for other environments like distributed systems, mobile computing etc then the requirements (or expectations) of the application would be different. Components written for **embedded systems** should have low memory and time constraint functionality. The basic functionality of the component will be same but there would be some variation for different environments. Hence, a **generic component** and its possible variants can be design and developed and stored in respective repositories and with the help of Component Generator function the component for desired environment may be delivered.

In many cases the components need to be made reusable by adding some required application specific code. A successful application of **Aspect Oriented Programming (AOP)** [Kiczales, et al., 1997] in **CBSE** has been demonstrated by [Gray, 2001 & Doclos et. al., 2002]. This application of **AOP** requires considerations of the internal code of the component for the replacement of the additional code and hence it is easily noticeable that this is applicable on white box components. It does not remove or modify the existing lines of code in the component. This is a good example of specialization of a component by a user of the component. Our model may make use of **AOP** by the component developer to perform specialization of the component by adding some aspect based code without modifying the component generated before its delivery to the application user. The other possibility is to generate and deliver a white box component to the user and leave the aspect oriented specialization of the component to the user as described in [Gray, 2001 & Doclos, et al., 2002]. We have attempted to go for making available components to a user as per the requirements of the application by placing only those attributes and functions in the component that are necessary and sufficient for satisfying the requirements of the application in hand.

Our proposal is different than **AOP** [Doclos et al, 2002] in the following manner.

1. Ours is the work to be done by the component developer for delivering a suitable components where as [Doclos et al, 2002] describes the specialization of a white box component by the user.

2. The developer of the component, in our approach, always has the possibilities of full knowledge of the internals of the components even if a black box component is to be delivered.

3. The method given in [Doclos et al, 2002] can not consider a black box component obtained from some **repository** as it will not be possible to insert any additional code into a black box component.

4. In [Doclos et al, 2002], there is a clear separation in between functional part of a component and its non-functional aspect. In our case, a **generic component** has basic functionality and the additional property (that is to be added later) may be a complementary part of the basic functionality or a non-functional property.

5. In [Doclos et al, 2002], it is considered that the source code of the component can not be modified only some aspect based code can be inserted at appropriate places. In ours case the **generic component** is defined as a 'component framework' and its internal code can be modified by the Component developer and addition of the aspect based code by insertion of the same can also be taken up

by the developer. If a white box component has to be generated and delivered then the component user may also insert aspect based code as described in [Doclos et al, 2002].

If a Component Developer delivers, as per our approach, a white box component then the matter described by the [Doclos et al, 2002] would be useful. The benefit of our approach is to provide a component that will not be a heavy weight component as the attributes and functions that are not required by the application of the user would not be included in the components. Normally a component is developed keeping in mind requirements of various applications and hence it carries some attributes and functions that may not be required in this deployment consequently making the component heavy from the point of view of this application in hand.

THE EXPLORATION OF THE "COMPONENT GENERATION" MODEL

We have proposed here the idea of *"Component Generation Model"* as follows.

1. In the first step, a "**Generic component**" would be worked out by identifying and implementing the common most attributes and functionalities required across, and common to all, the application types. There would be a part of **repository**, say R1, in which all identified "**generic component**s" will be stored.

2. There would be another part of the **repository**, say R2, which would have the possible functional/non-functional properties, required as variations in different application types.

3. A component developer will specify the requirements, that s/he receives from a component user, to be submitted to the

'Component Development Interface' being proposed as part of this Component Generation framework.

4. Now the proposed "*Component Generator*" function will choose the "**generic component**" (for example- Student mark-sheet) from **repository** R1 and the required properties (as desired by the component user) from the **repository** R2 (for example say Absolute grading mark etc) and then generate the component (by combining the both) according to the need of the specific application.

5. There would be a 'Verifier' that will verify the non-functional aspect of the developed component.

6. The Component Generator Framework may optionally receives some requests regarding aspect based specialization of the component and perform the **AOP** based specialization using for example AspectJ for Java components etc, as described.

7. Finally the Component Generation Model may deliver:

   (a) The black box component to the component user, or

   (b) The white-box component to the component user for its further specialization applying the method described in [Doclos et al, 2002].

Normally third party component vendors would not deliver a white-box component. It is only in-house developed components are always white-box and their specializations can be taken up in that organization making use of the method described and explained in [Gray, 2001 & Doclos et al, 2002]. In our approach we have included the aspect based specialization [Gray, 2001 & Doclos et al, 2002] as per the component user request in case the user does not have this expertise and it is feasible and possible for the component developer to take up this job. It should be obvious to note that inclusion of this aspect based specialization facility would be a big hindrance in automation of the Component Generation Framework. One can go for designing a Component Generation and Specialization (**AOP** based) Environment to be used by the professionals of the component development organization. The necessary tools for generation, specialization and delivery will also have to be designed and developed to be made available to the professionals of the component development organization. This idea may be very useful for the component development organization as it calls for sufficient interaction with the component users for delivery of appropriate components to the users as per their demand. It may further be extended to provide room for an Agile Component Development and Delivery Model.

The proposed "Component Generation Framework" would contain [Figure 4]:

- A **generic component repository**,
- A **repository** to store the variations and their properties,
- A 'Component Generator' function, and
- A 'Verifier'.

As shown in the above figures, R1 **repository** (figure 2) would have all the '**generic components**' and R2 **repository** (figure 3) would have the possible functional/ nonfunctional properties (for components in R1).

Figure 1. Refinement of the requirements

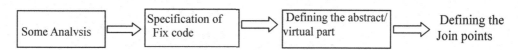

The 'Generic Component' would have a semi-code implementation and it can be accessed by its interface. A 'Generic Component' would have some 'Join-point' mechanism at which the code of its variant can be combined. Similarly, a proposed structure of a variant of a 'Generic Component' would have a Join-point and implementation of the particular property. A 'Generic Component' may have more than one Join-point e. g. at a time more than one variant can be combined with the corresponding 'Generic Code'.

Possible steps of the 'Component Generation' model have been shown in the figure (4). If a Component User requires a component with some specified properties then s/he will send the request to the 'Component Developer'. The Component Developer then refines the request of the Component User and sends it to the 'Component Development Interface'. The Component Development Interface then directs it to the 'Component Generator' function to pick up the required **Generic Component**, from **Repository** R1, and choose the specified functional/nonfunctional properties, from the **Repository** R2, and generate the desired component. The generated component then will be verified by the proposed 'Verifier' that will verify whether it fulfills the requirements of the Component User or not. It might be possible that some new errors may arise due to combining both of them (the **generic component** and its variants) and hence a verification process is necessary here. If the generated component

would not have desired functionalities then the 'Verifier' will give some exceptions otherwise it will give the output component. There would be separate 'Component Generator' function for different component development technologies like .NET, EJB, CORBA etc. The division of the work between 'Generic Component' and 'Component Generator' allows component developers to concentrate on the business logic rather than system level programming.

LIMITATIONS, OVERHEADS AND FUTURE TRENDS OF THE PROPOSED APPROACH

The description above has highlighted the need of light weight composable components and raises a few important questions concerning solution of the 'Component Generator' model. The idea of 'Component Generator Framework' is very useful to generate **lightweight components**. Realization of this idea will help a component development organization to develop components according to the requirements of a Component User and such components would be highly composable in that application (where into it will be plugged). The question is that weather the complete automation of the 'Component Generation Model' is possible or some software environment (to be handled by professionals with some human interaction) would be needed for the purpose. The Component

Figure 2. Repository of generic components

Repository of
'Generic
Components'
(Say R1)

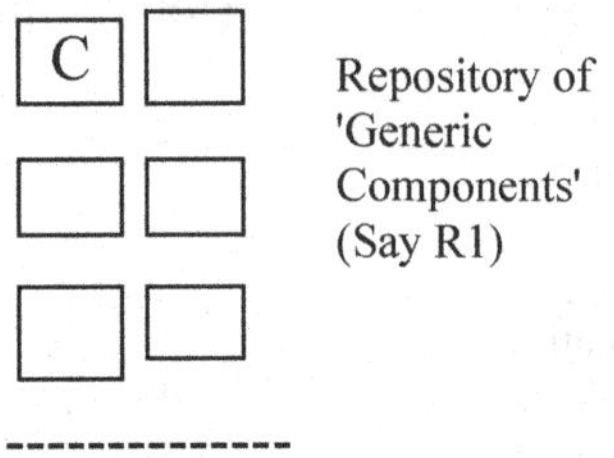

Figure 3. Repository of possible functional/nonfunctional properties corresponding to components in R2

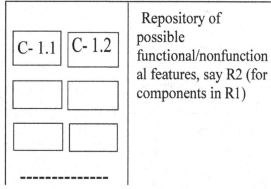

Figure 4. Component generation model

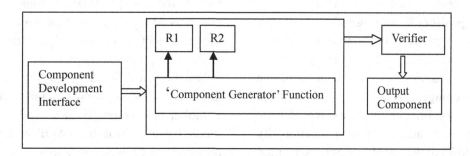

Development Life Cycle (identification, designing, coding & testing of a component) for such components would be different from the current development and delivery model. Domain analysis for identification of components would also be different. Requirements would be classified in two parts: the fix part and its variants. A clear separation of common attributes and functionalities of a **generic component** and its possible variants is necessary. It should be very clear that which information should be in **generic component**s and which should be in their variants. Design, coding and unit testing processes may have some newer issues that would not be there in conventional component development process. The question is that whether a '**generic component**' would be tested before depositing into the **repository** or the testing process will be performed after develop-

ment of a final component. We propose the idea of 'Component Generator' function which still has to be realized. An organized and well defined relationship should be established among the Component Development Interface, Component Generator function, the repositories and the Verifier. The process of design and development of the 'Component Generator' function is difficult. There should be some defined mechanism inside the Component Generator, in case if automation of the same has to happen, to select the **generic component** and its variants and combine them to deliver the final component. The process of combining the both, **generic component** and its variants, along with some common points (at which both can be combined) should be properly defined. The 'Component Generator' function should be defined in such a manner that it can work with

Figure 5.

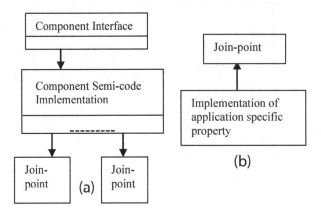

most component development technologies. The nature of **repository** for storing and methodology for searching a '**generic component**' and its variants would also be required. The management of these three repositories in the organization, one for **generic component**s, one for their variants, and the one for final components, would have some extra overheads. The proper functionality and mechanism of the 'Verifier' has to be worked out. The final component to be delivered, in most of the cases, would be a black box component. The delivery of components may take some time because the component developer will develop the component according to the requirements of the component user and especially for that application. This is also an important issue that how much time, effort and expertise will be needed to realize the idea of the 'Component Generation' model. The software component, stored in **repository**, should have information regarding memory requirement, Worst case execution time, dependencies on other components and environment assumptions.

Several technologies have been proposed to promote separation of functional and nonfunctional parts in programming languages. **AOP** provides a strategy for dealing with concerns that crosscut modularity [Kiczales, et al, 1997]. Software component containers also provide separation of concerns but they are predefined

and limited in scope. **AOP** promotes user defined concerns. Many researchers have used **AOP** concept in **CBSE**. Bruin and Vliet [Bruin & Vliet, 2002] have proposed a generation technique that is based on two pillars: Feature Solution Graph and Top down Component Composition. Duclos, Estublier and Morat [Doclos et al, 2002] have merged both approaches (**AOP** & **CBSE**) and allow aspect designers to define new aspects or services and aspect users to apply these aspects or services on components without the component code being available. Jeff Gray has given a "Meta-Weaver Framework" for generating a component by merging the functional code and non functional aspects [Gray, 2001]. Kieburtz et al have presented results of a software engineering experiment in which a new technology for constructing program generators from domain specific specification languages has been compared with a reuse technology that employs sets of reusable Ada program templates [Kieburtz, et al, 1996]. Our work mainly considers avoiding unnecessary code in a component to be delivered apart from easy and possible separation of concerns as described and used in the papers discussed in this section of the related work. Future work may include the development of a process model for such **Software Components** and study of other software component related issues.

CONCLUSION

The main motivation of '**Generic Components**', as proposed by us, is to reduce the size of components and produce lightweight composable components, that would not have wastage of memory and execution time as unnecessary properties and codes are not included. The aim of this work is to point out the possibilities of applying this approach for development of light weight components that would be suitable for composition. **CBSE** will be as successful as composable the components would be. When **CBSE** would be mature enough to provide components "on demand" then only the proper culture of software development with components would come into being. We propose here a model that addresses this question, though in a limited sense. The component generation model would be able to generate some component only if the corresponding template is available and that too of the automatic modification of the template to generate the components is possible. Future work may include the development of a process model for such **Software Components** and study of other software component related issues.

REFERENCES

Anderson, J. (2000). A Deployment System for Pervasive Computing. In *Proceedings of International Conference on Software Maintenance, ICSM'00*, San Jose, CA.

Banavar, G., et al. (2000). Challenges: An Application Model for Pervasive Computing. In *Proceedings 6th Annual International Conference on Mobile Computing and Networking (MobiCom 2000)*, August, Boston.

Barbier, F. (2002). Composability for Software Components- An Approach Based on the Whole Part Theory. In *Eighth IEEE International Conference on Engineering of Complex Computer Systems (ICECCS 02)*, December 2 - 4, (pp. 101), Greenbelt, MD.

Becker, C., Handte, G., Schiele, G., & Rothermal, K. (2004). PCOM: A Component System for Pervasive Computing. In *Proceedings of the 2ⁿᵈ IEEE International Conference on Pervasive Computing and Communication, PreCom04*, March 14-17, Orlando, FL.

Chakraborty., et al. (2002). A Reactive Service Composition Architecture for Pervasive Computing Environment. In C. G. Omidyar, (Ed.), *Proceedings of the IFTP Tc6/Wg 6.8 Working Conference on Personal Wireless Communications* (October 23-25), *IFIP Conference Proceedings*, (vol. 234, pp. 53-62). Deventer, The Netherlands: Kluwer B.V.

Councill, W. T., & Heineman, G. T. (Eds.). (2001). *Component Based Software Engineering: Putting the Pieces Together*. Reading, MA: Addison Wesley.

de Bruin, H., & van Vliet, H. (2002). The Future of component-Based Development is Generation, not Retrieval. In *proceedings of ECBS'02, Workshop on CBSE – Composing Systems from Components*. Lund, Sweden, April 8-11.

Doclos, F., Estublier, J., & Morat, P. (2002). Describing and Using Non Functional Aspects in Component Based Applications. In *Proceedings of the 1ˢᵗ international conference on Aspect Oriented Software Development*, Enschede, The Netherlands, April 22-26.

Endres, C., & Butz, A. (2005). A Survey of Software Infrastructure and Frameworks for Ubiquitous Computing. *Mobile Information Systems Journal, 1*(1).

Esler, M., et al. (1999). Next Century Challenges: Data Centric Networking for Invisible Computing. In *Proceedings of 5ᵗʰ Annual International Conference on Mobile Computing and Networking, Mobicom99*, August 15-19, Seattle, WA.

Eustice, K. (1999). A Universal Information Appliance. *IBM Systems Journal, 38*(4).

Flissi, A., Gransant, C., & Merle, P. (2005). A Component Based Software Infrastructure for Ubiquitous Computing. In *Proceedings of 4th International Symposium on Parallel and Distributed Computing*, Lille, France, July 04-06.

Garlan, D., & Schmerl, B. (2001). Component Based Software Engineering for Pervasive Computing Environment. In *Workshop on Component Based Software Engineering: Component Certification and System Prediction*, (held during ICSE'01), Toronto, Canada, May.

Gray, J. (2001). Using Software Component Generators to Construct a Meta-Weaver Framework. In *Proceedings of the 23rd international conference on Software Engineering*, Toronto, Ontario, Canada, May 12-19, Washington, DC, (pp. 789-790).

Henricksen, K., & Indulska, J. (2004). A Software Engineering Framework for Context Aware Pervasive Computing. In *Proceedings of the 2nd IEEE International Conference on Pervasive Computing and Communication, PreCom04*, March 14-17, Orlando, FL.

Henricksen, K., Indulska, J., & Rakotonirainy, A. (2001). Infrastructure for Pervasive Computing: Challenges . In Bauknecht, K., Brauer, W., & Muck, T. (Eds.), *Informatic 2001* (pp. 214–222). Vienna, Austria.

Kalasapur, S., & Shirazi, B. A. (2007). Dynamic Service Composition in Pervasive Computing. *IEEE Transactions on Parallel and Distributed Systems*, 18(7), 907–918. doi:10.1109/TPDS.2007.1039

Kiczales, G. lamping, J., Mendhekar, A., Maeda, C., Lopes, C., Loingtier, J. M., & Trwin, J. (1997, June). Aspect Oriented Programming. In *Proceedings of ECOOP'97*, (LNCS 1246). Berlin: Springer-Verlag.

Kieburtz, R. B., et al. (1996). A Software Engineering Experiment In Software Component Generation. In *Proceedings of the 18th international conference on Software Engineering*, Berlin, March 25-29.

Kulkarni, D., & Tripathi, A. (2008). Context Aware Role Based Access Control in Pervasive Computing Systems. In *Proceedings of the 13th ACM Symposium on Access Control Models and Technologies*, Ester Park, CO, June 11-13.

Muller, P. O., & Stich, C. M. & Zeidler, C. (2001). Component Based Embedded Systems. In I. Crnkovic & M. Larson, (Ed.), Building Reliable Component Based Software Systems, (pp. 303-324). Boston: Artech House.

Norman, D. (1998). *The invisible computer: why good products can fail, the personal computer is so complex, and information appliances are the solution*. Cambridge, MA: MIT Press.

Panfilis, S. D., & Berre, A. J. (2004). Open issues and concerns on Component Based Software Engineering. In *Proceedings of 'Ninth International Workshop on Component Oriented Programming (WCOP 2004)'*, 14-18 June, Oslo, Norway.

PECOS. (n.d.). PECOS Project Website. Retrieved from http://www.pecos-project.org

Pressman, R. (2001). *Software Engineering: A practitioner approach* (6th ed., pp. 847–857). New York: McGraw Hill.

Satyanarayanan, M. (2001). Pervasive Computing: Issues and Challenges. *IEEE Personal Communications*, 8(4), 10–17. doi:10.1109/98.943998

Schmidt, A., Spiekermann, S., Gershman, A. & Michahelles, F. (2006). Real World Challenges for Pervasive Computing. *IEEE Pervasive Computing*, 5(3), 91-93, C3.

Szyperski, C. (1999). *Component Software- Beyond Object Oriented Programming*. Reading, MA: Addison-Wesley.

Tripathi, A. K., Ratneshwer & Gupta, M. (2008). Some Observations on Software Processes for CBSE. *Software Process Improvement and Practice, 13*(5), 411–419. doi:10.1002/spip.356

Want, Z. & Garlan, D. (2000). *Task-Driven Computing*. Technical Report, CMU-CS-00-154, School of Computer Science, Carnegie Mellon University, May.

KEY TERMS AND DEFINITIONS

Composability: The ease with which a component can be integrated and perform the functionalities as desired by the specific application.

Context Awareness: Three important aspects of context are: where you are, who you are with, and what resources are nearby. In computer science it refers to the idea that computers can both sense, and react based on their environment. Devices may have information about the circumstances under which they are able to operate and based on rules, or an intelligent stimulus, react accordingly.

Stack Data Structure: A stack is a limited version of an array. New elements, or nodes as they are often called, can be added to a stack and removed from a stack only from one end. For this reason, a stack is referred to as a LIFO structure (Last-In First-Out).

Embedded System: An embedded system is a special-purpose computer system designed to perform one or a few dedicated functions, often with real-time computing constraints. It is usually embedded as part of a complete device including hardware and mechanical parts. In contrast, a general-purpose computer, such as a personal computer, can do many different tasks depending on programming. **Embedded systems** control many of the common devices in use today.

Aspect Oriented Programming: Aspect-oriented programming (**AOP**) is a programming paradigm that increases modularity by allowing the separation of cross-cutting concerns, forming a basis for Aspect-oriented software development. Separation of concerns entails breaking down a program into distinct parts (so-called concerns, cohesive areas of functionality).

Component Repository: Component **repository** management is a field of configuration management that seeks to ensure the safe storage of different components of a software product and all its versions.

ADDITIONAL READING

Pervasive computing systems are highly complex due to not only to vast heterogeneity but also to mobile, ad-hoc interactions. Some research challenges of pervasive computing are discussed in following papers.

GuX.MesserA.GreenbergI.MilojicicD.NahrstedtK. (2004, Jul.). Adaptive Offloading for Pervasive Computing.IEEE Pervasive Computing / IEEE Computer Society [and] IEEE Communications Society, 3(Issue 3), 66–73. 10.1109/MPRV.2004.1321031

ThompsonC. (2004, Jan.). Everything Is Alive.IEEE Internet Computing, 8(Issue 1), 83–86. 10.1109/MIC.2004.1260708

Welbourne, E., Balazinska, M., Borriello, G., & Brunette, W. (2007). Challenges for Pervasive RFID-Based Infrastructures. In Proceedings of the *Fifth IEEE international Conference on Pervasive Computing and Communications Workshops* (March 19 - 23, 2007), pp. 388-394.

AhamedS. I.SharminM. (2008, Dec.). A Trust-Based Secure Service Discovery (TSSD) Model for Pervasive Computing.Computer Communications, 31(18), 4281–4293. 10.1016/j.comcom.2008.07.014

Pervasive computing systems are interactive systems in the large, whose behavior must adapt to the user's changing tasks and environment using different interface modalities and devices. Development processes and design methodologies for a pervasive application need to be redefined in context of properties and requirements of pervasive computing. The following papers demonstrate this idea.

Thackara, J. (2001). The Design Challenge of Pervasive Computing. *Interactions, Volume* 8, Issue 3 (May. 2001), pp. 46-52.

Dobson, S. & Nixon, P. (2005). More Principled Design of Pervasive Computing Systems. *Lecture Notes in Computer Science,* Volume 3425/2005, DOI: 10.1007/b136790, Springer Berlin / Heidelberg.

Cano, J. C., Cano, J., Manzoni, P., & Kim, D. (2006). On the Design of Pervasive Computing Application Based on Bluetooth and a P2P Concept. *1st International IEEE Symposium on Wireless Pervasive Computing 2006*, (16 - 18 January 2006), Phuket, Thailand.

Kostakos, V., & O'Neill, E. (2004) Extending Traditional Design approaches for Pervasive Computing. *PREP2004*, 5-7th April, University of Hertfordshire, UK.

In pervasive applications, where a large number of wireless networked appliances and devices are becoming common place, there is a necessity for providing a standard interface to them that is easily accessible by any user. Boukerche and Ren, (2008) have given an approach to dynamic service management in pervasive computing systems.

Boukerche A. Ren Y. (2008, Dec.). A Trust-based Security System for Ubiquitous and Pervasive Computing Environments. Computer Communications, 31(Issue 18), 4343–4351. 10.1016/j.comcom.2008.05.007

A pervasive application has to be resilient to various kinds of faults and should be able to function despite faults. S. Chetan, et. al., have discussed various classes of failures, their implications to pervasive computing and the challenges to be addressed in designing a fault- tolerant pervasive computing system.

Chetan, S., Ranganathan, A., & Campbell, R. (2005). Towards Fault Tolerant Pervasive Computing. In *IEEE Technology and Society*, Volume: 24, No. 1, Spring 2005, pp 38-44.

Some challenges in location aware computing have been addressed in the following paper:

May, A., Mitchell, V., Bowden, S., & Thorpe, T. (2005). Opportunities and Challenges for Location Aware Computing in the Construction Industry. In Proceedings of *the 7th International Conference on Human Computer interaction with Mobile Devices & Amp*; Services (Salzburg, Austria, September, 19 - 22, 2005). MobileHCI '05, vol. 111. ACM, New York, NY, pp. 255-258.

S. Dobson, et. al. have addressed the need of an open source infrastructure for pervasive computing.

Dobson, S. (2008). An Open Source Infrastructure for Pervasive Computing. *PerAda Magazine* (2008). Web page: http://www.perada-magazine.eu/view.php?article=1262-2008-09-22&category=Middleware

Software architecture for a pervasive application should address the concerns of heterogeneous devices, limited connectivity, and autonomous administration in order to make it feasible to design, develop and deploy applications on a global scale. These concerns are discussed in following papers.

GRIMM. R. et. al. (2001). Programming for Pervasive Computing Environments. *Tech. Rep. UW-CSE*-01-06-01. Department of Computer Science and Engineering, University of Washington, Seattle, WA.

O'Sullivan, D., & Lewis, D. (2003). Semantically Driven Service Interoperability for Pervasive Computing. In Proceedings of the *3rd ACM international Workshop on Data Engineering For Wireless and Mobile Access* (San Diego, CA, USA, September 19 - 19, 2003). MobiDe '03. ACM, New York, NY, pp. 17-24.

Yamin, A. C. et. al. (2005). ISAM: A Software Architecture for Pervasive Computing. *CLEI Electronic Journal*, Volume 8, Number 1, Paper 3, August 2005.

Grimm, R., Anderson, T., Bershad, B., & Wetherall, D. (2000). A System Architecture for Pervasive Computing. In Proceedings of the *9th Workshop on ACM SIGOPS European Workshop: Beyond the Pc: New Challenges For the Operating System* (Kolding, Denmark, September 17 - 20, 2000). EW 9. ACM, New York, NY, pp. 177-182.

It is crucial to reform software engineering education in order to well prepare software engineers for the new challenges and opportunities presented by pervasive human-centric computing. The following paper discusses it.

Pour, G. (2006). Software Engineering for Pervasive Computing: An Outlook for Educational Reform. In Proceedings of the *5th IEEE/ACIS international Conference on Computer and Information Science and 1st IEEE/ACIS international Workshop on Component-Based Software Engineering, Software Architecture and Reuse* (July 10 - 12, 2006).

The following papers present testing framework for assuring pervasive software applications that overcomes the identified challenges faced by conventional testing techniques.

Lu, H. (2007). A Context-Oriented Framework for Software Testing in Pervasive Environment. In Companion to the Proceedings of the *29th international Conference on Software Engineering (May 20 - 26, 2007),* Minneapolis, MN, USA.

Lu, H., Chan, W., & Tse, T. (2008). Testing Pervasive Software in the Presence of Context Inconsistency Resolution Services. In Proceedings of the *30th international Conference on Software Engineering* (Leipzig, Germany, May 10 - 18, 2008). ICSE '08. ACM, New York, NY, pp. 61-70.

Memon, A. M. (2004). Developing Testing Techniques for Event-driven Pervasive Computing Applications. *OOPSLA'04 Workshop on Building Software for Pervasive Computing (BSPC'04),* Oct. 25, 2004, Vancouver, BC, Canada.

Germonprez, M., et. al. have investigated the impact of interface design standards on two essential aspects of pervasive computing: device independence and usability.

Germonprez, M., Srinivasan, N., & Avital, M. (2005). Using Interface Design Standards to Support Pervasive Computing. Case Western Reserve University, USA. Sprouts: *Working papers on Information Systems*, Volume 5, issue 14, 2005.

Section 2
Securing Pervasive Computing Environment

Chapter 5
Key Establishment for Securing Pervasive Wireless Sensor Networks

Anusree Banerjee
M S Ramaiah Institute of Technology, India

Divya P.
M S Ramaiah Institute of Technology, India

Jeevan E. L.
M S Ramaiah Institute of Technology, India

Jibi Abraham
M S Ramaiah Institute of Technology, India

ABSTRACT

Technological growth in embedded systems has given a leading growth for pervasive computing in today's human world. But the possibility of leakage of private information necessitates the need for security. Confidentiality service allows concealment of messages transmitted between communicating parties from the outsiders. To achieve confidentiality, it should be able to encrypt and decrypt the messages using a secret key. The key used must be agreed upon by the parties before start transmission. This chapter gives an overview of the issues in establishing a secret key, a scheme to establish the key and its implementation results. The scheme utilizes the fact that communication in sensor networks follows a paradigm called aggregation. Keys are split into shares and forwarded using disjoint paths in the network to reduce the effect of node compromise attack. The implementation results show that even though the scheme fits properly with the available memory with the sensor nodes, its communication overhead is high.

DOI: 10.4018/978-1-61520-741-1.ch005

INTRODUCTION

Pervasive computing extends computing anywhere at anytime using embedded systems. A Wireless Sensor Network (WSN) is the building block for many pervasive computing applications (Zheng Yuan Zheng, 2007). Each node in a WSN combines sophisticated sensing, computing and low-range communication in a low-power, low-cost system. WSNs can be easily deployed to various environments for tracking targets and monitoring various conditions. The applications include military sensing and tracking, environment monitoring, patient monitoring and tracking, smart environments, etc. (Akyldiz, 2002) When pervasive WSNs deals with information related to like military matters or human personal, security becomes extremely important, as the network and data are prone to different types of malicious attacks. Hence to provide security, communication should be authenticated and encrypted. An open research problem in this area is how to bootstrap secure communications among sensor nodes. That is how to set up secret keys (pair-wise keys) among the communicating nodes.

The various activities of key management service include initializing the end users of the key, generating the key, distributing the key to each user, installing the key at each user, controlling the usage of the key, updating the key, revoking the old key and destroying the old key. Key establishment is a fundamental prerequisite for secure communication and it includes the key generation and its distribution. The unavailability of network infrastructure, low cost requirement and node resource constraints make the security solutions currently existing for traditional networks useless in WSN. Many researchers have worked in this area and proposed key management solutions (Yang Xiao, 2007). But while choosing an appropriate key establishment scheme for a WSN, the foremost importance has to be given to choose a scheme which uses fewer node resources (to achieve energy efficiency) in order to provide

long network life. Hence we have chosen an approach proposed in the paper (Blaβ, 2006) to find whether it is energy efficient and secure against security compromise in sensor networks. It uses the concept of a '*master-device*' and the nodes in the network establish keys by using the concept of aggregation.

The remaining chapter is structured as follows: Section on "Key Management Issues in Pervasive WSNs" presents a brief introduction to various key management issues in pervasive wireless sensor networks. An overview of the selected key establishment scheme is available in Section "Overview of the Key Establishment Scheme" and its implementation, testing and results are given in the next Section. Conclusion and future works are suggested later.

KEY MANAGEMENT ISSUES IN PERVASIVE WSNS

The primary task of pervasive computing is to provide smart and continuous services designed according to specific requirements of users in order to enable them to live comfortably. The sensor networks used here are assumed to be collecting the context information like status of computing, resource availability, personal information of users, environmental information and temporal information. This context information may be accessed by intruders to breach their privacy. For example, a thief could analyze the wireless communication from a home automation system to find out whether there is anybody inside the house or not. Hence it is essential for a pervasive computing system to make the context information rapidly and continuously available along with preventing the unauthorized persons from blocking, impersonating, understanding or using the information.

In wireless sensor networks, data is transmitted between the nodes by using wireless communication and the wireless communication is prone to interception and eavesdropping. Due to constraints in cost and feasibility, sensor hardware is not tamper proof; therefore an attacker might compromise a loyal node for his purposes or add malicious nodes to the network. These compromised nodes may illegally or improperly collect data, wrongly analyze and misuse them to deviate from the purpose of the network. Data transportation starting from a sensor node which collects the data towards a data sink that transports the data to outside world has to be protected from such threats (Haowen Chan, 2003). Therefore cryptographic keys are employed to establish a security relation between communicating nodes.

The key establishment problem is a part of the key management problem. There are three types of general key establishment schemes: trusted-server scheme, self-enforcing scheme, and key pre-distribution scheme. The trusted-server scheme depends on a trusted server for key establishment between nodes, e.g., Kerberos (William Stallings, 2005). This type of scheme is not suitable for sensor networks because there is usually no trusted infrastructure available in sensor networks. The self-enforcing scheme depends on asymmetric cryptography, such as key establishment using public key certificates. However, limited computation and energy resources of sensor nodes often make it undesirable to use public key algorithms, such as Diffie-Hellman key establishment or RSA. The third type of key establishment scheme is key pre-distribution, where key information is distributed among all sensor nodes prior to deployment. If we know which nodes are more likely to stay in the same neighborhood before keys can be decided apriori. However, because of the randomness of the deployment, knowing the set of neighbors deterministically might not be feasible.

There exist a number of key pre-distribution schemes in the literature (Seyit, 2005). A naive solution is to let all the nodes carry a master secret key (Tassos Dimitriou, 2005). Any pair of nodes can use this global master secret key to achieve key establishment and obtain a new pair-wise key.

This scheme does not exhibit desirable network resilience because if one node is compromised, the security of the entire sensor network will be compromised. Some existing studies suggest storing the master key in tamper-resistant hardware to reduce the risk, but this increases the cost and energy consumption of each sensor. Furthermore, tamper-resistant hardware might not always be safe.

Another key pre-distribution scheme (Yu, 2005) is to let each sensor carry $N-1$ pair-wise keys, each of which is known only to this sensor and one of the other $N-1$ sensors (assuming N is the total number of sensors). The resilience of this scheme is perfect because compromising one node does not affect the security of communications among other nodes. However, this scheme is impractical for sensors with an extremely limited amount of memory when N is large. Moreover, adding new nodes to a pre-existing sensor network is difficult because the existing nodes do not have the new nodes' keys. All these issues reveal that achieving a key establishment scheme for wireless sensor networks is non-trivial.

Another set of key pre-distribution schemes relies on probabilistic key sharing among nodes within the network. This scheme uses distribution of a key ring to every node before deployment. Each key ring is a set of randomly selected keys from a larger pool of keys generated offline. In the shared key discovery phase, every two nodes sharing a common key in their key rings establish the pair-wise key between them. At the end of shared key discovery phase, if two nodes do not share a common key, a path key is established between them by taking help from already established secure links. Even though the scheme is not perfect as the probability of not finding a common key exists, the probability of having the shared-key connectivity is high for very large sensor networks. But generally, the communication overhead for key establishment is high for these schemes (Jibi Abraham, 2008). Hence, we look into a scheme which utilizes the inherent properties of sensor networks like hierarchical network tree organization and data aggregation.

OVERVIEW OF THE KEY ESTABLISHMENT SCHEME

In a sensor network which supports data aggregation service (Estrin, 1999), any intermediate node collects data from the neighbors and calculates an aggregation result from the collected data. The key management used here utilizes the network aggregation service. A trustworthy *master-device* *MD* is assumed to be available in the network and is never compromised. The base station in the network, which connects the network to the external world, can be considered as the *master-device*. The *master-device* has its own hard coded secret key value K_{MD}. The *master-device* is used to authenticate any new node entering the network. Authentication is done using an approach similar to Kerberos (William Stallings, 2005). Nodes establish pair-wise keys using only symmetric key cryptography, which is more energy efficient than public key cryptosystems.

When a new node '*i*' enters the network, it sends an authentication request to the *master-device*. All legal nodes are hard coded with the master key K_{MD} that is used only for authentication to the *master-device*. The authentication process consists of two steps protocol: transmission of an authentication-request and an authentication-reply. The authentication-request from node '*i*' to the *master-device* contains the source node ID encrypted with the master key K_{MD}. The authentication-reply from the *master-device* to node '*i*' contains the following:

- K_{MD-i}, a secret key between *i* and *MD*, using which node *i* securely communicate with *MD* in the future.
- Random node IDs *e* and *d* as well as respective secret keys with them K_{e-i} and K_{d-i} for node *i* to communicate securely with nodes *e* and *d* during the rest of the protocol.

- Two authentication tickets $T_e = EK_{MD-e}$ (*i*, "*is legal player*", K_{e-i}), $T_d = EK_{MD-d}$ (*i*, "*is legal player*", K_{d-i}) respectively to nodes *e* and *d* to confirm authentication of node *i*. Here, $EK(M)$ means encrypting the message *M* with the secret key *K*.

The key establishment uses the idea of key splitting to achieve better resilience against key capture. It splits a key *K* perfectly into two key shares K_1 and K_2 by choosing a random number *r* of the same size as *K* and computing $K_1 = r$, $K_2 = K \wedge r$ ($\wedge$ means XOR). Now K_1 and K_2 may be distributed to different nodes, but *r* is stored with the node itself or destroyed immediately. This technique allows $K = K_1 \wedge K_2$ to be restored only if K_1 as well as K_2 are known to the same node. Knowledge of only either K_1 or K_2 will not reveal anything about *K*.

When a node *i* has to establish a secret key with node *f*, it generates a random symmetric key K_{i-f}. Then it splits K_{i-f} into two shares K_1 and K_2. Because node *i* possesses the two authentication tickets T_e and T_d and two keys K_{e-i} and K_{d-i} for the random nodes *e* and *d*, it uses these nodes to forward both the key shares towards node *f*. Node *i* does the following:

- Node *i* sends T_e and T_d to nodes *e* and *d* respectively, using its normal wireless communication facilities. As both tickets are encrypted with the corresponding key between *MD* and *e* or *d*, both nodes assure that the tickets are originally coming from *MD*. The term '*is a legal player*' convinces them about node *i* going to be a legal node in the network. Using keys K_{e-i} and K_{d-i}, they can now securely communicate with node *i*. Tickets T_e and T_d can be discarded later.
- Node *i* creates $C_1 = (i, EK_{e-i} (i, K_1, f))$ and sends to node *e*. C_1 is a request from node *e* to forward K_1 to node *f*. The preceding node ID, *i* in C_1 helps the receiving node *e*

Figure 1. Distribution of Key shares up the tree

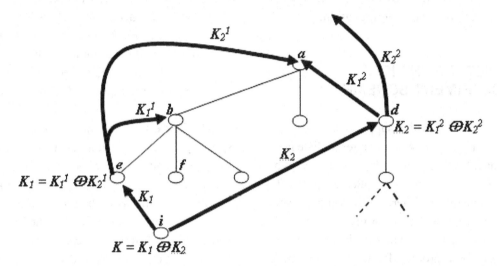

to understand that the following ciphertext is coming from node i and can be decrypted with K_{e-i}.

- Node i requests node d to forward K_2 to node f in the similar way. It creates and sends $C_2 = (i, EK_{d-i} (i, K_2, f))$ to node d.

Nodes e and d now accept node i as a legal new node, since both have shared keys with node i and then decrypt and possess node i's key shares for forwarding them to node f. Now, secure key forwarding begins. If node e already had a pairwise key with node f, say K_{e-f} it would simply send $Y_1 = (e, EK_{e-f} (i, K_1))$ to node f.

Let us assume that there is no key between nodes e and f. Consider an example key establishment scenario as given in figure 1. What node e now does is to gradually find one of its predecessors in the communication tree path with a secret key to node f, simply by asking them. Node e starts asking its father b whether it has a key with f. If node b did not have a key with node f then node e would go on and ask node a etc. As node f is taking part in the aggregation tree, one of node e's predecessors will have a key with node f in any case. Similar to the technique explained

above, these forward requests are secured with the pair-wise keys all nodes along a tree predecessor path possess.

By the induction hypothesis, e.g., nodes e and b share the key K_{e-b} or nodes e and a share the key K_{e-a} and so on. In our case however, node e's predecessor node b already has the common key K_{b-f} with node f and reports this fact back to node e. As node e now has knowledge that node b owns a key with node f, it is quite clear to node e that node b's predecessor node a must also have a common key with node f. On the other hand, node e knows node a, because node a is of course also along the path upwards the aggregation tree. And because node a is a predecessor in node e's aggregation tree, node e has a common key K_{e-a} with node a as well.

Now node e does the following:

- Node e splits K_1 into two shares, namely K_1^1 and K_2^1.
- It computes $C_1^1 = (e, EK_{e-b} (f, K_1^1))$ and $C_2^1 = (e, EK_{e-a} (f, K_2^1))$.
- Finally, node e sends C_1^1 to node b and C_2^1 to node a.

The key distribution is pictorially demonstrated as shown in Figure 1. After decryption, nodes b and a send to node f:

- b: $Y_1^1 = (b, EK_{b-f}(i, K_1^1))$
- a: $Y_1^2 = (a, EK_{a-f}(i, K_1^2))$

Node d carries out the same operations after receiving C_2 and generating K_2^1 and K_2^2. It will ask node a and a's father (not shown in Figure 1) to forward in a similar way K_2^1 and K_2^2 to node f. Note that there is no problem, if node a has no father but is the root node, that is, the sink. Eventually, node f receives the encrypted key shares, Y_1^1, Y_1^2, Y_2^1 and Y_2^2 and decrypts to K_1^1, K_1^2, K_2^1 and K_2^2 respectively. Then, it can compute K_{i-f} by $K_{i-f} = K_1^1 \wedge K_1^2 \wedge K_2^1 \wedge K_2^2$.

If one of the nodes e or d already had a key with node f, say e, then f would have received only Y_1, Y_2^1 and Y_2^2 giving K_1, K_2^1 and K_2^2. Yet, node f is able to compute K_{i-f} by simple XOR operation: $K_{i-f} = K_1 \wedge K_2^1 \wedge K_2^2$. As a result, a secret key K_{i-f} has been established between the two nodes. All the key establishment steps include only symmetric key operations which require very less computing power compared to asymmetric key operations.

IMPLEMENTATION, TESTING AND RESULTS

Berkeley based Mica motes (Crossbow, 2003) are the prominent sensor network hardware available in the market. TinyOS (Jason Hill, 2000) is the operating system for Mica motes and the software developments are done using the programming language known as NesC (David 2003), a dialect of C. A key concept in TinyOS is the use of event based programming in conjunction with a highly efficient component model. Among many available simulators like TOSSIM, NS-2 SensorSim, GloMoSim, Qualnet, OMNet++ etc., TOSSIM (Philip Levis, 2003) is chosen for creating simula-

tion environment since it bridges the gap between simulation and real time implementation in the hardware. The software code developed for TOS-SIM simulator can be directly used as the software under the real time hardware.

The key establishment scheme uses *multihop* component of TinyOS to establish the aggregation tree. The tree is created by evaluating the 'goodness' of links between nodes. *GenericComm* component in TinyOS is utilized to send and receive messages. RC5 (Rivest, 1995) algorithm is used for encryption and decryption operations. Our implementation uses 128 bit keys, 64 bit blocks and 12 rounds for the encipher operations. The pseudorandom generator available with TinyOS generates 128 bit unique random numbers.

Each node will maintain a key with two random nodes, the *master-device*, its parent and grandparent. When it establishes a key with another node, that key is also stored. Therefore the memory required to store the pre-distributed material in order to establish a secret key is very low compared to other schemes. But the memory required to store the keying material is directly depending upon the number of secret keys need to be established.

Incremental testing was carried out for the design and integration testing was carried after the integration of each module. The simulations are performed for various numbers of nodes in the network like 5, 10, 15, 20, 30 and 40. The scheme establishes keys successfully in the presence of a single intruder. The results mainly include communication overhead in terms of the message sent and computation overhead in terms of number of key splitting done. They are listed below for different cases.

Test Case 1: Table 1 shows the parameters chosen for Test Case 1. Only six nodes are alive in the network and the *master-device* is the parent of all the nodes. The network topology formed is shown in Figure 2.

Table 1. Test Case 1

No of nodes	Source	Destination	Random no 1	Random no 2	No of Key Splits	No of Messages Sent
30	16	13	17	18	1	6

Figure 2. Network topology formed for Test Case 1

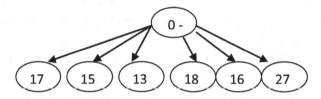

Test Case 2: Table 2 shows the parameters chosen for Test Case 2. Six nodes are alive and *master-device* is the parent of all the nodes. The corresponding network topology formed is shown in Figure 3.

Test Case 3: Table 3 shows the parameters chosen for Test Case 3. There are now 7 nodes in the network. Node 16 is the parent of node 22. The network topology formed is shown in Figure 4.

Test Case 4: Table 4 shows the parameters chosen for Test Case 4. There are now 8 nodes in

Table 2. Test Case 2

No of nodes	Source	Destination	Random no 1	Random no 2	No of Key Splits	No of Messages Sent
3	16	18	15	17	1	6

Figure 3. Network Topology formed for Test Case 2

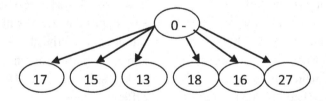

Table 3. Test Case 3

No of nodes	Source	Destination	Random no 1	Random no 2	No of Key Splits	No of Messages Sent
30	22	17	15	18	1	6

Figure 4. Network Topology formed for Test Case 3

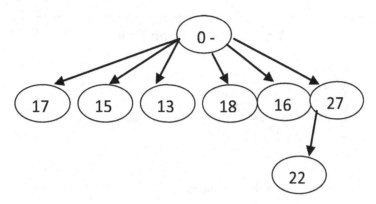

Table 4. Test Case 4

No of nodes	Source	Destination	Random no 1	Random no 2	No of Key Splits	No of Messages Sent
30	15	27	17	22	2	9

Figure 5. Network Topology formed for Test Case 4

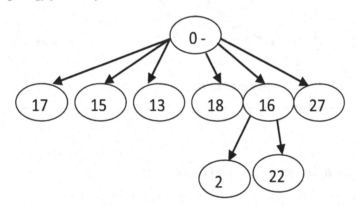

the network. Node 16 is the parent of node 22 and is also the parent of node 2. The network topology formed is shown in Figure 5.

Mica motes have 4 KB of RAM, where the data (Segment containing initialized data) and bss (Block Started by Symbol - Segment containing uninitialized data) of the compiled code are stored. The memory required for the optimized version of key management scheme by using a MICA

mote (Crossbow, 2003) is 3129 Bytes, which is less than 4K memory of available with a MICA mote, hence this scheme can be compiled and run in the MICA platform.

The following graphs indicate the test results. Figure 6 shows the total time taken to form the network aggregation tree. Figure 7 shows the time taken to establish key with the *master-device*. Figure 8 shows the time taken for authentication ticket generation and forwarding. Figure 9

Figure 6. Time taken to form the tree

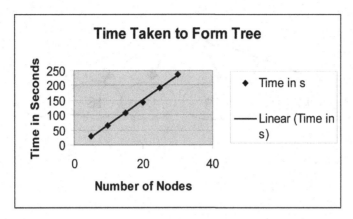

Figure 7. Time taken to establish key with master device

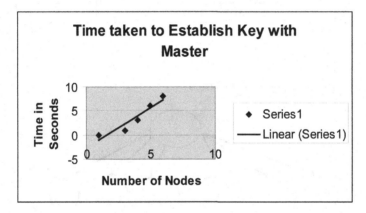

Figure 8. Time taken for ticket generation and forwarding

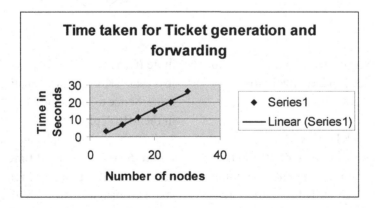

Figure 9. Time taken for splitting and distribution

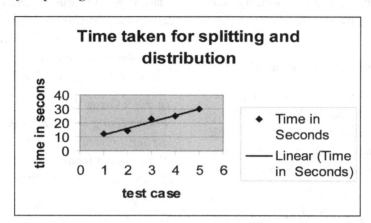

shows the time taken for splitting the key and its distribution. It is understood from the graphs that as the number of nodes increases, the time taken for various operations also increases.

CONCLUSIONS AND FUTURE WORKS

We have realized the need to secure sensor networks while use for pervasive computing applications. A key management scheme is implemented for establishing pair-wise keys with other nodes when a new node joins in a sensor network. The scheme permits aggregation operation and works effectively in the presence of a single intruder. It is more efficient than existing key management schemes like key pre-distribution scheme with respect to the number of keys that need to be stored at each node. The memory requirements show that the scheme can easily run on MICA platform and is suitable for wireless sensor networks.

During the simulations, two weaknesses about the scheme are observed. Firstly, a large number of messages need to be passed for key establishment when the network grows in size. Secondly, the security analysis is done assuming only one intruder. Possible improvements to this scheme can be made by considering upto k intruders, where

$k > 1$, assuring it be more resilient to DoS attacks and but limiting the number of times a key is split, in order to reduce the communication overhead in the network.

REFERENCES

Abraham, J., & Ramanatha, K. S. *(2008). Estimation of Communication Overhead during Pair-wise Key Establishment in Wireless Sensor Networks. In* 16th IEEE International Conference on Networks, *New Delhi, India.*

Akyldiz, F., Su, W., Sankarasubramaniam, Y., & Cayirci, E. (2002). Wireless Sensor Networks: A Survey. *International Journal of Computer and Telecommunications Networking, 38*(4), 393–422.

Blaß, E. O., & Zitterbart, M. (2006). An Efficient Key Establishment Scheme for Secure Aggregating Sensor Networks. In *ACM Symposium on Information, Computer and Communications Security,* Taiwan, (pp. 303-320).

Camtepe, S. A., & Yener, B. (2005). *Key Distribution Mechanisms for Wireless Sensor Networks: a Survey. TR-05-07.* Department of Computer Science, Rensselaer Polytechnic Institute.

Chan, H., & Perrig, A. (2003). Security and Privacy in Sensor Networks. *IEEE Computer*, *36*(10), 103–105.

Crossbow. (2003). Smarter Sensors in Silicon.

Dimitriou, T., & Krontiris, I. *(2005). A Localized, Distributed Protocol for Secure Information Exchange in Sensor Networks. In* 5th IEEE International Workshop on Algorithms for Wireless, Mobile Ad Hoc and Sensor Networks, *(pp. 1 – 8).*

Estrin, D., Govindan, R., Heidemann, J. S., & Kumar, S. *(1999). Next Century Challenges: Scalable Coordination in Sensor Networks. In* Proceedings of International Conference on Mobile Computing and Networking, *Seattle, WA, (pp. 263 – 270).*

Gay, D., Levis, P., von Behren, R., Welsh, M., Brewer, E., & Culler, D. (2003). *The NesC Language: A Holistic Approach to Networked Embedded Systems* (pp. 1–11). Proceedings of Programming Language Design and Implementation.

Hill, J., Szewczyk, R., Woo, A., Hollar, S., Culler, D., & Pister, K. (2000). System Architecture Directions for Network Sensors.In *Proceedings of International Conference on Architectural Support for Programming Languages and Operating Systems*, Cambridge, (pp. 93 – 104).

Levis, P., Lee, N., Welsh, M., & Culler, D. *(2003). TOSSIM: Accurate and Scalable Simulation of Entire TinyOS Applications. In* Proceedings of ACM Conference on Embedded Networked Sensor Systems, *(pp. 26 – 137).*

Rivest, R. L. (1995). The RC5 Encryption Algorithm. In *Proceedings of 2nd Workshop on Fast Software Encryption*, (LNCS 809, pp. 86 – 96). Berlin: Springer-Verlag.

Stallings, W. (2005). Cryptography and Network Security, Principles and Practice (4th, Ed.). Upper Saddle River, NJ: Pearson Education.

Xiao, Y., Krishna Rayi, V., Sun, B., Du, X., Hu, F., & Galloway, M. (2007). A Survey of Key Management Schemes in Wireless Sensor Networks. *IEEE Computer Communications*, *30*(11), 2314–2341. doi:10.1016/j.comcom.2007.04.009

Yu, Z., & Guan, Y. *(2005). A Key Pre-distribution Scheme Using Deployment Knowledge for Wireless Sensor Networks. In* Proceedings of 4th ACM/ IEEE International Conference on Information Processing in Sensor Networks, *(Poster Article No. 35).*

Zheng, Y., Cao, J., Chan, A. T. S., & Chan, K. C. C. (2007). Sensors and Wireless Sensor Networks for Pervasive Computing Applications. *Journal of Ubiquitous Computing and Intelligence*, *1*(1), 17–34. doi:10.1166/juci.2007.003

ADDITIONAL READING

Becher, A., Benenson, Z., & Dornseif, M. *(2006).* Tampering with Motes: Real-world Attacks on Wireless Sensor Networks, *Proceedings of 3rd International Conference on Security in Pervasive Computing, (pp. 104 – 118).*

Chan, H., Perrig, A., & Song, D. (2006). *Secure Hierarchical In-network Aggregation in Sensor Networks*, Proceedings of the 13th ACM Conference on Computer and Communications Security, USA, (pp. 278 – 287).

Chris Karlof & David Wagner. (2003). *Secure Routing in Wireless Sensor Networks: Attacks and Countermeasures*, Proceedings of IEEE International Workshop on Sensor Network Protocols and Applications, (pp. 113 – 117).

Dimitriou Dimitris T. & Foteinakis (2002). Secure and Efficient In-Network Processing for Sensor Networks, *Proceedings of 1st Annual International Conference on Broadband Advanced Sensor Networks.*

Jibi Abraham & Ramanatha K S. (2006). Wireless Sensor Networks Security: Current Research – A Survey [Macmillan India.]. *International Journal of Lateral Computing, 3*(1), 149–167.

Jibi Abraham & Ramanatha K S. (2007). Simulation of Distributed Key Management Protocols in Clustered Wireless Sensor Networks, International Journal on Security and its Applications, Vol. 1, No. 2, Republic of Korea, (pp. 21-32).

Jibi Abraham & Ramanatha K S. (2009). Energy Efficient Relaxed Rekeying Policies for Distributed Key Management in Sensor Networks, International Journal on Ad-Hoc and Ubiquitous Computing, Vol. 4, No.1, InderScience, (pp. 3-11).

Karlof, C., Sastry, N., & Wagner, D. *(2004)*. TinySec: A Link Layer Security Architecture for Wireless Sensor Networks, *2nd International Conference on Embedded Networked Sensor Systems, USA, (pp.162 – 175)*.

Laurent Eschenauer & Virgil D. Gligor. *(2002)*. A Key Management Scheme for Distributed Sensor Networks, *Proceedings of 9th ACM Conference on Computer and Communications Security, (pp. 41 – 47)*.

Lingxuan Hu & David Evans. *(2003)*. Secure Aggregation for Wireless Networks, *Proceedings of Symposium on Applications and the Internet Workshops, (pp. 384)*.

Liu, D., Ning, P., & Li, R. (2005). Establishing Pairwise Keys in Distributed Sensor Networks. *ACM Transactions on Information and System Security, 8*(1), 41–77. doi:10.1145/1053283.1053287

Madden, S., Szewczyk, S., & Franklin, M. J. & *Culler D. (2002)*. Supporting Aggregate Queries Over Ad-Hoc Sensor Networks, *Proceedings of 4th IEEE Workshop on Mobile Computing and Systems Application, (pp. 49 – 58)*.

Perrig, A., Stankovic, J., & Wagner, D. (2004). Security in Wireless Sensor Networks . *Communications of the ACM, 47*(6). doi:10.1145/990680.990707

Raymond, D. R., & Midkiff, S. F. (2008). Denial-of-Service in Wireless Sensor Networks: Attacks and Defenses . *IEEE Pervasive Computing / IEEE Computer Society [and] IEEE Communications Society, 7*(1), 74–81. doi:10.1109/MPRV.2008.6

Roosta, T., Shieh, S., & Sastry, S. (2006). *Taxonomy of Security Attacks in Sensor Networks and Countermeasures*, Proceedings of the First IEEE International Conference on System Integration and Reliability Improvements.

Sang & Hong Shen. *(2006)*. Secure Data Aggregation in Wireless Sensor Networks: A Survey, *7th IEEE International Conference on Parallel and Distributed Computing, Applications and Technologies, Taiwan, (pp. 315 – 320)*.

Sasha Slijepcevic. Miodrag Potkonjak, Vlasios Tsiatsis, Scott Zimbeck & Mani B Srivatsa (2002). On Communication Security in Wireless Ad-Hoc Sensor Networks, 11th IEEE International Workshops on Enabling Technologies, (pp. 139 – 144).

Shi, E., & Perrig, A. (2004). Designing Secure Sensor Networks . *IEEE Transactions on Wireless Communications, 11*(6), 38–43. doi:10.1109/MWC.2004.1368895

Solis & Obraczka K. (2004). The Impact of Timing in Data Aggregation for Sensor Networks, IEEE International Conference on Communications, (pp. 3640 – 3645).

Wood, A. D., & Stankovic, J. A. (2002). Denial of Service in Sensor Networks . *IEEE Computer, 35*(10), 54–62.

KEY TERMS AND DEFINITIONS

Wireless Sensor Networks: A wireless sensor network is an adhoc wireless network consisting of spatially distributed autonomous computing devices using sensors and communication facilities to cooperatively monitor physical or environmental conditions, such as temperature, sound, vibration, pressure or motion, at different locations.

Aggregation: In order to save energy, the data aggregation operation combines the data coming from different sensor nodes, eliminates redundancy among the data and minimizes the number of transmissions.

Network Security: Network security is a provision made by the underlying computer network system to protect the network system and the data flowing on the network from unauthorized access, data modification and its privacy.

Key Establishment: Key establishment a process or protocol whereby a shared secret becomes available to two or more communicating parties, for subsequent cryptographic use.

Authentication Ticket: An authentication Ticket is a small amount of encrypted data issued by a server to a client for verifying the client's identity during a communication session.

Secret Key: A secret key is a shared key known to the two or more communication parties to encrypt/decrypt the messages traversed between them in order to protect the privacy of the message.

Confidentiality: Confidentiality ensures that the information is accessible to whoever needs to know it.

TinyOS: TinyOS is an embedded, open source, component based operating system designed by University of California, Berkeley, intended for Wireless Sensor Networks.

Chapter 6
SRIP:
A Secure Hybrid Routing Information Protocol for WSN

Rajshree
Babasaheb Bhimrao Ambedkar University, India

Ravi Prakash Pandey
Dr. Ram Manohal Lohiya Awadh University, India

Sanjeev Sharma
Rajiv Gandhi Prodyogiki Vishwavidyalaya, India

Vivek Shukla
Rajiv Gandhi Prodyogiki Vishwavidyalaya, India

ABSTRACT

Security in Mobile Ad hoc Network (MANET)/ Wireless Sensor Network (WSN) is very important issue. Due to dynamic topology and mobility of nodes, Mobile Ad hoc Networks/ WSNs are more vulnerable to security attacks than conventional wired and wireless network. Nodes of Mobile Ad hoc Network communicate directly without any central base station. That means in ad hoc network, infrastructure is not required for establishing communication. In this chapter we are describing Route Falsification Attack which is easy to launch in MANETs or wireless ad hoc network. Route Falsification attack is referred to as a node with no special hardware capability can use packet encapsulation and tunneling to create bogus short-cuts in routing paths and influence data traffic to flow through them. This chapter shows the implementation of a Secure Hybrid Routing Information Protocol (SRIP) which can be used to prevent route falsification attack in MANETs. We evaluated performance of SRIP in Qualnet Simulator with and without route falsification attack. Our analysis indicates that SRIP is very suitable to stop this attack

DOI: 10.4018/978-1-61520-741-1.ch006

and performs well with low overhead in normal networks.

INTRODUCTION

Ad-hoc network is a collection of several wireless nodes that are capable of communicating directly with each other without having any infrastructure or any centralized administration. Multi hop communication can be created by making nodes as routers. That means all nodes which involve in ad hoc network can be act as router. The wireless node can give wide range of application because of node mobility and frequent topology changes. Especially in military operations and emergency & disaster relief efforts. Because of open wireless medium used, dynamic topology and distributed & cooperating sharing of channels, ad-hoc networks are more venerable to security attacks than conventional wired and wireless networks. B. Dahill, B. N. Levine, E. Royer & C. Shields. Aran (2002) stated that TCP/IP is unsuitable for sensor networks.

In this paper we are describing rout falsification attacks for MANETs. Sometimes this route falsification attack works as black hole attack. In a Route Falsification Attack, malicious node can work in both direction, source to destination during route request and destination to source during Route reply. When source sends request to destination node or when destination/ other node give reply for request. In this attack, malicious node falsify the route request and / or route reply packets to indicates a better/ shortest path to the source of a data connection for making large portion of the traffic go through them. Rajendra V. & Boppana Xu Su (2007) state that when the source selects the falsified path, the malicious nodes can drop data packets they receive silently (denoted Black hole attack), on forward the packets but keep the information to conduct the analysis of communication patterns such as sender-recipient matching, traffic timing volume and shape. After introduction the chapter includes the working of route falsification attack, description of the SRIP protocol, results that shows by SRIP route falsification attack can be totally removed and conclusion of the paper.

BACKGROUND

There are lots of researches have been going on and conducted on the topic of security. Wireless Sensor network is the very accepted area. Wireless sensor networks are often deployed in a hostile environment and work without human supervision, individual node could be easily compromised by the malicious node due to the constraints such as battery lifetime, smaller memory space and limited computing capability. Security in WSN has been one of the most important topics in the WSN research community. Here we only briefly review the reported works closely related to malicious node detection due to the limited space. To identify denial of service vulnerabilities, A.D. Wood and J. A. Stankovic (2002) analyzed two effective sensor network protocols that did not initially consider security. In their examples, they demonstrated that consideration of security at design time is the best way to ensure successful network deployment. Most recent ad hoc network research has focused on providing routing services without considering security. In their paper, B. Dahill, B. N. Levine, E. Royer & C. Shields. Aran (2002) detailed security threats against ad hoc routing protocols, specifically examining AODV and DSR. They proposed protocol, ARAN, that was based on certificates and successfully defeats all identified attacks. C.Karlof & D. Vagner (2003) proposed security goals for routing in sensor networks, showed how attacks against ad-hoc and peer-to-peer networks can be adapted into powerful attacks against sensor networks, introduced two classes of novel attacks against sensor networkssinkholes and HELLO floods, and analyzed the security of all the major sensor network routing protocols. H. Yang, H. Luo, F. Ye, S. Lu & L. Zhang (2004) focused on the fundamental security problem of protecting the multihop network connectivity between mobile nodes in a MANET. They identify the security issues related to this problem, discuss the challenges to security design, and review the state-of-the-art security proposals.

In their article A. Mishra, K. Nadkarni, and A. Patcha (2004, February) present a survey on the work that has been done in the area of intrusion detection in mobile ad hoc networks. Ad hoc networks use mobile nodes to enable communication outside wireless transmission range. Attacks on ad hoc network routing protocols disrupt network performance and reliability. Hu, Y.C. & Perrig, A. (2004) surveyed the state of research and its challenges in this field.

K. Balakrishnan, J. Deng & P. K. Varshney (March, 2005) proposed two network-layer acknowledgment-based schemes, termed the TWOACK and the S-TWOACK schemes, which can be simply added-on to any source routing protocol. Yih-Chun Hu, Adrian Perrig & David B. Johnson (2005) presented attacks against routing in ad hoc networks, and they presented the design and performance evaluation of a new secure on-demand ad hoc network routing protocol, called Ariadne. G. Acs, L. Buttyan & I. Vajda (2006) argued that flaws in ad hoc routing protocols can be very subtle, and they advocated a more systematic way of analysis. They proposed a mathematical framework in which security can be precisely defined, and routing protocols for mobile ad hoc networks can be analyzed rigorously.

ROUTE FALSIFICATION ATTACK AND ITS FUNCTIONING

Before going towards the functioning of Route Falsification Attack some aspects are necessary to learn-

We know that security aspect in MANETs is very challenging issue in the field of research. Because of the very dynamic character of the ad-hoc network a safe route between two nodes is very important. It is not guaranteed that a route, a node used one day ago to communicate with other node, is still present today. A very important security component is secure route discovering and establishing protocol. Route discovery is needed to find out new routes and update routs with new one.

A. Route Discovery

There are two types of route discovery-

- Proactive version i.e. table oriented- a discovered route is written into a table. This table gets updated in certain intervals.
- Reactive version- routes gets discovered when they are needed.

In this chapter, we are using 2nd version i.e. reactive version.

Route discovery is divided in to three phases

1. Route ask for Stage- in this stage, the source node (S) floods the network with route request (RREQ) packet and each intermediate node rebroadcast the RREQ the first time it hears.
2. - Route Acknowledge Stage- in this stage, upon receiving RREQ, the Destination (D) sends a RREP packet, which is prorogated to the source in reverse path of RREQ.
3. - Conversation Stage- in this stage on receiving RREP packet from destination node the source node starts sending data packet. Therefore the communication link can be established. During this phase the discovered route is used, that means source send data packet to its direct neighbors first and so on. All the nodes between the source & destination are called intermediate nodes.

B. Route Falsification Attack

In a Route Falsification Attack, malicious node can work in both direction, source to destination during route request and destination to source during Route reply. When source sends request to destination node or when destination/ other node give reply for request. In this attack, malicious node falsify the route request and / or route reply packets to indicates a better/ shortest path to the source of a data connection for making large portion of the traffic go through them. When the source selects the falsified path, the malicious nodes can drop data packets they receive silently (denoted Black hole attack), on forward the packets but keep the information to conduct the analysis of communication patterns such as sender-recipient matching, traffic timing volume and shape.

There are two types of route falsification attacks are possible.

- Route falsification attacks with single malicious node - only one malicious node is present in the ad hoc network
- Route falsification attacks with multiple malicious nodes - more than one malicious will be presented in the ad hoc network.

These two types of attacks are further classified into two as-

1. Reactive Attack- This attack is effective only when RREQs carry path list in clear text. That means the malicious node can take this RREQ and after modifying forward further.
2. Proactive Attack- in this attack, if the source doesn't send the RREQ, malicious node sends its own RREQ packet to the destination node.

When the malicious node is present in the ad hoc network they will always be nearer to the source node or destination node to get RREQ or RREP packet. Because in this attack the malicious node wants to modify the RREQ or RREP packet to attract the data traffic go through them.

SRIP PROTOCOL

Secure Hybrid Routing Information protocol supports only wireless interface. Through SRIP we create the routing table during the route discovery. This is called as hybrid protocol because for route discovery it can use either reactive version or proactive version. When we use SRIP, common settings of all nodes, which are making ad hoc network, are necessary. This is necessary, to find out that node which is not the part of the network. In this we also take some constrains for the outsider node. If the outsider node does not fulfill the requirement we say that this node is malicious. By this mechanism we restrict the Route falsification attack. Before implementing the algorithm we analyzed SAODV proposed by M. G. Zapata. (2001). The algorithm is describing under-

```
1. If WiredNetwork,
Send error report "SRIP supports
only wireless interfaces"
2. If number of Interfaces > 1,
Send error report "SRIP only
```

Figure 1. packet formate

Number of entries
Dest #1 nextHop #1 Distance #1
Dest #2 nextHop #2 Distance #2
. . .
Dest #n nextHop #n Distance #n

Table 1. Routing table1:- for node 1

Dest	NextHop	Distance
1	1	0
2	2	1
3	3	1
4	4	1
5	5	1

Table 2. Routing table2:- for node 2

Dest	NextHop	Distance
1	1	1
2	2	0
3	3	1
4	4	1
5	5	1

supports one interface of node"
3. chek the settings1 for the available node.
4. if settings are true.
allocate memory for SRIP's variables for this node.
Else
chek the settings2 for the available node.
if settings are true.
allocate memory for SRIP's variables for this node.
Else
Send error report" node is malicious node"
Stop.
otherwise
5. read parameter from the configuration file (required to find out the route between source and destination)
6. if new rout occurred
check update interval parameter
7. If update interval is false
Send error report" SRIP update interval is not specified"
8. prepare a route update packet according to the following format –
9. If any changes
Send the route update packet to MAC layer.
10. schedule the next route up-

date broadcast after a fixed delay of sripupdateInterval
11. scan the entry list and update routing table only with entries with shorter distance
12. if the entry is matched with destination node entry.
Msg"this is the packet final destination"
13. if the entry is not matched, msg "do not rout any SRIP control packet"

PERFORMANCE EVALUATION

To evaluate the performance of the SRIP we used Qualnet simulator version 4.0. In our simulation we created two scenario first scenario contains only 5 nodes and one wireless interface. This scenario has no malicious node. The routing table

Table 3. Routing table3:- for node 3

Dest	NextHop	Distance
1	1	1
2	2	1
3	3	0
4	4	1
5	5	1

Table 4. Routing table4:- for node 4

Dest	NextHop	Distance
1	1	1
2	2	1
3	3	1
4	4	0
5	5	1

Table 5. Routing table5:- for node 5

Dest	NextHop	Distance
1	1	1
2	2	1
3	3	1
4	4	1
5	5	0

Figure 2. Scenario with no malicious node

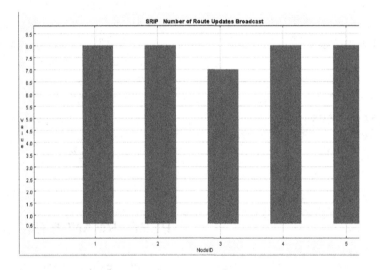

of all five nodes, which were the part of the ad hoc network are as-

If we take the routing table for the node 1, we can see that the first field dest define the destination from the node 1. Next hop tells the next neighbour of 1 through this hop we will reach to the selected node. Distance tells the distance of node from no.1 node. This simulation took 10 sec to complete its transaction. We have to take all nodes with same type. The result of this scenario in Qualnet simulator is shown in Figure 2 & 3.

The second scenario contains 6 nodes and one wireless interface and one malicious node. In the Figure 4, Figure 5 we can see that No. 6 node is a

malicious node and it is responsible for creating route falsification attack. From the figures it is clear that no. 6 node can't receive or broadcast any packet during communication between valid nodes.

CONCLUSION

Secure routing information protocol (SRIP) for ad hoc networks are designed to completely remove route falsification attack. From the results it is clear that SRIP is efficient approach for removing route falsification attacks. Though there have

Figure 3. Compare Metric Graph of Figure 2

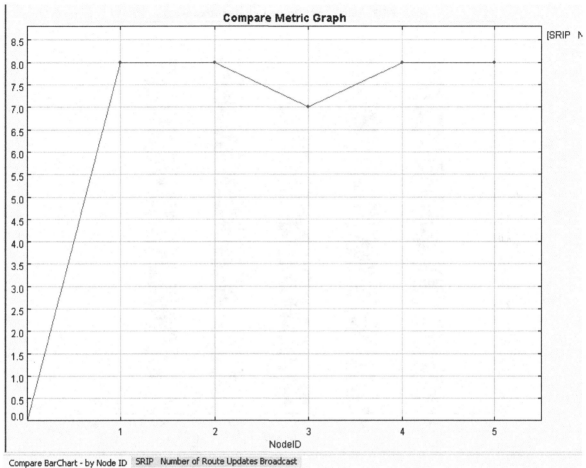

Compare BarChart - by Node ID   SRIP   Number of Route Updates Broadcast

been several SRPs proposed in literature, they do not handle route falsification attacks launched by malicious nodes. We described an attack in which malicious nodes can easily falsify routes, even when current secure routing protocols are used. Using simulations, we showed that the impact of malicious node in route falsification attack. In this paper, we proposed a secure and flexible protocol which can be tuned to meet desired security and performance constraints. Using simulations, we showed that SRIP performed well with low overhead and resists the described attack. In future, we wish to evaluate the performance of SRIP protocol with more complex scenario and more parameter we can take.

Further, we want to implement this algorithm on other types of malicious node centered attacks if possible. However, we believe that there are very good reason to hope so.

FUTURE TRENDS

Most of the attacks against security in wireless sensor networks are caused by the insertion of false information by the compromised nodes within the network. For defending the inclusion of false reports by compromised nodes, a means is required for detecting false reports. In this chapter, the Route Falsification Attack is simulated in the

Figure 4. Scenario with one malicious node

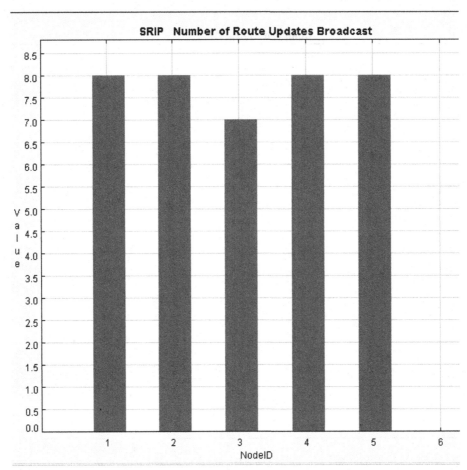

Ad-hoc Networks and applied S-RIP protocol to detect and remove malicious node from the network. A no. of techniques has been proposed by various researchers to detect malicious node. So the next logical outcome is to compare these techniques and evaluate them. However, developing such a detection mechanism and making it efficient represents a great research challenge. Many of today's proposed security schemes are based on specific network models. As there is a lack of combined effort to take a common model to ensure security for each layer, in future though the security mechanisms become well-established for each individual layer, combining all the mechanisms together for making them work in collaboration with each other will incur a hard research challenge. In this work, only malicious node is found out and block them to send or receive packets. In the future work researchers can use this protocol with more parameters. The cost-effectiveness and energy efficiency to employ such mechanisms could still pose great research challenge in the coming days. The mathematical modeling of different threats present in the WSN is another aspect of this work.

Figure 5. Compare Metric Graph of Figure 4

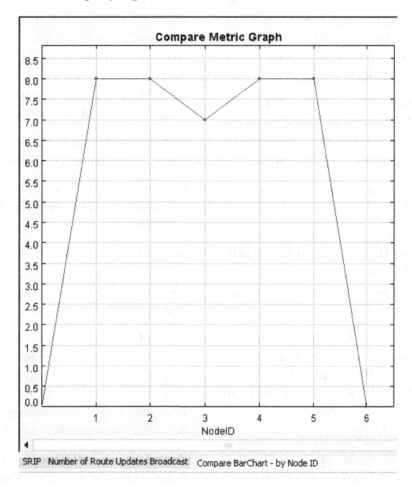

REFERENCES

Acs, G., Buttyan, L., & Vajda, I. (2006). Provably secure on-demand source routing in mobile ad hoc networks. *IEEE Transactions on Mobile Computing*, *5*(11), 1533–1546. Retrieved from http://ieeexplore.ieee.org/stamp/stamp.jsp?tp=&arnumber=1704818&isnumber=35972. doi:10.1109/TMC.2006.170

Balakrishnan, K., Deng, J., & Varshney, P. K. (2005, March). Twoack: preventing selfishness in mobile ad hoc networks. In *The IEEE Wireless Communications and Networking Conference(WCNC'05)*, (pp. 2137–2142), New Orleans, LA. Retrieved from http://ieeexplore.ieee.org/stamp/stamp.jsp?arnumber=01424848

Dahill, B., Levine, B. N., Royer, E., & Shields, A. C. (2002). A secure routing protocol for ad hoc networks. Technical Report UMass Tech Report (pp. 02-32), University of Massachusetts, Amherst, MA.

Deng, H., Li, W., & Agrawal, D. P. (2002). Routing Security in Wireless Ad Hoc Network. *IEEE Communications Magzine, 40*(10). Retrieved from http://ieeexplore.ieee.org/stamp/stamp.jsp?tp=&arnumber=1039859&isnumber=22296

Dunkels, A., Voigt, T., & Alonso, J. (2004). Making TCP/IP viable for wireless sensor networks. In *Proceedings of the European Workshop on Wireless Sensor Networks,* (pp. 364–379).

http://www.monarch.cs.rice.edu/monarch-papers/ariadne-winet05.pdf

Hu, Y. C., & Perrig, A. (2004). A Survey of Secure Wireless Ad Hoc Routing. *IEEE Security and Privacy Magazine, 2*(3), 28-39. Retrieved from http://ieeexplore.ieee.org/stamp/stamp.jsp?arnumber=01306970

Hu, Y.-C., Perrig, A., & Johnson, D. B. (2005). Ariadne: A secure on-demand routing protocol for ad hoc networks. [Retrieved from]. *Wireless Networks, 11*(1-2), 21–38. doi:10.1007/s11276-004-4744-y

Karlof, C., & Vagner, D. (2003). *Secure routing in wireless sensor networks: attacks and counter-measures. In 1st IEEE int'l workshop on sensor network protocols and applications.*

Mishra, A., Nadkarni, K., & Patcha, A. (2004, February). Intrusion detection in wireless ad hoc networks. *IEEE Wireless Communications, 11*(1), 48–60. Retrieved from http://ieeexplore.ieee.org/stamp/stamp.jsp?tp=&arnumber=1269717&isnumber=28409

Rajendra, V., & Su, B. X. (2007). Secure Routing Techniques to Mitigate Insider Attacks in Wireless Ad Hoc Networks. *IEEE proceedings.* Retrieved from http://www.cs.utsa.edu/faculty/boppana/papers/Whns07-preprint.pdf

Ramaswamy, S., Fu, H., Sreekantaradhya, M., Dixon, J., & Nygard, K. (2003). Prevention of Cooperative Black Hole Attack in Wireless Ad Hoc Networks. *International Conference on Wireless Networks (ICWN'03),* Las Vegas, NV. Retrieved from http://www.cs.ndsu.nodak.edu/~nygard/research/BlackHoleMANET.pdf

Retrieved from http://ieeexplore.ieee.org/stamp/stamp.jsp?arnumber=01181388

Retrieved from http://ieeexplore.ieee.org/stamp/stamp.jsp?tp=&arnumber=1203362&isnumber=27104

Wood, A. D., & Stankovic, J. A. (2002). Denial of service in sensor networks. *IEEE Computer, 35*(10), 54-62. Retrieved from http://ieeexplore.ieee.org/stamp/stamp.jsp?arnumber=01039518

Yang, H., Luo, H., Ye, F., Lu, S., & Zhang, L. (2004). Security in mobile ad hoc networks: challenges and solutions. *IEEE Wireless Communications, 11*(1), 38–47. Retrieved from http://ieeexplore.ieee.org/stamp/stamp.jsp?tp=&arnumber=1269716&isnumber=28409

Zapata, M. G. (2001). Secure ad hoc on-demand distance vector (SAODV) routing. In *IETF Internet Draft.* Retrieved from http://tools.ietf.org/id/draft-guerrero-manet-saodv-06.txt

ADDITIONAL READING

Buchegger, S., & Le-Boudec, J.-Y. (June 2004). A robust reputation system for p2p and mobile ad-hoc networks. *In Second Workshop on the Economics of Peer-to-Peer Systems, Harvard university, Cambridge, MA, USA.*

Buttyan, L., & Vajda, I. (October 2004). Towards provable security for ad hoc routing protocols. *In The ACM Workshop on Security in Ad Hoc and Sensor Networks SASN04, Washington DC.*

Capkun, S., Buttyan, L., & Hubaux, J.-P. (2003, January). Self-organized public-key management for mobile ad hoc networks. *IEEE Transactions on Mobile Computing, 2*(1), 52–64. doi:10.1109/TMC.2003.1195151

Chen, B., Jamieson, K., Balakrishnan, H., & Morris, R. (Number 5, 2002). An energy-efficient coordination algorithm for topology maintenance in ad hoc wireless networks. ACM Wireless Networks Journal, vol. 8. pp. 481-494.

Hu, Y.-C., Johnson, D. B., & Perrig, A. (Jun. 2002). *SEAD: Secure Efficient Distance Vector Routing for Mobile Wireless Ad Hoc Networks.* Fourth IEEE Workshop on Mobile Computing Systems and Applications (WM-CSA'02).

Y. -C. Hu, D. B. Johnson & A. Perrig (2002). *Ariadne: A Secure On-Demand Routing Protocol for Ad Hoc Networks.* Mobicom'02.

Y. -C. Hu, D. B. Johnson & A. Perrig (2003). *Rushing Attacks and Defense in Wireless Ad Hoc Network Routing Protocols.* WiSe 2003.

Y. -C. Hu, D. B. Johnson & A. Perrig (Feb. 2003). Efficient Security Mechanisms for Routing Protocols, The 10th Annual Network and Distributed System Security Symp. (NDSS).

Hu, Y.-C., Perrig, A., & Johnson, D. B. (2003). *Packet Leashes: A Defense against Wormhole Attacks in Wireless Networks.* Infocom.

D. B. Johnson & D. A. Maltz (1998). *Dynamic Source Routing in Ad hoc Wireless Network.* (pp 153-181) Kluwer Academics Publisher. C. Edward Chow & Paul J. Fong (2003) *Secure Mobile Ad-hocNetwork (SMANET).* A Midterm Report Submitted to Network Information and Space Security Center (NISSC) The University of Colorado at Colorado Springs, USA.

Karakehayov, Z. (2005). *Low-power design for Smart Dust networks. Handbook of Sensor Networks: Compact Wireless and Wired Sensing Systems* (Ilyas, M., & Mahgoub, I.CRC Press LLC., Eds.).

Lee, S. J., & Gerla, M. *AODV-BR: backup routing in ad hoc networks.* Proceedings of the IEEE Wireless Communications and Networking Conference. 1311–1316.

Marti, S., Giuli, T. J., Lai, K., & Baker, M. (2000). Mitigating Routing Misbehavior in Mobile Ad Hoc Networks. In *Proceedings of 6th ACM/IEEE International conf. on Mobile Computing and Networking* (pp. 255 – 265). Boston, Massachusetts, United States, ACM Press.

Murthy, C. S. R., & Manoj, B. S. (2004). *Ad Hoc Wireless Networks: Architectures and Protocols.* Prentice Hall PTR.

Newsome, J., Shi, E., Song, D., & Perrig, A. (2004). *The Sybil Attack in Sensor Networks: Analysis & Defenses. Proc.of the 3rd Intl.* Symp. on Information Processing in Sensor Networks.

Ramaswamy, S., Fu, H., Sreekantaradhya, M., Dixon, J., & Nygard, K. (2003). Prevention of Cooperative Black Hole Attack in Wireless Ad Hoc Networks. *International Conference on Wireless Networks (ICWN'03),* Las Vegas, Nevada, USA.

Sun, J.-Z. (2001). Mobile Ad Hoc Networking: An Essential Technology for Pervasive Computing. *Beijing International Conferences on, 3,* 316–321.

Wu, J., & Dai, F. (2004, Oct.). A Generic Distributed Broadcast Scheme in Ad Hoc Wireless Networks. *IEEE Transactions on Computers, 53*(10), 1343–1354. doi:10.1109/TC.2004.69

Zhang, Y., Lee, W., & Yi'an, H. (2003). *Intrusion Detection Techniques for Mobile Wireless Networks* (pp. 545–556). Wireless Networks, Kluwer Academic Publishers. Manufactured in The Netherlands.

KEY TERMS AND DEFINITIONS

MANETs (Mobile Ad hoc Networks): is a self-configuring network of mobile devices connected by wireless links.

WSN (Wireless Sensor Network): A wireless sensor network is a wireless network consisting of spatially distributed autonomous devices using sensors to cooperatively monitor physical or environmental conditions, such as temperature, sound, vibration, pressure, motion or pollutants, at different locations.

Route Falsification Attack: In this attack, malicious node falsify the route request and / or route reply packets to indicates a better/ shortest path to the source of a data connection for making large portion of the traffic go through them.

SRIP (Secure Route Information): protocol used to detect malicious node in WSN.

Security: Security is the degree of protection against danger, loss, and criminals. That means to protect the network from unauthorized access.

Attack: in the wireless sensor network there are different types of attacks that can harm or capture the information, node or network.

Chapter 7
A Progressive Exposure Approach for Secure Service Discovery in Pervasive Computing Environments

S. Durga
Karunya University, India

ABSTRACT

The dynamic property of pervasive computing hinders users to have complete knowledge of the relationship among services, service providers, and credentials. The involvement of only the necessary users and service providers for service discovery in pervasive computing environments is challenging. Without prudence, users' and service providers' requests or service information, their identities, and their presence information may be sacrificed. The problem may be as difficult as a chicken-and-egg problem, in which both users and service providers want the other parties to expose sensitive information first. In this chapter, the authors propose a progressive approach to solve the problem. Users and service providers expose partial information in turn and avoid unnecessary exposure if there is any mismatch. Although 1 or 2 bits of information are exchanged in each message, the theoretical analysis and experiments show that our approach protects sensitive information with little overhead.

INTRODUCTION

In pervasive computing environments, intelligent devices are ubiquitously embedded within our personal belongings, homes, offices, and even public environments. These devices provide us various network services (services for short). Via service discovery protocols, these services are discovered just in time. Client devices and services

DOI: 10.4018/978-1-61520-741-1.ch007

automatically configure themselves without users' involvement. Much research has been conducted on service discovery, as reviewed in (Zhu et al., 2005). However, the problem of involving only necessary service providers and users in a service discovery session has not been well addressed. If unnecessary users and service providers are involved, then security and privacy may be sacrificed. Services may be illegally discovered or accessed and personal privacy may be exposed and inferred.

For traditional network service accesses, it is not difficult to involve only necessary and legitimate service providers and users. Usually, a user explicitly specifies a service and supplies a credential such as a username and password pair to authenticate with a service provider. Then, the service provider verifies the user and checks the user's privilege. The user has prior knowledge of the service, service provider, credential, and relationship among them. Nevertheless, in pervasive computing environments, a user may not have such knowledge.

Challenges arise when environments change. First, a user may interact with many more services and service providers in pervasive computing environments than in conventional computing environments. For instance, a room may be saturated with hundreds of devices and services. Furthermore, everyone may become a service provider. For example, if Bob shares his MP3 player with Alice, then Bob becomes a service provider. A significant growth in the number of services and service providers makes it difficult to memorize the relationships among the services, service providers, and credentials. Second, pervasive computing environments are extremely dynamic. Devices and services may be unattended, services are added and removed, service providers' mobility causes the devices that they wear and carry to move, and partial failures cause services to be inaccessible. The dynamic property of pervasive computing hinders users to have complete knowledge of the relationship among services, service providers, and credentials.

Without such knowledge, the problem to involve only necessary service providers and users becomes difficult when users and service providers have privacy concerns. If a user is too cautious to interact with a service provider, then a user may miss the opportunity to access a service and a service provider misses an opportunity to serve a user. However, unnecessary interaction between a user and a service provider may expose a user's intent (what service a user is looking for), his credentials, and presence information. Similarly, a service provider may unnecessarily expose his service information, identity, and presence information.

Many service discovery protocols have been proposed, but it seems that no protocol addresses the problem without sacrificing security, privacy, or convenience. Several protocols and their security extensions adopt the traditional approach such that users start service discovery by supplying credentials

together with service discovery requests (Ellison, 2003, p.37) . The design is secure and only involves necessary users and service providers besides the server system. Nevertheless, both users and service providers expose their privacy to the central server system. In PrudentExposure (Zhu et al., 2006, p. 418), only users and service providers that share secrets discover and communicate with each other, but there is still a privacy leak among insiders. For example, if Bob only shares an MP3 player with Alice, then it is unnecessary to contact Bob when Alice discovers an electronic book.

We classify privacy concerns into four cases, as shown in Figure 1. The four cases are the combinations resulting from whether a user and a service provider have privacy concerns. Since there is no privacy concern in Case 1, we may directly apply authentication and authorization to secure services. In Case 2, service providers may announce their service information first because they do not have privacy concerns. Note that service providers can announce service information in an encrypted form, so only users who can decrypt messages will understand service information. If a service provider does not provide a desired service, then a user may keep silent and therefore protect the user's privacy. Similarly, in Case 3, users send their requests first. If a service provider provides the required service, and the user has privilege, then the service provider contacts the user. Otherwise, the service provider keeps silent. Nevertheless, we identify that Case 4 is as difficult as a chicken and- egg problem. That is, neither users nor service

Figure 1. Four cases of privacy concerns

Service provider / User	No	Yes
No	Case 1	Case 3
Yes	Case 2	Case 4

providers want to expose their information first when both parties have privacy concerns. Thus, users and service providers may not even want to communicate with each other. To the best of our knowledge, this is a new problem, and we have not yet seen any solution.

In this paper, we propose a progressive approach to solve the chicken-and-egg problem. Users and service providers exchange partial and encrypted forms of their identities and service information. They establish mutual trust over multiple rounds of communication. Any mismatch during the procedure stops the communication and indicates that further interaction is unnecessary. Because only partial information is exposed in the unnecessary cases, sensitive information is not exposed in an understandable way to inappropriate participants. Via simple strategies, users and service providers know the number of communication rounds and the number of bits to exchange in each round to reach mutual trust. The progressive approach not only properly identifies the legitimacy of users and service providers, but also differentiates to which legitimate service provider that a user should expose his sensitive information and determines whether a service provider should expose its sensitive information to a legitimate user. So the proposed approach provides an intelligent Service discovery since the device not only discovers the service providers which provides the service but also it identifies the service providers which known to the user.

BACKGROUND

In this section, we discuss some representative service discovery protocols that provide security and privacy features. Then, we discuss other related research. For a wider survey of service discovery protocols, refer to our survey paper published elsewhere (Zhu et al., 2005).

Existing secure and private service discovery protocols may be classified into three categories:

Traditional authentication and authorization solutions. In this category, a user or a device is responsible for supplying correct credentials to discover and access services, for example, Universal Plug and Play (UPnP) Security (Ellison, 2003, p.37) and Bluetooth Security (2002). UPnP Security provides many authorization methods including access control lists, authorization servers, authorization certificates, and group definition certificates, and users are assumed to supply correct credentials. In the trusted discovery mode of Bluetooth Security, services only interact with a device that shares a common secret. In this category, service providers may easily protect their privacy. If a user does not have the privilege to discover and access a service, then a service provider can remain silent. Users usually have to expose their identities and service requests to service providers. Therefore, users may unnecessarily expose their sensitive information when service providers do not provide the requested services. Moreover, users need to memorize the relation among services, service providers, and credentials.

Trusted central servers. In Secure Service Discovery Service (Czerwinski et al., 1999), servers are in a hierarchical structure. A server at the leaf level controls services at a place, whereas a server at a higher level aggregates information on the lower level servers. A user uses his public key to authenticate with a local server and discover services. Service providers specify user privileges and register services with local servers. Furthermore, communication among the parties is encrypted. With the help from the servers, only proper and necessary users and service providers will be involved in a service discovery session. The approach provides good usability because a user may only need one credential (his public key) to discover services. Using one credential, however, is also a disadvantage because a credential broken in an application will jeopardize other applications.

Automated service provider discovery and credential management. In our previous work, PrudentExposure (Zhu et al., 2006, p. 418) users do not need to actively identify existing services and service providers. Instead, a user's program discovers service providers from whom he acquires credentials via code words. Specifically, code words are in the Bloom filter format (Bloom, 1970, p. 422). The approach involves only users and service providers that share secrets, but a privacy leak still occurs when service providers do not provide requested services or users do not have privileges to access services. For example, Alice does not need to contact Bob when she is discovering electronic books if Bob does not share electronic books with her. In such cases, users' intents and presence information and service providers' identities and presence information are exposed, respectively. Although users and service providers share secrets, such exposure is not necessary. The progressive approach proposed in this paper distinguishes and avoids these unnecessary exposures during mutual partial exposures. Unlike the PrudentExposure approach, exposure in the progressive approach is based on both identities and service information.

Other work also influences our approach. Automated trust negotiation systems such as (Bonatti & Smarati, 2000), (Yu & Winsletti, 2003), and (Winslett et al., 2002) establish mutual trust between strangers on the Internet. Two parties, in turn, disclose part of their access control polices and submit required credentials until they reach mutual trust.

PROBLEM DEFINITION

In this paper, we focus on the chicken-and-egg problem and use the following formal model to discuss and analyze our exposure approach. We assume that a user and a service provider share a secret before they interact with each other. We also assume that each service has a standard name:

- A user, U, shares unique secrets with a set of service providers, $\{S_k\}_{k \in N}$. A service provider, S, may have a set of users, $\{U_l\}_{l \in N}$.
- When a user wants to discover a service, a set of service providers, $\{S_m\}_{m \geq 0}$, is in the vicinity. For a service provider, $S_a \in \{S_m\}$, it is possible that $S_a \notin \{S_k\}$. In addition, it is possible that, at different times, $\{S'_m\} \neq \{S_m\}$ because service providers may move around.
- A service provider in the vicinity has a subset of services, $\{V_n\}_{n \in N}$, which matches a user's request at the discovery moment. The set $\{V_n\}$ may change at any time because of the dynamic property in pervasive computing environments. For example, new services are added and granted access to a user or partial failures cause services to be inaccessible.
- Service providers and users have privacy concerns. They want to protect their identities, existence information, service information, and service requests. We define that a user is legitimate if the user shares a secret with the service provider and the

Figure 2. Design goal of the progressive approach (find Case D)

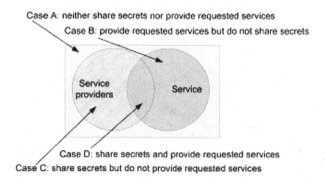

user has privilege to access the service. Similarly, a service provider is legitimate if the service provider shares a secret with a user and provides the requested service. Note that, even if a user and a service provider share a secret, they may not be legitimate and exposure is not necessary. This situation is not addressed in existing solutions.

- The constraints are that users and service providers want to interact with each other, whereas their privacy is protected. Figure 2 shows our design goal from a user's perspective: Find Case D, in which a service provider provides the service that a user is looking for, and they share a secret. That is, for some service providers, $S_c \{S_k\} \cap \{S_m\} \neq_\varphi$, and for those S, $\{V_n\} \neq_\varphi$ (from a service provider's perspective, the diagram is similar). In addition, when the numbers of elements in $\{S_k\}$, $\{U_j\}$, and $\{V_n\}$ are large, Case D still needs to be identified efficiently.

A PROGRESSIVE EXPOSURE APPROACH

To solve the chicken-and-egg problem (find Case D), users and service providers expose partial (several bits of) encrypted information in turn, as shown in Figure 3. Users partially provide their identities and service requests, and service providers partially provide their identities and service information. During each round of message exchange, both the user and service provider verify the partial information. If there is a mismatch, then the communication stops. If matches repeatedly occur, then at some point, the service provider and the user believe that the other party is legitimate with high probability. Finally, the two parties establish a connection for service usage. During each round, the progressive protocol identifies and excludes unnecessary exposures (Cases A, B, and C).

For those cases, sensitive information is preserved because only a few bits of sensitive information are exposed. A service provider usually provides a small set of services in comparison to all different types of services. Suppose that a unique ID represents each type of service and all IDs have the same length. On the average, each bit of a service ID excludes half of the types of services provided by a service provider. Thus, an unnecessary exposure is identified in several bits of service information exchange. However, to learn the requested service and available services, the whole IDs are needed.

Moreover, when a mismatch is found in a message, neither a user nor a service provider is certain about the true reason of the mismatch. That is, neither users nor service providers can discern

Figure 3. Users and service providers expose partial identities and service information in turn

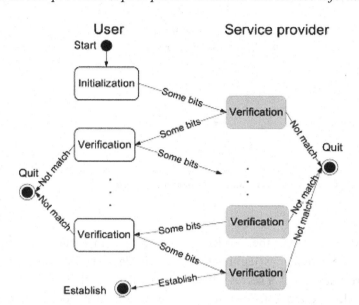

Case A, Case B, or Case C in Figure 2. For example, a user finds a match on identity information and a mismatch on service information, but maybe the true reason is a false-positive match on the identity information and a mismatch on the service information. Thus, in this case, the mismatch looks like Case B, but it is Case A. In the remainder of this section, we first discuss how we can exchange encrypted sensitive information, so users and service providers that do not share secrets do not even acquire partial sensitive information. Then, we present the message formats and the security protocol. Next, we illustrate that unnecessary exposure can be quickly detected by exchanging a few bits. An analysis of the unnecessary exposure in terms of the probabilities is given. The probabilities are known for each state in the communication. Last, we show the strategies that users and service providers use to expose their information.

Exchange Identity Information in the Code Word Form

Users and service providers exchange code words without explicitly specifying their identities in the messages. A code word is generated from a unique secret shared between a user and a service provider. A user says several bits of a code word, and a service provider checks this. If the service provider does not recognize the code word, he keeps silent.

- Otherwise, he says another several bits of the code word and the user checks this. Via the interaction over multiple rounds, a user identifies existing service providers within the vicinity (for all S, $S \subseteq \{S_k\} \cap \{S_m\}$), and a service provider identifies a user (U_i). Eavesdroppers, however, do not understand who is talking to whom. To protect against replay attacks, a user and a service provider speak one-time code words. During the code word generation, we use a time-variant parameter (TVP), which consists of a time stamp and a random number. A TVP is transmitted from a user to a service provider in the first message. Thus, each time, a user and a service provider speak a different code word and a replay attack can be easily detected (our approach requires loosely synchronized clocks).

Figure 4. (a) Generating a one-time code word to identify a user and a service provider. (b) Generating a one-time secret to protect service information

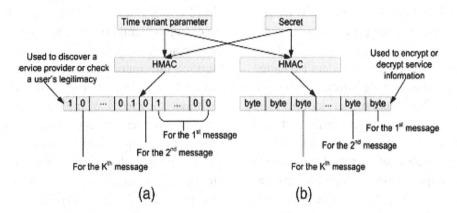

(a)   (b)

Figure 4a illustrates the generation of a code word. A TVP and a unique secret shared between a user and a service provider are the two inputs to a hash function. Specifically, we use hash-based message authentication codes (HMACs), as proposed in (Kezywinski, 2003):

h(Secret,XORpadding1,h(Secret,XOR padding2,Time Variant Parameter))

• Therefore, a code word is the hash result. The nature of the HMAC ensures that it is computationally difficult to find the shared secret from the hash results [18]. Thus, only a user and a service provider who share a secret can correctly generate and verify the code words. For any service provider, $S_{a \notin}\{S_k\}$, the user does not know who the service provider is, even if false-positive matches happen. Similarly, for any user, $U_{b \notin}\{U_j\}$, a service provider does not know who the user is.

Exchange Encrypted Service Requests and Available Services

• Services are identified by unique IDs with the same length. Users and service providers use one-time secrets to protect service requests and service information, respectively. The generation of a one-time secret is shown in Figure 4b. Unlike a code word that uses bits of the hash result, in each message, a user and a service provider use a byte to encrypt and decrypt the service information. To be precise, the encryption is *cipher = service $_\oplus$ one-time secret*, and the decryption is service = cipher $_\oplus$ one-time secret. The encryption method is known as the Vernam cipher [18]. According to (Winsborough & Li, 2002), if the bytes (generated one-time secrets) that we use to encrypt service information are random, then our encoding method is computationally secure.

Users and service providers exchange service requests and service information in the encrypted form. Thus, users and service providers who share secrets understand service requests and available services. Among those users and service providers, only a subset of users and service providers whose requests match available services will find the subset $\{V_n\}$. The encryption method is known as the Vernam cipher (Winsborough & Li, 2002). According to (Winsborough & Li, 2002), if the bytes (generated one-time secrets) that we use to encrypt service information are random, then our encoding method is computationally secure Users and service providers exchange service requests and service information in the encrypted form.

Thus, users and service providers who share secrets understand service requests and available services. Users and service providers exchange service requests and service information in the encrypted form. Thus, users and service providers who share secrets understand service requests and available services. Among those users and service providers, only a subset of users and service providers whose requests match available services will find the subset $\{V_n\}$. At a service provider's side, since partial information is exchanged, more than one type of service with the same initial bits may match a user's request. For example, if a user requests a service 10001, a service provider has two services: 10001 and 10101.

If a user says the first 2 bits, 10, then the service provider will find two services starting with 10. To inform the user that there is more than one service that matches his request, we encode the possible combinations of 1 and 2 bits, as shown in Figure 1a and 1b, respectively. In this example, if the service provider replies with 1 bit of service information, then he will send the coding 10. If the service provider replies with 2 bits of service information, then he will send the coding 0101.

The Message Formats

In a discovery message, users and service providers exchange several bits of code words and service information. Only if the bits of a code word and service information match would one provide more bits. A user starts a discovery process. Without knowledge of the existing services and service providers, he may specify all code words and the encrypted service request, along with a TVP. Figure 6a shows the message format. In the following messages, a user and service provider exchange 1 or 2 more bits of the code word and service information, as shown in Figure 6b. The first message is sent as a broadcast message or a User Datagram Protocol (UDP) multicast message for the minimum configuration overhead. The following messages between a user and a service provider are sent via Transmission Control Protocol (TCP) unicast to guarantee delivery. In addition, a service provider indicates the code word for which he finds the match in the second message.

The discussion so far is based on the condition that a user and a service provider share a unique secret. When a user interacts with many service providers and a service provider has many users, false-positive matches are very likely to

Figure 5. The Encoding Scheme for Services

Next one bit	Coding
0	00
1	01
0 and 1	10

(a)

Next two bits	Coding
00	0000
01	0001
10	0010
11	0011
00 and 01	0100
00 and 10	0101
00 and 11	0110
01 and 10	0111
01 and 11	1000
10 and 11	1001
00, 01, and 10	1010
00, 01, and 11	1011
00, 10, and 11	1100
01, 10, and 11	1101
00, 01, 10, and 11	1110

(b)

Figure 6. Message formats. (a) First message. (b) Following messages. (c) Alternative second message

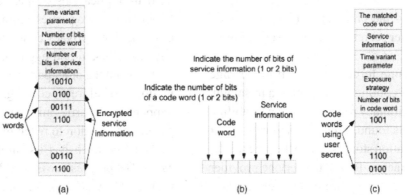

happen because only several bits are exchanged initially. The problem might be addressed for a service provider by sharing a secret among all users. The shared secret, however, is difficult to revoke from an individual user. Our solution is that service providers and users may use two types of shared secrets: domain secrets and user secrets. A domain secret is used in the first message to identify a service provider. A user secret is used in the following messages to identify a user within a service provider. Figure 6c shows that a service provider specifies a list of code words generated from user secrets in the second message along with a TVP that he selects. Afterward, the user indicates the matched code word and the two parties exchange bits of information, as shown in Figure 6b. To revoke a user's service discovery privilege, the user secret is invalidated by the service provider, whereas updating the domain secret may not be imminent.

Figure 7. The security protocol using domain secrets and user secrets

Notation:
U is a user; S is a service provider.
T_X is a timestamp that X attaches. R_X is a random number that X attaches.
CB_{USi} is bits of a code word generated from the domain secret shared between U and the ith S.
CW_{SUl} is bits of a code word generated from the user secret shared between l^{th} U and S.
K_{USi} is a secret generated from the domain secret that U and i^{th} S use to encrypt and decrypt messages.
K_{SUl} is a secret generated from the user secret that l^{th} U and S use to encrypt and decrypt messages.
SRB is bits of the requested service information.
SAB is bits of the available service information.
Y^j is the element Y that is sent in the jth message.
ES is an exposure strategy.
$\{\}^n$ is a set of n elements, where $n \in N$.
Q is a message indicates the communication stops.
P is a message instructs a user to prepare for service usage.

Message number	Sender/Receiver	Message
1	U→S:	R_U, T_U, $\{CB^1_{USi}, (SRB^1)_{KUSi}\}^n$
2	S→U:	R_U, T_U, R_S, T_S, CB^1_{USi}, $(SAB^2)_{KUSi}$, $\{CW^2_{SUl}\}^m$, ES
3	U→S:	R_S, T_S, CW^2_{SUl}, CW^3_{SUl}, $(SRB^3)_{KSUl}$
4	S→U:	R_S, T_S, CW^4_{SUl}, $(SAB^4)_{KSUl}$
A	U→S: or S→U:	R_S, T_S, Q
B	S→U:	R_S, T_S, P

The Detailed Security Protocols

Figure 7 shows the protocol that uses a domain secret and a user secret. After the first three messages, a user and a service provider send messages in the same format, as shown in message 4. The process continues until either a mismatch is found or legitimacy reaches a high probability. If a mismatch is found, a message indicating that the communication stops is sent to the other party. If high legitimacy is found, the service provider instructs the user to prepare for service access.

FUTURE TRENDS

Pervasive Computing has many names including ubiquitous computing and it forms an environment in which intelligent devices are networked together in order to share services. The key element of pervasive computing is the omnipresence of information devices. These devices can be embedded into cars, airplanes, ships, bikes, posters, signboards, walls and even clothes. This chapter focuses on secure communication between independent information devices including wearable computers, mobile phones, screen phones, PDAs and the services made available by them.

CONCLUSION AND FUTURE WORK

In this chapter, we identified that involving only the necessary users and service providers for service discovery in pervasive computing environments may be as difficult as a chicken-and-egg problem. We designed a progressive approach to protect sensitive information effectively and preserve privacy for users and service providers. Users and service providers, in turn, expose bits of information to determine whether further exposure is necessary. Performance measurements show that our protocol runs efficiently on devices such as PDAs.

The progressive exposure approach might be used in applications besides service discovery. In general, if two parties communicate with each other and have privacy concerns, then they might have the chicken-and-egg problem. That is, both parties want the other party to expose some information first before proceeding. When the problem happens, both parties might progressively expose partial information to reach mutual trust.

Our approach has its limitation in extreme cases. The progressive is not efficient when many users and service providers are present in a place, for example, a stadium. But this approach is good for a private and secure service discovery.

REFERENCES

Bloom, B. (1970). Space/Time Trade-Offs in Hash Coding with Allowable Errors. *Communications of the ACM*, *13*, 422–426. doi:10.1145/362686.362692

Bluetooth, S. I. G. *Specification of the Bluetooth System*. (2004). Retrieved November 2004, from http://www.bluetooth.org/

Bluetooth SIG Security Expert Group. *Bluetooth Security white paper*. (2002). Retrieved 2002, from http://grouper.ieee.org/groups/1451/5/Comparison %20of%20PHY/Bluetooth_24Security_Paper.pdf

Bonatti, P., & Samarati, P. (2000). Regulating Service Access and Information Release on the Web. In *Proc. Seventh ACM Conf. Computer and Comm. Security (CCS '00)*.

Czerwinski, S., Zhao, B. Y., Hodes, T., Joseph, A., & Katz, R. (1999). *An Architecture for a Secure Service Discovery Service*. Proc. MobiCom.

Ellison, C. (2002). Home Network Security. *Intel Technolog*, *6*, 37–48.

Ellison, C. (2003). *UPnP Security Ceremonies*. V1.0, Intel Co. Retrieved October 2003.

Krzywinski, M. (2003). Port Knocking: Network Authentication across Closed Ports. *SysAdmin Magazine, 12*, 12–17.

Winsborough, W. H., & Li, N. (2002). Towards Practical Automated Trust Negotiation. In *Proc. Third Int'l Workshop Policies for Distributed Systems and Networks (POLICY '02)*.

Winslett, M., Yu, T., Seamons, K. E., Hess, A., Jacobson, J., & Jarvis, R. (2002). Negotiating Trust on the Web. *IEEE Internet Computing*, 30–37. doi:10.1109/MIC.2002.1067734

www.upnp.org/download/standardizeddcps/UPnPSecurity Ceremonies_1_0secure.pdf. (2003, October).

Yu, T., & Winslett, M. (2003). A Unified Scheme for Resource Protection in Automated Trust Negotiation. In *Proc. IEEE Symp. Security and Privacy*.

Zhu, F., Mutka, M., & Ni, L. (2005). Service Discovery in Pervasive Computing Environments. *IEEE Pervasive Computing / IEEE Computer Society [and] IEEE Communications Society, 4*, 81–90. doi:10.1109/MPRV.2005.87

Zhu, F., Mutka, M., & Ni, L. (2006). A Private, Secure and User-Centric Information Exposure Model for Service Discovery Protocols. *IEEE Transactions on Mobile Computing, 5*, 418–429. doi:10.1109/TMC.2006.1599409

ADDITIONAL READING

Adam Greenfield. (2006). *Everyware: The Dawning Age of Ubiquitous Computing*. New Riders.

Alfons Schuster. (2007). *Intelligent Computing Everywhere*. Springer.

Dieter Hutter. (2003). *Security in Pervasive Computing: First International Conference, Boppard, Germany*, Springer Pub.

ebiquity.umbc.edu/paper/html/id/186/**Service-Discovery**-and-Compsition-in-**Pervasive**-Environments - 20k

Mohammad Ilyas & Imad Mahgoub. (2004). *Mobile computing handbook*. CRC Press.

Mohsen Guizani. (2004). *Wireless communications systems and networks*. Springer Pub.

portal.acm.org/citation.cfm?doid=570705.570708

www.computer.org/**pervasive**

www.cs.utah.edu/~sgoyal/**pervasive**/ - 9k

www.inf.ethz.ch/news/spotlight/visit_**pervasive**_comp - 32k

www.**pervasivecomputing**.net/

www.**pervasive**.dk/

www.**pervasive**health.org/

www.**pervasive**.jku.at/ - 23k

www.smartmobs.com/ - 51k

www.webopedia.com/TERM/P/**pervasive_computing**.html

Yang Xiao. (2007). Security in Distributed, Grid, Mobile, and Pervasive Computing.CRC Press.

KEY TERMS AND DEFINITIONS

Authentication: The process of identifying an individual, usually based on a username and password. In security systems, authentication is distinct from authorization, which is the process of giving individuals access to system objects based on their identity.

Pervasive Computing: Intelligent devices are networked in order to share services.

Privacy: Concealment of what is said or done

Progressive Exposure: Devices expose partial information in turn and avoid unnecessary exposure. During the progress of communication both can identify each other.

Security: In the computer industry refers to techniques for ensuring that data stored in a computer cannot be read or compromised by any individuals without authorization. Most security measures involve data encryption and passwords.

Chapter 8
Security in Pervasive Computing:
A Blackhole Attack Perspective

Sunita Prasad
Centre for Development of Advanced Computing, India

Rakesh Chouhan
Centre for Development of Advanced Computing, India

ABSTRACT

Pervasive computing has wide application in military, medical and smart home domain. In pervasive computing, a large number of smart objects interact with one another without the user intervention. Although the technology is promising but security needs to be addressed before the technology is widely deployed. Pervasive networks are formed spontaneously and the devices communicate via radio. Thus, mobile ad hoc networking is an essential technology for pervasive computing. An ad hoc network is a collection of wireless mobile nodes, which acts as a host as well as a router. The communication between the nodes is multihop without any centralized administration. AODV (Ad Hoc On demand Distance Vector) is a prominent on-demand reactive routing protocol for mobile ad hoc networks. But in existing AODV, there is no security provision against well-known attack known as "Black hole attack". Black hole nodes are those malicious nodes that agree to forward the packets to destination but do not forward the packets intentionally. Thischapter extends the watchdog mechanism for the AODV routing protocol to detect such misbehavior based on promiscuous listening. The proposed method first detects a black hole node and then gives a new route bypassing this node. The experimental results show that in a lightly loaded, hostile environment, the proposed scheme improves the throughput compared to an unprotected AODV protocol.

INTRODUCTION

In 1991, Mark Weiser, father of ubiquitous computing, described the vision for 21st century computing.

DOI: 10.4018/978-1-61520-741-1.ch008

He stated that "The most profound technologies are those that disappear. They weave themselves into the fabric of everyday life until they are indistinguishable from it" [Weiser 1991] He named it ubiquitous computing aka pervasive computing. Pervasive computing is a rapidly developing area of Information and Communication Technology (ICT). The term refers to the increasing integration of ICT into people's lives and environment. This is made possible by the growing availability of wireless embedded systems with inbuilt communication facilities. Pervasive computing has many potential applications from health care and home care to environmental monitoring and intelligent transport systems. Consider a heart patient wearing an implanted monitor that communicates wirelessly with computers trained to detect and report deviations from the normal behavior. The monitor should know when to raise the alarm, based on its knowledge about the environment. Pervasive computing is not just wireless communication but a complex system. The goal is to meet the claim of computing anytime anywhere. Millions of embedded microprocessors allow the technology to recede into the background. A pervasive computing technology involves three converging areas of ICT namely computing devices, connectivity and user interfaces. The technology involves embedded devices, which may be stationary as well as mobile. These components are linked to each other and communicate via radio. The pervasive system forms the network spontaneously. Mobile networking is the key technology to pervasive computing.

Pervasive computing systems (PCS) are complex as there are billions of processors having complex interaction. Integrating the pervasive computing components raises severe security issues. The complex system is a paradise for hackers and virus in absence of any security measures. The system may propagate false information, selective information or completely block the information of individuals or organizations. Pervasive computing cannot become a reality until these issues are addressed. Security involves preventing unauthorized persons from viewing and/or manipulating the data and also protection from both internal and external attacks. Thus secure communication is of vital importance in these networks. This paper discusses a specialized

attack known as the blackhole attack in ad hoc networks, which is the underlying technology for connectivity in PCS. A mobile ad hoc network (MANET) is an autonomous system of mobile hosts connected by wireless links. There is no static infrastructure such as base station. The hosts are free to move around randomly, thus changing the network topology dynamically. Thus routing protocols must be adaptive and able to maintain routes in spite of the changing network connectivity. Such networks are very useful in military and tactical applications such as emergency rescue or exploration missions, where cellular infrastructure is unavailable or unreliable. Commercial applications include home area networking, on-the-fly conferencing applications, networking intelligent devices or sensors, communication between mobile robots, etc. Ad hoc networks are ideal in situations where installing an infrastructure is not possible because the infrastructure is too expensive or too vulnerable.

The communication in a MANET is essentially multihop due to limited transmission range. This decentralized operation relies on the cooperative participation of all nodes. Thus security becomes an essential component even for the basic network operation like packet forwarding and routing (Deng, 2002). The malicious node could simply block or modify the traffic traversing through it by refusing to cooperate. Security in wireless ad hoc network is a challenging task. In general, the MANET is vulnerable due to its fundamental characteristic of open medium, dynamic topology, and absence of central authorities, distributed cooperation, and constrained capability.

Security Requirements

Routing in ad hoc network is trivial and based on implicit "Trust your neighbor" relationship. If all the nodes are within the transmission range, then the destination can be reached by a single hop. However, when the destination is not within a single hop then multi-hop routing is required.

This means that the source now routes the packets through some intermediate nodes, which may be malicious. The generic security requirements for an ad hoc network are:

1. Authentication – It is verifying the identity and the privileges of the user.
2. Confidentiality – The data sent by the sender must be comprehensible only to the intended receiver.
3. Integrity – The data sent by the source node should reach the destination node unaltered.
4. Non-repudiation – To guarantee that the sender of a message cannot later deny having sent the message and that the recipient cannot deny having received the message.
5. Availability – The network should remain operational all the time. It must be robust enough to tolerate link failures and also be capable of surviving various attacks mounted on it.

Attacks and Threats on Ad Hoc Networks

The use of wireless links makes MANETs susceptible to attack. The attack on an ad hoc network may vary in strength and intention. The attack on an ad hoc network can be categorized into active and passive attacks

In a passive attack the malicious node only listens to the traffic without modifying or disturbing it in any way. The main threat by such an attack is that confidential information is leaked to the attacker.

In an active attack, the malignant node actively disturbs the normal operation of the network. This can be done in different ways, for e.g. by foraging packets, disrupting normal routing or consuming network and node resources.

The existing security solutions for wired networks cannot be directly applied in MANET's due to its dynamic topology. Although a mali-

cious node can deploy a variety of attacks, this chapter considers only the attacks caused by the failure to perform packet forwarding when the node participates in routing. This is known as the blackhole attack. Blackhole attack is a sequence number attack launched at the network layer. In this attack, the node falsely advertises as having the shortest path to the node whose packet it wants to intercept by fabricating the sequence number of the "Route Reply" packet and thus pretending to have the shortest and freshest route to the destination. The nodes may route the packet through the malicious node because it seems to be the most effective route. The malicious node then simply drops the packet. Unlike the classical network, the nodes in a MANET cannot be trusted for correct execution of the network function. The security mechanism based on *a priori* trust relationship between the nodes requires entity authentication for correct execution of network functions. However, in large networks entity authentication raises key management issues. In the absence of *a priori* trust, cooperative security schemes seem to offer the best alternative (Argyroudis, 2005).

In this chapter we extend a mechanism based on promiscuous listening to detect misbehaving nodes. For a given node, we use a combination of the direct and the indirect observation to find the ratio of the number of dropped data packets to the number of successfully forwarded data packets by the node that represents a metric to mark the node as either misbehaving or well behaving. If this ratio exceeds a certain threshold, the node is marked as misbehaving else marked as well behaving. Upon detecting a misbehaving node, the detecting node tries to avoid the misbehaving node and route the packets along another path. This decision is taken locally without informing the sender or the receiver. Thus the misbehaving nodes are isolated transparently from the sender and the receiver.

BACKGROUND

In this section, we survey some of the current attempts at solving the problem of routing misbehavior in ad hoc networks.

The Watchdog and Pathrater components attempt to detect and mitigate the effect of nodes that do not forward the packets although they have agreed to do so (Marti, 2002). The method was built on top of DSR. Watchdog is responsible for monitoring of packet forwards by listening in the promiscuous mode. It labels the node as misbehaving if it fails to do so. The watchdog of the node maintains copies of the recently forwarded packets and compares it with the overheard transmissions by neighboring nodes. If a node that was supposed to forward a packet fails to do so within a certain timeout period, the watchdog of an overhearing node increments the failure rating for a specific node. When the failure rating for the misbehaving node exceeds a certain threshold, the node is labeled as misbehaving. The pathrater assesses the result of the watchdog and selects the most reliable path for packet delivery. This chapter extends the method for mitigating the effect of the blackhole in the on-demand reactive AODV routing protocol. Our mechanism uses the combination of the direct and indirect observation of the ratio of the dropped and the forwarded packets to label the node as misbehaving or legitimate. This is because the communication in a mobile ad hoc network is multihop and the nodes have to forward the packets coming from different nodes. We assume that the node may fail to forward the packet of a specific node within a certain timeout period due to congestion or it may be forwarding the packets of other nodes. In our opinion using the ratio of the dropped and forwarded packets can prevent labeling of the legitimate nodes as blackhole nodes.

The CONFIDANT stands for Cooperation Of Nodes: Fairness In Dynamic Ad hoc Networks (Buchegger 2002). The scheme extends DSR and includes the following components – the monitor, the reputation system, the path manager and the trust manager. The monitor component is responsible for monitoring passive acknowledgements for each packet it forwards. When a node forwards a packet, it monitors the transmissions of its next hop neighbors trying to detect deviations from the expected normal behavior. The trust manager deals with the sending and receiving of alarm messages. These messages are generated and sent when the local node concludes that another node is misbehaving. Such messages are exchanged only between friend nodes. The conclusion is reached based on the passive acknowledgement mechanism of the monitor component or received alarm messages form another node. The reputation system component maintains a table of node identities and associated ratings. Ratings are modified according to a rate function that uses small weights for reported alarms of malicious behavior and greater weights for direct observation. If the rating falls under a certain threshold, the path manger component is called in order to remove the path containing the identified malicious node. Further, the path manager ignores routing packets from the attacker and alerts legitimate nodes when they request a route that uses a compromised path.

Deng et al. (Deng, 2002) proposed a solution for single black hole problem for ad hoc on-demand distance routing protocol. This method requires the intermediate node to send Route Reply (RREP) packet with next hop information. When a source node receives the RREP packet from an intermediate node, it sends a *FurtherRequest* packet to the next hop to verify that it has a route to the intermediate node who had sent back the RREP packet and that it has a route to the destination. When the next hop receives the *FurtherRequest*, it sends a *FurtherReply* that includes check result to the source node. Based on the information in the *FurtherReply*, the source node judges the validity of the route. However, this method greatly increases the routing overhead and therefore the authors suggest using this method be used only when a node is suspected of malicious behavior, which can be detected using an Intrusion Detection System (IDS).

The CORE scheme is based on collaborative monitoring technique and reputation mechanism (Michiardi, 2002). Each node of the network monitors the behavior of its neighbors and collects observations for a requested function. Based on the collected observations, each node computes a reputation value for every neighbor using a complex reputation mechanism. The overall reputation comprises of subjective reputation (based on observations), indirect reputation (positive reports by others) and functional reputation (task specific behavior), which are weighted to give a combined reputation value. The formula used to evaluate the reputation value gives more relevance to past observations to avoid false detections. A node attains a negative reputation only when its neighbor detects its misbehavior and this negative value is kept local to the detecting neighbor. A misbehaving node will eventually be isolated from the network when all its neighbors detect its misbehavior and thus stop forwarding packets to/from it. With mobility in mind, one would expect this mechanism to fail if the misbehaving node's neighbors continuously change allowing for a new chance for the malicious node to drop more packets.

AODV WATCHDOG MECHANISM

AODV Routing Protocol

AODV routing protocol is purely a reactive algorithm and gathers route information only on demand. There are two main phases in AODV routing protocol. The phases are described as follows.

- Route Discovery -The process of finding a new route between two nodes.
- Route Maintenance -The process of repairing a broken route or finding a new route in case of route failure.

Route Discovery

In this, a source node that wants to send a message to the destination for which it does not have a route, broadcasts a Route Request (RREQ) packet across the network. A node that receives a RREQ can send a Route Reply (RREP) packet if it is either the destination or has a route to the destination. The RREP is sent back to the source along the reverse path. Each node sets up a forward pointer to the node it received the RREP from. This sets up a forward path from the source to the destination. Nodes receiving the RREQ packet set up backward pointers to the source node in the route tables. The sequence number is used to maintain the freshness information about the route.

Route Maintenance

In case of link failure, the node generates a Route Error (RERR) packet that is sent to all sources using the broken link. The RERR packet renders all routes using that link as invalid. The source then initiates a new route discovery process.

The time complexity of AODV is O(2D) where D is the network diameter and the communication complexity is O(2N) where N is the number of nodes in the network [Royer, 1999].

Black Hole Attack

Black hole attack is an active insider attack. It is also known as the sequence number attack. In this, the malicious node advertises falsely as having the shortest and freshest path to the node whose packet it wants to intercept. This is done by fabricating the sequence number of the "route reply" packet. The node may route their packets to the destination via the malicious node because it seems to be the most efficient route. The adversary then consumes the intercepted packets without any forwarding (Hu, 2004).

Based on original AODV protocol, any intermediate node may respond to the RREQ message

Figure 1. The Black hole problem

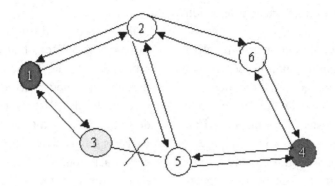

if it has fresh enough route, which is checked by the destination sequence number contained in the RREQ packet. In figure 1, node 1 is source node and node 4 is the destination node. The source node broadcasts RREQ packet to find a route to destination node. Assume that node 3 acts as black hole. When node 1 broadcasts a RREQ packet, it is received by both node 2 and node 3. Node 3, being a malicious node, does not check with its routing table for a path for the requested destination node. Hence it immediately sends a RREP packet to the source node. Since the RREP from node 3 reaches to source node before any other intermediate node, source node sends the data packet for the destination node through node 3 assuming that the shortest path to the destination exists through node 3. Being a blackhole node, node 3 does not forward the packet further and drops it. Since the source node is not aware of the malicious intentions, therefore it continues to send packet to the node 3. In this way the data, which has to reach the destination, fails to reach there. There is no way to find out such kind of attack. These nodes can be in large number in a single MANET, which makes the situation more critical.

Watchdog Mechanism

In the proposed solution, each node maintains two tables, the pending packet table and the noderating table. In pending packet table, each node keeps track of the sent packets. It contains a unique packet ID, the address of the next hop to which the packet was forwarded, address of the destination node, and an expiry time after which a still existing packet in the buffer is considered not forwarded by the next hop.

In noderating table, each node keeps rating of nodes, which lies within its communication range. This table contains the node address, a counter of dropped packets observed at this node and a counter of successfully forwarded packets by this node. Each node listens to packets that are within its communication range. If it overhears the transmission of a data packet with the same source address, then it removes this data packet from pending packet table and increments the packet forwarding value in the noderating table. An expired packet in the pending packet table causes the dropped packet counter to increment for the next hop associated with the pending packet table entry.

The fourth field of the noderating table calculates the ratio of data packets forwarding failure to the successfully forwarded packets. However, this ratio is not directly used to mark the node as misbehaving or legitimate as the method suffers from the limitation of partial dropping. In this method, the misbehaving node will not be detected as long as it keeps the ratio of the dropped packets to the forwarded packets below the threshold. This limitation of direct observation is overcome by incorporating indirect observation i.e. observation by the neighbors. In the modified method, if the ratio is greater than a given threshold value then the node is labeled as suspicious node. This direct observation is confirmed with the other neighbors' observation. To accomplish this, a request packet is forwarded to the suspicious node requesting to send its neighbor table. If the suspicious node sends the neighbor table, then a further request packet is sent to the neighbors of the suspicious node requesting for the marking of the suspicious node. If the neighbor table is not sent by the suspicious node then the node is marked as misbehaving and the misbehave value is set to '1'. Upon receiving the neighbor table, the total marking is considered. If the total number of marking as suspicious node is greater than the number of marking as non-suspicious or legitimate node, then the node is marked as misbehaving and the misbehave value is set to "1" otherwise it is considered as a legitimate node.

The decision to label the node is misbehaving or well behaving, depends on the selection of threshold value (threshold value have been chosen on the basis of experimental results). In this, we set the threshold value to 0.5. A lower threshold value increases the percentage of false positives. To avoid constructing routes, which traverse through the misbehaving nodes, nodes drop/ignore all RREP messages coming from nodes currently marked as misbehaving. Thus the misbehaving node is segregated and cannot participate actively in a network process. The pseudocode of the proposed algorithm is given in figure 2.

RESULTS

We use the NS2 simulator (Fall, 1997) to build a module for our AODV watchdog mechanism. The module inherits from the AODV module already

Figure 2. Pseudocode of the Proposed Algorithm

```
Data packet forwarded or sent.
Copy and keep the data packet in pending packet table until it is expired or forwarded
If (data packet forwarded) {
   Increment the corresponding forwarded packet in the noderating table and remove the data packet
   from pending packet table
}
If (data packet expires in the pending packet table) {
   Increment the corresponding dropped packet in the noderating table and remove the data packet
   from pending packet table
   If (total no. of dropped packets > threshold(th1)) then {
       If ((no. of dropped packet / no. of forwarded packet) > threshold(th2)) {
       Mark the node as suspicious node
       Request for the Neighbor Table from the suspicious node
          If (Neighbor Table sent) {
              Request the neighbors to send the marking i.e. ratio of dropped packets to forwarded
              packets of the suspicious node
          If ( no. of marking as suspicious node > no. of marking as non-suspicious node) {
              Node is misbehaving
              Discard RREP message coming from the misbehaving node
          else {
              Resend the packets}
          else {
              Node is misbehaving
              Discard RREP message coming from the misbehaving node}

       }
   }
}
```

integrated in NS2. It adds the two tables: the pending packet table and the noderating table. The experimental setup consists of 50 nodes moving in an area of 1000x1000 m² with speed varying between 0 to 5 m/s using the random waypoint mobility model. Each simulation is run for 200 seconds. The pause times of the nodes is varied between 0 to 160 seconds. The lower bound of the pause time signifies high mobility and the upper bound indicates low mobility. There are five CBR traffic generators with a rate of 4 packets/second each and a packet size of 512 bytes. Finally, we set the number of misbehaving nodes as 0, 3 and 5 nodes in the network.

Simulation Metrics

The metrics are the important determinants of network performance, which have been used to compare the performance of the proposed scheme in the network with the performance of the original protocol. This study has been done to show that the proposed scheme enhances the security of the routing protocol without causing substantial degradation in the network performance. The performance is gauged in terms of the following metrics:

* Throughput – It is the total number of packets received per unit time.
* Packet Delivery Ratio – It is the ratio of number of packets received by the CBR sink at the final destination to the number of packets originated by the CBR sources.

Performance Evaluation

This section consists of the results for the test cases. The recorded values are obtained by averaging over three runs for each test case. The performance evaluation of the proposed scheme involves two different aspects as given below

* Performance of the AODV protocol in the presence of compromised nodes and watchdog inactive.
* Performance of the AODV protocol in the presence of compromised nodes and watchdog active.

Figure 3. Throughput vs. Mobility for 3 misbehaving nodes

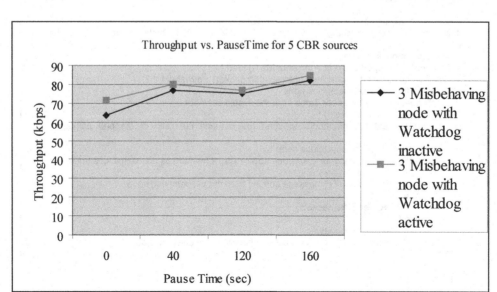

Figure 4. Throughput vs. Mobility for 5 misbehaving node

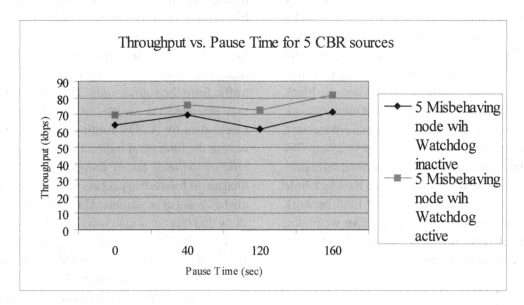

Figure 3 and figure 4 shows throughput at different pause times with 3 and 5 misbehaving nodes respectively. The number of CBR sources is 5. The experimental results shown in figure 3 indicates that for a lightly loaded network when the number of blackhole nodes is increased upto 6% of total network nodes, then in the presence of active watchdog, the throughput increases up to 3% to 8% for different pause times. The experimental results shown in figure 4 shows that when the blackhole nodes is increased up to 10% of total network nodes, then in the presence of active watchdog the throughput increases up to 10% to 18% for different pause times.

Figure 5. PDR vs. Mobility for 3 misbehaving nodes

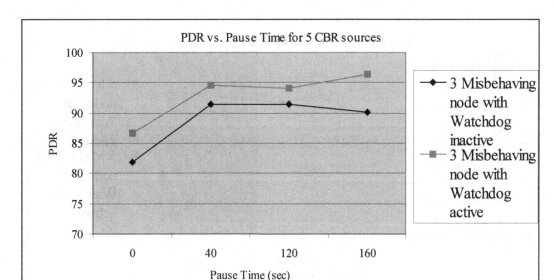

The experimental results for packet delivery ratio (PDR) at different pause times with 3 and 5 misbehaving nodes respectively, when the number of CBR sources is 5 is shown in figure 5 and figure 6 respectively. The experimental results shown in figure 5 indicates that when the black hole nodes is increased up to 6% of total network nodes, then in the presence of active watchdog packet delivery ratio increases up to 2% to 7% for different pause times. The experimental results shown in figure 6 shows that when the black hole nodes is increased up to 10% of total network nodes, then in the presence of active watchdog packet delivery ratio increases up to 6% to 17% for different pause times.

CONCLUSION AND FUTURE TRENDS

Mobile ad hoc networks is one of the most important and essential technologies that support future pervasive computing scenario. The characteristics of MANET make these networks vulnerable to many types of attacks. This chapter presented a mechanism to mitigate blackhole attack in mobile ad hoc network. In this attack, a malicious node impersonates a destination node by sending forged RREP to the source node that initiates route discovery and consequently deprives data traffic form the source node. The proposed solution extended the watchdog and the pathrater mechanism for AODV routing protocol. In this, we use the direct and indirect observation of the ratio of the total no. of dropped packets to the total no. of forwarded packets to mark the node as misbehaving or legitimate. The simulation results show that this technique increases throughput by 10% to 18% and packet delivery ratio by 6% to 17% in the presence of 10% misbehaving nodes in a network with moderate mobility.

There are great research challenges in the area of security of pervasive computing. Without security pervasive computing will be more a hype than a reality. Security should be treated as an integral element of PCS. Keeping this in view, there is a need to study various types of other attacks like wormhole attacks, DoS attacks, sinkhole attack etc in pervasive networking.

Figure 6. PDR vs. Mobility for 5 misbehaving nodes

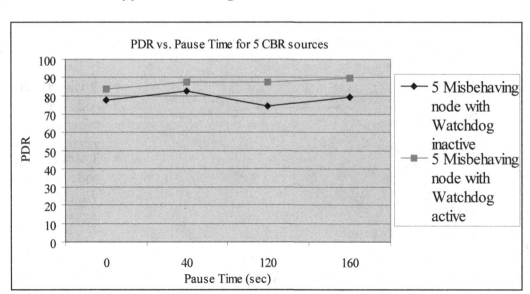

REFERENCES

Argyroudis, P. G., & O'Mahony, D. (2005). Secure Routing for Mobile Ad Hoc Nteworks. *IEEE Communications Survey and Tutorials, 2*(3), 2–21. doi:10.1109/COMST.2005.1610547

Buchegger, S., & Boudec, J. L. (2002). Nodes Bearing Grudges: Towards Routing Security, Fairness and Robustness in Mobile Ad Hoc Networks. In *Proceedings of Tenth Euromicro Workshop on Parallel, Distributed and Network based Processing* (pp. 403-410), Canary Islands, Spain. Washington, DC: IEEE Computer Society.

Deng, H., Li, W., & Agarwal, D. P. (2002). Routing Security in Wireless ad hoc Networks. *IEEE Communications Magazine, 40*(10), 70–75. doi:10.1109/MCOM.2002.1039859

Fall, K., & Varadhan, K. (1997). *Ns Notes and Documentation*. Technical Report, UC Berkeley, LBL USC/ISI and Xerox PARC.

Hu, Y. C., & Perrig, A. (2004). A Survey of Secure Wireless Ad Hoc Routing. *IEEE Security and Privacy Magazine, 2*(3), 28–39. doi:10.1109/MSP.2004.1

Johnson, D. B., & Maltz, D. A. (1996). Dynamic Source Routing in Ad hoc Wireless Networks. In T. Imielinski & H. Korth (1st Ed.) Mobile Computing (pp. 153-181). Amsterdam: Kluwer Academic Publishers.

Marti, S., Giuli, T. J., Lai, K., & Baker, M. (2000). Mitigating Routing Misbehavior in Mobile Ad Hoc Networks. In *Proceedings of 6th ACM/IEEE International conf. on Mobile Computing and Networking* (pp. 255 – 265), Boston. New York: ACM Press.

Michiardi, P., & Molva, R. (2002). CORE: A collaborative reputation mechanism to enforce node cooperation in mobile ad hoc networks. In *Proceedings of Sixth IFIP conference on Security Communications and Multimedia*, (pp. 107-121), Portoroz, Slovenia. Amsterdam: Kluwer Publisher.

Perkins, C.E., Royer, E. & Das, S.R. (2003). *Ad hoc On Demand Distance vector (AODV)*. RFC 3561.

Royer, E. M., & Toh, C. K. (1999). A Review of Current Routing Protocols for Ad Hoc Mobile Wireless Networks. *IEEE Personal Communication, 6*(2), 46-55.

Weiser, M. (1991). The Computer for the 21st Century. Scientific American, (pp. 94-104). Reprinted in IEEE Pervasive Computing, March 2002, (pp. 19-25).

ADDITIONAL READING

Agarwal, P., Ghosh, R. K., & Das, S. K. (2008). Cooperative Black and Gray Hole Attacks in Mobile Ad Hoc Networks. *In Proceedings of 2nd Intl Conference on Ubiquitous Information Management and Communication* (pp 310-314), Suwan, Korea. ACM Press

Deng, H., Li, W., & Agarwal, D. P. (2002). Routing Security in Wireless Ad Hoc Networks. *IEEE Communications Magazine, 40*(10).

Dokurer, S., Ert, Y. M., & Acar, C. E. (2007). Performance Analysis of Ad Hoc Networks under Blackhole Attcaks. *In Proceedings of IEEE Conference* (pp 148-153).

Frodigh, M., & Johansson, P. & Larsson. (2000). Wireless Ad Hoc Networking: The Art of Networking Without a Network. *Ericsson Review, 4*, 248–263.

Hollick M., Schmitt J., Seipl C. & Steinmetz (2004). The ad hoc on demand distance vector protocol: an analytical model of the route acquisition process. *In Proceedings of Second Intl Conference on Wired/Wireless Internet Communication* (pp 201-204), Frankfurt, Germany.

Hollick M., Schmitt J., Seipl C. & Steinmetz (2004). On the effect of node misbehavior in ad hoc networks. *In Proceedings of IEEE Intl Conference on Communication* (pp 3759-3763), Paris, France.

Hongsong, C. Zhenzhou Ji & Mingzeng H. (2006). A Novel Security Agent for AODV Routing Protocol Based on Thread State Transition. In Asian Journal of Information Technology, Vol 5(1), pp 54-60.

Huang, Y. A., Fan, W., Lee, W., & Yu, P. (2003). Cross Feature Analysis for detecting ad hoc routing anomalies. *In Proceedings of 23ʳᵈ IEEE Intl Conference on Distributed Computing Systems.*

Huang, Y. A., & Lee, W. (2004). Attack analysis and detection for ad hoc routing protocols. *In Proceedings of Seventh Intl Symposium on Recent Advances in Intrusion Detection* (pp 125-145).

Jeong, J., Lee, G., & Hass, Z. J. (2008). Prevention of Blackhole Attack Using One Way Hash Chain Scheme in Ad Hoc Networks. *LNCS, 5200,* 564–573.

Kurosawa, S., Nakayama, H., & Kato, N. (2007). Detecting Blackhole Attack on AODV based Mobile Ad Hoc Networks by Dynamic Learning Methods. *Intl Journal of Network Security*, 5(3), 338–346.

Ramaswamy S., Fu H., Sreekantaradhya M., Dixon J. & Nygard Kendall (2003). Prevention of Cooperative Blackhole Attack in Wireless Ad Hoc Networks. *In Proceedings of Intl Conference on Wireless Networks* (pp 570-575), Las Vegas, Nevada, USA.

Ray, I., & Chakraborty, S. (2009). An Interoperable Context Sensitive Model of Trust. *Journal of Intelligent Information Systems*, *32*(1), 75–104. doi:10.1007/s10844-007-0049-9

Saha D., Mukherjee A. & Bandopadhyay (2002). Networking Infrastructure for Pervasive Computing: Enabling Technologies and Systems. *Kluwer Academic Publisher.*

Satyanarayanan, M. (2001). Pervasive Computing: Vision and Challenges. *In IEEE Personal Communication,* pp 10-17.

Stamouli, I. (2003). Real Time Intrusion Detection for Ad Hoc Networks. Masters Thesis, University of Dublin.

Stamouli, I., Argyroudis, P. G., & Tewari, H. (2005). Real Time Intrusion detection for ad hoc networks. *In Proceedings of Sixth IEEE Intl Conference on a World of Wireless Mobile and Multimedia Networks* (pp 374-380).

Stanford, V. (2002). Using Pervasive Computing to Deliver Elder Care. *IEEE Pervasive Computing / IEEE Computer Society [and] IEEE Communications Society*, 10–13. doi:10.1109/MPRV.2002.993139

Sun, B., & Guan, J. Chen & Pooch U.W. (2003). Detecting Black Hole Attack in Mobile Ad Hoc Networks. *In Proceedings of 5ᵗʰ European Personal Mobile Conference* (pp 490-495).

Tamilselvan L. & Sankarnarayanan (2008). Prevention of Blackhole Attack in MANET. *In Journal of Networks*, Vol 3(5), pp 13-20.

TERMS AND DEFINITIONS

Pervasive Computing: Pervasive computing is a proactive form of computing which aims to achieve the goal of computing anytime anywhere.

Promiscuous Listening: Listening to the packets sent by adjacent nodes within the wireless range.

Network Diameter: It is the maximum shortest distance between any two pair of nodes in the network.

Intrusion Detection System (IDS): Hardware or software designed to detect unwanted attempts at accessing and/or manipulating the systems in the network.

Blackhole Attack: In a black hole attack, a malicious node spuriously announces a short route to the destination node to attract additional traffic through itself and then drops them.

Watchdog: Mechanism to detect misbehavior of the nodes by overhearing transmission.

Pathrater: Rates the path based on the observation of the watchdog and also avoids routing the packets through the misbehaving nodes.

A Priori Trust: A pre-existing relationship built outside the context of the network.

Section 3
Applications of Pervasive Computing

Chapter 9
The Causes of Developing a Wireless City:
Singapore vs. Taipei (Taiwan)

Mei-Chih Hu
National Tsing Hua Univeristy, Taiwan

Chien-Hung Liu
Feng Chia University, Taiwan

Ching-Yan Wu
Macquarie University, Australia

ABSTRACT

This study examines the causes of developing a wireless city, with Singapore and Taipei taken as examples. The examination is extended to include consideration of how the factors influencing consumer usage behavior have variable impacts on the development of wireless cities with diverse resource bases. The empirical results show that the internal and external influencing factors are related to each other and to the innovation adoption intentions during the development of a wireless city. From the cases of Singapore and Taipei, it is evident that the factors influencing innovation adoption intentions have varying impacts on the development of a wireless city given the diverse resource bases available.

INTRODUCTION

Along with the mature development of fixed-line Internet services, wireless broadband Internet access was rapidly developed and has flourished in the market, especially as a consequence of all the newly produced laptop computers since 2000 being equipped with wireless networking devices. Other mobile electronic products, such as palm digital assistants (PDAs) and cellular phones, have boosted the demand for and the resulting growth of the wireless Internet service industry. The critical contribution of becoming a wireless city to economic development is thus readily apparent. By 2006, cities that have launched or announced wireless city plans include Singapore, Taipei in Taiwan, Philadelphia in Pennsylvania, San Francisco in California, Osseo in Minnesota, Boston in Massachusetts, Perth in Western Australia, and London in the United Kingdom. Nevertheless, the government involvement of Singapore and Taipei does not represent

DOI: 10.4018/978-1-61520-741-1.ch009

the same kind of private-sector buy-in evinced by the work of Google and Earthlink on wireless projects in U.S. cities like Philadelphia and San Francisco.

Amongst these cities, Taipei was the first in the world to construct the facilities that constitute a large-scale wireless city. Singapore plans to complete its nationwide wireless Internet installation by 2008. In 2004, the Taipei city government outsourced the wireless city project to Q-Ware Communications with the intention of providing wireless Internet hot spots throughout the city. Targeting public use of the system, the city government mainly utilized the low-cost Wi-Fi technology and opened up access to all sky bridges, traffic lights, bus stops, subway stations, other public infrastructure, and commercial centers to the equipping of these wireless hot spots. Their aim was to offer residents and tourists a ubiquitous wireless Internet environment and they coined the term 'WIFLY' to refer to it.

Singapore built its wireless broadband Internet system two years after that of Taipei in 2006. However, the Singapore government has incorporated various additional wireless technologies into the building of its wireless city and these have helped in the rapid deployment of its planned facilities. They adopted dual parallel technologies for public access and for government and business sector access, respectively. For public access by its citizens and tourists, Singapore used Wi-Fi technology, while WiMAX technology was utilized in both the government and business sectors. In this way, both WiFi and WiMax wireless technologies are utilized in a manner that best exploits their respective advantages of lower cost and higher security protection. The construction of Singapore's wireless hot spots was spearheaded in 2006 by three companies, namely Singtel, iCell, and QMax. The network attracted 60,000 users within one year, while this number had increased more than seven times to 425,000 (approximately 10% of the total population of Singapore) by the end of 2007 (IDA, 2007).

Taipei's 'WIFLY' plan was opened to the public for a free trial period from October 2004 to December 2005. According to data released by Q-Ware, a total of 50,000 users were registered as soon as the free trial opened. However, after one and a half years of free public access, the number of users had only increased to just more than double this at 110,000 by the end of 2007 (Taipei City Council, 2007). This registered number represents only 4% of the Taipei city population. From a marketing perspective, the number of new technology users needs to break through the 'critical mass' of the adoption rate so that the new technology has a better chance of entering the growth stage of the product life cycle (Moore, 1991; Rogers, 1962). In particular, the rate of diffusion during the introduction stage is the key to pushing the new technology into the growth stage (Olson, 1995; Betz, 1993; Foxall and Bhate, 1993). Such new technology diffusion is to be considered as a critical element in the development of an emerging wireless city. Given the equivalent size of their populations and of the geographic areas they cover, Taipei and Singapore are utilized as key examples of wireless cities to be investigated and compared in the present study of the determinants of innovation adoption intentions.

The infrastructure of a wireless city not only depends upon the hardware supplying hot spots, but also relies extensively upon various software service applications. Through wireless broadband provision, economic efficiency and competitiveness are expected to be greatly enhanced. This study utilizes the Technology Acceptance Model (TAM), along with the three external variables of service quality and content, government policy and business strategy, and price of usage to examine the direct and indirect determinants of innovation adoption intentions in the emerging wireless cities of Singapore and Taipei. The wireless city concept aims to provide a new experience and better products and services to the people and businesses in each city as a whole. This can be seen as a new technology product for all its customers. Consequently, the pertinent research questions for us to pose here are the following: (1) what are the causes of developing a wireless city?; (2) to what extent can consumer usage behavior be expected to be different in Singapore and Taipei as wireless cities?; and (3) how do government initiatives affect the extent of developing a wireless city?

The study is organized as follows. Section 2 introduces the guidelines for wireless city establishment in Singapore and Taipei, builds a baseline research framework, and posits hypotheses derived from the extant literature regarding the factors influencing new technology acceptance and the related customer behavior. Section 3 presents the method to be applied and data available for use in this study. Empirical results are analyzed in Section 4, followed by the drawing of conclusions in Section 5.

RESEARCH BACKGROUND

The 'WIFLY' City: Taipei

The Taipei wireless city plan was the first of its kind in the world. From its inception in January 2004, it has adopted the BOT (Build-Operate-Transfer) model. The plan was implemented by a process of public bidding for the contract. This was won by Q-Ware Communications, a company operating under the auspices of one of Taiwan's syndicates, the Uni-President Corporation. The company invested TWD30 billion (approximately USD1 billion) to deploy the infrastructure required for the wireless broadband Internet service. It was this early movement on the project that enabled Taipei to be the first city worldwide to enjoy a large-scale wireless city network.

Taipei has two primary wireless service providers. One is Q-Ware (a new and small private sector company) and the other is Chunghwa Telecom (a large state-run company). These two companies provide different extended programs for different customers. Whereas Chunghwa Telecom provides two subscription programs: (1) a per-minute basis service, and (2) a fixed monthly subscription combination, Q-Ware's BOT plan offers fixed and pre-paid combinations to its subscribers.[1]

Even though the Taipei wireless city was initiated at the beginning of 2004, a series of promotions, such as 3G (mainly linked to mobile phone services) and M-Taiwan (mainly WiMAX, but also promoted by the Ministry of Economic Affairs, MOEA), were not launched until 2007. These were to operate in conjunction with other telecommunication applications as integral to the development of the wireless city. At that time, the National Communications Commission (NCC) finally announced the opening up of 2.5 to 2.69 GHz (for WiMAX) spectrum licenses. This announcement was two years later than in some other Asian countries, such as South Korea and Singapore. They opened up and launched their spectrum license in 2005 and immediately turned them towards commercialization in 2006.

Wireless in Singapore

This Wireless@SG plan was launched by the Singapore Prime Minister, Lee Hsien Loong, in October 2006. Singapore's Infocomm Development Authority (IDA) has commissioned three service providers, namely iCell (specializing in Wi-Fi technology), QMax (specializing in WiMax technology), and SingTel (a large, state-run telecom-company), to operate Wireless@SG. The intention of Wireless@SG is to provide Singapore with widespread broadband wireless Internet access. The goal of the first stage is mainly focused on coverage for public areas and the plan is to expand the existing hot spots from 900 to 5,000 by September 2007 (IDA, 2007). With such a goal set to be achieved within only nine months, a quick and simple online registration process was designed to ensure rapid adoption of the service by both Singapore citizens and tourists. In conjunction with the Intelligent Nation (iN2015) plan, the ultimate goal of these extensions of Singapore's information communication infrastructure is to provide the whole city-state with a universal connection service.

In developing these wireless communication blueprints, the Singapore government has been collaborating with the infocomm industry to integrate its wireless broadband services with the available wireless communication technologies. Compared to Taipei, Singapore has focused more on applying both Wi-Fi and WiMax technologies in deploying its wireless city facilities, with the lower cost Wi-Fi technology mainly open to public access, while the wider coverage of WiMAX is mainly designed for government services and business operations.

The wireless city concept thus can be seen as a new technology and innovation product, which contains a series of processes of diffusion and adoption. Even though diffusion perspective (focus on acceptance and adoption decisions) is used to considered as opposite and competing with domestication perspective (focus on the use and appropriation), both considerations have been proved complementary (e.g. Pierson, Jacobs, and Dreessen, 2008; Pierson, 2005). As emerging technology applications and derived business models and services are critical key factors for developing a successful wireless city, we look at the enrichment from an explorative diffusion and adoption tradition as applied in the diffusion and Technology Acceptance Model, as follows.

Diffusion of Innovations

The diffusion of innovations theory was first proposed by Rogers (1962). Its argument is that a successful innovation or new technology could have its pattern of diffusion through a society represented as a mathematically-based 'S curve'.

The rate of diffusion is affected by the role of network externalities in a society where one individual's action affects the intentions of another individual in ways that may accelerate or deceler-

ate the rate of adoption (Jang, et al., 2005). These arguments have been confirmed in the cases of many practical new technology applications and have been extended to explain how and why technology companies and industries have succeeded in OECD countries (Bijwaard, et al., 2008; Moore, 2005; Dalglish and Newton, 2002) and in developing countries such as Taiwan and India (Lin, 2006; Kaushik and Singh, 2004). Consequently, diffusion of innovations theory has become one of the most important theories in cross-area research concerned with the rapidly evolving phenomena of technological innovation.

Technology Acceptance Model (TAM)

The TAM posits that perceived usefulness and perceived ease of use act as mediating factors in determining an individual's intentions with respect to using any newly introduced technological system or device (Davis, 1986; 1989). Subsequent attempts to extend the TAM concept have generally taken one of three approaches: introducing external factors from related models, introducing additional or alternative internal belief factors, and examining antecedents and moderators of perceived usefulness and perceived ease of use (see, for example, Wixom and Todd, 2005 and Venkatesh, et. al., 2003). Both external factors and antecedents and moderators could influence a user's internalization of the perceived usefulness and perceived ease of use factors (Gefen et. al., 2003; Szajna, 1996; Igbaria et. al., 1995).

Compared to diffusion theory, the TAM places more emphasis on subjective and psychological predispositions and social influences on behavioral intentions to adopt an innovation. In this respect, the TAM is similar to institutional theory in which public policy plays an important role in governance through networks and also in helping to construct the symbols and meanings by which such networks are perceived by those involved (Frederickson, 1999; March and Olsen, 1984). By utilizing the TAM, the present study intends to investigate how external institutional factors have an impact on the internalized beliefs that subsequently influence innovation adoption intentions within the wireless cities of Taipei and Singapore.

Consumer Usage Behavior

Even though the causes and effects of consumer behavior vary when examined from the different points of view in psychology, sociology, anthropology, and economics, one common perception is that such behavior is a dynamic process that encompasses purchasing by means of strategic activities. Consequently, the focus of this paper is on a dynamic and stepwise strategic process within which there are three external variables influencing the two internalized innovation and technology acceptance beliefs of perceived usefulness and perceived ease of use in the emerging wireless city cases cited above. These variables are (1) service quality and extended applications (Lee, 2007; Chaudhuri, et al., 2005; Reeves and Bednar, 1994), (2) price of usage (Flamm and Chaudhuri, 2007; Rao and Monroe, 1989), and (3) government policy and business strategy. Inclusion of the third variable reflects the essential role of government-led strategic industry development in Asian catch-up latecomer countries, whereas the technology and innovation is mostly 'new-to-the-country' (Amsden, 2007; Hu and Mathews, 2005). These three variables are discussed in turn below

Service Quality and Extended Applications

The quality of goods and services and customer satisfaction are prominent among the factors cited as relevant in the extant customer behavior research literature (see, for example, Sousa and Voss, 2006; Ahire and Dreyfus, 2000; Hardie, 1998; and Reeves and Bednar, 1994). Some studies have confirmed the assumption that improving

quality and customer satisfaction leads to better business performance ((Ittner and Larcker, 1998; Fornell, 1992), while other studies have exposed evidence that quality and customer satisfaction improvement may become a negative influence in this context (Grandzol and Gershon, 1997; Kordupleski, et al., 1993). These debates are indicative of the importance of further investigating the impact of service quality and extended applications on the emerging service-oriented wireless and communications industry (Lee, 2007).

According to one survey, 60% of Taiwanese citizens frequently use mobile phones to go online to use Internet service applications and undertake information searches (Marketing Intelligence Center, 2006). These observations provide evidence that the public has high expectations regarding service quality and extended applications with respect to wireless communication facilities.

Price of Usage

The role of price in the market has been identified in two ways. One is that it acts to determine resource allocation in order to maximize the benefits accruing to and the welfare of consumers, and the other is that it acts as an information provider that serves to deliver maximum efficiency in production (Dolan and Simon, 1996; Olshavsky et al., 1995). Pricing is thus the most complicated strategy among the 4Ps of marketing cited as product, promotion, place, and price. Even though other factors, such as market demand, government policy and regulations, and the goal of the company, are critical in the real business world, pricing is nonetheless an important influencing factor in the process of decision making that determines consumer usage behavior.

From a firm's perspective, price is one of the tools used when engaged in market competition, as well being the source of income and profit. To a customer, price represents the claimed value of a product and influences his/her willingness and capacity for its purchase and adoption (Flamm and

Chaudhuri, 2007; Monroe and Lee, 1999; Rao and Monroe, 1989). In the present particular context, when the marketing target of the wireless city is the broad mass of customers, the availability of various pricing programs enables different customer preferences and desires to be met so that the overall willingness and capacity for taking up the service on offer will be increased. As a consequence, the ensuing study focuses on price of usage as one of the key factors affecting the innovation adoption intentions that underpin the development of a wireless city.

Government Policy and Business Strategy

Cities such as San Francisco, Oseo, Boston, and Philadelphia in the US, Perth in Australia, London in the UK, Taipei in Taiwan, and Singapore either have already established or have under construction some system of wireless broadband Internet access. Taipei was the first to accomplished wireless city status, with Singapore aiming to complete its city-state wireless infrastructure by 2008. The funds required for these projects are raised from diverse sources, such as by establishing a mutual fund, through low-interest bank financing, or by issuing government bonds. Despite the fact that each government involved has different purposes in promoting the wireless city, one common aim is to employ wireless Internet access as a low cost enabler to provide support for public services and the education system, as well as to increase government services efficiency. Here, government policy, along with business promotion strategies, as these relate to licensing, regulation, related technology and industry development, and financial subsidization are crucial in influencing consumers' adoption intentions in developing an emerging wireless city (Wang, 2005; McGregor and Holman, 2004).

Main Focus of the Chapter

In order to explore the three research questions cited above, the present study utilizes the TAM model, along with the associated factors affecting consumer usage behavior, to design a survey questionnaire and to carry out a two-stage Structural Equation Model analysis. From a customer's perspective, the three elements of awareness, relative advantage, compatibility, and complexity, are counterparts of or equivalent to the perceived usefulness and ease of use factors. Capacities to observe and to try out the service then act as catalysts in the deployment of wireless city facilities (Bijwaard et al., 2008; Veryzer Jr., 1998; Holak and Lehmann, 1990). Accordingly, the research framework that defines the undertaking of this study is designed to investigate the direct and indirect causes of innovation adoption intentions as between and amongst the three external factors of consumer usage behavior cited above as service quality and its extended applications, price of usage, and government policy and business strategy, and the two internalized beliefs concerned with degree of perceived usefulness and ease of use. The specific focus is on their respective impacts on the innovation adoption intentions of customers in the wireless cities of Taipei and Singapore.

MAIN RESULTS

Table 1 reports mean scores and *t*-test results for each of the measured items from the respondent ratings. The influencing factors for developing a successful wireless city exert various impacts in Singapore and in Taipei. In Singapore, except for 'business marketing promotion' that was rated as less important, all other items were judged important in contributing to the innovation adoption intentions of customers in the wireless city. By comparison, 'service contents and applications' was the least influential factor in Taipei. Notably, 'public initiatives' in Singapore was rated most important, followed by 'proper infrastructure' and 'availability of free trials', all factors that were grouped within the 'government policy and business strategy' variable.

Maximum likelihood estimates were used for each parameter as shown in Table 2. This table presents the analytical results for the hypothesized research model and suggests that the determinants of innovation adoption intentions are largely related in the theoretically predicted manner. The χ^2 value, goodness of fit index (GFI), and comparative fit index (CFI) are 78.742, 0.912, and 0.952 in Singapore and 69.458, 0.908, and 0.973 in Taipei,

respectively. All indicate an acceptably relevant fit for the research model used.

The β coefficients of the estimated parameters in Table 2 demonstrate the effect of the paths hypothesized. It is apparent that only service quality and extended applications influence perceived usefulness, and service quality and extended applications influence perceived ease of use are not supported in the case of the Taipei wireless city, while all other hypotheses are significantly supported with various magnitudes for both cities. In the case of the Singapore data, the relationships between service quality and extended applications

Table 1. Mean scores and t-test results for measured items

Items	Mean		t scores
	Singapore (n=100)	Taipei (n=348)	Difference between Singapore and Taipei
Service quality and extended applications			
Connection stability	3.42	**2.98**	0.71*
Transmission speed and security	3.15	**2.65**	0.24*
Ease of operation	4.23	3.03	0.68
Location of receiving	3.93	3.38	0.32
Service contents and applications	3.54	2.84	0.61**
Price of usage			
Alternatives of pricing	3.37	3.57	-1.87*
Payment programs	3.55	**4.32**	-0.50
Value of services provided	4.07	3.49	-1.24
Government policy and business strategy			
Proper infrastructure	4.52	3.31	0.54*
Reliable implementation	4.32	3.13	1.08**
Availability of free trials	4.39	4.22	0.16
Public initiatives	**4.54**	3.12	2.45*
Business marketing promotion	**2.95**	3.14	-0.97
Perceived of usefulness			
Beneficial to easier lifestyle	3.24	4.02	-0.54**
Perceived ease of use			
Ease in using	4.36	4.12	1.04
Innovation adoption intentions			
Degree of intending usage	4.26	4.52	-0.36**
Willingness of continue to use	4.39	4.64	0.67**

**: $p<0.01$, *: $p<0.05$.

Table 2. Parameter estimates in SEM

Path description	β coefficient	
	Singapore	**Taipei**
Service quality and applications →Perceived usefulness	0.195*	-0.061
Service quality and applications→Perceived ease of use	0.183**	0.039
Price→Perceived usefulness	0.434**	0.248**
Price→Perceived ease of use	0.453**	0.258**
Government and business strategy→Perceived usefulness	0.333**	**0.555****
Government and business strategy→Perceived ease of use	0.379**	**0.610****
Perceived usefulness→Innovation adoption intention	**0.655****	0.146*
Perceived ease of use →Innovation adoption intention	0.025*	0.104*

**: $p<0.01$, *: $p<0.05$.

and perception of usefulness and ease of use, even though not as essential as other external factors, are significantly supported.

All five variables (service quality and applications, price of usage, government and business strategy, perceived usefulness, and perceived ease of use) have contributed significantly to reinforcing the innovation adoption intentions with respect to the wireless city facilities in Singapore. In this case, it is the impact of perceived usefulness that exerts itself as the most important driver (coefficient 0.655), with perceived ease of use listed as having the least impact (coefficient 0.025). By comparison, the impact of government and business strategy in Taipei includes the perception of ease of use (coefficient 0.610) as the most essential determinant, followed by perceived usefulness (coefficient 0.555). It is evident, then, that the development of the Taipei wireless city has overwhelmingly relied on the external influences diffused from government policy and business strategy, while in Singapore, greater reliance has been on the internal impact derived from perceived usefulness.

FUTURE TRENDS

The emerging business models of heterogeneous wireless networks are integrated with the Internet and cellular infrastructures to offer innovative services (data and voice) to individuals and businesses (Gunasekaran and Harmantzis, 2007; 2008). These new innovative services derived from wireless and mobile infrastructure are not only creating significant value networks in the developed countries but also acting as the PC base in the developing countries to help people with banking, education and business (Funk, 2009; Marshall, 2007). The various magnitudes of the impacts experienced in the cases of Singapore and Taipei as shown in Table 2 further suggest that the internal and external influencing factors are related to each other and to the innovation adoption intentions during the development of a wireless city. However, these relationships may differ from city to city due to different resources endowments.

Telecommunications technological applications and service models have become a critical driver of competitive advantages in a city and in a nation, the future research may like to provide comparison cases from both the developed cities and the catching-up developing cities, whereas the causes of developing a wireless city, from different resources endowments, may be able to further differentiated and evidenced. This study thus provides useful insights on the impacts of innovation diffusion and adoption for the emerging cities in the latecomer countries who are attempting to build as a wireless city as Singapore and Taipei. The policy makers should pay greater attention to understanding the significance of the variation of consumer behaviors and public initiatives along with its magnitude and the direction of technology diffusion in that city.

CONCLUSION

This study has given emphasis to examining the relationships between and among the causes of developing wireless cities of Singapore and Taipei. For the three research questions posed in this study, the results obtained suggest that the causes of developing a wireless city are largely consistent with those theoretically predicted. All three external/indirect factors, services quality and extended applications, price of usage, and government policy and business strategy, along with the two internal beliefs, perceived usefulness and perceived ease of use, have been found to make positive contributions to the development of the wireless city in Singapore. However, this full support for the model is not found in the case of Taipei. The service quality and extended applications factor does not show any importance in influencing the internalized beliefs cited. And, the descriptive statistics in Table 1 indicate that there are differences in the determinants of innovation adoption intentions as between the Singapore and Taipei wireless cities.

Even though the communication services and contents sector is strongly supported by Taiwan's government, it is found that only the smaller sized companies with 3 to 10 employees have survived in the market (Science and Technology Indicator, 2007). Thus, it is no surprise that the input factor service quality and extended applications item shows up as insignificant among the influences on technology adoption intentions in Taipei's wireless city. This weakness is also apparent in the stagnant growth of the number of wireless subscribers in Taipei. For while the registered number rapidly reached 50,000 soon after the launch in 2004, it has not increased significantly since then. Indeed, it took two years until 2007 to reach 110,000.

Telecommunications related technological applications and service models are among the inevitable drivers of economic development in a city and in a nation. From the cases of Singapore and Taipei, it is evident that the factors influencing innovation adoption intentions have varying impacts on the development of a wireless city given the diverse resource bases available. However, despite the various causes and effects associated with innovation adoption intentions, the customers in both Singapore and Taipei have sustained a high level of intentions regarding their continuing use of the wireless city services.

REFERENCES

Ahire, S. L., & Dreyfus, P. (2000). The impact of design management and process management on quality: an empirical investigation. *Journal of Operations Management*, *18*, 549–575. doi:10.1016/S0272-6963(00)00029-2

Amsden, A. H. (2007). *Escape from Empire: the Developing World's Journey Through Heaven and Hell*. Cambridge, MA: The MIT Press.

Betz, F. (1993). *Managing Technology Competing Through New Ventures, Innovation and Corporate Research*. Upper Saddle River, NJ: Prentice Hall.

Bijwaard, G. E., Janssen, M. C. W., & Maasland, E. (2008). Early mover advantages: an empirical analysis of European mobile phone markets. *Telecommunications Policy*, *32*(3-4), 246–261. doi:10.1016/j.telpol.2007.08.006

Chaudhuri, A., Flamm, K., & Horrigan, J. (2005). An analysis of the determinants of internet access. *Telecommunications Policy*, *29*, 731–755. doi:10.1016/j.telpol.2005.07.001

Dalglish, C., & Newton, C. (2002). Relationship between firm survival and innovation: an introduction to the literature. *Innovation: Management . Policy & Practice, 4*(2-3), 209–214.

Davis, F. D. (1986). *A technology acceptance model for empirically testing new end-user information systems: theory and results.* Doctoral dissertation, MIT Sloan School of Management, Cambridge, MA.

Davis, F. D. (1989). Perceived usefulness, perceived ease of use, and user acceptance of information technology. *Management Information Systems Quarterly, 13*, 319–339. doi:10.2307/249008

Dolan, R. J., & Simon, H. (1996). *Power Pricing: How Managing Price Transforms the Bottom Line.* New York: The Free Press.

Flamm, K., & Chaudhuri, A. (2007). An analysis of the determinants of broadband access. *Telecommunications Policy, 31*(6-7), 312–326. doi:10.1016/j.telpol.2007.05.006

Fornell, C. (1992). A national customer satisfaction barometer: the Swedish experience. *Journal of Marketing, 55*(1), 1–21.

Frederickson, H. G. (1999). The repositioning of American public administration. *Political Science and Politics, 32*(4), 701–711. doi:10.2307/420159

Funk, J. L. (2009). The emerging value network in the mobile phone industry: The case of Japan and its implications for the rest of the world. *Telecommunications Policy.* Available online.

Gefen, D., Karahanna, E., & Straub, D. W. (2003). Trust and TAM in online shopping: An integrated model. *Management Information Systems Quarterly, 27*(1), 51–90.

Gunasekaran, V., & Harmantzis, F. (2007). Emerging wireless technologies for developing countries. *Journal of Technology in Society, 29*(1).

Gunasekaran, V., & Harmantzis, F. (2008). Towards a Wi-Fi ecosystem: technology integration and emerging service models. *Telecommunications Policy, 32*, 163–181. doi:10.1016/j.telpol.2008.01.002

Holak, S. L., & Lehmann, D. R. (1990). Purchase intentions and the dimensions of innovation: an exploratory model. *Journal of Product Innovation Management, 7*, 59–73. doi:10.1016/0737-6782(90)90032-A

IDA (Infocomm Development Authority). (2007). *Singapore's vibrant telecoms market.* The China Telecom (Singapore) Inauguration Ceremony on 31 January 2007, Singapore. Retrieved September 2008, from http://www.ida.gov.sg/News%20and%20Events/20060814181223.aspx?getPagetype=21

Jang, S. L., Dai, S. C., & Sung, S. (2005). The pattern and externality effect of diffusion of mobile telecommunications: the case of the OECD and Taiwan. *Information Economics and Policy, 17*(2), 133–148. doi:10.1016/j.infoecopol.2004.05.001

Lee, S. (2007, October). *The determinants of the global broadband deployment: an empirical study.* Paper presented at the Pacific Telecommunications Councils 2008 Conference, Washington, DC. Retrieved from www.ptc.org/ptc08/participants/speakers/papers/SangwonLee_FullPaper.pdf

Lin, J. M. (2006). *Industrial spatial distribution phenomena of technological innovation diffusion — a case study of IC industry in Taiwan.* Unpublished master dissertation, National Chung Kung University, Taiwan. Retrieved November 12, 2008, from http://0-etdncku.lib.ncku.edu.tw.lib1.npue.edu.tw/ETD-db/ETD-search/view_etd?URN=etd-0725106-013137

March, J. G., & Olsen, J. P. (1984). The new institutionalism: organizational factors in political life. *The American Political Science Review, 78*(3), 734–749. doi:10.2307/1961840

Market Intelligence Center. (2006). *The Taiwanese WiMax industry. Statistics report*. Taipei, Taiwan: Institute for Information Industry.

Marshall, J. (2007). Smartphones are the PCs of developing world. *New Scientist, 195*(2615), 24–25. doi:10.1016/S0262-4079(07)61964-2

McGregor, M. A., & Holman, J. (2004). Communication technology at the Federal Communications Commission: E-government in the public interest? *Government Information Quarterly, 21*(3), 268–283. doi:10.1016/j.giq.2004.04.005

Monroe, K. B., & Lee, A. (1999). Remembering versus knowing: issues in buyers' processing of price information. *Journal of the Academy of Marketing Science, 27*(1), 207–225. doi:10.1177/0092070399272006

Moore, G. A. (2005). *Dealing with Darwin: How Great Companies Innovate at Every Phase of Their Evolution*. New York: Portfolio.

Moore, G. C., & Benbasat, I. (1991). Development of an instrument to measure the perception of adopting an information technology innovation. *Information Systems Research, 2*(3), 192–222. doi:10.1287/isre.2.3.192

Olshavsky, R. W., Aylesworth, A. B., & Kempf, D. S. (1995). The price-choice relationship: A contingent processing approach. *Journal of Business Research, 33*(3), 207–218. doi:10.1016/0148-2963(94)00070-U

Olson, E. M. (1995). Organizing for effective new product development: the moderating role of product innovativeness. *Journal of Marketing, 59*, 48–62. doi:10.2307/1252014

Pierson, J. (2005). Domesticaion at work in small businesses . In Berker, T., Hartmann, M., Punie, Y., & Ward, K. (Eds.), *Domestication of media and technology* (pp. 205–226). Berkshire, UK: Open University Press.

Pierson, J., Jacobs, A., Dreessen, K., & De Marez, L. (2008). Exploring & designing wireless city applications by way of archetype user research within a living lab. *Observatorio Journal, 5*, 99–118.

Rao, A. R., & Monroe, K. B. (1989). The effect of price, brand name, and store name on buyers' perceptions of product quality: an integrative review. *Journal of Marine Research, 26*, 351–357. doi:10.2307/3172907

Reeves, C. A., & Bednar, D. A. (1994). Defining quality: alternatives and implications. *Academy of Management Review, 19*(3), 435–440. doi:10.2307/258934

Rogers, E. M. (1962). *Diffusion of Innovation* (3rd ed.). New York: Free Press.

Taipei City Council. (2007). *Taipei City WIFLY plan*. Retrieved June 10, 2008, from http://www.tupc.taipei.gov.tw

Venkatesh, V., Morris, M. G., Davis, G. B., & Davis, F. D. (2003). User acceptance of information technology: Toward a unified view. *Management Information Systems Quarterly, 27*(3), 425–478.

Veryzer, R. W. Jr. (1998). Key factors affecting customer evaluation of discontinuous. *Journal of Product Innovation Management, 15*, 136–150. doi:10.1016/S0737-6782(97)00075-1

Wang, J. L. (2005). Two-stage channel assignment scheme in wireless networks. *International Journal of Communication Systems, 18*(6), 571–584. doi:10.1002/dac.718

Wixom, B. H., & Todd, P. A. (2005). A theoretical integration of user satisfaction and technology acceptance. *Information Systems Research, 16*(1), 85–102. doi:10.1287/isre.1050.0042

ADDITIONAL READING

Agarwal, R. A., & Prasad, J. (1999). Are individual differences germane to the acceptance of new information technologies? *Decision Sciences*, *30*(2), 361–391. doi:10.1111/j.1540-5915.1999.tb01614.x

Bar, F., & Park, N. (2006). Municipal Wi-Fi networks: the goals, practices, and policy implication of the US case. *Communications and Strategies*, *61*, 107–125.

Belch, G. E., & Belch, M. A. (2004). *Advertising and Promotion: An Integrated Marketing Communications Perspective* (6th ed.). New York, NY: McGraw-Hill.

Bouillet, E., Mitra, D., & Ramakrishnan, K. G. (2004). The structure and management of service level agreements in networks. *Journal on Selected Areas in Communications, IEEE*, *20*(4), 691–699. doi:10.1109/JSAC.2002.1003036

Bryne, B. M. (2001). Structural Equation Modeling with AMOS, EQS and LISREL: comparative approaches to testing for the factorial validity of a measuring instrument. *International Journal of Testing*, *1*(1), 55–86. doi:10.1207/S15327574IJT0101_4

Camponova, G., Heitmann, M., Slabeva, K. S., & Pingneur, Y. (2003, June). *Exploring the WISP industry: Swiss case study*. Paper presented at the 16th Bled electronic commerce e-transformation conference, Bled, Slovenia.

Centonza, A., Casagranda, P., Owens, T. J., Cosmas, J., & Song, Y. H. (2007). Management of Digital Video Broadcasting services in open delivery platforms. *International Journal of Mobile Communications*, *5*(2), 186–214. doi:10.1504/IJMC.2007.011818

Chun, S. Y., & Hahn, M. (2008). A diffusion model for products with indirect network externalities. *Journal of Forecasting*, *27*(4), 357–370. doi:10.1002/for.1058

Corderio, C., Gossain, H., Ashok, R., & Agarwal, D. (2003). The last mile: wireless technologies for broadband and home networks. In proceedings of 21th Brazilian symposium on computer networks, pp.19-23.

Davis, F. D., & Venkatesh, V. (1996). A critical assessment of potential measurement biases in the technology acceptance model: three experiments. *International Journal of Human-Computer Studies*, *45*, 19–45. doi:10.1006/ijhc.1996.0040

Gillett, S., Lehy, W., & Osorio, C. A. (2004). Local broadband initiatives. *Telecommunications Policy*, *28*(7/8), 537–558. doi:10.1016/j.telpol.2004.05.001

Huang, K. C. (2008). Can citywide municipal WIFI be a feasible solution for local broadband access in the US? An empirical evaluation of a techno-economic model. PhD Dissertation, University of Pittsburgh, USA. Retrieved January 28, 2009, from http://etd.library.pitt.edu/ETD/available/etd-07242008-151444/unrestricted/HuangKuangChiu07242008.pdf

Igbaia, M., Iivari, J., & Maragahh, H. (1995). Why do individual use computer technology? A Finnish case study. *Information & Management*, *29*, 227–238. doi:10.1016/0378-7206(95)00031-0

Katzand, M. L., & Shapiro, C. (1986). Technology adoption in the presence of network externalities. *The Journal of Political Economy*, *94*(4).

Lehr, W., Sirbu, M., & Gillett, S. (2006). Wireless is changing the policy calculus for municipal broadband. *Government Information Quarterly*, *23*, 435–453. doi:10.1016/j.giq.2006.08.001

Oliver, S., & Poiraud, P. (2002). Public WLAN for mobile operators. White paper, Alcatel. Retrieved August 26, 2008, from http://www.bitpipe.com/data/detail?id=1074104553_856&type=RES&src=hdl_aa

Omar, A. (2007). Service model and resource allocation scheme for multimedia traffic in 3G wireless systems. *International Journal of Mobile Communications*, *5*(6), 677–691. doi:10.1504/IJMC.2007.014181

Pearson, I. (2006). The role of future ICT in city development. *Foresight*, *8*(3), 3–16. doi:10.1108/14636680610668036

Pierson, J., Jacobs, A., Dreessen, K., & De Marez, L. (2008). Exploring and designing wireless city applications by way of archetype user research within a living lab. Observatorio, 5, 99-118. Retrieived February 20, 2009, from http://obs.obercom.pt/index.php/obs/article/view/205/172

Skouby, K. E., & Tadayoni, R. (2006). Future networks and user requirements- A techno-economic analysis. *Wireless Personal Communications*, *38*, 89–101. doi:10.1007/s11277-006-9066-1

Tapia, A., Maitland, C., & Stone, M. (2006). Making IT work for municipalities: building municipal wireless networks. *Government Information Quarterly*, *23*, 359–380. doi:10.1016/j.giq.2006.08.004

Venkatesh, V., & Davis, F. D. (1996). A theoretical extension of the technology acceptance model: Four longitudinal studies. *Management Science*, *46*(2), 186–204. doi:10.1287/mnsc.46.2.186.11926

Wong, A., & Schal, A. (2002). An examination of the relationship between trust, commitment and relationship quality. *International Journal of Retail and Distribution Management*, *30*(1), 34–50. doi:10.1108/09590550210415248

KEY TERMS AND DEFINITIONS

Wireless City: It is city-wide wireless broadband networks. The service is a municipal high-speed wireless network, provided by the city as a public service to residents, businesses and visitors within the city.

WiFi: Wi-Fi is a trademark of the Wi-Fi Alliance, based on the IEEE 802.11 standards (also called Wireless LAN (WLAN) and Wi-Fi). A Wi-Fi enabled device such as a PC, game console, mobile phone, MP3 player or PDA can connect to the Internet when within range of a wireless network connected to the Internet.

WiMax: WiMAX, meaning *Worldwide Interoperability for Microwave Access*, is a telecommunications technology that provides wireless transmission of data using a variety of transmission modes. The technology is based on the IEEE 802.16 standard (also called Broadband Wireless Access).

Diffusion of Innovation: is a theory of how, why, and at what rate new ideas and technology spread through certain channels over time among the members of a social system.

Technology Acceptance Model (TAM): The Technology Acceptance Model (TAM) is an information systems theory that models how users come to accept and use a technology. The model suggests that when users are presented with a new technology, a number of factors influence their decision about how and when they will use it.

ENDNOTE

[1]   Q-Ware's subscription programs are multiform. For example, fixed subscription rates are separated into monthly and yearly periods and pre-paid subscribers are given more options with pre-paid cards, day cards, monthly cards, and rechargeable cards. Moreover, different programs are applied to different targeted subscribers, such as students, households, and enterprises (Chunghwa Telecom, www.pwlan.hinet.net/index).

Chapter 10

Knowledge Super Corridors in Developing Countries:
A Critical Perspective

Chun Kwong Han
Universiti Putra Malaysia, Malaysia

ABSTRACT

Developing countries in Asia are in the process of transitioning from a production economy to a knowledge-based economy (k-economy). Various new knowledge and information communications technology (ICT) mega-projects aimed at pervasive computing are being designed and executed at the international, national, state and industry levels to sustain competitiveness. The structures and processes by which these so-called "knowledge super corridors" are developed and implemented are complex economic-social-political decisions. An in-depth understanding is illustrated and assessed using two case studies concerned with formulating and implementing a k-economy blueprint and decision making to develop a knowledge portal in emerging k-economies in Southeast Asia. From analyses based on the structurational framework, practical implications are drawn for success strategies and implementation of pervasive computing.

INTRODUCTION: A NEW WORLD OF KNOWLEDGE, INNOVATION AND DREAM ECONOMIES

An increasing number of countries around the world are embracing the concept and practice of the knowledge-based economy (hereafter refer to as the k-economy). Just before the beginning of the new millennium, the US, UK, Canada, Ireland, Finland,

France, Japan, South Korea, Australia, New Zealand and Singapore have already articulated national positions and strategies for their k-economies. Although each country defines its k-economy somewhat differently, all of these definitions revolved around the New Growth Theory of an economy based on the production, distribution and utilization of knowledge, which constitutes the primary engine of economic growth and wealth creation. More than 50% of the Gross Domestic Product in the major OECD economies is now based on the

DOI: 10.4018/978-1-61520-741-1.ch010

production and distribution of knowledge. In the US, more than 60% of workers are classified as knowledge workers, defined as symbolic analysts who manipulate symbols rather than machines, and they include architects, bank workers, fashion designers, pharmaceutical researchers, teachers and policy analysts.

Developing countries, not wanting to be left behind in these developments, are also formulating policies and strategies to transform their production economies (p-economies) based on the conventional inputs of land, labor and capital into the k-economies (Rosenberg 2002). The strategy documents produced in developing countries, however, are fairly similar to those of the developed economies, giving the impression that k-economy and innovation strategies are readily transferable across different countries (Makishima 2002; Masuyama and Vandenbrink 2003; Saperstein and Rouach 2002). An example is Malaysia's developmental strategy known as the Ninth Malaysia Plan 2006-2010 heavily underscored by the concept and practice of the k-economy. First articulated in the 2002 Knowledge-based Economy Master Plan, the country defines its own k-economy and the rationale for the transition as follows:

"….k-economy is one in which knowledge, creativity and innovation can play an ever-increasing and important role in generating and sustaining growth. This differs from the conventional production-based or p-economy where economic growth was driven largely by the accumulation of the traditional factors of production, namely, land, labor and capital. The most valuable asset in the k-economy is human capital or the pool of educated and skilled human resources, whose core competency is the ability to create, acquire and exploit knowledge. ….Why is it imperative that our country makes the transition towards the k-economy? Our international competitiveness has been on the decline, as indicated in the slip in the *World Competitiveness Report*. Increasing foreign competition from countries such as China,

India and Vietnam means that the country has to re-position itself in niches with distinct competitive advantages. Globalization and liberalization make local and world markets indistinguishable, and this requires the country to differentiate its offerings in the marketplace. Furthermore, as costs escalate and profit margins shrink in traditional industries, we would have to seek higher value-added to its products and services, seek new sources of growth, and move into both pre- and post-production stages. The development of the k-economy will enable our country to enhance its international competitiveness and sustain socioeconomic development…."

In the last two years, Malaysia's 'k-economy' concept is expanded to capture and highlight the critical aspects of innovation which entails using existing building blocks of knowledge to create new value and customer intimacy, thus encapsulating the innovation and dream economies in which pervasive computing would be embedded. But, the reading of any government public domain document is an interpretive act that reveals to the reader as much as it conceals from him/her. The social-political-organizational dynamics that underpinned the decisions and processes embedded and reflected in strategy and action plan documents are not fully known to those outside the government policy making bodies. Authors such as Hearn and Rooney (2002) argued that "….to provide an appropriate starting point for policy makers, we must first set out a theory of knowledge or, more specifically, of knowledge systems…. and specify key behaviors of such systems….that provide insights about how policy should be formulated". They further asserted that instead of a diminishing role, governments have an important strategic role in designing the policy systems of the twenty-first century, by virtue of the relational nature of knowledge and k-economy. Bhatnagar (2004) used a multi-disciplinary approach covering economic, managerial, public administration and technical dimensions to provide practical guidelines for electronic government (e-government) based on best practices in sixteen developing countries.

While I concur with the need for prescriptive tools based on a post-industrial analytical framework for designing policy and monitoring implementation of knowledge and information communications technology (ICT) projects and pervasive computing, I would suggest that better prescription have to be derived from a rich and thick description of the contexts and processes of specific countries. Indeed, being critical is a prerequisite for the transformation of a developing country into a developed country. In this chapter, I develop an account of the k-economy policy formation, project design and implementation processes in Southeast Asia (hereafter referring the countries to "MyCountry" and "MyCountry2" as the pseudonyms) using an interpretive research approach, and illustrate how new concepts and theories are developed that in turn provide a basis for enhancing practice.

LIMITS TO KNOWLEDGE AND WAYS OF SEEING AND DOING

Although MyCountry has been embarking on k-economy mega-projects in the past decade, and MyCountry2 is beginning to get onto the k-economy, the contributions to the development of knowledge, innovation and dream economies have come largely from government policy makers, consultants and businesspersons. Their academic fraternity has not been at the forefront of these developments, although a number of researchers were doing research on various aspects of ICT developments in that country MyCountry, in particular the progress of the Knowledge Super Corridor and National Knowledge-ICT Agenda (both are pseudonyms for large-scale national initiatives, starting with e-business, borderless marketing, cyberlaws, e-government, single multi-purpose smart card and now pervasive computing in government, industry and society). Thought

leadership for MyCountry's knowledge, innovation and dream economies could only be attained if it was supported by empirical management research at the national, society, industry, organization and the individual, besides technological research and development. Analyses of the transition towards the k-economy, however, are not restricted to the West as evident from a collection of research articles in Masuyama and Vandenbrink (2003). These papers provide statistics, information, accounts and anecdotal evidence on the various dimensions of development of ICT sectors and strategic plans for the transition towards the k-economy in their respective countries. At least one of the papers has a theoretical structure to frame the analysis, namely, the Singapore paper which uses the Fujita, Krugman and Venables (1999) model for assessing influences of industry-specific inputs and transaction costs on agglomeration, and Porter (1998) model for assessing competitive advantages in cluster location. Bunnell (2006) and Ramasamy et al. (2004) made an evaluation of Malaysia's national ICT initiative. Unlike in the West, long ago, there has been an intense debate between researchers and practitioners. For example, Michael Porter (2001) and Don Tapscott (2001, 2002) discussed intensively on the meaning of strategy in the internet-based economy. Both sides provided empirical evidence on the types of organizations that are winners in the new economy. Porter argued for the traditional vertically integrated firm that uses the Internet as a complement to traditional ways of competing, while Tapscott believed that the Internet is a qualitatively new infrastructure for economy activity that enables the business web a network of partners that are more competitive because each focuses on its core competence and reducing transaction costs by using the Internet, and more recently mass collaboration in wikinomics (2006). Such conceptual and theoretical developments have a direct and significant impact on practice because managers subscribing to a theoretical position organize resources to achieve corporate objectives according to the theories they espouse and use.

In the area of information systems (IS), in the past two decades, the research literature had shown much interest in the process of managing compared to earlier emphasis on technical issues of system design and development. One stream of work draws on social theories and philosophies to analyze social, political, organizational and cultural issues in the innovation, design, development and implementation of ICT, as documented in Mingers and Willcocks' (2004)*Social Theory and Philosophy for Information Systems*. In this chapter, I am drawing on the increasingly influential stream of work in the area of structuration theory as the theoretical basis. Structuration theory is a general theory of the social sciences which aims to grasp the importance of the concept of action in the social sciences without failing to highlight the structural components of social institutions. The approach was primarily developed by the sociologist Anthony Giddens (1984), and has become highly influential throughout the social sciences. It seeks to reinstate the importance of the concepts of time and space in social and political analysis. Central to structuration is the notion of the duality of structure. All social action consists of practices, located in time-space, which are the skilful, knowledgeable accomplishments of human agents. However, this 'knowledgeability' is always 'bounded' by unacknowledged conditions and unintended consequences of action. The duality of structure therefore attempts to convey the idea that structure is both the medium and outcome of the practices which constitute social systems. Structuration theory is the latest in a long line of attempts to grapple with one of the central problems in social analysis, the agency-structure dilemma. Phipps (2001) reviewed and classified fifty-three empirical applications of structuration theory in the social sciences and geography between 1982 and 2000. But the five dimensions he used, namely representable type of social behavior, methodological bracketing, data, roles of time-space, and interpretation of duality of structure, captured only seven applications in the area of business and organizational studies.

Structuration theory, in its original formulation, pays little attention to technology (Jones 1997; Orlikowski 1992, 2000; Jones et al 2004). However, given the pervasiveness of technology in organizations' everyday operations, and especially the role of information technology in the process of enactment and reality construction in contemporary organizations, various attempts have been made to extend Giddens's ideas by including an explicit ICT dimension in social analysis. Based on use of structuration theory as the primary or secondary theoretical foundation, Pozzebon (2004) and Pozzebon and Pinsonneault (2005) made an assessment of the increasingly application of structuration theory on management and IS research and noted that structuration theory has often been appropriated as a broad framework or to complement and augment other approaches. In recent years, only several studies such as Brocklehurst (2001), Nicholson and Sahay (2001), Orlikowski (2000), Stillman (2006), Walsham (2002) used structuration theory as the sole theoretical foundation in empirical inquiries, especially in the IS field. Stones (2005) further strengthened the conceptual orientations to a "strong" structuration theory.

The use of structuration theory as the guidance and first-order sensitizing device in this research is subjected to the usual limitations of employing and thereby emotionally fixating on a particular way of thinking and a particular way of seeing and perceiving the world, as we generally tend to see what we want to see and the empirical material largely confirming the theory. In reporting on my research, I attempt to circumvent this somewhat by emphasizing on reflexivity and being creative rather than mechanistic interaction between the theoretical framework and empirical research. Reflexivity means interpreting one's own interpretations, looking at one's own perspectives from other perspectives, and turning a self-critical eye onto one's own authority as interpreter and author. Reflexivity is particularly significant because as researchers we are carrying our own implicit social-political-ideological assumptions, and far from being detached observers. Alvesson et al (2000, 2008) provides a useful starting point to operationalize a reflexive methodology in intensive research. The use of structuration theory, and possibly augmented by other theoretical perspectives such as complexity theory (Jacucci, Hanseth and Lyytinen 2006, Wallace, Fertig and Schneller 2007), actor network theory (Heeks and Stanforth 2007) and critical theory (Stahl 2008), combined with a careful application of reflexive methodology should increase significantly our ability to develop a more sophisticated understanding of the real world, which would provide a strong foundation to develop new theories of the human condition in different contexts.

In order to illustrate the application of the structuration theory, the reflexive methodology and being a critical researcher, and to assess its value in analyzing real problem situations and prescribing pragmatic solutions, I will draw on two case examples on k-economy experiences during the 2002-2008 period. In both MyCountry and MyCountry2, the methodological difficulty of breaking-in and getting access as a researcher has been tremendous, as government meetings and minutes were classified as confidential and secrets. But in all the two case studies, I was engaged in both as an academic researcher as well as practitioner role where I formally stated that I would employ various theoretical frameworks including complexity theory, actor network theory and critical theory for analyzing the issues and problems. The first case was a MyCountry's initiative to transition to the k-economy and I was the chairman of the committee responsible for preparing the blueprint over a period of nearly two years. The second case was about MyCountry2 in BIMP-EAGA (Brunei-Indonesia-Malaysia-Philippines East Asia Growth Area) where the government attempted to address unemployment through an integrated knowledge portal. I shall disguise the identities of individuals and organizations as much

as I can for reasons of confidentiality and I am stating upfront that my analyses are based on my own and other individuals' subjective interpretations of events and processes, which might not concur with the views and interpretations of the various key players who were the subjects of the case studies.

CASE STUDY 1: K-ECONOMY BLUEPRINT

Empirical Evidence

A state-level government in MyCountry decided to launch a pioneering k-economy blueprint to transform the state into a Knowledge Super Corridor in the Asian region. I shall call this state IntelligentState to reflect the stated intention of its government to make the state fully wired with electronic intelligence by the turn of the decade. Unlike many other strategy documents of the federal government of MyCountry, IntelligentState's K-Economy Blueprint (hereafter refer to ISKE Blueprint) was a public domain document. The justification statement for the new strategy was a message of urgency positioning IntelligentState at a "defining moment and critical turning point in its history and development efforts". The business case was the diminishing competitiveness of IntelligentState caused by new technologies, competition from lower wage countries in the region, liberalization pressures from WTO, APEC and AFTA, and globalization. These factors were said to erode the profitability of IntelligentState's traditional strength in manufacturing, and the turnaround strategy was the seamless transition to the k-economy. The targets to be achieved within a ten-year period covered all aspects of business, education, government, society and the individual. Examples of these targets read as follows: "The people of IntelligentState will practice life-long learning and are life-long employable. With an innovative education and training system, high quality knowledge workers who are adaptable, creative, flexible and responsive will be produced for the workforce" and "E-business will be the prevalent mode of conducting business transactions in all sectors of the economy". The respective roles of the government, the private sector and the community were defined, with the government playing an enabling role, the private sector in the vanguard driving the development, and community sector a full partner, as the stated approach was one of inclusiveness of all affected parties in planning and implementation. The strategic goals included producing a critical mass of quality knowledge workers, creating the learning economy and organizations, and promoting the widespread adoption of e-business.

The Governor of IntelligentState decided to re-activate the state-level ICT coordinating mechanism, which was the administrative arrangement recommended by the National ICT Board in the mid-1990s to all state governments for managing ICT projects. For some time now, the Governor of IntelligentState had recognized the importance of ICT at the state level, no doubt seeing the various mega-projects that have been undertaken on a grant scale in the Knowledge Super Corridor. Five strategic initiatives were formulated to achieve the vision, targets and goals. The Knowledge Work and Connectivity Flagships were the basic building blocks of IntelligentState's k-economy. Under these five flagships, a total of 30 programmes were outlined for implementation over three phases during the ten-year period. The ISKE Blueprint was a compelling strategy document even by international standards, available in book form, CD format and at the government website. It was launched in a ceremony attended by some 800 people, and made IntelligentState the first state government to articulate a strategy for the k-economy. Subsequently, other state governments declared similar strategic intents.

Structurational Analysis

Throughout the production of the ISKE Blueprint, broader structures were drawn upon to justify the rationale for the transition to the k-economy, allocation of resources and responsibilities, and ensuring alignment with national and state policies. The committee structure, both the Central ICT Committee and its working committees, was the common organizational mechanism used for ICT strategies and implementation monitoring purposes. Everywhere in MyCountry, the ICT community has been talking about the Knowledge Super Corridor projects and the k-economy. The ISKE Blueprint can be considered both a top-down and bottom-up document. It was noted earlier that during the 18 months period of its production, existing and new projects were championed by various stakeholders and these got grafted into the blueprint document. There was no grand design on the portfolio of ICT projects and neither would it be possible for the blueprint committee or central ICT committee to draw up the project portfolio. Formulation and implementation occurred concurrently, with sources of innovations and new projects coming from the national government, international agencies and multinational corporations. The chairman of the central ICT committee, being the head of state government, also means that both strategy and projects would have to be seen politically viable. Indeed, he was extremely realistic about what was feasible and realizable given the resources at his disposal. It would be politically disastrous to launch an overly ambitious project, found that its achievement fell short of expectations and thereby giving ammunitions to his political opponents. The ISKE Blueprint document, seen from these vantage points, can be considered a patchwork and a template for both change and continuity.

Reflexive monitoring of actions, in particular, actions and decisions undertaken by powerful players was endemic to the way the different aspects of strategy and execution were crafted. Final

Table 1. Structuration Analysis of K-Economy Blueprint

Analytic Devices	Key Aspects
Duality of Structure	Regional competitive pressures to the state's traditional manufacturing-led strategy necessitated a review of developmental options. The k-factor provided a new structure of signification The Central ICT Committee, chaired by the governor and have leaders of key agencies and institutions in its membership, became the strategy formulation and implementation coordination mechanisms The focus on k-economy and ICT resonated with national strategic directions, was politically correct, and formed the structure of legitimization
Knowledge and Information Communications Technologies	Knowledge and ICT became the new variables underlying the state socio-economic development, embodying a new system of meaning for enhancing significantly the competitive advantages of the state, encapsulating norm of aligning with the stated national strategic intent regarding the k-economy, and providing a new engine for wealth creation through reengineering and k-intensification
Contradiction and Conflict	The committee structure ensured that the views of multiple players were represented But it also meant that influential players from diverse positions and platforms could influence policy to their own organizational interests. Working groups produced reports that support the different perspectives and, in some cases, predetermined projects of their leaders
Dialectic of Control	State-level policy formulation for the k-economy was a top-down and bottom up, learning and re-learning process The committee structure facilitated drawing from the knowledge domains and perspectives of more than 100 persons. Knowledgeability and interests of influential players became a critical determinant of the design, diffusion and implementation of policy
Reproduction and Change	The production of the blueprint spanned more than 18 months from inception to launch. During that period, strategy formation and implementation occurred concurrently In addition to new projects initiated by the state and federal governments, MNCs and international agencies, existing projects in the state were re-conceptualized and re-framed to retrofit with the emerging strategic map The final blueprint document was a historical account of a stream of incremental decisions across time, and a template for change and continuity

decisions on project tended to be more a political decision rather than based predominantly on technical economic rationale. Industry players would want to connect directly to politicians. In the case of IntelligentState, the central ICT committee was chaired by the governor and getting the ears of the governor was the goal of many a businessman. This change came about, surprisingly, not from what was standard project management practice in the government machinery but from unexpected project presentations for approval during the central ICT committee meetings. Table 1 below captures the structurational analytics.

CASE STUDY 2: BIMP-EAGA KNOWLEDGE CENTRE

In this case, I developed an interpretive critical account of decision making processes on an e-government project in one of the countries in

BIMP-EAGA (hereafter refer to "MyCountry2" as the pseudonym). The data were collected from the players in various ministries and the ICT players directly involved in the decision making process over the period 2006-2008.

Empirical Evidence

MyCountry2 aimed to rapidly increase its economic and technological development in order to participate in globalization. Its capability and capacity in acquiring and utilizing new knowledge and technologies was to further develop the quality of its human capital in the country's economic thrust areas, identified in their vision statement as agriculture, manufacturing and tourism. A recent study indicated that MyCountry2 seemed to have one of the higher rates of unemployment in BIMP-EAGA. The provision of education and training to school leavers was pivotal in preparing them for gainful employment, alleviating the poverty situation in their family socio-economic structure and the rural areas, and reducing MyCountry2's dependency of a large number of migrant labour, including knowledge workers.

The Knowledge Centre of MyCountry2 was an integrated network to provide the latest information on education and employment, and accurately solve the unemployment problems. It consisted of a contact centre, an education centre, a job centre and a human capital research and development centre, depicted in Figure 1. The Knowledge Centre was located at the Ministry of Knowledge and Information Communications Technology (K+ICT Ministry). The contact centre was to act as the nexus for all employers, job seekers and education and training providers to interactively exchange and provide easy access to information and services. The job portal was the official job website to provide accurate online information on the labour market, the search engine that would enable job-seekers to access job listings by different search criteria. Employers could search for employees with the required skills from the portal. The education centre was an on-line educational portal to provide information on education and training courses and job opportunities to as many potential skilled workers in different settings. It played a complementary role in creating awareness and understanding on high potential work organizational skills and selected common qualities of a good worker. The human capital research and development centre aimed to conduct empirical analysis of education and training programmes at all levels of government and private providers in order to feed crucial information into the knowledge centre.

The *Major Players*: The main player was a private company, Dung.Com (disguised name) which has been doing construction jobs for the government and familiar with the bureaucratic procedures. The CEO had just completed a PhD in e-Business, and has conducted together with his PhD supervisor a consultancy study on human resource development in MyCountry2. Following the macro-analysis report, the CEO has proposed to the Minister of K+ICT Ministry the new project on Knowledge Centre, as well as other ICT projects. In recruiting the consultants to prepare the technical proposal, Dung.Com CEO has called for his PhD supervisor, a retired director of a government ICT department and an ICT professor of a local university. The idea was to convey to the government that the team comprised experienced senior officials with reputations.

BestCall was the contact centre consulting company engaged in the knowledge centre project. An international contact centre company overseas has earlier suggested to MyCountry2 government of the need for the government's contact centre, but charging at international rates. Major local contact centre developers were contacted by the retired government ICT director for request for proposals but not considered by the CEO. BestCall was chosen and this was the first job they were doing for the government in the whole of the country. The project members from BestCall developing the contact centre on site were not allowed to show their own business cards but declared that they were from Dung.Com. The numbers and figures in the proposal were Dung.Com proprietary decisions and the BestCall leader said that the costs were "above the seas !".

The proposals on job centre, education centre and human capital R & D centre were done by university lecturers in the same school as Dung.Com CEO's PhD supervisor. They were in the education fields but either retired or about to retire. Again, none of them knew about the numbers and figures in the proposals until the day when presented to the Government Steering Committee chaired by the permanent secretary of K+ICT Ministry.

The *Government Players*: The Steering Committee comprised representatives from the major government departments and agencies. When the proposals were heard, the several government officials requested that Dung.Com was to leave the meeting room so the committee could provide their assessments and views. However, the

Figure 1. Technological Context and Components of the Knowledge Centre

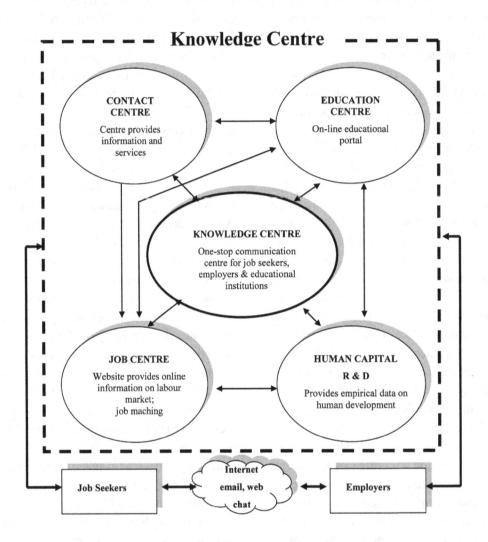

permanent secretary did not agree for a variety of reasons, including the K+ICT Ministry decision to quick-start the project and used up the funds allocated for the budget year, decision to use the negotiated party rather than an open tender, and the experienced professional team. Then, the government officials remained silent as questions were cynically commented by the permanent secretary. The most senior ICT director of MyCountry2 later said "Since the K+ICT Ministry already made the decision to employ Dung.Com in the first meeting, there was no need for me to attend further meetings. Instead I am dispatching my deputy director to attend future meetings of the Steering Committee". The deputy director of ICT in K+ICT Ministry said "Our IT unit did not agree for the project as similar government and private portals were already existing in the country, and the need for MyCountry2 to set up new websites were unnecessary. But since our bosses (K+ICT Minister and the permanent secretary) wanted the project, we have no choice but remain silent in their presence".

Structurational Analysis

An analytical description for MyCountry2 deci-sion making processes for the Knowledge Centre, is shown in Figure 2.

The human players were the K+ICT Ministry particularly the Minister and his permanent sec-retary, the ICT players notably Dung.Com, and the targeted unemployed of the public. They were operating in a developing country cultural context where the government senior officials made all the strategic decisions and lower level officials abided by those decisions. There were various political parties in the ruling coalition and hence the ministry was given a certain amount of budget for their respective roles in politics.

The non-human actors were the technological dimensions of the ICT project. In this case the cur-rent interest was on the contact centre, e-learning

and human capital development. These were new to the country, and hence captured interest. Indeed, Dung.Com claimed that MyCountry2 was the first to develop this unique knowledge centre which tapped on a range of new applications and technologies.

The key actor was the CEO of Dung.Com. He was closely linked to the K+ICT Minister, and indeed freely called the minister on the mobile phone. He and the Minister were in strategically alignment, in that by getting the funds for the project he could then provide financial support to political and personal activities of the Minister. The knowledge centre was approved by the Finance Ministry, although the project was not in the annual budget for that year. The budget was approved according to the pre-determined allocation for the K+ICT Ministry. Hence, Dung.Com set the figures for the different sub-proposals to suit the overall

Figure 2. Structurational Analytics

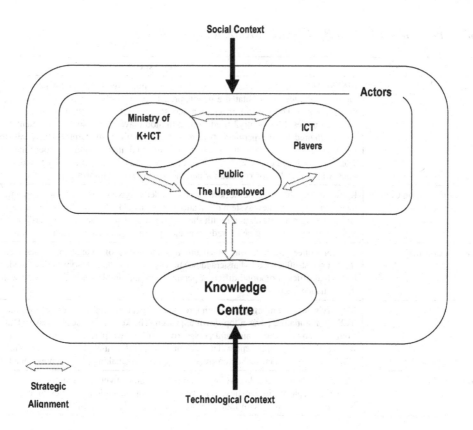

budget. All the other consultants were linked to the Dung.Com CEO's PhD supervisor, and paid an emolument by that professor. Hence, at the end of the job, the retired ICT government department was unsatisfied that he was paid the equivalent of his last monthly salary, similar to other lower level jobs, at the end of the six months.

The technological context, as depicted in Figure 2, were designed by the retired ICT government director (with a master degree in computer science) who "patched" together the different components so that a unified frame could be exhibited to the Steering Committee. The different components were initially proposed by the different consultants from their own areas of expertise, and were aiming at separate budget allocations. The social context is one where a private company was closely linked to the government officials and politicians in order to get the project. This was common knowledge to the public, and consequently government officials generally remain silent on decision making during boardroom meetings. The detailed structurational analytics are summarized in Table 2 below:-

FUTURE TRENDS

The two case studies highlighted a more sophisticated lens of seeing the difficulties of developing and implementing "knowledge super corridors" and ICT projects in developing countries. In both MyCountry and MyCountry2, the governments have had injected huge amounts of funding into the projects over the last few years. Yet, the beneficiaries seemed not to be the masses but skilful players directly connected to politicians. Hence, it has not been a corridor of knowledge, ICT and pervasive computing but more precisely a corridor of power, with the strategic alignment of the vested interests of the ICT actors and political players. The insider knowledge of who benefited from the projects and the modus operandi of the key actors

Table 2. Structuration Analysis of BIMP-EAGA Knowledge Centre

Analytic Devices	Key Aspects
Duality of Structure	BIMP-EAGA's regional growth and competitive pressures to MyCountry2's traditional agriculture-based strategy necessitated a new approach, particularly to address high unemployment and migrant labour. The k-factor provided a new structure of signification, as in most other Southeast Asian countries. MyCountry2 tried to be a me-too player. The usual governmental steering committee, chaired by the permanent secretary and involving government officials from key and related ministries, became the decision making and implementation coordination mechanism The focus on an integrated approach to k-economy and ICT resonated with national strategic directions, was politically correct, and formed the structure of legitimization
Knowledge and Information Communications Technologies	Knowledge and ICT became the new variables underlying MyCountry2 socio-economic development theme, embodying a new system of meaning for enhancing the competitive advantages of the state, encapsulating norm of aligning with the stated national strategic intent regarding the k-economy, and providing a new engine for reducing unemployment as well as wealth creation
Contradiction and Conflict	The committee structure was to ensure that the views of related ministries were represented But the interests of the K-ICT Minister and the Ministry's permanent secretary were the key to decision making. Individual officials reported different perspectives and, in all cases, their views were rejected by the permanent secretary
Dialectic of Control	Ministry's decision making, although having a long-established ICT unit responsible for MyCountry2's ICT initiatives, was a top-down approach. The key private sector player, Dung.Com, drew from the knowledge domains and perspectives of his own players rather than best of knowledge workers through an open tender. The self-interests of influential players in particularly the Ministry of K+ICT became a critical determinant of the decision making on the Knowledge Centre
Reproduction and Change	The production of the knowledge Centre was done over a 9-month period but it remains a "white elephant" in the next one year for implementation and yet to become operational No change except for use of funds for design and technical implementation

are well known among the government officials, businesspersons and whosoever involved in these projects, but the public remained silent. By using an approach such as structuration theory, a systematic critical analysis was done and brought to light to policy makers the underlying structures and processes of decision making. An enlightened understanding and knowledge for action were developed and indeed a new model was constructed that could directly impact future decision making on the development and implementation of ICT mega-projects. As Ghoshal (Birkinshaw & Piramal 2005) stated, bad theories are destroying good practices. In order to develop good theories that can capture the complexity of real world decisions, a more sophisticated theoretical framework is required to guide data collection and critique of taken-for-granted assumptions underpinning practices. In the context of developing countries, researchers doing critical research with the higher aim of providing knowledge for action and constructive change to decision making is necessary. A range of theories on the social, economic and organizational aspects of ICT are now available and could be a first step in developing good theories. Increasingly, complexity theory, structuration theory, actor network theory, critical theory and grounded theory are being used to provide different ways of seeing, and thereby to reconstruct new ways of doing and working compared to conventional approaches in developing countries. Generating good theories of ICT that could enable transformation would be a quantum of solace for MyCountry and MyCountry2.

CONCLUSION: PERVASIVE COMPUTING IN THE NEW WORLD OF COMPLEXITY

In MyCountry and MyCountry2, the ICT sector was widely perceived by the government and local industry as an engine of economic growth. Hence, its national development program was allocated

a huge proportion of funding for ICT-related programmes. Its key players were allocated substantive budgets for capital investments and research and development. Various assessments of the performance of the ICT sector, however, have been mixed. Previous assessments of selected aspects by international consulting corporations were not positive. Over the years, the press has reported specific cases of failures on ICT, resulting in a general public perception of the non-performance of government spending on ICT. Internationally, rankings conveyed different messages. The United Nations' Global E-Government Readiness Report 2007 ranked MyCountry and MyCountry2 as beyond the number 40th, in spite of the Knowledge Super Corridor in MyCountry. Yet A.T. Kearney Global Services Location Index of 2004, 2005, 2006 and 2007 rated MyCountry as one of the best for outsourcing in the world.

The performance of the ICT sector and decision making of the government would need to be assessed from a combination of economic, managerial, organizational, social and technological criteria. The conventional economist, technologist, management scientist and sociologist would project a limited rather than a sophisticated perspective. For example, rather than the conventional methods of economics, the rogue economist Levitt (2005) used an expanded approach to uncover the "hidden sides". Marglin (2008) dissected how thinking like an economist's ideology of knowledge would undermine the community and the need to celebrate on social connections, an essential dimension in pervasive computing. Indeed, "transformation" has been a recurring pervasive nametag to all MyCountry and MyCountry2 government initiatives, but transformation as significant change and making a difference to human life could only happen if activated from a combination of economic, managerial, organizational, social and technological dimensions. Good research, rather than "excellent research" of the Nobel Laureate category, is needed in the developing countries discussed in this chapter. In the complex problematical world, more sophisticated approaches are needed to assist in generating deeper and richer insights on structuring contexts and activities and thereby spurring the requisite action for transformation. The aim of this chapter was to demonstrate that an approach using structuration theory with an emphasis on being critical for social transformation could provide a greater degree of sophistication in the ways of seeing and hence enhance ways of doing. The analyses in the two cases were far from a desktop conventional scholarly exercise of ICT evaluation but grounded on in-the-trench experience as a practitioner and hard-soft evidence as a senior professor on the real world complexity of decision making in a developing country.

The study of developments of k-economies in Southeast Asian countries has been extremely limited. My analysis of structures and actions in the two cases suggested that "altered states" are better understood as outcomes of complex processes whereby reflexive actions of various stakeholders who shape and reshape actions and strategies and create and recreate institutions according to their perceived interests. Long ago, a description of Asian ICT initiatives in *Newsweek, December 2002 – February 2003* presented Asian projects as "....at best hollow replicas of the real Silicon Valley, mere real-estate developments.... high-technology-related sweatshops where cheap local labor does simple programming or call processing for foreigners. But there's no sign that any Asian country is rethinking...". Evidently, from the cases on the attempts to develop a knowledge super corridor in MyCountry, and developing and implementing a knowledge portal in MyCountry2, such a sweeping statement failed to consider the reflexive monitoring of contexts and situations and their implications done by skilful actors as they constantly rethink, reinvent and recreate their strategies and projects by mobilizing the access to resources and opportunities to their own best interests. Indeed, the players of MyCountry and MyCountry2 were "world-class competent great players" operating the duality of structure in everyday activities to achieve their strategic intents and personal higher aims.

Practitioners are characterized by their wealth of practical hand-on experiences. However, when asked to share the wisdom of their experiences, a general tendency is that they retreat to an "academic" mode so that their self-presentations appear intellectual and hence respectable. I reproduce below a piece of written prescription from a practicing technopreneur:

"So, MyCountry and MyCountry2 policy makers, take heed. Efforts of leapfrogging to a knowledge-based economy does not involve tinkering with only a few parts of the national development system, derived from a short-sighted emulation of American technological hubs and funding systems. It involves tinkering with all of the system, removing the unnecessary impediments to transformation. It involves creating the same strong basic foundation they have built upon, gradually, and remedying any indigenous weaknesses or shortcomings. It entails that Asian governments must be able to handle all these issues simultaneously. It is a painful process indeed especially for countries with insular, entrenched, sometimes institutionalized, negative cultures. Last but not least, policy making in the transitional stage must involve the proactive participation of all parties including the government, private and community sectors. Therefore, the players must consist of people who are collaborative in nature and unafraid to conduct frank, open dialogues, debates and analysis, to come to the right questions and subsequently, the right answers. Turf wars and personal agendas should be eliminated and observance of the Asian concept of face be reduced, lest we lose our heads in the process."

The above prescription was doubtlessly naïve but it has been based on presumptions of a world where diverse interpretive schemes, asymmetrical relations of power, divergent values, contradictions and conflicts in human relations were non-significant and non-correlations. The two cases on the interplay of structure and action by competent players generated empirical evidence to the contrary.

In everyday practice, a variety of implicit and explicit theories influences our thinking on particular topics and impacts our decisions. A greater measure of reflexivity on the part of the decision maker is required in order to generate more powerful mental models for enhancing practice. Structuration theory, combined with being critical or used in combination with complexity theory, actor network theory, critical theory, offers the potential for the design of practical frameworks for effective management of nations and organizations and the development of high-performing reflexive practitioners. In a world of complexity, highly effective decision makers, skilful strategists and creative innovators are those who develop a sophisticated knowledgeability of problem situations. This new breed of knowledge workers, not those with simplistic worldviews but knowledgeability of simplicity and sophistication shall inherit the new worlds of knowledge, innovation and dream economies.

REFERENCES

Alvesson, M., Hardy, C., & Harley, B. (2008). Reflecting on Reflexivity: Reflective Textual Practices in Organization and Management Theory. *Journal of Management Studies*, *45*(3), 480–501. doi:10.1111/j.1467-6486.2007.00765.x

Alvesson, M., & Skoldbergg, K. (2000). *Reflexive Methodology: New Vistas for Qualitative Research*. London: Sage Publication.

Bhatnagar, S. (2004). *E-governmnent: From Vision to Implementation*. New Delhi: Sage Publications India Pte Ltd.

Birkinshaw, J., & Piramal, G. (Eds.). (2005). *Sumantra Ghoshal on Management: A Force for Good*. Harlow, UK: FT Prentice Hall.

Bunnell, T. (2006). *Malaysia, Modernity and the Multimedia Super Corridor*. London: RoutledgeCurzon.

Giddens, A. (1984). *The Constitution of Society: Outline of the Theory of Structuration*. Cambridge, UK: Polity Press.

Hearn, G., & Rooney, D. (2002). The Future Role of Government in Knowledge-based Economies. *Foresight*, *4*(6), 23–33. doi:10.1108/14636680210453461

Heeks, R., & Stanforth, C. (2007). Understanding e-Government Project Trajectories from an Actor-Network Perspective. *European Journal of Information Systems*, *16*(2), 165–177. doi:10.1057/palgrave.ejis.3000676

Jacucci, E., Hanseth, O., & Lyytinen, K. (2006). Taking complexity seriously in IS research. *Information Technology & People*, *19*(1), 5–11. doi:10.1108/09593840610649943

Jones, M. (1997). Structuration theory. In W. J. Currie, & R. D. Galliers (Eds.), Re-thinking Management Information Systems, (pp. 103-135). Oxford, UK: Oxford.

Jones, M., Orlikowski, W., & Munir, K. (2004). Structuration Theory and Information Systems: A Critical Reappraisal . In Mingers, J., & Willcocks, L. (Eds.), *Social Theory and Philosophy for Information Systems* (pp. 297–328). Chichester, UK: John Wiley & Sons.

Levitt, D. S., & Dubner, J. S. (2005). *Freakonomics: A Rogue Economist Explores the Hidden Side of Everything*. New York: HarperCollins.

Makishima, M. (Ed.). (2002). *Human Resource Development in the Information Age: The Cases of Singapore and Malaysia. ASEDP 61, Institute of Developing Economies*. Chiba, Japan: Japan External Trade Organization.

Marglin, S. A. (2008). *The Dismal Science: How Thinking Like an Economist Undermines Community*. Cambridge, MA: Harvard University Press.

Masuyama, S., & Vandenbrink, D. (2003). (Eds.). Towards a Knowledge-based Economy: East Asia's Changing Industrial Geography. Singapore, Nomura Research Institute, Tokyo and Institute of Southeast Asian Studies.

Mingers, J., & Willcocks, L. (Eds.). (2004). *Social Theory and Philosophy for Information System*. Chichester, UK: John Wiley & Sons.

Nicholson, B., & Sahay, S. (2001). Some political and cultural issues in the globalization of software development: case experience from Britain and India. *Information and Organization*, (11): 25–43. doi:10.1016/S0959-8022(00)00008-4

Orlikowski, W., & Barley, S. R. (2001). Technology and institutions: what can research on information technology and research on organizations learn from each other? *Management Information Systems Quarterly*, 25(2), 245–265. doi:10.2307/3250927

Orlikowski, W. J. (1992). The Duality of Technology: Rethinking the Concept of Technology in Organizations. *Organization Science*, 3(3), 398–427. doi:10.1287/orsc.3.3.398

Orlikowski, W. J. (2000). Using Technology and Constituting Structures: a Practice Lens for Studying Technology in Organizations. *Organization Science*, 11(4), 404–428. doi:10.1287/orsc.11.4.404.14600

Phipps, A.G. (2001). Empirical Applications of Structuration Theory. *Geografiska Annaler, 83 B*(4).

Porter, M. E. (2001). Strategy and the Internet. *Harvard Business Review*, 79(3), 62–79.

Pozzebon, M. (2004). The Influence of a Structurationist View on Strategic Management Research. *Journal of Management Studies*, 41(2), 247–272. doi:10.1111/j.1467-6486.2004.00431.x

Pozzebon, M., & Pinsonneault, A. (2005). Challenges in Conducting Empirical Work Using Structuration Theory: Learning from IT Research. *Organization Studies*, 26(9), 1353–1376. doi:10.1177/0170840605054621

Ramasamy, B., Chakrabarty, A., & Cheah, M. (2004). Malaysia's leap into the future: an evaluation of the multimedia super corridor. *Technovation*, 24, 871–883. doi:10.1016/S0166-4972(03)00049-X

Rosenberg, D. (2002). *Cloning Silicon Valley: The Next Generation High-Tech Hotspots*. London: Reuters.

Saperstein, J., & Rouach, D. (2002). *Creating Regional Wealth in the Innovation Economy: Models, Perspectives, and Best Practices*. Upper Saddle River, NJ: Financial Times Prentice Hall.

Seno, A. A. (2003). A Wide-Open Valley but Not Much Silicon. *Newsweek: The International Magazine*, 90-93.

Stahl, B. C. (2008). *Information Systems: Critical Perspectives*. New York: Routledge.

Stillman, L. J. H. (2006). *Understandings of Technology in Community-Based Organisations: A Structurational Analysis*. Unpublished doctoral dissertation, Faculty of Information Technology, Monash University, Australia.

Stones, R. (2005). *Structuration Theory*. New York: Palgrave MacMillan.

Tapscott, D. (2001). Rethinking Strategy in a Networked World. *Strategy + Business*, 24.

Tapscott, D., & Williams, A. D. (2006). *Wikinomics: How Mass Collaboration Changes Everything*. New York: Penguin Group.

Wallace, M., Fertig, M., & Schneller, E. (2007). *Managing Change in the Public Services*. Maldan, MA: Blackwell Publishing.

Walsham, G. (2001). *Making a World of Difference: IT in A Global Context*. Chichester, UK: John Wiley & Sons.

Walsham, G. (2005). Learning about being critical. *Information Systems Journal, 15*, 111–117. doi:10.1111/j.1365-2575.2004.00189.x

ADDITIONAL READING

Abend, G. (2008). The Meaning of 'Theory'. *Sociological Theory, 26*(2), 173–199. doi:10.1111/j.1467-9558.2008.00324.x

Briand, L., & Bellemare, G. (2006). A Structurationist Analysis of Post-Bureaucracy in Modernity and Late Modernity. *Journal of Organizational Change Management, 19*(1), 65–79. doi:10.1108/09534810610643695

Creswell, J. W., & Tashakkori, A. (2008). How Do Research Manuscripts Contribute to the Literature on Mixed Methods? *Journal of Mixed Methods Research, 2*(2), 115–120. doi:10.1177/1558689808315361

Demers, C. (2007). *Organizational Change Theories: A Synthesis*. Thousand Oaks, California: Sage Publications.

Etzkowitz, H. (2008). *The Triple Helix: University-Industry-Government Innovation in Action*. New York: Routledge.

Flyvbjerg, B. (2006). Five Misunderstandings About Case-Study Research. *Qualitative Inquiry, 12*(2), 219–245. doi:10.1177/1077800405284363

Government of Malaysia. (2002). *Knowledge-Based Economy Master Plan*. Kuala Lumpur: Institute of Strategic and International Studies.

Han, C. K. (2003). *Blueprint for Transformation or Business as Usual? A Structurational Perspective of the Knowledge-Based Economy in Malaysia, Inaugural Lecture Publication No. 64, Serdang*. Selangor, Malaysia: Universiti Putra Malaysia.

Han, C. K., & Walsham, G. (1993). *Government Information Technology Policies and Systems: Success Strategies in Developed and Developing Countries*. London: Commonwealth Secretraiat.

Jack, L., & Kloleif, A. (2007). Introducing Strong Structuration Theory for case studies in Organization, Management and Accounting Research (Working Paper WP 07/01). School of Accounting, Finance & Management, University of Essex.

Johnson, P., Buehring, A., Cassell, C., & Symon, G. (2006). Evaluating Qualitative Management Research: Towards a Contingent Criteriology. *International Journal of Management Reviews, 8*(3), 131–156. doi:10.1111/j.1468-2370.2006.00124.x

Jones, M. R., & Karsten, H. (2008). Giddens's Structuration Theory and Information Systems Research. *MIS Quartery, 32*(1), 127–157.

Kitching, G. N. (2008). *The Trouble with Theory: The Educational Costs of Postmodernism*. New South Wales: Allen & Unwin.

Lauer, C. (2008). *The Management Gurus*. London: Penguin Books.

McGrath, K. (2005). Doing Critical Research in Information Systems: A Case of Theory and Practice Not Informing Each Other. *Information Systems Journal, 15*, 85–101. doi:10.1111/j.1365-2575.2005.00187.x

Mitev, N. N. (2006). Postmodernism and Criticality in Information Systems Research: What Critical Management Studies Can Contribute. *Social Science Computer Review, 24*(3), 310–325. doi:10.1177/0894439306287976

Prahalad, C. K., & Krishalad, C. K. (2008). *The New Age of Innovation: Driving Cocreated Value through Global Networks*. New York: McGraw-Hill.

Richardson, H., & Robinson, B. (2007). The mysterious case of the missing paradigm: a review of critical information systems research 1991-2001. *Information Systems Journal*, *17*(3), 251–270. doi:10.1111/j.1365-2575.2007.00230.x

Shah, R. C., & Kesan, J. P. (2007). Analyzing Information Technology & Societal Interactions: A Policy Focused Theoretical Framework. Illinois Public Law Research Paper No. 07-12 from http://papers.ssm.com/abstract=1028129.

Vaujany, F. (2008). Caputuring Reflexity Modes in IS: A Critical Realist Approach. *Information and Organization*, *18*(1), 51–72. doi:10.1016/j.infoandorg.2007.11.001

KEY TERMS AND DEFINITIONS

Knowledge-Based Economy: All definitions of a knowledge-based economy revolve around the notion of an economy based on the production, distribution and utilization of knowledge, which constitiutes the primary engine of growth and wealth creation in the economy. In both MyCountry and MyCountry2, the k-based economy was defined as an economy in which knowledge, creativity and innovation play an ever-increasing and important role in generating and sustaing growth.

Knowledge Super Corridor: Terminology used in MyCountry and MyCountry2 for the national and government initiated mega-projects in the area of information communications technology. These projects are aimed at pervasive computing in specified geographical regions.

Information and Communications Technology (ICT): an umbrella term that includes all technologies for the manipulation and communication of information. ICT encompasses any medium to record information, technology for broadcasting information - radio, television, and technology for communicating through voice and sound or images - microphone, camera, loudspeaker, telephone to cellular phones. It includes the wide variety of computing hardware, the rapidly developing personal hardware market comprising mobile phones, personal devices, MP3 players, and much more, the full gamut of application software from the smallest home-developed spreadsheet to the largest enterprise packages and online software services, and the hardware and software needed to operate networks for transmission of information.

Information Systems Research: the study of the effects of information systems on the behavior of individuals, groups, and organizations. Since information systems is an applied field, industry practitioners expect information systems research to generate findings that are immediately applicable in practice. However, that is not always the case. Often information systems researchers explore behavioral issues in much more depth than practitioners would expect them to do. This may render information systems research results difficult to understand, and has led to criticism.

Structuration Theory: the theory developed by Lord Anthony Giddens to explain and integrate agency and structure. For Giddens, human agency and social structure are not two separate concepts or constructs, but are two ways of considering social action. Structure is what gives form and shape to social life, and exists only in and through the activities of human agents. Agency does not refer to people's intentions in doing things but rather to the flow or pattern of people's action.

Duality of Structure: The relationshiship between agency and structure. One side is composed of situated actors who undertake social action and interaction, and their knowledgeable activities in various situations. At the same time, the other side is the rules, resources, and social relationships that are produced and reproduced in social interaction.

Critical Research: Critical researchers assume that social reality is historically constituted and that it is produced and reproduced by people. Although people can consciously act to change their social and economic circumstances, their ability to do so is constrained by various forms of social, cultural and political domination. The main task of critical research is seen as being one of social critique, whereby the restrictive and alienating conditions of the status quo are brought to light. Critical research focuses on the oppositions, conflicts and contradictions in contemporary society, and seeks to be emancipatory, that is, it should help to eliminate the causes of alienation and domination.

Interpretive Research: Interpretive researchers start out with the assumption that access to reality (given or socially constructed) is only through social constructions such as language, consciousness and shared meanings. The philosophical base of interpretive research is hermeneutics and phenomenology. Interpretive studies generally attempt to understand phenomena through the meanings that people assign to them. Interpretive research does not predefine dependent and independent variables, but focuses on the full complexity of human sense making as the situation emerges.

Chapter 11
An Intelligent Framework for Automatic Question Set Generation

Joydip Dhar
Indian Institute of Information Technology and Management, India

Abhishek Vaid
Indian Institute of Information Technology and Management, India

Manyata Goyal
Indian Institute of Information Technology and Management, India

Shilp Gupta
Indian Institute of Information Technology and Management, India

ABSTRACT

Automated question selection is an emerging problem in the industry of Online Test Management. The Test Management Suites, offer administration of question sets, either precompiled by experts, or randomized over the database of questions. Presently available literature in this domain is sparse and primarily focuses on automated question classification problem. This paper proposes a novel technique for administering question sets in an intelligent and automated approach. Artificial Intelligence, in the form of Self Organizing Feature Maps is utilized for question selection process. Finally, results from experiments are compiled for an illustration of the whole technique. Optimal design parameters for further research are also proposed alongside plausible future direction in pervasive computing.

INTRODUCTION

Need for conducting examinations/tests for the purpose of academic performance evaluation is manifold. Several reputed institutes offer admissions to candidates after assessing their performance in a self conducted examination. CAT, BITSAT, IIT-JEE, AIEEE, PET, PMT are examples of a few examinations held at National level. Troubled by the heavy cost requirements pertaining to management of such examinations, concerned authorities are looking ahead into the option of conducting examinations in an online manner as mentioned

DOI: 10.4018/978-1-61520-741-1.ch011

by Mukherji (2008). CAT, BITSAT, GMAT are examples of such online tests.

One of the important issues faced by most authorities while conducting online examinations is the formulation of question set creation policy. Most online test management suits offer random automated question set creation, or self administered question sets. Literature on automated test management is sparse and techniques for intelligent and automated question set creation are few.

This paper proposes a novel technique for administering question sets in an intelligent and automated fashion. The authors use the clustering capabilities of Self Organizing Maps explained by Haykin (1999) for achieving this purpose. But before any technique can be applied, it is necessary to generate meta-data on questions to make sure the machine understands the question's context. Modeling the context of questions in the form of a Feature Map also explained by Haykin (1999) and Kohonen (1982) is also proposed alongside.

Related Work

The academic research attention to automated intelligent question set creation is sparse. There is positive research focus on automated classification of questions in the work of Li (2002) and Hacioglu (2003). Feature based classification, that forms the basis of the Feature Map Model presented in next section, has been proposed and explored by Huang (2007). Applications of Self Organizing Feature Maps (or simply Self Organizing Maps) for feature based clustering are mentioned by Zhang (1993) and Vars (1992). A technique for generation of playlists from a music collection using SOMs has been explored by Pohle (2007), Rauber (2002) and Stavness (2005), which serves as a major guideline for the work in this paper. In several ways, the authors perceive the problem of question set generation solvable in a similar fashion to automated music playlist generation. The authors envision software solutions that bring

together automated feature extraction performed by Hacioglu (2003) from questions and question set creation techniques to produce a fully automated Online Test Management Suite.

Dynamic programming and stochastic algorithms for constraint satisfaction can be applied for solving the problem of question selection to a large extent. The novelty of the approach set forth for question selection, lies in the fact that the authors harness the abilities of Artificial Intelligence in imitating human procedure of question selection and offer greater prospects for adaptability.

A FEATURE MAP MODEL FOR QUESTIONS

This section proposes a novel mathematical model for abstraction of questions. Such abstraction provides the mathematical language for defining a question in terms of: the subject of the question, the intent of the question and the ease of evaluation of the question. The objective of such abstraction is to unify the validation process for the questions. Preparation of questions for the purpose of survey has been studied by McColl (2001) and Martin (2006). Huang (2007) explains the application of a similar model, but is done so in the context of automated question classification.

Domain of Evaluation (DoE)

Let there be a set,

$$D = \{t_1, t_2, ..., t_n\} \ ... \tag{1}$$

Each 't' is representative of a feature of the question. A feature is either one of the subject, the intent or the ease of evaluation. A set of these features forms the domain of evaluation for the questions [1].

Questions in DoE

Every question should be carefully worded and checked for integrity and accuracy. Also, it is important to assure that the system of questionnaire preparation understands the meaning of each question. This is conveyed to the system by providing the system, a mapping onto the DoE for every question. This mapping is in 'n-tuple' format. There are n values in an 'n-tuple', each corresponding to a feature defined in the DoE.

Weight of Feature Representation

In the DoE, every question is represented in an 'n-tuple' format. Each value in this 'n-tuple' signifies the weight of representation of that feature, by a question. It can be assumed that these values are integers from 0-5, though the technique presented in Section 3 is equally applicable to any such scale [1].

$$t_1, t_2, \ldots, t_n \in \{0, 1, 2, 3, 4, 5\} \ \ldots \quad (2)$$

[1] For example, let a question be represented as,

$$q_1 = (3, 2, 4, 2)$$

for some domain of evaluation with four features. If the third feature in this DoE is "how significantly does a question judge mathematical ability", then this question is said to be biased towards mathematical ability. If the second feature in this DoE is "how significantly does a question judge proficiency of English", then it can be inferred that this question is not biased towards judging the proficiency of English. This is similar to feature weights specified by Huang (2007).

Measure of Disparity

The set of questions are arranged in the DoE by a set of corresponding 'n-tuple's. We propose a measure of the disparity of two such questions to be the Euclidean distance (5) between their 'n-tuple' representations. That is,

If,

$$Q_1 = (x_1, x_2, \ldots, x_n) \ \ldots \quad (3)$$

$$Q_2 = (y_1, y_2, \ldots, y_n) \ \ldots \quad (4)$$

then,

$$\Delta(Q_1, Q_2) = \sqrt{\sum_{i=1}^{n}(x_i - x_i)^2} \ \ldots \quad (5)$$

where

$\Delta(Q_1, Q_2)$ = disparity between Question 1 and Question 2

The Question Bank

A set of questions, worded and created for a database formulate a question bank. Every question has only its ID and its statement associated with it. The only assumption made for the question bank is that the questions are coherent.

$$QB = \begin{Bmatrix} \langle QID_1, QuestionStatement_1 \rangle, \\ \langle QID_2, QuestionStatement_2 \rangle, \ldots, \\ \langle QID_m, QuestionStatement_m \rangle \end{Bmatrix}$$

The Feature Map

After the formulation of DoE for a Question bank, every question is then mapped to an 'n-tuple' in the

DoE. This mapping is many to one from questions to the set of all 'n-tuple's. Both forward and reverse mapping is preserved, such that, upon presentation of a question's ID, we can retrieve its 'n-tuple', and, upon the presentation of an 'n-tuple', we can get the IDs of all the questions that are mapped to it. This set of mappings for all the questions is collectively known as Feature-Map.

Clusters of Questions – Theory of Good Question Selection

A set of questions, such that Disparity (eqn. 5) among any two questions from the set is below a predefined threshold (T), is called a cluster. It is desirable to set the value of threshold, such that, each cluster consists of all questions that are similar in context. If we set the threshold too low, it will result in closely related questions appearing in various clusters. Consequently setting it too high results in over generalization of the clusters. For example, let a, b, c be three questions in a DoE with 3 features, such that,

$$a = (2, 2, 4)$$

$$b = (3, 2, 4)$$

$$c = (3, 3, 2)$$

a, b will be in the same cluster at threshold of 1, while at threshold of 3, all a, b, c will be in the same cluster. Notice how a, b are almost alike. They will also be alike in their context to the test giver and are not likely to produce any extra effort.

A good question selection strategy would be to opt for questions from different contexts and also presents questions in an order that does not abruptly change the context of the questions.

SELF ORGANIZING FEATURE MAPS (SOFM) FOR QUESTION SET EXTRACTION

There are a large number of questions 'n' and a small number of neurons 'm'. We create a feature mapping from these questions to neurons such that we have a uniform many to one mapping from questions to neurons. This is described as the learning process by Haykin (1999). Principle component analysis for dimensionality reduction of the problem can be conducted prior to the application of the SOFM as mentioned by López-Rubio (2004).

A completely trained SOFM would map each question to some neuron. A neuron's synaptic weights as mentioned by Haykin (1999) represent an 'n-tuple' in the DoE. All questions with small Measure of Disparity (as described above) to this 'n-tuple' are then associated to this neuron. By virtue of the topology preserving nature of SOFM as developed by Kohonen (1982), questions mapped to adjacent neurons in SOFM are closer in context. While those questions mapped to Neurons far apart in SOFM would be of different topics and purpose.

An exploration of how this training occurs is explained by Haykin (1999) and Kohonen (1982). The mathematical rigor and derivation of the truth of observations is not in the interest of this paper, and can be followed to its original source. At the same time, the reader is also motivated to explore the works of Haykin (1999) and Kohonen (1982) to gain further insights into the accomplishment of SOFMs in the case of question bank modeling, and the solution we offer to question set creation through them.

SOFMs were introduced as a competitively learning Neural Networks by Kohonen (1982). Use of SOFMs for clustering (similar to the clustering discussed in last section) in multidimensional spaces is discussed by Vesanto (2005), Zhang (1993) and Vars (1992). SOFMs as a tool for playlist generation are introduced by Rauber (2002).

Box 1.

```
• Let Q[N] = Map of Node (N) to Questions
• Let n = No. of Ques. Required
• Let f = No. of Features in Questions
• Let M[f] = Maximal Feature Values Vector Required by Set
• Let V[f] = Vector of Feature Values of Current Set (Initial-
ized to 0)
• Let T = 0, P = Node at (1,1)
• Let S = null ; S is the Final Question Set
• While T < Total Number of Ques. Required
• Do
o Let q = null
o For Each q' in Q[P]
o If FeatureSet[q'] + V <= M Then Set q = q'
o if q != null Then Add q to S, T = T + 1, augment V
o For Each node P' adjacent to P
o If Disparity(P',P) > Threshold Then P = P'
o If P does not change, backtrack to the Previous Selection of P
• End Do
```

Question Set Extraction from SOFM

A completely trained SOFM outputs a Layer of neurons (henceforth mentioned as nodes) and questions associated with them as given by Haykin (1999).

The Question Set Extraction Procedure then resembles a traversal over these nodes and selection of questions during the traversal. As suggested by Pohle (2007) a traversal should select questions from a diversity of nodes to make sure that the entire feature space of questions is represented – therefore making a good question set that covers most topics. For the purpose of this paper, we selected a depth first heuristic that selects questions from nodes that have feature space disparity above a particular threshold.

The above Algorithm explains the procedure used to select the question set over repeated trials.

- The algorithm's backtracking step asserts that the algorithm ends with a valid selection of questions.
- The validity of a Question Set is defined as V <= M.
- A Valid Question Set hence asserts that the maximal requirement of feature representation is met. For example, If the requirement is to represent questions on Logic, more than those of Percentages, Then M[Logic] > M[Percentages] will assert that a valid question set represents so.

EXPERIMENTAL ANALYSIS

Experiments were performed on a test Dataset of 1000 Questions. The Domain of Evaluation for

Figure 1. Histogram of question dataset spread on SOFM layer of 10x10 neurons. Larger squares represent dense clusters while empty spaces represent absent tuples in feature space, as explained by Principe (1999)

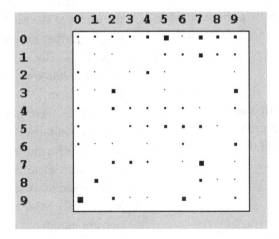

Figure 2. The graphical representation of the unified distance of unsupervised synapse over the test dataset of questions. Darker areas represent neurons close together in feature space as explained by Principe (1999)

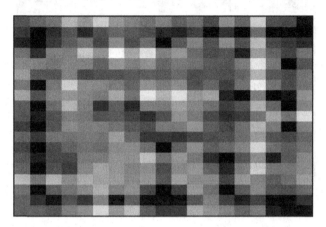

the questions was chosen to have a cardinality of 5. Every question was hence represented as a '5-tuple' of 5 weight values for each feature similar to as given by Huang (2007). The target of the experiment was to produce question sets of 20 questions each. The experiments were done using clustering techniques in software called "Neuro Solutions".

Using the weights obtained post-training; the algorithm was implemented for production of desired result - a question set with 20 questions. The range of values of each variable in the DoE was chosen as [1, 5] (closed interval). Figure 3 highlights a sample path that the depth first traversal might take through the feature space. We take shorter jumps from regions which have lighter color in Figure 2, as neighboring neurons would be far apart in such regions. On the other hand, longer jumps are taken from regions with darker color, as neighboring neurons are closer to this neuron as mentioned by Principe (1999).

Results of the one of the experiment at a specified Maximal Feature Value Set vector are outlined in Table 1.

It should be noticed that low average disparity (<3.0), of the sequence of questions indicates our goal to achieve a question set where consecutive questions are not too separated in feature space. This assures that consecutive questions are related in context and transition from one context to another is taking place smoothly. Also, this value is not too low to suggest that consecutive questions

Table 1. Results of a run of the algorithm over SOFM trained with a test Dataset of 1000 questions with a DoE of 5 features

Features	F1	F2	F3	F4	F5
Maximum Feature Value Specified	80	40	60	40	50
Total Sum of Feature Value	71	40	52	36	40
Mean Feature Value	3.55	2300	2.60	1.80	2.50
Standard Deviation of Feature Values	1.51	1.37	1.29	0.67	1.07
Average Disparity of the Order of Questions	2.9567				

Figure 3. Path marked by a traversal (in red) alternate path possible by a second traversal (in blue)

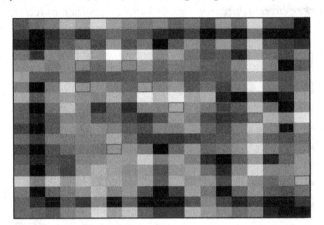

are very similar.

Given that the goal is to achieve a question set biased to Feature 1, we have achieved a mean feature value of 3.55, which shows how often questions rich in context pertaining to Feature 1 occur in the prepared question set.

Optimal Parameters for Design

The number of questions to the number of neurons ratio must be small (<0.1), to assure that each neuron has high probability of associating to multiple question. If the number of questions required is N, the number of rows in the SOFM layer is R and the number of columns is C, a good relation among these values is suggested to be:

$$R = C = N/2$$

This can be complemented with a depth first traversal from one corner to another corner, and selection of one question from each node encountered. Such a traversal would guarantee good average case question set which is unbiased to any topic.

The SOFM should be trained each time the feature space of questions changes. Events that suggest retraining the network are addition / deletion of questions to the Question Bank. Deletion

does not strictly require retraining, however, this may result in large gaps in the histogram (Figure 1).

FUTURE DIRECTIONS

The suggested technique proves effective for question set extraction, but like any other random question set creating technique, is plagued with bad question bank selection. Research in optimal feature map modeling of questions for various examinations would assist coordinators of such examinations to easily use SOFM for more efficient question set creation. Further research in techniques for traversal, such as by Pohle (2007) would help explore question sets with stylistic attributes to complement reputed online tests.

Combination of the technique specified in this paper with constraint satisfaction algorithms (such as using dynamic programming) should prove effective in generation of more balanced automated question sets.

Online Tests in a Pervasive Environment

The ability of this framework to model questions in several contexts is useful, and not only for the purpose of selecting questions for online tests. Questions are highly appropriate constructs in conversation. SOFM can map questions on features of the last response. Combination of this question selection framework with one of question feature detection framework - in which much progress has already been achieved - would constitute a verbose system. Psychometric analysis through automatically generated questionnaires would allow companies to better nurture their employees at all times at minimal costs and man power required to do so.

REFERENCES

Hacioglu, K., & Ward, W. (2003). Question Classification with Support Vector Machines and Error Correcting Codes. In the *Proceedings of HLT-NACCL 2003, Edmonton, Alberta, Canada,* (pp. 28-30).

Haykin, S. (1999). *9. Self-organizing maps. Neural Networks - A comprehensive foundation* (2nd ed.). Upper Saddle River, NJ: Prentice-Hall.

http://www.nd.com/ (n.d.). Retrieved July, 2008.

http://www.questionmark.com/us/index.aspx (n.d.). Retrieved July, 2008.

http://zohochallenge.com/OnlineTest/Candidate. do (n.d.). Retrieved July, 2008.

Huang, P. B. Jiajun, Chen, Chun, Qiu, Guang (2007). An Effective Feature-Weighting Model for Question Classification. In *Proceedings of the 2007 International Conference on Computational Intelligence and Security,* (pp. 32-36).

Kohonen, T. (1982). Self-organized formation of topologically correct feature maps. In Biological Cybernetics, (pp. 43-69).

Li, X., & Roth, D. (2002). Learning Question Classifiers. In COLING'02.

López-Rubio, E., Ortiz-de-Lazcano-Lobato, M., Muñoz-Pérez, J. J., & Gómez-Ruiz, A. J. (2004). Principal Components Analysis Competitive Learning. *Neural Computation, 16*(11), 2459–2481. doi:10.1162/0899766041941880

Martin, E. (2006). Survey Questionnaire Construction. *Survey Methodology, 13.*

McColl, E. (2001). Design and use of questionnaires: a review of best practice applicable to surveys of health service staff and patients. *Health Technology Assessment, 5*(31).

Mukherji, A. (2008, April). Retrieved from http://timesofindia.indiatimes.com/article-show/2915234.cms.

Pohle, T., Knees, P., Schedl, M., Pampalk, E., & Widmer, G. (2007). Reinventing the Wheel: A Novel Approach to Music Player Interfaces. *IEEE Transactions on Multimedia, 9*(3). doi:10.1109/TMM.2006.887991

Principe, J. C., Euliano, N. R., & Lefebvre, W. C. (1999). *Neural and Adaptive Systems: Fundamentals through Simulations.*

Rauber, A., Pampalk, E., & Merkl, D. (2002). Using Psycho-Acoustic Models and Self-Organizing Maps to Create a Hierarchical Structure of Music by Sound Similarity. In *Proc. Int. Conf. Music Information Retrieval (ISMIR)*, Paris, France, (pp. 71–80).

Stavness, I., Gluck, J., Vilhan, L., & Fels, S. (2005). The music table: A map-based ubiquitous system for social interaction with a digital music collection. In *Int. Conf. on Entertainment Computing (ICEC05).*

Vars, A., & Versino, C. (1992). *Clustering of socio-economic data with Kohonen maps.* Neural Network World.

Vesanto, J., & Alhoniemi, E. (2005). Clustering of the Self-Organizing Map. *IEEE Transactions on Neural Networks, 11*(3), 586–602. doi:10.1109/72.846731

Zhang, X., & Li, Y. (1993). Self-organizing map as a new method for clustering and data analysis. In *Proceedings of International Joint Conference on Neural Networks (IJCNN '93)*.

ADDITIONAL READING

Azghadi, S. M. R., Bonyadi, M. R., & Shahhosseini, H. (2007). Gender Classification Based on FeedForward Backpropagation Neural Network. Artificial Intelligence and Innovations 2007: from Theory to Applications. Volume 247. Pages 299-304. ISBN 978-0-387-74160-4

Egmont-Petersen, M., de Ridder, D., & Handels, H. (2002). Image processing with neural networks - a review. *Pattern Recognition, 35*(10), 2279–2301. doi:10.1016/S0031-3203(01)00178-9

Gardner, E. J., & Derrida, B. (1988). Optimal storage properties of neural network models . *Journal of Physics, 21*, 271–284.

Mandic, D., & Chambers, J. (2001). *Recurrent Neural Networks for Prediction: Architectures, Learning algorithms and Stability*. Wiley. Devireddy S. K. & Rao S. A. (2009). Hand Written Character Recognition Using Back Propagation Network. *Journal of Theoretical and Applied Information Technology., 5*(3).

Nguyen, T. M., Sarwer, M. G., & Wu, Q. M. J. (2008). *A New Probability Neural Network for Image Classification Problem*. Proceeding Signal and Image Processing.

Wong, E. S. K. (2009). Cognitive Pattern Analysis Employing Neural Networks: Evidence from the Australian Capital Markets. *International Journal of Economics and Finance., 1*(1).

TERMS AND DEFINITIONS

Domain of Evaluation (DoE): The set of features that help quantify the characteristics of the questions that need to be considered. These are pre decided by experience or experimentation. Each feature in the DoE acts as a dimension in the feature map.

Feature Map: Each question is mapped to a point in the n-dimensional space, where there are n-features. This mapping forms the feature map that helps quantify the difference between questions.

Measure of Disparity: The Euclidean distance between two questions in their feature map representations.

Self Organizing Map: An advanced clustering technique based on artificial neural networks. Each processing unit (or neurons) arranges itself in the feature map to a set of neighbouring questions. Selecting questions from processing units farther apart result in questions that differ vividly in context and vice versa. Also called, Kohonen Maps.

Depth First Traversal: A traversal technique that explores deeper nodes, (that are farther from the starting point) before others.

Training: Presenting the system with exemplars to pre-process, learn, qualify or classify, to be able to generate useful and/or interesting results in the production mode.

Automated Question Selection: The process, independent of continuous human intervention, of selecting questions from a question bank for the purpose of a test, especially, online tests.

Section 4
Pervasive Healthcare

Chapter 12
Neuro Linguistic Programming:
Towards Better Understanding of Human Computer Interaction

Ankur Choubey
Institute of Technology & Management, India

Ramesh Singh
National Informatics Centre, India

ABSTRACT

The power of computers is now beginning to be exploited in subjective areas of human study like those related to human psychology in order to make the interaction between humans and computers more natural. An effective interaction must involve automatic analysis of human behavior by the computer, and responding to it. Neuro-Linguistic Programming was developed, drawing its inspiration from the computer programs, so as to change the perception of the human brain to a more successful behavior. In addition to that, Neuro Linguistic Programming gave an algorithmic approach to 'observe' and analyze human behavior, both verbal and non-verbal, and serve to effectively perceive the human behavior and interaction. The interaction is a more deep rooted cognitive interaction. With the use of Neuro Linguistic Programming and the fundamentals of cybernetics, the humans and computer can be brought closer, with automatic transfer of valuable information between the two. This chapter describes the fundamentals of Neuro Linguistic Programming and aims at developing a hypothetical model on how Neuro Linguistic Programming can be used to better understand the interaction between the humans and the computers.

INTRODUCTION

With the increased use of computers and computing system being assimilated into every human aspect,

the cognitive interaction of computers and robots with the humans is a new research domain. Recent developments in field of Human-Computer Interaction and other cognitive sciences have enabled man to interact more naturally with the computer. However to further enhance the Human Computer

DOI: 10.4018/978-1-61520-741-1.ch012

Interaction, some new techniques need to be designed and incorporated. Not only verbal but also non-verbal behavior is a major factor in the efficient communication between the two.

One of the techniques that gained a lot of momentum in the recent years, especially in the field of communication, is the Neuro-Linguistic Programming abbreviated as NLP. It originated as a therapy and was earlier used in Psychotherapy (*A Dictionary of Psychology 2nd ed.*, 2006). An information scientist Richard Bandler and a linguist John Grinder, at Santa Cruz, created NLP in the early 1970's.

This technique evolved so as to duplicate and model highly successful behavior of three psychotherapists (Dilts R & Erickson R.K, 2006). Later on, apart from psychotherapy, it was implemented in fields of communication, management, sales, marketing, public relations, education and many others. NLP primarily aims at changing the "perception" of the real world through our 'maps of reality' created by the brain. It tends to change the state of the mind, the brain's 'programming' (analogous to a computer program, the source of inspiration for NLP) and the maps of reality so as to 'reprogram' the brain and consequently change one's behavior to a more useful and efficient one.

With the help of Neuro-Linguistic Programming and the advances made in computer sciences, the interaction and communication between Humans and the computers can further be developed, more efficiently and naturally.

Humans interact with each other generating meaningful information and communicating it to others. To enter this information to a computing system or probably a robot, the system must extract it directly from observing the human interactions. The proposed work presents a model that uses NLP to analyze and perceive the human behavior effectively, thereby also enhancing effective human and computer interactions.

There certainly needs to be a shift from data processing to knowledge processing and this model may be considered as an integrated application of pervasive computing and A.I coupled with V.R concepts etc.

OBJECTIVES

In this paper we try to develop a hypothetical model to study the use of Neuro-Linguistic Programming and computing system as an aid to cognizance and perception of human interactions. By successful modeling the interaction between humans and the computers, including robots can be made more natural. Understanding efficiently human behavior, need, feelings etc., with the use of Neuro-Linguistic Programming, by computers can lead us to new applications in cognitive science.

BACKGROUND OF NLP – A FEW APPLICATIONS

Neuro-Linguistic Programming is a concept that evolved so as to study and duplicate highly successful human behavior, skills and competence and then modeling it. This model could then be further developed or enhanced such that a transferable model could be developed and learnt by the humans so as to improve their skills, creativity etc. or to cure patients with phobias. It is also being employed in a big way in Management Concepts like Sales and Marketing, Advertisements and Organizational behaviors etc. Education sector is another potential area for NLP to be applied, once the computer models are ready and implemented.

NLP was developed in early 1970's by an information scientist Richard Bandler and a linguist, John Grinder (John Grinder, http://en.wikipedia.org/wiki/John Grinder, n.d) at University of California, Santa Cruz. They observed that people having similar education, training, background and experience had widely varied results. They wanted a reason for this and know their secrets of success, and how they achieved it.

They wanted to duplicate the behavior and competence and model human excellence. They could make out some common patterns of thinking and communication that accounted for their success. They perceived that the brain could learn healthy patterns and behaviors and this would bring some positive changes in humans. What emerged from their work came to be called NLP, Neuro-linguistic Programming

NLP was invented to apply some concepts from programming to psychotherapy, where it has enjoyed considerable success. It has also been used to help people with personal development, again with considerable success. Educators who need a method to observe the learning styles of students have used it. Managers who want to understand the communications have used it and cognitive styles of their people so as to best interact with them. Although there are skeptics about whether the brain is really a "computer" that can be "programmed", NLP has produced useful interventions in a number of areas and cannot be written off pure speculation.

USES AND APPLICATIONS

Psychotherapy

One of the major uses of NLP was found in psychotherapy. NLP is widely being applied as an efficient technique to treat phobias, and other psychological disorders, using techniques like anchoring. Moreover by modeling oneself, one can change his unhealthy habits or traits, or simply his beliefs, views, perception. Study of NLP also helps psychiatrists to understand their client better and to get to the core of the problem.

Interpersonal Communication Skills

The second major use of NLP is found in improving one's communication skills. By modeling the communication patterns of highly effective people, one can study the common characteristics and behavior of these people and then can use it to try improving one's own communication skills and creativity. This has been used extensively in fields like Business, Mass communication, sales, marketing etc. Also by a technique called Anchoring, in NLP, one can reduce the fear of public speaking or some kinds of phobias. Similarly, with other techniques, one can further reduce his/her phobias of public speaking and behavior. Also techniques like mirroring help a lot. Thus, NLP can be used to improve oneself. One notable personality who has used NLP to his benefit is the former U.S. President, Mr. Bill Clinton. (Moudgil Manu, 2008)

Artificial Intelligence – NLP can be used to impart efficient and in fact the best possible traits into robots and thus we can have a live virtual human model. The robots cannot only model them virtually, but also they can be used in various fields, as having the required characteristics in terms of communication skills. Also using NLP they won't be having any kind of phobias, or wrong perception, or beliefs, views, unlike humans and hence automatically the effectiveness of robots will surely increase.

B.P.O. – Customer Satisfaction

NLP has also lately found its use in Business Process Outsourcing (BPO's), call centers and companies dealing with customers and their satisfaction (Anirvan Ghosh, 2008). By NLP the client and the companies can have better understanding and also a good rapport can be maintained between them. The client's requirements can be better understood by analyzing the verbal content of the user especially in mode of communication like telephone, e-mail etc. Similarly search-oriented companies are also applying NLP to better understand the user's given search query, as in case of "Communicate2" company (Communicate2, http://www.communicate2.com, n.d).

As a Profession in I.T Industry – I.T industry nowadays solely relies on Communication, Customer Requirements, Customer satisfaction etc. NLP can help IT industrialists to better understand their customer's requirements and satisfaction. Moreover, the communication skills of software engineers and others can be improved, since the era of IT industry requires communication with other countries and origins over a common language. All these will help them to further enhance their managerial skills and the prosperity of the company and business. Moreover one can impart training and other NLP-related services, which then again becomes a new profession in itself, and have also been found recently. Furthermore, NLP concepts have been visualized to be applied in Education sector also, so as to impart 'effective' characteristics in both teachers and the students.

Entertainment

In the recent years, NLP has found a great use and is further being popularized by the media, namely mass communication like television. Generally NLP is mentioned in the context of "achieving something" or "power of brain" etc. For example, NLP can be used to get rid of say smoking etc. or unleash the power of your mind etc. Although these may be useful but NLP practitioners however say that it will not always be true. But also, if used properly, it may impart a certain level of improvement in one's skills or communication etc. However scientists warn the clients not to get carried away by some of the false advertisements by some people or group, as it may lead to some adverse effect.

One program telecasted on the T.V, The Oprah Winfrey Show is a chat show, wherein the Host, uses NLP techniques to being a great communicator and winning over her audiences and also motivating people to confess the details of their private lives. (Moudgil Manu, 2008).

There have been two other notable programs telecasted on the T.V that closely refers to NLP and its applications. Paul McKenna, a celebrity hypnotist anchored a show called, "I can change your life" to assist people with phobias or wrong habits. Similarly another program called "I can make you Thin" used the same theory ("Paul McKenna will make" from http://www.skyone. co.uk/mckenna, n.d).

Furthermore, some audio programs were also launched; those of Anthony Robbins being famous and his famous book 'Unlimited power' (Robbins, Anthony, 1986). There are several books available in the market that use some form of NLP to change one's habits.

Many sports persons form India like Rajyavardhan Rathore and Robin have used NLP to their benefit. One can find many other real-life testimonies to the benefits of NLP, some of them in the newspaper reference mentioned here. (Moudgil Manu, 2008)

HUMAN INTERACTIONS AND NLP: A PERSPECTIVE

Neuro-Linguistic Programming aims at changing one's behavior to a certain stimulus by changing the perception of the brain, and enhancing it for a more efficient one. The most important use of NLP has been found in communications. It is also applied to analyze human behaviors and better perception of the real world entities.

"How perceptions are formed, how they govern the way we see, how the way we see governs how we behave." (Covey, Stephen R, 1999)

In a nutshell, NLP technique tries to change the 'programming' done by the brain and the 'internal models of the world' (or 'maps of reality' as is usually said in NLP), which ultimately changes the way the brain responds and thereby affecting the 'Behavior' of the body.

Action is nothing but one's behavior. This behavior is instructed by the brain to be performed by the body or its part, based on certain 'inputs'. Now, if we have two or more humans (or likewise computers), and they together perform certain actions or behavior, observing each other and giving feedbacks to one's own body (brain), we have an interactive system.

The brain works on a stimulus-response model similar to a computer's I/O model (Covey, Stephen R, 1999) wherein the response is nothing but the behavior. Behavior thus is the source of interactions. Now comes the use of NLP in analyzing the behavior and perceiving the behavior effectively by the other one (human, computer or robot). And with effective behavior, one can achieve efficient interaction, especially when dealing with the computers or robots.

NLP focuses on several factors. Both the verbal and non-verbal behavior is taken into consideration. Moreover, NLP aims first at developing "independent" (one's own) behavior skills and then also at "inter-dependence" (group) (Covey, Stephen R, 1999) behavior skills. Hence by affecting one's own behavior by every one in the group and some of the other behavior of the group, an efficient interaction or communication can be achieved among the group.

Hence finally NLP will be useful in analyzing and perceiving the behavior and affecting it so as to have a better interaction among other members of a group, be it computers or even robots. For automatic analysis of human (or likewise other) interactions by the computer, NLP is of great aid. One more advantage will be the aid for computer to *understand humans and their needs more effectively*.

NLP serves as an aid to better understanding as may be used in the old Turing test (Rich, Elaine & Knight, Kevin, 1991) or imitation game referred in various Artificial intelligence concepts. NLP is the driving force for "understanding human behavior and improving human inter-action"

COMPUTERS AND THEIR ROLE IN INTERACTIONS

If NLP is the engine then computers are the *cars*. As stated, NLP is the engine for understanding and analyzing human behavior. Every interaction produces some valuable information, which here needs to be automatically perceived, and cognized by the computer. Thus computer is the *car*, abstracting engine, but performing all the desired purposes and effectively interact with the humans.

A typical computing system will accept some input from the human by interacting with the humans. This includes automatically observing human behavior or with explicit instructions and other forms of input. The computer then performs the desired task.

Some Applications

Moving a step forward, these computing systems could be best replaced by the *Robots*. Using robotics, one can achieve numerous tasks involving and related to cognizance of human interactions. This of course makes use of NLP as the engine. One of the most exciting applications of robots may be to represent robots as a natural human being. Apart from perceiving its entire interaction with the humans, it will be able to respond as well, as would another human might do. Moreover the robots can also duplicate highly successful behavior as well or probably impart training to others, using a NLP principle, "seek first to understand and then to be understood" (Covey, Stephen R, 1999) Alternatively, they can be more like friends, understanding our moods, behavior etc. or like 'perfect' employees. One can think of lots more other applications that make use of this model, if successful.

A typical computer or rather computing system requires certain inputs, follows some algorithms and finally produces some output. In this case, some 'feedback' of one's own action might also be required as is required a normal human interaction. There are quite a lot of *similarities* between the functioning of the computer and human brain, which NLP utilizes. One can easily find/observe them however discussing them here is avoided in this case.

Assuming necessary materials are available, we try making a hypothetical model to further illustrate this entire system.

HYPOTHETICAL MODEL: USING NLP AND COMPUTING SYSTEM

Before developing a model, one interesting thing to note is the use of Cybernetics - the Control Theory. Any cybernetic system has most importantly a feedback mechanism (Cybernetics, http://en.wikipedia.org/wiki/Cybernetics, n.d), apart from input, output, memory and interfaces. Using Computers, Cybernetics theory and NLP together, we might be able to finally develop our model of the '*car*' referred earlier as the metaphor, encapsulating all the three, to be an aid to "cognizance and perception of human interactions."

In case of a human body, it's the 'mind'/'brain' and 'body' that works as a perfect cybernetic system, working together in a *synchronized* manner with regular feedbacks and self-regulation. Also as an example failure of a behavior is the feedback (Moudgil Manu, 2008) for the knowledge base of the brain. Other characteristics of a pure cybernetic system, like the working of the mind and body may be observed. This though requires some basic knowledge of cybernetics, however may be skipped without loss of generality.

In a similar analogy to mind and body, is the body behavior and interactions. The Brain instructs the body to perform a certain behavior, which results in interactions, while simultaneously, receiving a feedback and based on which next behavior or a "Pro-Active" one may be instructed to the body.

We proceed systematically now to develop a hypothetical model.

REPRESENTATIONAL SYSTEMS OF NLP (SENSORS): INTERFACE BETWEEN HUMANS AND COMPUTERS

To receive inputs, both the NLP and the computers require some 'senses'. A usual Computer uses certain input devices, such as a keyboard, in simple applications. NLP uses "Representational Systems" – the most important human senses, namely Visual (Sight), Auditory (Hear), Kinesthetic (Touch and internal feelings). To analyze any non-verbal behavior, NLP requires input 'signals' from these representational systems. Moreover, to get a detailed 'input' NLP further uses *sub-modalities* – the sense of finer details by the representational systems.

Analogously, the computing system also requires "sensors" as an "Interface" from Humans, to receive input signals for processing. In the case, of Robots it is easier to *visualize* these sensors. However the computers or any other computing system may utilize similar sensors and sensing technology.

Using special cameras fitted as *eyes* in the case of robots, or using a group of those similar to CCTV cameras can capture visual information. Microphones can capture auditory information. Related circuits in addition to this technology can obtain feedbacks. Pressure sensors can obtain 'touch' and a combination of these can obtain *kinesthetic* feelings.

As an illustration, consider the following figure, to observe a group of people on a meeting table, interacting with each other.

The auditory signals that would be received in the above figure would be somewhat like this:

With the technological advancements made till today, this task could easily be carried out, at a much more detailed level, from a simple one illustrated above.

Some of the sensors may look in a robot like as shown in Figure 3:

Figure 1. (McCowan I, et al., n.d)

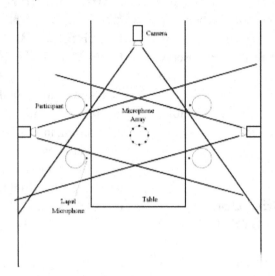

Figure 2. Microphone array directivity patterns at 1000 Hz (speaker 1 direction in bold) (McCowan I, et al., n.d)

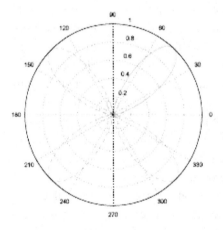

All these are finally connected to a central processor that does all the processing and also implementing NLP techniques.

ALGORITHM FOR THE WORKING OF THE HYPOTHETICAL MODEL

a) General Algorithm For The Model:
1. Identify the concerned person
2. Locate it and focus more on the input streams, in detail (see Algorithm b.)
3. Recognize the action of the located person
4. Follow the delete distort generalize model, similar to working of a brain
5. Send the signals to the processor
6. The processor, on receiving the signals then implements the NLP techniques and algorithms
7. Analyze the input signals and then perform the required task
8. Send the output to the 'body' (like in case of robots) or any other output

Figure 3.

1. Eye – Visual sensor using cameras (Patrick M., n.d)

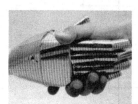

2. Skin – Touch sensor using micro pressure sensors (Flexible Sensors Make Robot Skin http://radio.weblogs.com/0105910/ 2004/09/22.html, n.d)

3. Auditory sensor fitted with microphone (Siegwart R., 2008)

device.

9. Obtain a feedback and again repeat step 5.

b) Algorithm To Locate The Person

1. For each person present in the field of view, follow the step 2-6 till the required person is found

2. Track any person based on input signals from the sensor

3. For each and every located person follow step 4-5

4. Enhance the audio and visual streams or even kinesthetic, if necessary

5. Identify the person based on its characteristics.

6. If found then return to step 2 of the general algorithm above else the person is not there.

Neuro-Linguistic Programming, deriving its inspiration from Computer Programs, also works on certain algorithms. However, mentioning and discussing these algorithms for NLP techniques, is itself a vast and a detailed topic, which would be inappropriate here.

But, in practice, these NLP techniques and algorithms will be well implemented by the "Processor" of the system, on receiving input signals as mentioned in the general algorithm given above, using a specific programming done.

SUMMARY AND FUTURE DIRECTIONS

Perception as interpreted by the brain refers to creating a *map of 'reality'* (outside world) in our *own views*. By using NLP that tends to change this

Figure 4. Block diagram showing the hypothetical model

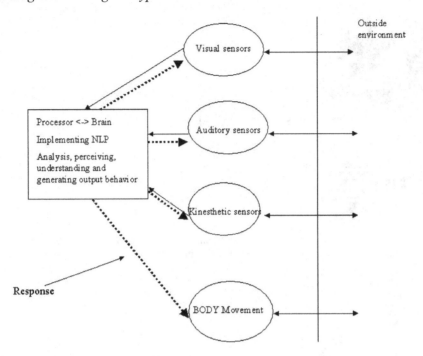

perception, one can achieve successful behavior and efficient cognizance of human interactions. By modeling NLP and implementing it on to a computing system, even robots; the human – computer interaction could be made more natural. An efficient understanding and cognizance of human behavior, needs, feelings etc. can be obtained using this system, which induces many applications. The role of NLP is as important as an engine of a *car* – it provides the driving force. The computers, due to the algorithmic nature of NLP technique, can easily implement the NLP techniques. As stated, the model developed allows automatic analysis of the human behavior and interaction or even computer-computer interaction and fed into the computing system. This serves as an aid to analyzing human behavior (verbal and non-verbal) and effectively responding to it.

The model discussed here is a purely hypothetical one, but provides a base upon which real applications can be built implementing the system. However, the proposed system would require an extensive use of cognitive sciences, intelligent sys-

tems, fast and parallel processing, multimedia and virtual reality etc. With the increasing technology these factors should not pose much problem. The NLP techniques however could not be discussed here but it has been abstractly used here. Further work is going on in this field and improvements can be made. The model is yet to be tested.

REFERENCES

Covey, S. R. (1999). *The 7 Habits of Highly effective People*. New York: Pocket Books.

Cybernetics. (n.d). Retrieved August 10, 2008, from http://en.wikipedia.org/ wiki/Cybernetics

Dictionary of Psychology. (2nd ed.).(2006). neurolinguistic programming. New York: Oxford University Press, USA.

Dilts, R., & Erickson Klein, R. (2006). Neurolinguistic Programming . In *The Milton H. Erickson Foundation: Newsletter, Summer, 26(2)*. Historical.

Flexible Sensors Make Robot Skin. (n.d.). Retrieved August 10, 2008, from http://radio.we-blogs.com/0105910/ 2004/09/22.html

Ghosh, A. (2008 May 12). Neuro-linguistic programming is the newest fad in BPOs. *The Economic Times. Communicate2.* (n.d). Retrieved July 30, 2008, from http://www.communicate2.com

Grinder, J. (n.d). Retrieved July 28, 2008, from http://en.wikipedia.org/ wiki/John Grinder

Knight, K., & Rich, E. (1991) Artificial Intelligence (2 ed.), (pp. 24). New York: McGraw-Hill.

McCowan, I., et al. (n.d.). *Towards Computer Understanding of Human Interactions,* 3. Retrieved August 10, 2008, from http://www.idiap. ch/~mccowan/publications/mccowan-eusai.pdf

McCowan, I., et al. (n.d.) *Towards Computer Understanding of Human Interactions, 8.* Retrieved August 10, 2008, from http://www.idiap. ch/~mccowan/publications/mccowan-eusai.pdf

Moudgil, M. (2008 November 11) Tapping into your full potential. *The Mail Today,* (pp 27).

Patrick, M. (n.d.). *How to Build a Computerized Android Robot Head.* Retrieved August 10, 2008, from www.howtoandroid.com/HowToBuildRobotHead.html

Paul McKenna will make you thin. (n.d.). Retrieved July 30,2008, from http://www.skyone. co.uk/mckenna

Robbins, A. (1986). *Unlimited power: the new science of personal achievement.* New York: Simon & Schuster.

Siegwart, R. (2008, June 26). *Design and Realization of an Ear for Robot,* (p. 1). Retrieved August 10, 2008, from http://www.asl.ethz.ch/education/ proj_apps/gifs/doku29.pdf

ADDITIONAL READING

Bandler, R., Andreas, S., & Andreas, C. (1985) *Using Your Brain--for a Change.* Real People Press McCowan I, et al. (n.d) *Towards Computer Understanding of Human Interactions,* retrieved from http://www.idiap.ch/~mccowan/publications/mccowan-eusai.pdf

Card, S. K., Moran, T. P., & Newell, A. (1986). *The psychology of human-computer interaction.* Lawrence Erlbaum Associates.

Covey, S. R. (1999). *The 7 Habits of Highly effective People* (introductory pages). New York: Pocket Books Alan Dix, Janet E. Finlay, Gregory D. Abowd, Russell Beale(2004) *Human-Computer Interaction (3rd Edition).* Pearson. *Parallel Computing* retrieved from http://en.wikipedia.org/ wiki/Parallel_computing

Dilts, Robert B & Judith A DeLozier (2000). Encyclopaedia of Systemic Neuro-Linguistic Programming and NLP New Coding. NLP University Press.

Druckman, Daniel & John A Swets, (Eds) (1988). *Enhancing Human Performance: Issues, Theories, and Techniques.* Washington DC: National Academy Press.

Facial recognition, how it works retrieved from http://electronics.howstuffworks.com/facial-recognition.htm

Feature recognition retrieved from http://feature. geometricglobal.com/

Hans-W., G., Want, R., & Schmidt, A. (2005) *Proceedings of the Pervasive Computing*: Third International Conference, PERVASIVE 2005, Munich, Germany. Springer. *The newest code of NLP* retrieved from http://www.neurosemantics. com/index.php?option=com_content&task=view&id=486&Itemid=199

Knight, K., & Rich, E. (1991) *Artificial Intelligence* (2 ed.). McGraw-Hill John D. Woodward, Jr., Christopher Horn et al. *Biometrics - A Look at Facial Recognition*, retrieved from http://www.rand.org/pubs/documented_briefings/DB396/DB396.pdf

Lawton, Teri B, *Dynamic object-based 3D scene analysis using multiple cues*,. published in Proc. SPIE Vol. 2054, p. 194-210, Computational Vision Based on Neurobiology, Teri B. Lawton; Ed.

Maltz, M. (1968). *Psycho-Cybernetics, A New Way to Get More Living Out of Life*. Simon & Schuster, Inc.

NeuroLinguistic Programming retrieved from http://en.wikipedia.org/wiki/Neuro-linguistic_programming

O'Connor, J., & Seymour, J. (1993). *Introducing Neuro-Linguistic Programming: Psychological Skills for Understanding and Influencing People*. London, UK: Thorsons.

Online journal on Human Computer Interaction retrieved from http://hci-journal.com/

The structure of magic: a book about language and therapy By Richard Bandler, John Grinder, Published by Science and Behavior Books, 1975

William Ross Ashby. (1964). *Introduction to Cybernetics (University Paperbacks)*. Methuen.

KEYWORDS AND DEFINITIONS

Neuro-Linguistic Programming: A model of interpersonal communication chiefly concerned with the relationship between successful patterns of behavior and the subjective experiences (esp. patterns of thought) underlying them

Computing System: A system of one or more computers and associated software with common storage

Cognizance: Conscious knowledge or recognition; awareness

Perception: the act or faculty of apprehending by means of the senses or of the mind; cognition; understanding.

Interactions: A mutual or reciprocal action

Cybernetics: The study of human control functions and of mechanical and electronic systems designed to replace them, involving the application of statistical mechanics to communication engineering.

Robots: A mechanical device that sometimes resembles a human and is capable of performing a variety of often-complex human tasks on command or by being programmed in advance.

Chapter 13

Tele-Immersive Psychotherapy:
Stepping Towards Pervasive Computer Aided Healthcare

Anubhav Kumar Singh
National Institute of Technology, India

Ramesh Singh
National Informatics Centre, India

ABSTRACT

As our world progresses into ever more competitive stressful environments and life styles, various mental and psychological disorders have come to manifest themselves increasingly among the general human population. As our knowledge has advanced various methods and techniques have been developed to combat these disorders. One such method is the use of immersive technologies for controlled exposure to certain environments as part of the treatment process. Tele-Immersion is a technology which enables such immersive cooperative environments over long distances. Thus it has an immediate application in psychotherapy where psychologists can control and monitor their patients and their immersive treatments over long distances. This chapter shows one such application model based in a tele-immersive environment and is based on the ongoing research on Tele-immersive systems and their applications at National Informatics Centre, New Delhi, India

INTRODUCTION

Various studies report that the occurrence of psychological disorders is among the rise today among the general population. This has been attributed to several factors such as more stressful lives with more competition due to increasing population and ever decreasing sources, more responsibilities etc. The problem is that the increase in the number of

doctors and psychiatrists has not been in proportion with the increase in population and occurrence of these disorders. Thus in many places it becomes difficult to obtain services of a competent psychiatrist without actually travelling long distances to established centres and big cities etc leading to big expenditures. This is especially true in developing and poor countries.

The problem then is the development of methods to effectively provide psychiatric services to far flung areas and possibly more number of patients

DOI: 10.4018/978-1-61520-741-1.ch013

per psychiatrist to cope with the ever increasing demands. In other words we need to create methods of achieving patient psychiatrist interaction without requiring the patient or psychiatrist to move to the other's location. The difficulty in this problem arises from the fact that we are in the domain of mental diseases in which there is no substitute for traditional "face to face" communication between the psychiatrist and patient. Thus we need methods using computing and communication technologies which simulate real interpersonal communication to a very high degree to essentially convince the patient's mind in a manner of speaking.

Essentially the problem goals are:

1) Development of methods for Travel Free Psychiatric Care
2) Development of a Software model for the above methods

Specifically, the problem taken up here is the description of the software running on top of the hardware which will interact with the patient and psychiatrist over the Internet.

Thus the main objectives of this chapter are as follows:-

- Familiarization with the problem of psychotherapy coverage expansion.
- Background review of Computer aided Psychotherapy and previous work in field
- Review of existing hardware technologies required for new model.
- Development of solution requirements or judging yardstick to measure the model's capability.
- Development of new model based on application of Tele-immersive technology to Psychotherapy alongwith a typical scenario for usage.
- Review of the CAVERNSoft Toolkit for implementation of model on given hardware requirements.

- Understanding the problems associated with proposed model implementation.
- Analysing future trends and possible solutions to encountered problems.

BACKGROUND

Tele-immersion was originally defined in 1996 by Thomas A. Defanti of the Electronic Visualization Laboratory (EVL), as The integration of audio and video conferencing, via image based modelling, with collaborative virtual reality in the context of data mining and significant computations" [Leigh, et. al., 1997]. Since then, research on Tele-immersion has outgrown most of its system and performance-related issues and now focuses on supporting collaborative interaction and usability. Tele-immersion now deals with the "Creation of persistent virtual environments enabling multiple, globally situated participants to collaborate over high-speed and high-bandwidth networks connected to heterogeneous supercomputing resources and large data stores" [Leigh, et. al., 1997].

Similarly "Webopedia" defines Tele-immersion as: "Tele-immersion is a technology to be implemented with Internet2 that will enable users in different geographic locations to come together in a simulated environment to interact. Users will feel like they are actually looking, talking, and meeting with each other face-to-face in the same room." Basically, Tele-immersion can be explained as the ultimate synthesis of media technologies like:

- 3D environment scanning - 3D reconstruction based on display
- Projective and display technologies
- Tracking technologies
- Audio technologies
- Robotics and Haptics and
- Powerful networking

In laymen terms tele-immersion can be said to be virtual reality over the internet. It is the integration of immersive technologies with high speed network infrastructure leading to cooperative multiple person immersion over huge distances.

While there has been previous research conducted into Computer aided psychotherapy, it has mostly focused on Virtual Reality based psychotherapy involving the patient interaction with a virtual world controlled by a psychiatrist. However this requires both the patient and psychiatrist to be present in the lab together in reality, thus defeating the purpose of our problem of expanding psychotherapy care over long geographical distances without travel and actual physical meeting between psychiatrist and patients. It is here that Tele-immersion combining Virtual Reality and Internet provides us with a method to approach the problem in a new way.

TELE-IMMERSIVE PSYCHOTHERAPY

We propose a solution to the stated problem based on the upcoming technology of Tele-immersion. Assuming availability of the hardware requirements (listed below) we develop a software model and scenario for Tele-immersion based psychotherapy.

Hardware requirements:

1)   CAVE™/BAT CAVE™ System
2)   High Speed internet link (gigabit)

CAVE™

CAVE is a recursive acronym that stands for CAVE Automated Virtual Environment. Until 1992, when EVL developed the CAVE, the VR community used mainly head-mounted displays-heavy and clumsy helmets with liquid crystal

displays or cathode ray tubes (CRTs) mounted in front of eyepieces. The CAVE-VR system is a 10 × 10 sq. ft. room in which CRT projectors project stereoscopic images.

The images give the CAVE occupants or users the illusion that objects surround them. Users wear lightweight liquid crystal shutter glasses to resolve the stereoscopic imagery and hold a three-button pressure sensitive wand for interaction with the virtual environment in three dimensions. An electromagnetic tracking system attached to the glasses and the wand lets

the CAVE determine the location and orientation of the user's head and hand at any given moment. This information instructs the Silicon Graphics Onyx that drives the CAVE to render the images from the user's point of view. [2]

Specifically, the CAVE is a theater 10x10x9 feet, made up of two rear-projection screens for walls and a down-projection screen for the floor. Electrohome Marquis 8000 projectors throw full-color workstation fields (1024x768 stereo) at 96 Hz onto the screens, giving approximately 2,000 linear pixel resolution to the surrounding composite image. Computer-controlled audio provides a sonification capability to multiple speakers. A user's head and hand are tracked with Ascension tethered electromagnetic sensors. Stereographics' LCD stereo shutter glasses are used to separate the alternate fields going to the eyes. A Silicon Graphics Onyx with three Reality Engines is used to create the imagery that is projected onto the walls and floor. The CAVE's theater area sits in a 30x20x13-foot light-tight room, provided that the projectors' optics are folded by mirrors.

The first CAVE (Cave Automated Virtual Environment) was developed by the Electronic Visualization Laboratory at University of Illinois at Chicago and was announced and demonstrated at the 1992 SIGGRAPH. The CAVE was developed in response to a challenge from the SIGGRAPH 92 Showcase effort for scientists to create and show off a one-to-many visualization tool that utilized

Figure 1. The CAVE (Cave Automated Virtual Environment).CRT projectors project stereoscopic computer images onto the CAVE's translucent walls, giving the occupant (user), who is wearing special glasses, the illusion that objects surround him. The user interacts with the environment through a wand (not shown). —Image courtesy of the Electronic Visualization Laboratory

large projection screens. The CAVE answered that challenge, and became the third major physical form of immersive VR after goggles and gloves and vehicle simulators. This became the most widely used system in Tele-Immersion Systems later on.

BRIGHT ADVANCED TECHNOLOGY (BAT) CAVE™

In June 2001, EVL built the next-generation Bright Advanced Technology CAVE™, or BAT CAVE, using Christie Digital Systems' Mirage 5000 projectors--the first DLP-based Active Stereoscopic projector--and near-black screens for higher contrast. The BAT CAVE's brightness, clarity and enhanced depth perspective produce more captivating real-time, real-life projection simulations than previous CAVE™ technology.

Apart from the hardware requirements, based on our problem analysis we came up with the following minimum requirements or goals to be met by the software:

The software in essence -

- Should run on above mentioned hardware and be compatible with other platforms too
- Should be easy to use with intuitive controls for both patient and psychiatrist requiring only very basic training or tutorial to master.
- Should produce realistic illusion of face to face communication
- Should allow the Psychiatrist to manipulate the patients projected environment as required. (for example transfer the patient into a soothing resort scene etc seamlessly.
- Should allow the patient to exit the illusion unconditionally in case of emergencies as well as temporary breaks for essential activities like toilet etc.
- Should record the session for examination by psychiatrist
- Should offer basic privacy protection measures to the patient so only he/her and an authorized psychiatrist can view his/her records.

SCENARIO

Based on the above requirements we give a potential scenario highlighting key points in a typical therapy session.

In this scenario, The Psychiatrist Dr Sharma is immersed in a CAVE located in his office at A. The patient Mr Rao is immersed in a CAVE located at his home or some nearby centre B. The two are connected via a land line based digital voice and data network which enables them to co-inhabit a virtual theatre of therapy and communicate with each other in real time. For the current therapy session the environment is populated by Mr Rao, Dr Sharma and a background environment decided by Dr Sharma. Dr Sharma views the environment as a *deity or god*. Thus, he sees the world from a bird's eye perspective. This puts him in a position to make high-level observations and decisions and modify the environment as he wishes. However he can also switch to an *avatar* form to interact directly with the patient. Mr Rao views the environment as a *mortal* and takes enters the world in an avatar form through which he can interact directly with his surroundings like a human in the real world. Since the chosen environment can be large, in the deity form the psychiatrist can choose any detail level using an adjustable zoom factor.

Dr Sharma has logged in with his user ID. The system recognises his ID and logs him in as a deity. Dr Sharma clicks ready on his interface (using the CAVE wand for interacting with the interface) and the systems starts broadcasting that Dr Sharma is online. Mr Rao logs in as a guest or patient requiring the id number of his counsellor or psychiatrist Dr. Sharma. If Dr Sharma is online the system asks him to verify the request on his interface and initiate the session by choosing a background world from available choices pre-stored and/or modified ones stored by Dr. Sharma on his local storage. After initiating the session (by Accepting Mr Rao's therapy request and choosing a world scene of a garden), Dr. Sharma can speak face to face initially with Mr. Rao while the session loads the scenario on both ends. After completion of loading, Dr Sharma can choose to shift himself and/or Mr Rao to predetermined locations in the world or continue direct chat for now. Dr Sharma chooses to enter the world with Mr Rao and continue the conversation there in avatar form. These avatars are digitally created at the moment of loading by the software using the cameras mounted in the CAVE environment at both ends and basic human skeletons stored in system memory. The system takes facial images of the participants and maps them onto the basic structures in 3D creating a human body avatar with the face of the participant.

While the therapy session continues Dr. Sharma receives an alert in his mailbox about an incoming request from another patient. Dr Sharma asks Mr Rao to take a stroll in the garden while he comes back in a moment. He then switches to deity mode and exits the environment which minimizes itself onto his interface workspace. He then initiates the session with another patient. Now he can switch back and forth between the two environments as per his wish. This allows him to multitask. He can also deny the other request if he wishes to take one session at a time by setting his status to Busy which would make the system tell the requesting patient to wait some time while Dr Sharma gets free.

In the meantime, Mr Rao feels the need to go to toilet. So he sends a message to Dr. Sharma telling him that he needs to visit the restroom and will be back in a moment. After that he uses the wand button for temporary exit which saves his avatar information and world information on the local system in his profile and stops the simulation till Mr Rao comes back.

After toilet Mr Rao returns and logs in again and continues the session which notifies Dr Sharma of his return. The rest of the session proceeds normally and at the end of an hour; Dr. Sharma decides that it is time to end the session for the day. Both users exit the world and Mr Rao gets the bill in his account which he authorizes to pay

Figure 2.

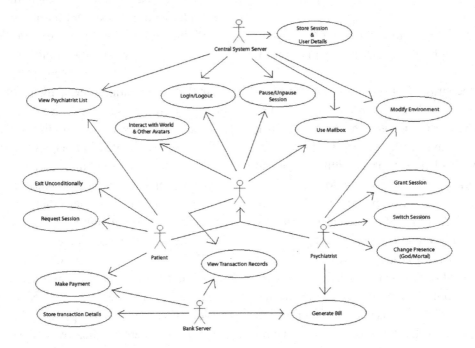

electronically. Thus at the end of the session, the fees is automatically transferred to Dr. Sharma's account electronically using an e-banking plug-in. The session gets recorded and stored on both ends for future use and now Dr. Sharma having received confirmation of payment can concentrate on the other patient or take up more patients as he wishes.

The Central Database Server storing ID and account information responsible for broadcasting information shall be maintained at an independent site by an independent agency such as a Govt body etc.

USE-CASE UML DIAGRAM FOR PROPOSED MODEL

The Above scenario highlights the average case runtime scenario of the tele-immersive therapy session technology.

Summary

1) This scenario captures several key features of tele-immersion: Accessing stored data while immersed, synchronous verbal and visual exchange, archiving of sessions, environment sharing etc

2) This scenario highlights the potential benefits of tele-immersion based psychotherapy: No travelling costs, multiple environments can be used instead of just a standard clinic, Multiple patients can be handled by the psychiatrist without interfering with or invading the privacy of individual sessions etc

3) This scenario shows the use of electronic commerce and banking in future medicine.

4) This scenario shows how psychiatric treatment care can be accessed by people who may not have a competent psychiatrist in their neighbourhood without compromising on the competence of the practitioner.

Figure 3.

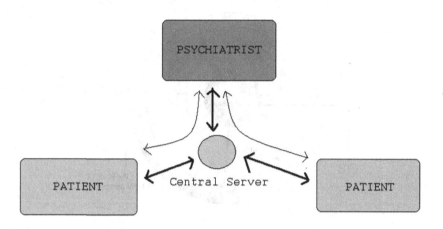

CLIENT SERVER ARCHITECTURE FOR THE MODEL

The presented framework is undergoing ongoing implementation and simulation using the **CAVERNsoft** G2 toolkit [1] and at the NIC software lab.

CAVERNsoft is a C++ toolkit for building collaborative networked applications or logistical networking applications. It has low and mid level networking classes to support general collaborative application building, and it has higher level modules to specifically support Tele-Immersion [2].

At its core is the Information Resource Broker (IRB), which was inspired by the CORBA (Common Object Request Broker Architecture) object request broker (ORB), but has a lower overhead. Like the ORB, it emulates both a distributed shared-memory system and a message passing system, but unlike the ORB and traditional systems, it does not unify the two systems. Instead, data distribution can occur over either reliable TCP, UDP, or multicast, which Tele-immersive applications usually need to distribute their many data classes. The IRB also allows shared-memory

segments to persist so that client programs can cache frequently used data at local sites. Applications built with the IRB are client-server symmetric i.e. all client programs are automatically server programs without the need for additional programming. This symmetry means that a collection of clients can easily form arbitrary collaborative topologies and thus that collaborators can initiate spontaneous sessions. [Defanti et. al]

DIAGRAM OF CAVERNSOFT SHOWING THE IRB IN THE CENTER, SURROUNDED BY INCREASINGLY HIGHER LEVEL LAYERS

CAVERNsoft also provides a suite of IRB-based libraries that support basic Tele-immersion needs, such as avatars, audio-conferencing, collaborative interfaces, and virtual e-mail. However, from almost a decade of experience with technology transfer, developers learnt that it is not enough to simply provide a suite of tools. A higher level tool organization must also be provided as an application framework so that users can conceptualize how to use the tools in a specific scenario. To

Figure 4.

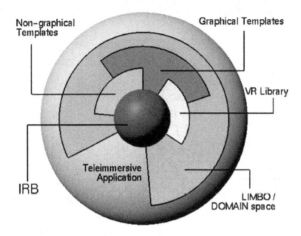

provide that support, EVL created Limbo, a Tele-immersion application framework. Limbo and its successor Tandem, support audio-conferencing, avatar rendering, model importing, and data distribution and manipulation. Collaborators use a basic Limbo space to quickly begin working in a shared virtual space without programming. As users import 3D models (car designs, scientific data sets, and so on) into the space, Limbo distributes them to all remote participants, who can begin to collectively modify them. EVL has also made the source code available so that application developers can jump-start the development of their own domain-specific tele-immersive applications.

The toolkit contains the following classes which are very helpful:

Low/Mid-level networking classes
- TCP, UDP, multicast, HTTP classes.
- UDP reflector and multicast bridge class.
- TCP reflector.
- Remote procedure calls classes.
- 32 and 64 bit remote file I/O classes.
- Client/Server database classes.
- Parallel socket TCP classes.
- Parallel socket 32 and 64 bit remote file I/O classes.
- 32 and 64 bit remote file I/O classes using parallel sockets
- Cross-platform data conversions.
- Mutual exclusion and threading classes.
- Network performance monitoring abilities

Higher level modules
- Audio streaming.
- Basic avatar classes without graphics.
- Performer articulated avatars.
- Performer navigation and collision detection.
- Performer menus.
- Performer Pick and Move
- Performer NetDCS
- Collaborative widget interface.
- Collaborative framework for animating data sets.
- LIMBO- basic collaborative framework for building other collaborative applications.
- Manipulative coordinate system class for programming transformations.

Figure 5.

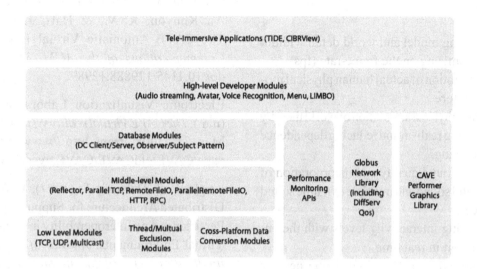

DIAGRAM OF CAVERNSOFT G2 SHOWING NETWORKING, DATABASE, GRAPHICAL MODULES AND TELE-IMMERSIVE APPLICATIONS

While performing further implementation and analysis of the model, the following problems/tradeoffs were identified when using this approach:

1) Accurate Scene and user modelling generates millions of points and datasets. Current technology cannot cope up with such a large amount of data and processing time as well as lag time increases dramatically beyond practical application for usage by common people.
2) Handling and minimizing packet losses and reducing collisions.
3) Simulation on non CAVE hardware reduces accuracy.
4) Usage of avatars and scripted animation for hand movement etc to substitute for actual human motion modelling increases frame rates and responsiveness at the cost of reducing the level of realism drastically thereby reducing effectiveness.
5) The initial hardware and setup cost is too high making it infeasible for private purchase as of now.
6) Comprehensive real-time interaction with the virtual environment or world is not included thereby reducing realism.
7) Following security protocols for the electronic monetary transactions along with the need for lesser response times presents a difficult trade-off.

FUTURE TRENDS AND WORK

This area of Tele-immersion is likely to see more and more research and development work as the technology becomes more commonplace. The main focus of research is likely to be achievement of higher and higher levels of realism approaching actual reality while at the same time minimization of costs.

Towards that end, some of the areas that we would like to work on in the future to refine this project are:

1) Improving model and world detail without compromising on the frame-rate (fps)
2) Incorporation of actual human physical motion capture
3) Greater physical simulation of world thereby improving realism and reducing dependence on scripting.
4) Greater sound quality and incorporation of surround sound and multiple dynamic sound sources.
5) Improving interactivity levels with the environment in real time.
6) Incorporation of advanced haptic devices and tactile feedbacks to improve realism and generate sensation of touch, smell etc.
7) Exploring both peer to peer (p2p) linkage and network based linkage options.

CONCLUSION

We can conclude by saying that the model proposed above satisfactorily complies with all the identified solution requirements. However it still lacks the realism of actual reality leading to possible loss of immersion. Apart from this, it is also quite costly to setup Tele-immersive hardware as required by the model. Thus, much research needs to be done in this area and further refinements to the approach need to be made. The approach of using Tele-immersion in psychotherapy offers a novel method for expanding the coverage area of psychiatric services as well as reducing costs. However with current technology and costs, the technique is still in its infancy and is too inaccurate and costly for practical acceptance and feasibility for common usage as of dateHowever, with upcoming advances in technology and reducing cost of hardware, it will very soon become competent with even the best practices.

REFERENCES

Cruz-Neira, C., Sandin, D. J., DeFanti, T. A., Kenyon, R. V., & Hart, J. C. (1992). The CAVE Automatic Virtual Environment. *Communications of the ACM, 35*(2), 64–72. doi:10.1145/129888.129892

Electronic Visualization Laboratory (EVL). (n.d.). *The CAVE Virtual reality system.* Retrieved May 31, 2008, from http://www.evl.uic.edu/pape/CAVE/oldCAVE/CAVE.overview.html

Leigh, J. & DeFanti, T. (1997). CAVERN: A Distributed Architecture for Supporting Scalable Persistence And Interoperability in Collaborative Virtual Environments. *Journal of Virtual Reality Research, Development and Applications, 2*(2.1).

Leigh, J., Johnson, A., DeFanti, T., et al. (1999). A Review of Tele-Immersive Applications in the CAVE Research Network. In IEEE VR '99, Houston TX.

Leigh, J., Rajlich, P., Stein, R., Johnson, A. E., & DeFanti, T. A. (1998). A Tool for Rapid Tele- Immersive Visualization . In *IEEE Visualizaton '98.* Research Triangle Park, NC: LIMBO/VTK.

Park, K., Cho, Y. J., Krishnaprasad, N., Scharver, C., Lewis, M., Leigh, J., & Johnson, A. (2000). CAVERNsoft G2: a Toolkit for High Performance Tele-Immersive Collaboration. In *ACM 7th Annual Symposium on Virtual Reality Software & Technology (VRST)*, Seoul, Korea.

Schiefele, J., Dörr, K., Olbert, M., & Kubbat, W. (1999). Stereoscopic Projection Screens and Virtual Cockpit Simulation for Pilot Training. In *Proceedings of the 3rd Annual Immersive Projection Technologies Workshop*, (pp. 211-222).

Singh, G., Serra, L., Png, W., Wong, A., & Ng, H. BrickNet. (1999). Sharing Object Behaviors on the Net. In IEEE VRAIS '95, Research Triangle Park, NC, March 11-15, (pp. 19-25).

Singh, R. & Singh, A.K. (2008). Transcending from Virtual Reality into TELE-IMMERSIVE Technologies and Applications – A Perspective. *ACM Ubiquity, 9*(23).

Stevens, W. R. (1994). *TCP/IP Illustrated* (*Vol. 1*). Reading, MA: Addison Wesley.

KEY TERMS AND DEFINITIONS

Avatar: An avatar is a computer user's representation of himself/herself or alter ego, whether in the form of a three-dimensional model used in computer games, a two-dimensional icon (picture) used on Internet forums and other communities, or a text construct found on early systems such as MUDs. It is an "object" representing the embodiment of the user. The term "avatar" can also refer to the personality connected with the screen name, or handle, of an Internet user. N our current context it is the three dimensional human figure representing the clients inside the virtual world during the therapy sessions [Wikipedia 2008].

Deity: User mode involving incorporeal or non-avatar based existence and interaction inside the world with full privileges. It is similar to the administrator user mode of Operating Systems. It allows high level observations, decision making and environment modifications.

Mortal: User mode involving solid, corporeal or tangible existence and interaction inside the world with limited privileges restricted to viewing and avatar movement, similar to the guest user mode of Operating Systems.

Psychotherapy: Psychotherapy is an interpersonal, relational intervention used by trained psychotherapists to aid clients in problems of living. This usually includes increasing individual sense of well-being and reducing subjective discomforting experience. Psychotherapists employ a range of techniques based on experiential relationship building, dialogue, communication and behaviour change and that are designed to improve the mental health of a client or patient, or to improve group relationships (such as in a family).

Tele-Immersion: The technology involving integration of audio and video conferencing, via image based modelling, with collaborative virtual reality in the context of data mining and significant computations.

Chapter 14
Optimal Resource Allocation Model for Pervasive Healthcare Using Genetic Algorithm

Lutfi Mohammed Omer Khanbary
University of Aden, Yemen

Deo Prakash Vidyarthi
Jawaharlal Nehru University, India

ABSTRACT

Number of mobile devices, equipped with sophisticated services apart from communication, is increasing day by day. Today a vast set of high speed network infrastructure, both wired and wireless, exists. This work studies the mobility management model for healthcare services developed for the efficient utilization of the network infrastructure. The model assumes that the physicians (doctors) are highly mobile and are periodically changing their location to perform their daily work, which includes serving patients at different nodes (serving as health centre). The mobility information about these doctors dependents on their current location. A location-aware medical information system is developed to provide information about resources such as the location of a medical specialist and patient's records. In the author's previous work, a framework is developed to describe the relations between types of hospitals and specialists with the use of Hospital Information Systems (HIS). The model for pervasive healthcare is to manage the specialists' movements between the hospital nodes with the objective to serve the maximum number of patients in minimum amount of time. In this work, they carried out simulation experiments to evaluate the performance of the proposed model towards servicing the patients. It has been observed that the model performs better in servicing the patients in the service area.

INTRODUCTION

Governments all over the world are increasingly concerned about their ability or inability to meet their social obligations in the health sector. The situation is of concern in light of rapidly increasing costs for medical care, aging population, lack of government funds, and so on. Also the quality of medical services delivered to the end users are not up to the mark. The hospital management is seriously concerned about the lack of medical infrastructure and resources to provide satisfactory service (Ramani, 2004).

DOI: 10.4018/978-1-61520-741-1.ch014

Traditionally, hospitals are provided for the congregation of various medical professionals, nurses, medical technicians, diagnostic and therapeutic equipment that work together to bring the best possible quality of medical care to the patient. With the development of medical and communication technologies, the quality of healthcare delivered by hospital has improved a lot. Hospitals are struggling hard to contain costs without sacrificing the quality of care. Medical technology, though indispensable to patient care, is suppose to consider creating some of the greatest costs and risks that a hospital encounters. The purpose of service quality management between the hospitals is to establish a system that measures and manages patient care and provides an optimal medical service to the patients. An attention is to be given to the contents of the healthcare services management from the view of a patient. (Davis, 1996)

Life is priceless, so evaluation and management is important in medical services to enhance the quality of medical services (Mei-Ju, 2005). The common person is mobile and his health

travels with him. It is needed to support the person's health mobility requirements along with other needs. The current situation in the healthcare domain is affected by the exciting fields of medical and technological improvement and increasing patient's requirements. The utilization of health services is going to be a regular service available anywhere and anytime i.e. the healthcare services should be available pervasively (Loos, 2002).

With the development of new information and communication technologies, the environment is more congenial for the installation and diffusion of services, allowing a better exchange of information between the physicians and hospitals of a geographical sector. Communication between professionals is a key element for the quality of care (Clemmer, 1995). The strategy for the diagnosis and a patient's treatment is elaborated after exchange of data between cooperating doctors and hospitals. Networks particularly focus

on the development of data exchanges between hospitals. The main objective of these healthcare networks is to ensure the rapid exchange of data between the participants of the system in a geographic sector. These exchanges facilitate the communication of the data which may be beneficial not only for the doctors but also for the patient (Beuscart, 1999).

Many national and regional healthcare plans have been floated in the past, in order to control the costs, the quality, and the availability of healthcare for all citizens. For instance, hospital management can focus on co-ordination of the primary medical processes, or on external networking with other hospitals for medical services. Healthcare usually consists of primary care (provided by general practitioners, dentists etc.) and hospital and special care provided by hospitals and medical specialists. Most medical specialists are not employees of a hospital, but work as private practitioners, making use of hospital facilities. The excessive pressure experienced by the hospitals can be transformed into 'functional specialization' thus to reduce costs and to improve the quality of specialized medical services. A more recent response of hospitals is to move into 'network management'. In this organizational type a hospital is seen as a piece of an elaborate network of medical care (Wulff, 1996). This can be used to improve the efficiency and effectiveness of hospital services. The communication processes are critical for improving the links between healthcare demands and providers (Smits, 1999).

Hospitals are facilities that provide both urgent and special medical care. The hospital staff may provide diagnosis and treatment for those persons who arrive at the facility and then release them back to the community. Some patients may need further treatment. Following the triage evaluation, treatment of the person's medical needs is administered to on an assessed priority of need basis (Tawney, 2005). The system should consider the connection between physicians (hospital doctors), specialists, when a patient consults a specialist (ophthalmology, gynecology, etc.), connection with other hospitals, appointment system that can share agenda between different hospitals (Beuscart, 1999). With the rapid growth in the network and mobile computing technology, the time is an important factor for life saving that should be considered. Further, the medical facility, on the tip, is also of concern. It is an important problem and requires careful planning and attention. A system approach to the planning of healthcare is essential to facilitate understanding of the process and to develop a holistic method of management (McClean, 2006).

Personal digital assistants (PDAs), wirelessly connected to a Hospital Information System (HIS), can give physicians access to patient medical records from anywhere, this handheld system provides medical staff with information based on their context of work, mainly their location [Fischer, 2003), (Lapinsky, 2001) and (Rodríguez, 2004). The use of the (PDA) in a 2001). Through this mobile system, the professionals will be able to manage the treatment of patients more efficiently and quickly as a result of real-time sharing of medical data and delivery of medical records and image data (Pavlovski, 2004). We utilized the PDA to improve the overall performance of the healthcare service in the network.

In recent past, the applications of Genetic Algorithm (GA), a useful search procedure for optimization problems, have attracted the attention of researchers of numerous disciplines for problem solving. The GA has been applied successfully for various optimization problems for which no straight forward solution exists. Researchers of mobile computing have used GA for channel allocation problem (Mahapatra, 2006), (Tripathi, 2006) and (Ioannis, 2000). GA has also been applied extensively for the task scheduling problem in distributed computing system (Tripathi, 2006; Vidyarthi, 2003; Vidyarthi, 1997). In the present work we utilize the GA to simulate the mobility management model for healthcare services.

The rest of this work is organized as follows. In section 2, a brief discussion on genetic algorithm is presented .The GA-based mobility model for healthcare is described in section 3. In section 4, the performance of the model is evaluated by carrying out the simulation experiments and the observations based on the results of the experiments. Concluding remarks are given in section 5.

GENETIC ALGORITHM

The GA is a search procedure based on the principle of evolution and natural genetics. GA combines the exploitation of past results with the exploration of the new areas of the search space by using the survival-of-the-fittest technique combined with a structured, yet randomized, information exchange. In each new generation, a set of strings is created using information from the previous ones. Occasionally, a new part is tried from the good measure. GA is randomized, but they are not simple random walks. GA efficiently exploits historic information to speculate on new search points with expected improvement (Khanbary, 2008; Mitchell, 1999; Zomaya, 2002).

In GA we start with an initial population, derived from the solution space, and then apply the genetic operators on it for the appropriate mixing of exploitation and exploration. A simple genetic algorithm consists of an initial population followed by selection, crossover and mutation operations (Mitchell, 1999), as shown in figure 1.

Initial Population

Initial population is the set of potential solutions to the problem. To start with number of solution is generated using any method (greedy etc.). Borrowing the terminology from genetic engineering, the population is also called chromosome or string. On the initial population various genetic operators are applied in GA.

Figure 1. Operations in GA

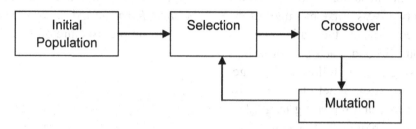

Figure 2. Crossover operations in GA

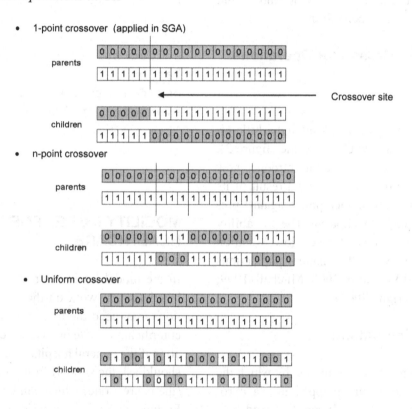

Selection

Selection operation selects good results among the chromosomes through some objective function (fitness function) used to rank the quality of the chromosomes. A fitness value is assigned to the chromosome using a fitness function and the chromosome is evaluated with this value for its survival. So the fitness of the chromosome depends on how well that chromosome solves the problem at hand. Strings with a higher value have a higher probability of contributing one or more offspring in the next generation. This operator is an artificial version of natural selection; the objective function is the final arbiter of the string-creature's life or death. (Khanbary and Vidyarthi, 2008; Mitchell, 1999).

Crossover

The idea of crossover is to swap part of the information between a pair of chromosomes to obtain the new chromosome. Simple crossover may proceed in two steps. First, members of the newly reproduced strings in the mating pool are mated at random. Second, each pair of strings undergoes crossing over as follows: an integer position k along the string is selected uniformly at random between 1 and the string length less one [1, l-1] as shown in figure 2. Two new strings are created by swapping all characters between positions k + 1 and l inclusively (Khanbary and Vidyarthi, 2008; Goldberg, 2005).

Examples of Crossover Operations

Mutation

In mutation a chromosome is altered a little bit randomly to get a new chromosome (figure 3). The mutation operator is used to introduce new genetic material (e.g. 0 or 1). As a result of its generality, it is an insurance policy against premature loss of important notions. The probability of applying mutation is often very low. Mutation rates are normally small in natural populations (Khanbary and Vidyarthi, 2008; Mitchell, 1999; Zomaya and Wright, 2002).

The Encoding Scheme

The encoding refers to the method by which the problem parameters are mapped into a chromosome. There are many ways to encode the chromosome. Most GA applications use fixed-length, fixed-order bit strings to encode candidate solutions. Though *Binary* encodings (bit strings)

are the most common encodings; there are also *Many-Character* and *Real-Valued* encodings.

The simple structure of the GA is as below.

```
GA()
{
Initial population ;
Evaluate population ;
While termination criterion not
reached
{
select solutions for next popu-
lation ;
perform crossover & mutation ;
evaluate population ;
}
}
```

MOBILITY MODEL FOR HEALTHCARE

In the model, as in the real world, the general hospitals that work on the primary care conditions may need the help from the expert one in complicated, acute or advance cases. In this situation if the general hospital needs the help then it should ask the support from the expert hospitals (the nearest one) which can be fixed or mobile. Further, we introduced the idea of mobility for the general and expert doctors. The time is a critical factor in expert selection. The general hospital should search and based on the time required

Figure 3. Mutation operations in GA

for the mobile experts to reach to its positions, selects the one with the minimum time (T_{min}), (Khanbary, 2008).

The model simulates these interaction and communication between the different kinds of hospitals and doctors so as to obtain better utilization of them in the geographic area.

In the real medical world the expert hospitals and doctors are limited resources. The objective of the work is to obtain from the designed model, the utmost utilization of available hospital nodes and doctors (resources) in the network area. The aim is to maximize the number of services requested by the patient at a minimum time and minimize the number of dropped requests by the expert doctors that have been directed by the general hospitals.

Assumptions

We assumed the following assumptions in the model.

- There are two types of doctors *General* and *Expert*.
- The doctors are classified as *fixed* and *mobile*.
- No two mobile experts of the same specialization are allowed being at the same node at the same time (this is to improve the resource utilization).
- Experts have PDAs with authorized access to patients' records over a mobile wireless area network.
- The moving difficulties due to the geographic obstacles and barriers are not considered.

Description of the Model

In the model, the geographic area covered is called the *service area*. The medical treatment provided to the patients in the presented area is given by two types of hospitals *General* and *Expert*.

General Hospitals provide the medical support to the patient from primary or basic treatment up to medium level of treatment. In this type of hospitals there are:

- *Fixed General (FG)* doctors: These doctors are fixed and cannot move or change their positions.
- *Mobile General (MG)* doctors: these doctors have the ability to move and change their positions within the service area.

Expert Hospitals provide the expert and advance medical support to the patient. In this type of hospitals there are:

- *Fixed Expert (FE)* doctors: these doctors are fixed and cannot move or change their positions.
- *Mobile Expert (ME)* doctors: these doctors have the ability to move and change their positions within the service area.

The experts have different specializations, S_1, $S_2 S_3 S_4$.... We assumed the mobile doctors (*General* and *Expert*) are moving amongst the nodes of the service network area, as shown in figure 4. The nodes are numbered to specify its positions. The initial distribution of the nodes may be done according to the distribution of the population areas, information for which is obtained manually or using the GPS data. This is to achieve better utilization of the nodes. The positions of the fixed and mobile nodes are traced and updated using the Global Positioning System (*GPS*).

All the nodes and mobile doctors are supported by GPS transceivers, so it receives the data about the locations of all the other nodes and doctors movements in the service area and hence updating its data about all other nodes.

As shown in figure 5, experts with different specializations are roaming between the specialist

Figure 4. Representation of the mobile and fixed nodes inthenetworkservicearea

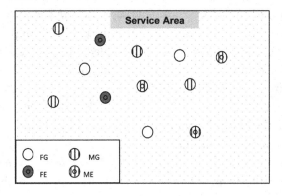

Figure 5. Network system of the service area with different MG priorities and ME specializations

nodes S_1, S_2, S_3, etc. and some general hospitals nodes having different priorities to be served, P_1, P_2, P_3, etc. in the service area.

The ME and FE use the PDAs to know the medical history of the patient, clinical information, laboratory results, including X-rays, etc. This is less time consuming for both the expert and the patient. Also the patient will avoid repeating useless clinical tests and wasting money.

Also experts will get helpful advantage by using PDAs in the countryside and rural areas since these nodes don't have advanced laboratories but the expert still can use the PDA to check for the patient medical history and decides the suitable treatment. The medical treatments given by the experts are updated automatically to the patient's record for future utilization. The general nodes request the help of experts when necessary. The

Figure 6. Network nodes of Experts and Generals at different distances

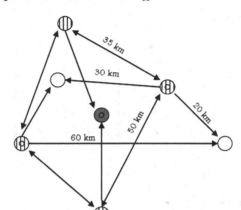

Figure 7. Dividing the service area into zones according to the population

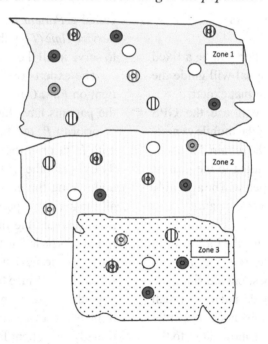

expert node accepts the request if it is not busy. So any request during busy time of the expert will be queued. A request from a general one has two levels of priority, emergency request (P_1) and normal request (P_2).

The mobile doctors, general and expert, are at various distances and are mobile with different velocities as shown by a graph in figure 6. Distances may not be straight as shown in the figure and may be zig-zag also.

Further, for better management and utilization of the resources, the service area is divided into zones according to the population density. A group of hospitals and doctors cover each of these zones as shown in figure 7.

When a patient moves to the nearest general hospital a doctor in the hospital evaluates his/her condition. If his/her condition needs expert advice then the general hospital will guide the patient to the appropriate node using the GPS technology.

Figure 8. Total Service Time distribution in the service area for a mobile expert

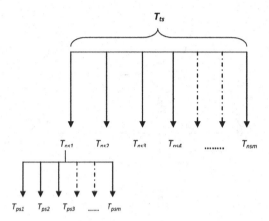

Two scenarios are possible here:

(1) The nearest required expert can be a fixed one, so the general hospital will guide the patient to the position of that expert.

(2) The general hospital will use the GPS about the movements of the mobile experts amongst the nodes for the required specialization. It guides the patient to the nearest node that the mobile expert will be available at lesser time, i.e. the shortest path.

The general hospital should take into account the fact that the nearest node from the patient's position is not always the best choice since the ME may be so far from this node and needs much time to reach it. While another node at a little far distance from the patient is more close to the required ME, so the ME will reach that node at lesser time. Hence the time required to the patient to get the service is less. Here, both the time for the patient to reach a node in addition to the time required for the ME to be at that node should be taken in to consideration.

The ME stays in each node for a specific time called a *Node Service Time (T_{ns})*, for serving the patients at that node before moving to the next node. The time required to serve one patient is called a *Patient Service Time (T_{ps})*. The *Total Service Time (T_{ts})* is the time required for the expert to serve in all the nodes as shown in figure 8.

The experts (ME and FE) will serve the patient on *First Come First Serve (FCFS)* basis, if the patients have the same priority. If a patient of priority P_1 reaches to a queue of patients all with P_2 priority then this P_1 will have the priority over all other patients except the one already undergoing the expert check. If the ME serves all the available patients in one node before the node service time finishes, i.e. no more patients required service at that node then the ME may move to the next node for better utilization of service time. Since the FE is not moving to serve any other node, its node service time is assumed to be at least four times to the ME node service time. If the patient fails to get service for his/her case in the nearest node, due to the nearest Expert's *Node Service Time* is full, then he/she is guided to the next nearest node which has the required expert and so on. If the *Total Service Time (T_{ts})* is finished then the service to this patient is failed. The movements of patients and experts amongst the node of the service area are shown in figures 9 and 10 respectively.

Encoding

The following encoding is used to simulate the designed model.

- The chromosome structure is an array of length 5, as shown in figure 11.
- The first location of the chromosome array represents the number of success services in the node.
- The second location of the chromosome array is for the number of nodes to be visited by the expert.
- The third location of the chromosome contains the information about the number of patients in that node.
- The fourth location of the chromosome represents the total service time T_{ts} of the expert.
- The fifth location of the chromosome represents the number of experts in that node.
- The chromosomes are combined together to give information about the whole network area.

Figure 9. Flow control of patients' movement

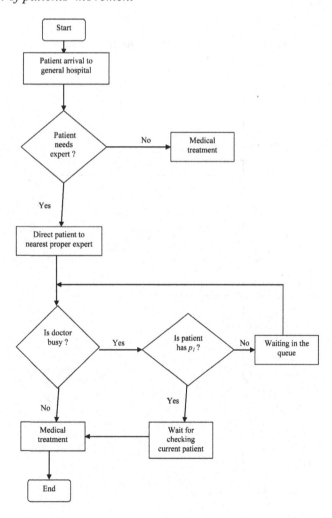

Fitness Function

The fitness function is used to measure the fitness value of each chromosome. The chromosome with the best fitness value will be selected. The fitness function used in this model is as follows:

Fitness = Patients_no + hot_nodes – expert_no – specialization_no – current_success_services

.... (1)

The *hot_node* is the node that full of patients for all the node service time T_{ns}. The *current_success_services* is the number of services successfully provided to the patients. The fittest chromosome is the one with the lowest fitness value.

ALGORITHM

The algorithm used in the pervasive healthcare model is as follows.

```
1. Input the total number of pa-
tients and experts.
2. Input number of nodes in the
service area. // to be visited
by the experts
3. Input number of specializa-
tions. // specializations number
divided randomly among experts
4. Distribute the patients ran-
```

Figure 10. Flow control movement for a mobile expert amongst nodes

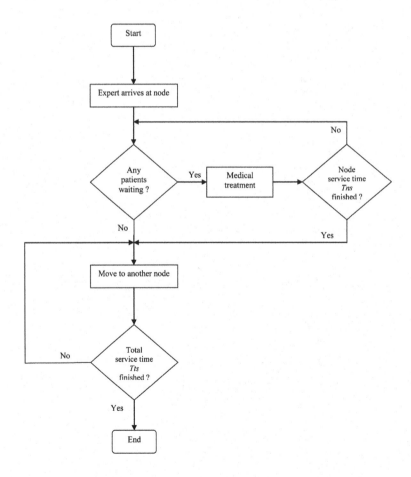

Figure 11. Chromosome structure

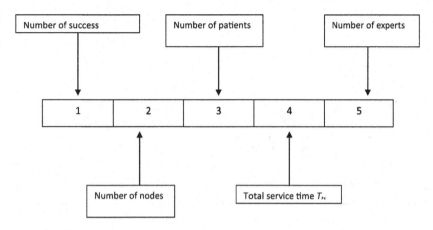

domly in the service area.
5. Assign experts to nodes as per initial demand. // based on priory knowledge
6. Input generation_ no. // for how many generations to carry out the experiment
7. Initialize generation_index=0. // used as index
8. Initialize max_success_services=0.
9. Create initial population.
10. Calculate the Total number

of current_success_services in the service area.
11. Repeat steps 12-17 until generation_index= generation_no.
12. Perform crossover ().
13. Perform mutation ().
14. Calculate the fitness (). // based on equation (1)
15. Select the best_ chromosome as the current_ chromosome.
16. Increment generation_index.
17. if (current_success_services

Figure 12. Uniform distribution of patients

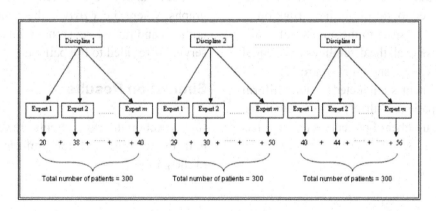

Figure 13. Non-uniform distribution of patients

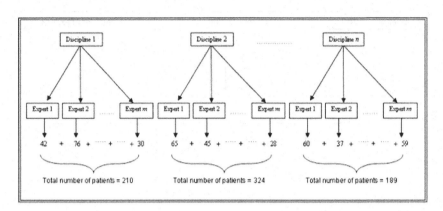

```
> max_success_services)
max_success_services = current_
success_services.
18. Output max_success_services.
```

The algorithm is designed to be executed for a number of generations, which is the termination criterion used for the simulated experiment.

SIMULATION EXPERIMENTS

In this section, the performance of the proposed algorithm is evaluated. The experiment is conducted up to 40, 50 and 60 generations to have clear observation of the convergence of the result. Total number of experts and the patients in the network are varying. To observe the effect of the patients distribution in the service area, the experiment is conducted for the uniform distribution of the patients with respect to the number of available disciplines i.e. all the disciplines have equal number of patients as shown in figure 12.

Also, experiment is conducted for non-uniform distribution of patients with respect to the available disciplines i.e. number of patients is not equal as shown in figure 13.

Simulation Parameters

The simulation parameters used in the experiment are as follows.

- The simulated network service area consists of 20 nodes.
- The different disciplines of experts are *5*.
- The input values of experts are *50, 100, 150.*
- The input values of patients are *500, 1000, 1500.*
- The average no. of patients with same type of illness is *100, 200* and *300* for the input values respectively.
- The crossover probability is *1*.
- The mutation probability is *.03*.

The results are represented in the performance graphs, where the *x-axis* is the number of generations and the *y-axis* is the number of success services provided to the patients.

Simulation Results

In this section the experiments are conducted for both the uniform and non-uniform distribution of the patients.

Figure 14. Results for 500 patients and varying experts in 60 generations

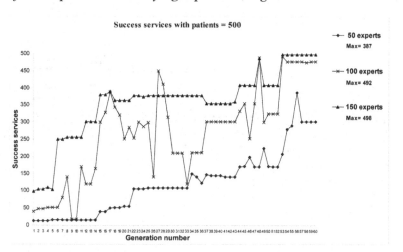

Uniform Distribution Experiment

We performed the experiment with the uniform distribution of patients to calculate the maximum number of success services up to 60 generations. The graph for the experiment with 500 patients is shown in figure 14.

The graph for the experiment with 1000 patients is shown in figure 15.

The graph for the experiment with 1500 patients is shown in figure 16.

Results obtained for the maximum success services in figures 14, 15 and 16, are summarized in the graphs shown in figures 17, 18 and 19.

Figure 15. Results for 1000 patients and varying experts in 60 generations

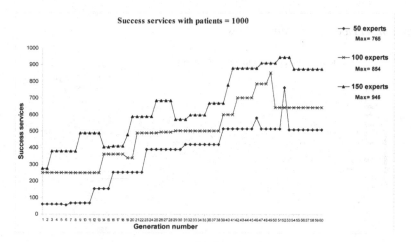

Figure 16. Results for 1500 patients and varying experts in 60 generations

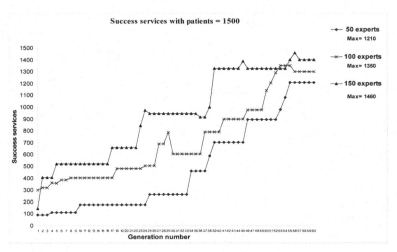

Figure 17. Maximum services in 40 generations

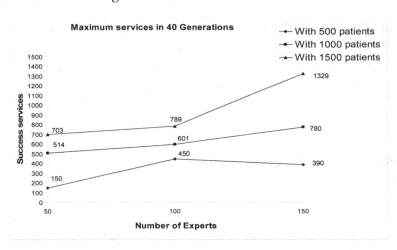

Figure 18. Maximum services in 50 generations

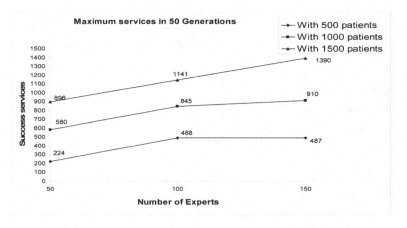

Figure 19. Maximum services in 60 generations

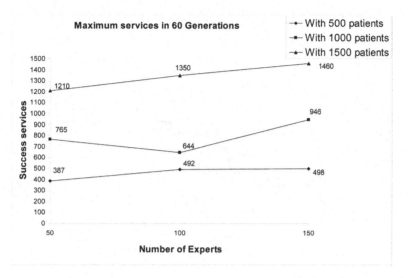

Figure 20. Results for 500 patients and varying experts in 60 generations

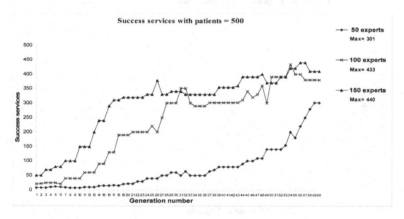

Figure 21. Results for 1000 patients and varying experts in 60 generations

Figure 22. Results for 1500 patients and varying experts in 60 generations

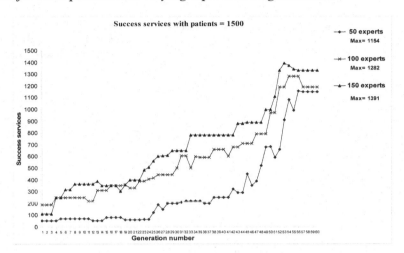

Figure 23. Maximum services in 40 generations

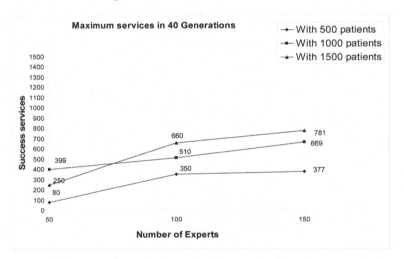

Non-Uniform Distribution of Patients

The following experiments performed with the non-uniform distribution of patients. The graph for the experiment with 500 patients is shown in figure 20.

The graph for the experiment with 1000 patients is shown in figure 21.

The graph for the experiment with 1500 patients is shown in figure 22.

Results obtained for the maximum success services in figures 20, 21 and 22, are summarized in the graphs shown in figures 23, 24 and 25.

Observations

From the performance graphs, the following observations are made.

There is an obvious maximization in the number of success services provided to the patients over the generations, in both uniform and non-uniform distribution of the patients i.e. there is an improvement in the resource utilization.

The efficient distribution and well-managed movements of the experts among the nodes, produce good results by increasing greatly the number of success services over the generations (figures 17-19, 23-25).

Figure 24. Maximum services in 50 generations

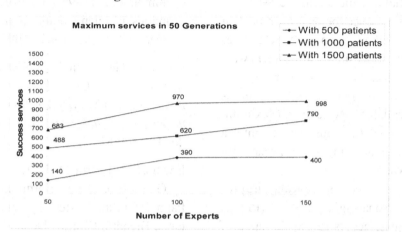

Figure 25. Maximum services in 60 generations

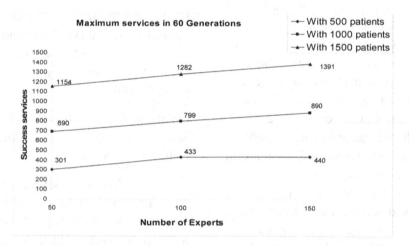

The convergence in the values of success services is remarkable only when the number of patients is very high compared to the available experts.

The initial distribution of the experts in the service area, based on the past experience, greatly increases the number of success services.

Although in some cases the number of experts is small compared to the number of patients, still the model performs better, as shown in figure 16, where the success services for 50, 100 &150 experts are 80.7%, 90% & 97.3% respectively.

The non-uniform distribution of patients may result, in some cases, in less number of success services compared to the uniform distribution but it is more realistic and proves the importance of the initial distribution of specialists from past experience.

CONCLUSION

In this work a GA based mobility management model for healthcare services has been simulated. The work shows the utilization of the mobility of the devices, with the aid of the GPS, to service the patients in the medical service area.

It is shown how a limited number of experts directed by the general hospitals are utmost utilized. The initial distribution to the resources (fixed and mobile) produces better utilization than the conventional methods. Also the model utilizes the available total service time in an efficient way. The model maximizes the usage of the resources, general and experts, with more emphasis on utilization of the available service time. Maximum number of patients will get medical treatment in a lesser time, i.e. without losing time for searching or waiting the experts.

It is also obvious that equipping healthcare professionals, with personal digital assistants (PDAs) that enable adequate access to a wide range of patients' medical records over a wireless network is an important step in better serving larger number of patients and hence improves the efficiency and utilization of the healthcare services.

A simulation study to observe and evaluate the performance of this model to serve the patient has been carried out. It is found that over the generations, the number of success services increases and result converges after certain generations. Conspicuous is the success rate when the number of patients is large in both uniform and non-uniform distribution of the patients.

This model may prove to be a useful one when it is used for the healthcare services. With the rapid increase in mobile devices, it will be possible to utilize them for healthcare. This model will set fourth a direction for these services.

REFERENCES

Beuscart, R., Renard, J.-M., Delerue, D., & Souf, A. (1999). Telecommunication in Healthcare for a Better Coordination between Hospitals and GP's: Routine Application of the "ISAR- Telematics" Project. *IEEE Transactions on Information Technology in Biomedicine*, 3(2), 101–108. doi:10.1109/4233.767085

Clemmer, T. P. (1995). The role of medical informatics in telemedicine. *Journal of Medical Systems*, 19, 47–58. doi:10.1007/BF02257190

Davis, K., Heitmann, L., Kollatschny, S., & Lessard, C. (1996). Challenges Facing Technology Assessment in Modern Health Care. *IEEE Engineering in Medicine and Biology*, 15(5), 55–59. doi:10.1109/51.537058

Enders, S. J., Pharm, D., Enders, J. M., & Holstad, S. G. (2002). Drug-Information Software for Palm Operating System Personal Digital Assistants: Breadth, Clinical Dependability and Ease of Use. *Pharmacotherapy*, 22(8), 1036–1040. doi:10.1592/phco.22.12.1036.33601

Fischer, S., Stewart, T., Mehta, S., Wax, R., & Lapinsky, S. (2003). Handheld computing in medicine. *Journal of the American Medical Informatics Association*, 10(2), 139–149. doi:10.1197/jamia.M1180

Goldberg, D. E. (2005). *Genetic Algorithms in Search, Optimization, and Machine Learning*. Delhi, India: Pearson.

Ioannis, E., Maria, K., Markaki, E., & Vasilakos, A. V. (2000). A Hybrid Genetic Approach for Channel Reuse in Multiple Access Telecommunication Networks. *IEEE Journal on Selected Areas in Communications*, 18(2), 234–243. doi:10.1109/49.824804

Khanbary, L. M. O., & Vidyarthi, D. P. (2008). A GA Based Fault-Tolerant Model for Channel Allocation in Mobile Computing. *IEEE Transactions on Vehicular Technology*, 57(3), 1823–1833. doi:10.1109/TVT.2007.907311

Khanbary, L. M. O., & Vidyarthi, D. P. (2008). Mobility Management Model for Healthcare Services. In *Proceedings of the International Conference on High Performance Computing, Networking and Communication Systems* (pp.47-53), Orlando, FL.

Lapinsky, A., Weshler, J., Mehta, S., Varkul, M., Hallett, D., & Stewart, T. (2001). Handheld computers in critical care. *Critical Care (London, England)*, 5(4), 227–231. doi:10.1186/cc1028

Loos, C. (2002). E-Health with Mobile Grids: The Akogrimo Heart Monitoring and Emergency Scenario. *Akogrimo consortium, Information society*. Retrieved from http://www.Akogrimo.org/download/White_Papers_and_Publications.

Mahapatra, S. S., Roy, K., Banerjee, S., & Vidyarthi, D. P. (2006). Improved Genetic Algorithm for Channel Allocation with Channel Borrowing in Mobile Computing. *IEEE Transactions on Mobile Computing*, 5(7), 884–892. doi:10.1109/TMC.2006.99

McClean, S. M., F., & Millard, P. (2006). Using Markov Models to assess the Performance of a Health and Community Care System. In *Proceedings of the 19th IEEE Symposium on Computer-Based Medical Systems*, (pp.777-782).

Mei-Ju, S., et al. (2005). Application of Wireless Network in a Medical Emergency Service Network. In *IEEE Proceedings of 7th International Workshop on Enterprise Networking and Computing in Healthcare Industry, 23-25 Jun*, (pp.45-50).

Mitchell, M. (1999). *An Introduction to Genetic Algorithms*. London: MIT Press.

Pavlovski, C., Kim, H., & Wood, D. (2004). Ubiquitous Mobility in Clinical Healthcare. *IEEE Proceedings of the IDEAS Workshop on Medical Information Systems: The Digital Hospital, 1-3 Sept.* (pp.147 – 153).

Ramani, K. V. (2004). IT Enabled Applications in Government Hospitals in India: Illustrations of telemedicine, e-governance, and BPR. In *IEEE Proceedings of the 37th International Conference on System Sciences, 5-8 Jan*, (pp.8), Hawaii.

Rodríguez, M. D., Favela, J., Martínez, E. A., & Muñoz, M. A. (2004). Location-Aware Access to Hospital Information and Services. *IEEE Transactions on Information Technology in Biomedicine*, 8(4), 448–455. doi:10.1109/TITB.2004.837887

Smits, M., & Pijl, G. (1999). Developments in Hospital Management and Information Systems. In *IEEE Proceedings of the 32nd International Conference on System Sciences, 5-8 Jan*, 9, Hawaii.

Stolworthy, Y. & Suszka-Hildebrandt, S. (2001). Mobile Information Technology at the Point-of-Care. *Medscape Nurses*, 3(1).

Tawney, B. (2005). Analyzing the Patient Load on the Hospitals in a Metropolitan Area. In *IEEE Proceedings of Systems and Information Engineering Design Symposium, 29 April*, (pp. 215-221).

Tripathi, A. K., Sarker, B. K., Kumar, N., & Vidyarthi, D. P. (2000). A GA Based Multiple Task Allocation Considering Load. *International Journal of High Speed Computing*, 11(4).

Tripathi, A. K., Vidyarthi, D. P., & Mantri, A. N. (2006). A Genetic Task Allocation Algorithm for Distributed Computing System Incorporating Problem Specific Knowledge. *International Journal of High Speed Computing*, 8(4), 363–370. doi:10.1142/S0129053396000203

Vidyarthi, D. P., Tripathi, A. K., & Mantri, A. N. (1997). Task Partitioning Using Genetic Algorithm. *International Conference in Cognitive Systems*, India, New Delhi.

Vidyarthi, D. P., Tripathi, A. K., Sarker, B. K., & Rani, K. (2003). Comparative Study of Two GA based Task Allocation Models in Distributed Computing System. *Fourth International Conference on Parallel and Distributed Computing, Applications and Technologies*, China, Chengdu.

Wulff. (1996). *Design of Hospital Organizations*. Doctoral dissertation, Eindhoven Technical University.

Zomaya, A. Y., & Wright, M. (2002). Observation on Using Genetic Algorithms for Channel Allocation in Mobile Computing. *IEEE Transactions on Parallel and Distributed Systems, 13*(9), 948–962. doi:10.1109/TPDS.2002.1036068

ADDITIONAL READING

Charles, B. H., Hough, J., & Binshan, L. (2005). Virtual Health/Electronic Medical Record: Current Status and Perspective. *International Journal of Healthcare Technology and Management, 6*(3), 257–275. doi:10.1504/IJHTM.2005.006523

Daiping, H., et al. (2005). Study on Information System of Healthcare Services Management in Hospital. *IEEE International Conference on Services Systems and Management, 13-15 June, 2*, (pp. 1498-1501).

David, Y., & Jahnke, E. G. (2004). Planning Hospital Medical Technology Management. *IEEE Engineering in Medicine and Biology Magazine, 23*(3), 73–79. doi:10.1109/MEMB.2004.1317985

Decker, K., & Jinjiang, L. (1998). Coordinated Hospital Patient Scheduling. *IEEE Proceedings of the International Conference on Multi Agent Systems, 3-7 July*, (pp. 104-111).

Evans, J. (1992). Handling Real-World Motion Planning: A Hospital Transport Robot. *IEEE Control Systems Magazine, 12*(19), 15–19. doi:10.1109/37.120445

Favela, J., Rodriguez, M., Preciado, A., & Gonzalez, V. M. (2004). Integrating Context-Aware Public Displays into a Mobile Hospital Information System. *IEEE Transactions on Information Technology in Biomedicine, 8*(3), 279–286. doi:10.1109/TITB.2004.834391

Gagnon, M., et al. (2004). The Impact of Organizational Characteristics on Telehealth Adoption by Hospitals, *IEEE Proceedings of the 37th Annual Hawaii International Conference on System Sciences, 5-8 Jan*, (pp. 10).

Giraldo, B. F., Martinez, P., & Caminal, P. (2000). Parametric Modeling of The Hospital Activity Applied to The Simulation of Patients in Waiting-List. *IEEE Proceedings of the 22nd Annual International Conference on Engineering in Medicine and Biology Society, 23-28 July, 3*, (pp. 2334-2334).

Heng-shuen, C. (2005). Mobile Hospital: Healthcare for Anybody in Anywhere. *IEEE Proceedings of the 7th International Workshop on Enterprise Networking and Computing in Healthcare Industry, 23-25 June*, (pp. 144-149).

Jay, J. (2007). Health Information Technology: Will It Make Higher Quality and More Efficient Healthcare Delivery Possible? *International Journal of Public Policy, 2*(3), 281–297. doi:10.1504/IJPP.2007.012908

Jiahua, L., Yue, Z., & Fukuya, I. (2008). Using Simulation to Improve Outpatient Appointment System with Minimum Change. *Proceeding of the 17th Annual International Conference on Health Sciences Simulation: Health Services*, (pp. 507-512), Ottawa, Canada.

Khorramshahgol, B., Al-Barmil, J., & Stallings, R. W. (1995). TQM in Hospitals and The Role of Information Systems in Providing Quality Services. *IEEE Proceedings of the Annual International Conference in Global Engineering Management: Emerging Trends in Asia Pacific, 25-28 June*, (pp. 196-199).

Kreutzer, M., Kharner, M., & Falk, H. (2004). Service Discovery with Higher Order Services in Mobile Hospitals. *IEEE Proceedings of the 17th Symposium on Computer-Based Medical Systems, 24-25 June*, (pp. 460-465).

Maass, M., & Eriksson, O. (2006). Challenges in the Adoption of Medical Information Systems. *IEEE Proceedings of the 39th Annual Hawaii International Conference on System Sciences, 04-07 Jan, 5*, (pp. 95b-95b).

Manlu, L., & Xiangnan, L. (2000). Healthcare Quality Management in China Hospitals. *IEEE Proceedings of the International Conference on Management of Innovative and Technology, 1, 12-15 Nov.*, (pp. 12-15).

McClean, S., & Millard, P. (2006). Using Markov Models to Manage High Occupancy Hospital Care. *IEEE Conference Intelligent Systems*, (pp. 256-260).

Prajakta, K., & Yusuf, O. (2007). Requirements and Design Space of Mobile Medical Care. *ACM SIGMOBILE Mobile Computing and Communications Review, 11*(3), 12–30. doi:10.1145/1317425.1317427

Qiang, S., & Xiaoyun, Y. (2006). Simulation and Optimization of the Hospital Registration Process Using MedModel. *IEEE International Conference on Service Operations and Logistics, and Informatics, 21-23 June*, (pp. 102-106).

Shaw, B., & Marshall, A. H. (2005). A Bayesian Approach to Modeling Inpatient Expenditure. *IEEE Proceedings on the 18th Symposium Computer-Based Medical Systems, 23-24 June*, (pp. 491-496).

Xinsheng, L., Yonghong, Z., & Jing, B. (2000). Development of A Healthcare Service Network for Community Residents. *IEEE Proceedings of the 22nd Annual International Conference in Engineering in Medicine and Biology Society, 23-28 July, 1*, (pp. 271-274).

Yanbing, J., Aihua, W., & Fengchun, Z. (2006). Analysis of One Hospital Using Simulation. *IEEE international Conference on Service Operations and Logistics, and Informatics, 21-23 June*, (pp. 170-174).

Yao-Yang, S., Roberson, G. H., Wenyaw, C., & Dung-Tsa, C. (1998). A Stochastic Model for Scheduling Programs to Maximize Outcome [of hospital profits]. *IEEE Proceedings of the 11th Symposium on Computer-Based Medical Systems, 12-14 June*, (pp. 113-116).

Yaw-Jen, L., Cheng-Chin, H., & Chin-Dar, F. (2007). A Hospital Applied Circuit Back Up Framework for External Network Services, *IEEE 9th International Conference on e-Health Networking, Application and Services, 19-22 June*, (pp. 156-161).

KEY TERMS AND DEFINITIONS

Healthcare: Refers to the treatment and management of illness, and the preservation of health through services offered by the medical, dental, pharmaceutical, clinical laboratory sciences (in vitro diagnostics), nursing, and allied health professions. Healthcare embraces all the goods and services designed to promote health, including "preventive, curative and palliative interventions, whether directed to individuals or to populations".

Hospital Information System: (HIS): Is a comprehensive, integrated information system designed to manage the administrative, financial and clinical aspects of a hospital. This encompasses paper-based information processing as well as data processing machines.

Mobility Models: Represent the movement of mobile users, and how their location, velocity and acceleration change over time.

Optimization: Improving a system to reduce runtime, bandwidth, memory requirements, or other property of a system.

Genetic Algorithm (GA): Is a search technique used in computing to find exact or approximate solutions to optimization and search problems. GA uses techniques inspired by evolutionary biology such as inheritance, mutation, selection, and crossover (also called recombination).

Chromosome: Is a set of parameters which define a proposed solution to the problem that the genetic algorithm is trying to solve. The chromosome is often represented as a simple string although a wide variety of other data structures are also used.

Selection: During each successive generation, a proportion of the existing population is selected to breed a new generation. Individual solutions are selected through a fitness-based process.

Crossover: Is a genetic operator used to vary the programming of a chromosome or chromosomes from one generation to the next. It is analogous to reproduction and biological crossover, upon which genetic algorithms are based.

Mutation: Is a genetic operator used to maintain genetic diversity from one generation of a population of chromosomes to the next. It is analogous to biological mutation.

Fitness Function: Is a particular type of objective function that quantifies the optimality of a solution (that is, a chromosome) in a genetic algorithm so that that particular chromosome may be ranked against all the other chromosomes.

Global Positioning System (GPS): Is a global navigation satellite system (GNSS) developed by the United States Department of Defense and managed by the United States Air Force 50th Space Wing. It is the only fully functional GNSS in the world, can be used freely, and is often used by civilians for navigation purposes. It uses a constellation of between 24 and 32 medium Earth orbit satellites that transmit precise radio wave signals, which allow GPS receivers to determine their current location, the time, and their velocity.

Personal Digital Assistant (PDA): Is a hand-held computer, also known as a palmtop computer. Newer PDAs also have both color screens and audio capabilities, enabling them to be used as mobile phones (smart phones), web browsers, or portable media players. Many PDAs can access the Internet, intranets or extranets via Wi-Fi, or Wireless Wide-Area Networks (WWANs). Many PDAs employ touch screen technology.

Section 5
Pervasive Education

Chapter 15

Student Learning in an Online Environment:
Differences in Study Approaches

Rodney Arambewela
Deakin University, Geelong, Australia

ABSTRACT

The increasing class sizes, changing expectations, diversity and mobility of students and the use of computer technology in teaching have challenged universities, world over, to review educational courses and delivery to provide a more satisfying learning experience to students. Understanding how students learn is essential in this process and continuous enquiry into teaching practices for their effectiveness towards enhancement of student learning outcomes is therefore considered a vital strategy. This chapter discusses an exploratory study on the differences in the learning approaches of a group of students in a second year marketing course in an Australian university. E-learning system remains the primary communication and the learning resource of these students. Results indicate that there are no significant differences in the study approaches of students but on average they seem to demonstrate deep learning than surface learning although they may differ in terms of the learning contexts. The study also reveals that in comparison female students and older aged students seem to demonstrate deep learning orientations than surface learning orientations.

INTRODUCTION

The higher education sector, the world over, is faced with the challenging task of servicing an increasingly diverse and mobile student community in the globally competitive education market. The significant growth in the number of international

students from different backgrounds entering universities has made the task more demanding. The different study approaches and learning styles of students influenced by their prior learning backgrounds (Ramburuth and McCormick 2001; Prosser and Trigwell, 1999) and their exposure to a variety of teaching methods while studying in universities (Biggs, 1999 & 1987) are among the major pedagogical challenges faced by universities

DOI: 10.4018/978-1-61520-741-1.ch015

in its efforts to ensure effective learning outcomes for students. Additionally, the increased use of computer based technologies for the delivery of teaching material has posed further challenges to the academia.

The issue therefore is how universities should address the learner differences in designing curricula and modes of delivery to improve the quality of teaching and learning. In this context, understanding how students learn is essential and continuous inquiry into teaching methods and strategies to assess their effectiveness becomes vital. Biggs (2003) argues that teaching quality is a joint responsibility of the teachers and the institutions; while the individual teacher takes responsibility for improvement in teaching, institutions will need to take responsibility for the quality enhancements in the whole delivery system.

The aim of this chapter is to discuss a research study on learning orientations of a group of students in an Australian university and their variances based on age and gender. The chapter is structured as follows. Following a brief background and a literature review, it will discuss the research design and the research findings before outlining the implications and directions for further research.

BACKGROUND

The students participated in the study belong to a second year marketing course in an undergraduate commerce degree. The subject is offered each year in multiple campuses both as on campus and off campus modes with face to face teaching supported by an E-learning system (WebCT equivalent) as the primary communication and learning resource for both modes. The course attracts around 300 students each semester. Two hour lectures and one hour tutorial classes are conducted each week and the tutorials are focussed on discussions on topics and concepts covered in the lecture of the previous week, chapter end questions and selected

case studies. Students are able to access the suggested answers to tutorial questions discussed in each tutorial the following week and to engage in a discussion with teachers and their peers via the E-learning system discussion folder. The assessment regime comprise of well paced three progressive assessment tasks – multiple choice test, learning reflections and the final exam. The first two assessment tasks are conducted online.

The increased dependency of some students on the E- learning system as their only learning resource and less exposure to face to face teaching has been of concern to many academics (Saunders and Klemming, 2003;Jackson, 2003). This is due to the fact that many students work either full time or part time although they are enrolled as full time day students or they consider internet based learning resources are more than adequate to achieve a pass. This would inevitably have implications on student learning environment, teaching strategies, and the uniformity of assessment. Less face to face contact for some students has reduced opportunities for the application of different teaching and learning contexts which cannot be delivered successfully to students who depend entirely on the online environment for all their learning resources. For the purpose of this study, lectures and tutorial classes are considered as the learning environment and tutorial discussions, group work and assessment processes are regarded as the learning context.

LITERATURE REVIEW

There is a large body of literature in relation to how students learn and are taught and the impact of social, cultural and past educational background on their own learning. According to learning theories individual learning differs in view of the different ways of processing information. This has prompted the educators and researchers to identify different learning styles or approaches which are useful in understanding the learning needs of students.

Universities and teachers have responded to the challenge of improving the quality of the learning outcomes of students with various internal reforms, strategies and practices. However, the teaching quality improvement represents a major challenge requiring continuous adjustment to teaching methods particularly with the increasing internationalisation of higher education. This has resulted in a greater diversity of the student population with varying demands and expectations. While it is a challenge common to all countries of the world and particularly those attracting large numbers of international students, Australian experience has been extraordinary given its large intake of international students. During 2002-2003, international students represented 18% of Australia's tertiary enrolments; highest among all other international education service providers in the world (UNESCO, 2005). A recent report by Banks et al (2007) indicates that Australia attracts students from more than 120 countries in the world. In addition, the migration trends, greater access to higher education (Ramsden, 1999), particularly the diversification of access to disenfranchised groups and new 'clients' such as working adults, older learners and learners at a distance (Middlehurst, 2004) have contributed to this increasing diversity in Australian student population.

The literature suggests that planning courses and teaching methods require a strong alignment with different learning approaches of students which relates to changes in curricula and how they are delivered (Smith, 2002). Several different learning approaches and styles have been identified in the literature although there appears to be a consensus that students in higher education show a limited number of different approaches to learning, albeit with some cultural variations (Kalantzis and Cope, 2000; Richardson, 1990). Although different views have been expressed on variances in student learning orientations and study approaches, very few writers have been explicit in terms of the matching strategies to

improve teaching and learning outcomes. In one of the earliest contributions in the area, Marton and Saljo (1976) identified "two levels of processing" of the material to be learned, namely under-surface- and deep-level learning. Kolb (1976; 1984) classified students into four groups of learners - divergers, convergers, assimilators and accommodators. Honey and Mumford (1982) also identified four groups of learners - activists, reflectors, theorists and pragmatists. Vermunt (1996, 1998) suggested that learning styles are also related to culture and social environment, meaning that program structure or curriculum design may not be able to be global in nature. Kalantzis and Cope (2000, p47) stated that the "curriculum experience needs to include explicit strategies to negotiate differences".

It is unlikely that an educational program could cater to each student's individual learning style or approach, but there may be opportunities for some degree of *congruent customization,* whereby a variety of teaching styles are used to address variation in learning approaches (De Vita, 2001). This requires a high degree of integration across subjects within a degree where coordinated program development caters for heterogeneous student groups. In this context, the investigation of how cultural background influences the development of individual learning style preferences and how educational institutions utilise this information to diversify delivery methods become relevant (De Vita, 2001). A good understanding of how students learn is important not only in terms of improving the teaching quality but also to dispel the misconceptions surrounding non traditional and international students. Research conducted by Sillitoe et al (2002) indicated that cultural stereotyping of students' approaches to learning has produced unsustainable positions regarding Asian students when they are labelled as shallow learners, non analytical, conservative and who demonstrate surface approach to learning with tendency towards regurgitation of teaching. Their findings however indicate that Asian students possess requisite analytical skills and the abilities of deep learning, though the new learning environment may act as a barrier for independent learning behaviour expected from tertiary students, at least in the early stages of their university life.

Three broad learning approaches (deep, surface and achieving) with two other subscales – motivation and strategy were conceptualised by Biggs (1987) in his Study Process Questionnaire (SPQ). The theoretical basis was that the students' approach to learning is not a stable trait and is subject to change with the learning environment and the learning context (Zeegers, 2002). As a result students learn differently in different situations and their study approaches (surface or deep) vary according the academic task. Ramsden (1992) has confirmed that the context of learning and learning orientations influence the learning outcomes of students.

Biggs (1987) original 3P model of learning emphasised the interrelationships and interactions between three phases – *presage, process* and *product* factors of learning. *Presage* relates to student experiences before learning takes place, *process* accounts for strategies while learning is taking place and *product* focuses on outcomes after learning has taken place. SPQ 3P model which comprised 42 scale items in 6 sub-scales has been used in several research projects including cross cultural studies (Zhang, 2000) with consistent results confirming its scale reliabilities.

The model however was subject to criticism for not representing the changed educational environment since 1970's when it was first developed. Zeegers (2001) and Richardson (1990) proposed revisions with reductions in the scale items. In 2001, Biggs himself decided that the original model needs further refinements to accommodate the new developments in the university educational sector following his collaborative research with Kember and Leung (Biggs et al, 2001). This resulted in a 2 factor, 2 sub-scale model (SPQ2F) representing only deep and surface with motive and strategy sub-scales. The revised model with only 20 items was rationalised on the basis of practicality in terms of quicker and easier administration by regular teachers to monitor teaching context, apart from the need for adaptation for the new educational environment. In encouraging the use of the revised model for inquiry into teaching practice, Biggs et al (2001, p. 145) indicate that the new model "will be an ideal tool for teachers to us in evaluating and researching their own classrooms" with a view to promoting deep approaches to learning.

Deep approach to learning is defined as the intention to establishing mastery of the material and integration of it into the learner's existing knowledge base while surface approach is identified as the intention to achieve short-term memorisation of the material so that it may be reproduced, for example in an assessment (Cuthbert, 2005). However, as Ramsden (2003) pointed out learning approach cannot be considered as a characteristic of an individual person and something that can be inferred from observing one's behaviour. It is also incorrect to associate 'low ability' with surface approaches or to consider deep approach in a complementary fashion. Research has proved that students are capable of both deep and surface approaches and it should be viewed in the relational point of view. Therefore the intention to adopt a surface (reproduce information) or a deep approach (seek meaning) is seen as a consequence of how students interpreted the context of learning i.e. the learning approach adopted by a student can vary with demands of the tasks. Nonetheless, there is consensus among educational researchers that deep approach to learning leads to better outcomes and it should be the focus of tertiary education (Ramsden, 2003; Biggs, 2003). Students' approach to learning and learning outcomes are interconnected with their previous experiences, content to be learned, and the methods of teaching and assessment associated with the content, and therefore it is through establishing points of interventions within these connections that the quality of students can be enhanced (Ramsden,

2003). These may be achieved by changing the curricula, teaching methods and assessment methods. The success of this intervention however will be dependent on the institutions ability to change policies and practices related to rewarding reproductive approaches while providing inducements for meaningful learning (Ramsden, 2003).

The impact of computer technology on teaching and student learning outcomes has been investigated by a number of researchers albeit most of the studies were focussed on students in science and mathematics courses (see Williams, 2002; Aberson et al, 2000; Mason and Weller, 2000; Heines, 2000). There is general consensus among researchers that the use of information and communication technology and computer mediated delivery of study resources (e.g. WebCT) has a positive influence on study outcomes of students. However they express caution that effectiveness of technology integration in teaching and learning should not be considered as given because it depends on specific learning scenario and context. Teachers and students face a number of challenges in coping with technology integration including technical and management issues and uncritical acceptance of computer mediated learning is therefore not encouraged.

AIMS OF THE STUDY

The study had two major aims. First was to ascertain the overall study orientations of students and second to investigate whether there are differences in these learning orientations based on gender and age variables.

METHODOLOGY

The study was based on a self administered survey in two classes using the 20 item SPQ2F instrument (Biggs et al, 2001) to obtain an insight into the learning approaches of students. In order to capture students' perceptions of the delivery of the unit, additional qualitative questions were added as part two of the questionnaire. In this section, students were expected to respond to several open ended questions expressing their personal views, and experiences in relation to their learning in the unit.

The selection of students was based on convenience sampling and only students volunteering for the study was included in the sample. The sample comprised of a total of 41 students – 43% were of Asian origin. In the first section of the questionnaire, students were asked to rate each of the question on a Likert scale of 1-5, higher rating indicating a positive inclination towards a particular study approach. Indices were constructed for each of the study approach domains: Deep Approach (DA), Surface Approach (SA), Deep Motive (DM), Surface Motive (SM), and Deep Strategy (DS), Surface Strategy (SS) followed by T tests of equality of means and cross tabulations on the demographic characteristics (Age and Gender). The data was analysed using SPSS.

RESULTS

Results indicated that there were no significant differences among students in regard to the study approach domains of deep and surface learning except for minor variation related to specific questions. The analysis of responses to items as shown in Table 1 and 2 provides insight into some of the differences.

As seen in the tables above, the average indices for each student response on each of the study approaches were less than 3 (out of 5) except for some questions. The indices higher than 3 were found to be associated with questions related to deep learning approach. Though not conclusive, it would indicate that these students appear to show a tendency towards a deep learning approach.

The two sub scales (motivation and strategy) results suggested that, in the main, students seem

Table 1. Deep Approach and cross tabulation with gender and age

Deep approach	Rarely true of me	True of me	Gender Mean Age Mean Male Female 17-20(yrs) 21-24(yrs) 25-29 (yrs)		
Average	42.6	57.4	2.7 2.9 2.8 2.7 3.3		
Motivation	Gender Mean Male Female 2.8 2.9		Age Mean 17-20 (yrs) 21-24 (yrs) 25-29 (yrs) 2.8 2.7 2.6		
Strategy	Gender Mean Male Female 2.7 2.8		Age Mean 17-20 (yrs) 21-24 (yrs) 25-29 (yrs) 2.9 2.6 3.0		
Deep motivation			Rarely true of me	True of me	
Work hard if interesting			26.8	73.2	
Deep personal satisfaction			34.1	65.9	
Any topic can be interesting			36.6	63.4	
Exciting as a good book or movie			48.8	51.2	
Come to class with questions			56.1	43.9	
Average			**40.5**	**59.5**	
Deep strategy			Rarely true of me	True of me	
Test self until understand			29.3	70.7	
Need to form own conclusions			34.1	65.9	
Spend time on interesting topics			56.1	43.9	
Do suggested readings			34.1	65.9	
Use free time on interesting topics			70.7	29.6	
Average			**44.8**	**55.2**	

to adopt deep learning than surface learning though their learning orientations differ in terms of the learning contexts. This is demonstrated by the high percentages of students indicating both deep and surface learning approaches. In the case of deep learning approach there were differences in subscales of motivation and strategy indicating the influence of the learning context on student learning orientation. For example, high scores were recorded in subscale items such as "working hard is interesting" (DM), "learning provide deep personal satisfaction" (DM), "any topic can be interesting" "self test until understand" (DS), "need to form own conclusions" (DS), "come to class with questions" (DM) "Spend time on interesting topics (DS), and "use free time in interesting topics" (DS). In the case of surface approach, all

students seemed to adopt similar motivation (SM) in learning such as doing minimum work as possible, and all claimed to have used the strategy (SS) of "learning by rote". It is clear that surface learning is used as a strategy when required which supports the argument that student study approaches differ according to the tasks and the learning context.

The cross tabulation of data related to Gender and Age indicated that on average female students and older aged students seem to demonstrate deep learning approaches and less surface learning approaches. These two groups of students also showed greater motivation and strategic intent in their learning (see Table 1 and 12). An interesting finding is that the youngest age group (17-20 years) showed greater motivation and strategy than the older age group (21-24 years).

Table 2. Surface Approach and cross tabulation with gender and age

Surface approach	Rarely true of me	True of me	Gender Mean Age Mean Male Female 17-20(yrs) 21-24(yrs) 25-29 (yrs)		
Average	42.9	57.1	2.6 2.3 2.6 2.4 2.0		
Motivation	Gender Mean Male Female 2.4 2.1		Age Mean 17-20 (yrs) 21-24 (yrs) 25-29 (yrs) 2.4 2.2 2.0		
Strategy	Gender Mean Male Female 2.8 2.5		Age Mean 17-20 (yrs 21-24 (yrs) 25-29 (yrs) 2.7 2.6 2.4		
Surface motivation			Rarely true of me	True of me	
Little work as possible to pass			73.2	26.8	
Not study topics in depth			65.9	34.1	
Do minimum work to pass			63.4	36.6	
Get by memorising key sections			65.9	34.1	
Un-examined material not learnt			51.2	48.8	
Average			**63.4**	**36.6**	
Surface Strategy			Rarely true of me	True of me	
Not study un-examinable material			41.5	58.5	
Do what is set and no extra			41.5	58.5	
Remember answers to questions			39.0	61.0	
Learn some by rote			58.5	41.5	
Only study what's given in class			41.5	58.5	
Average			**44.4**	**55.6**	

Table 3. Tests of means (2 tailed): Significance

Group variable	Deep Approach	Surface Approach
Gender Age	.021 (I find most topics interesting and often spend extra time trying to obtain more information about them .018 (I find that at times studying gives me a feeling of deep personal satisfaction)	.041 (I find it is not helpful to study topics in depth. It is a waste of time, when you all need is passing acquaintance with topics) not significant
	Deep Motivation	**Surface Motivation**
Gender Age	.017 (I find that studying academic topics can at time be as exciting as a good novel or movie not significant	not significant not significant
	Deep Strategy	**Surface Strategy**
Age	not significant	not significant

Table 3 shows the 2 tailed tests of means related to Gender and Age variables and the significance of some of the scale items. It was clear that the significant differences were more prominent in deep learning approaches than in surface learning approaches. There were no significant differences in the strategy subscale, indicating that students seem to change their learning strategies according to the learning contexts.

CONCLUSION

Using the revised SPQ2 instrument (Biggs et al, 2001), this study focussed on identifying the learning approaches of students in a second year marketing course in an Australian university and the differences of these approaches between males and females and age groups.

The results indicated that there were no significant differences in the broad learning approaches of students though some variations were noted. A greater percentage of students appeared to be more inclined towards deep learning though students differed in terms of their study motivations and strategies. Based on the literature this could be interpreted as students' adaptations to different learning contexts.

Two key findings in relation to gender and age differences were that on average female students and older aged students appear to demonstrate deep learning orientations while younger students seem to change their learning orientations depending on learning tasks. Gender and age therefore remain key variables in the analysis of learning orientations of students as it was confirmed in a study by Rautopuro and Vaisanen in 2001.

Although the study was not directly related to an evaluation of the impact of the use of information and communication technology, the qualitative feedback from students on the open ended questions revealed that majority of students supported the e-learning system as a valuable learning resource. Some were, however, critical about technical breakdowns and user friendliness of the service. It appeared that none of the students seemed to have had any prior training in the use of the service which had contributed to the overall dissatisfaction. It was clear therefore that the technological environment in which the course was delivered had a significant influence on the learning orientations and outcomes of students. This area requires further research.

LIMITATIONS AND FUTURE RESEARCH

The study provided insights into the study orientations of students and their perceptions of learning experience which would be useful in assessing and reviewing the current teaching practices for their effectiveness in providing positive learning outcomes. However the small sample size and heavy focus on the investigation of one single subject and class would have an effect on the replicability and generalisation of its findings to all learning contexts. The small sample size also had an effect on the opportunities available for more rigorous statistical analysis.

Given the increased use of computer technology and E-learning systems in higher education more research should be directed towards assessing the effectiveness of the technologies currently used and the adaptability of the new and emerging technologies to meet the changing expectations and demands of student learning. This should be supplemented with research on curriculum design to maximise the effectiveness of technology adaptation in teaching.

REFERENCES

Aberson, C. L., Berger, D. E., Healy, R., Kyle, D. J., & Romero, V. L. (2000). Evaluation of an Interactive Tutorial for Teaching the Central Limit Theorem. *Teaching of Psychology*, *27*, 289–291. doi:10.1207/S15328023TOP2704_08

Banks, M., Olsen, A., & Pearson, D. (2007). *Global Student Mobility – An Australian Perspective Five Years On. IDP Australia*. New York: Prentice Hall.

Biggs, J. B. (1987). *Student approaches to learning and studying*. Camberwell, Australia: Australian Council for Educational Research.

Biggs, J. B. (1999). *Teaching for Quality Learning at University*. Buckingham, UK: The Society for Research into Higher Education and Open University Press.

Biggs, J. B. (2003). Teaching for quality learning at university, (2nd ed.). Milton Keynes, UK: SRHE and Open University Press.

Biggs, J.B., Kember, D, & Leung, D, Y, P. (2001). The revised two-factor Study Process Questionnaire: R-SPQ-2F. *The British Journal of Educational Psychology*, *71*, 133–149. doi:10.1348/000709901158433

Coffield, F., Moseley, D., Hall, E., & Ecclestone, K. (2004). Should we be using learning styles? What research has to say to practice? Report published by the Learning and Skills Research Centre, UK.

Entwistle, N. (1989). Approaches to studying and course perceptions: the case of the disappearing relationship. *Studies in Higher Education*, *14*(2), 155–156. doi:10.1080/03075078912331377466

Heines, J. M. (2000). Evaluating the effect of a course web site on student performance. *Journal of Computing in Higher Education*, *12*, 57–83. doi:10.1007/BF03032714

Jackson, P. (2003). Ten Challenges for introducing Web-supported learning to overseas students in the social sciences . *Active Learning in Higher Education*, *4*(1), 87–106. doi:10.1177/1469787403004001007

Kalantzis, M., & Cope, B. (2000). Towards an inclusive and international education . In King, R., Hill, D., & Hemmings, B. (Eds.), *University Diversity*. Wagga Wagga, Australia: Keon Publications.

Keefe, J. W. (1979). Learning Style: an Overview . In Keefe, J. W. (Ed.), *Student Learning Styles: Diagnosing and Prescribing Programs*. Reston, VA: NAASP.

Marton, F., & Säljö, R. (1976). On qualitative differences in learning: Outcome and Process. *The British Journal of Educational Psychology*, *46*, 4–11.

Marton, F., & Säljö, R. (1997). Approaches to learning . In Marton, F., Hounsell, D., & Entwistle, N. (Eds.), *The experience of learning: Implications for teaching and studying in higher education*.

Mason, R., & Weller, M. (2000). Factors Affecting Students Satisfaction on a Web Course. *Australian Journal of Educational Technology*, *16*(2), 173–200.

Mc Keachie, S. J. (1995). Learning styles can become learning strategies. *The National Teaching and Learning Forum*, *4*(6), 1–2.

Mc Keachie, S. J. (1995). Learning styles can become learning strategies. *The National Teaching and Learning Forum*, *4*(6), 1–2.

Middlehurst, R. & Woodfied, S. (2003). *The role of transnationals, private and for profit provision in meeting global demand for tertiary eduction: mapping, regulation and impact*, Centre for Policy and Change in Tertiary Education, University of Surrey, Report commissioned by the Commonwealth of Learning and UNESCO.

Ramburuth, P., & McCormick, J. (2001). Learning Diversity in Higher Education: A comparative study of Asian international and Australian Students. *Higher Education*, *42*, 333–350. doi:10.1023/A:1017982716482

Ramsden, P. (2003). *Learning to Teach in Higher Education* (2nd ed.). London: RoutledgeFalmer.

Richardson, J. T. E. (1990). Reliability and replicability of the approaches to studying questionnaire. *Studies in Higher Education*, *15*(2), 155. doi:10.1080/03075079012331377481

Saunders, G., & Klemming, F. (2003). Integrating technology into traditional learning environment: Reasons for and risks of success. *Active Learning in Higher Education*, *4*(1), 74–86. doi:10.1177/1469787403004001006

Smith, J. (2002). Learning Styles: Fashion Fad or Lever for Change? The Application of Learning Style Theory to Inclusive Curriculum Delivery. *Innovations in Education and Teaching International*, *39*(1), 63–70. doi:10.1080/13558000110102913

Trigwell, K. H., & Prosser, M. (1996). Perceptions of the learning environment and approaches to learning university science at the topic level. In *HERDSA Conference,* Melbourne.

Williams, P. (2002). The learning web: The development, implementation and evaluation of internet-based undergraduate materials for the teaching of key skills. *Active Learning in Higher Education*, *3*(1), 40–53. doi:10.1177/1469787402003001004

Zhang, L. F. (2000). University students' Learning approaches in three cultures: An investigation of Biggs 3P model. *The Journal of Psychology*, *134*(1), 37–55. doi:10.1080/00223980009600847

ADDITIONAL READING

Alavi, M., Yoo, Y., & Vogel, D. R. (1997). Using Information Technology to Add Value to Management Education . *Academy of Management Journal*, *40*(6), 1310–1333. doi:10.2307/257035

Barome, C. A., & Hager, P. R. (2001). *Technology enhanced teaching and learning: Leading and supporting the transformation on your campus.* NY: Jossey-Bass Publication.

Bates, A. W., & Poole, G. (2003). *Effective teaching with technology in Higher Education: Foundation for success.* Indianapolis, USA: Jossey-Bass.

Berge, Z. L. (1999). Interaction in Post-Secondary Web-Based Learning . *Educational Technology*, *39*(1), 5–11.

Butler, D. L., & Selborn, M. (2002). Barriers to Adopting Technology for Teaching and Learning . *EDUCAUSE Quarterly*, *25*(2), 22–28.

Fry, H., Ketteridge, S., & Marxhall, S. (2009). *A Handbook for Teaching and Learning in Higher Education: Enhancing Academic Practice* (3rd ed.). Taylor & Francis Group.

Garrison, D. R., & Kanuka, H. (2004). Blended learning: Uncovering its transformative potential in higher education. *The Internet and Higher Education*, *7*(2), 95–105. doi:10.1016/j.iheduc.2004.02.001

Graham, C., Cagiltay, K., Craner, J., Lim, B., & Duffy, T. M. (2000). *Teaching in a Web-based distance learning environment: An evaluation summary based on four courses. Center for Research on Learning and Technology Technical Report No. 13-00.* Indiana University Bloomington

Groves, M. M., & Zemel, P, C. (2000). Instructional Technology Adoption in Higher Education: An Action Research Case Study. *International Journal of Instructional Media*, *27*(1), 57–65.

Jason, L. F. (2000). The information-age Mindset: Changes in students and implications for Higher Education . *EDUCAUSE Review*, *35*(5), 16.

Jonassen, D. H., & Peck, K. L & Wilson, B.G. (1999). Learning with technology: A constructivist perspective, Merill Columbus, OH.

Knight, P. (2002). *Being a teacher in Higher Education*. Maidenhead, UK: Society for Research in Higher Education and the Open University Press.

Laurillard, D. (2002). *Re-thinking University Teaching* (2nd ed.). RouledgeFarmer.

Mishra, P., & Koehler, M. J. (2006). Technological Pedagogical Content Knowledge: A Framework for Teacher Knowledge [Columbia University.]. *Teachers College Record, 108*(6), 1017–1054. doi:10.1111/j.1467-9620.2006.00684.x

Oblinger, D. G., & Iblinger, J. L. (2005). *Educating the next generation*. USA: Educause.

Privateer, P. M. (1999). Academic Technology and the future of Higher Education: Strategic Paths taken and not taken . *The Journal of Higher Education, 70*(1), 60–79. doi:10.2307/2649118

Roblyer, M. D., Edwards, J., & Havriluk, M. A. (1997). *Integrating educational technology into teaching*. NJ: Prentice Hall.

Rogers, P. L. (2000). Barriers to Adopting Emerging Technologies in Education . *Journal of Educational Computing Research, 22*(4), 455–472. doi:10.2190/4UJE-B6VW-A30N-MCE5

Schacter, J. (1999). *The Impact of Education Technology on Student Achievement: What the Most Current Research Has to Say*, Milken Exchange on Education Technology, Milken Family Foundation, California, www.milkenexchange.org

Stephenson, J. (2001). *Teaching and Learning Online: New pedagogies for new technologies*. RoutledgeFarmer.

Tolmie, A., & Boyle, J. (2001). Factors influencing the success of computer mediated communication (CMC) environments in university teaching: A view and case study . *Computers & Education, 34*(2), 119–140. doi:10.1016/S0360-1315(00)00008-7

Young, J. R. (2002). "Hybrid" Teaching Seeks To End the Divide between Traditional and Online Instruction. *The Chronicle of Higher Education, 48*(28), 33–34.

KEY TERMS AND DEFINITIONS

Study Process Questionnaire (SPQ): An instrument developed by Biggs (1987) to examine learning approaches of students. The original version SPQ3P (Study Process Questionnaire with three phases – Presage, process and product and used to identify three broad learning approaches (deep, surface and achieving with two other subscales of motivation and strategy). The original model was subject to criticism and the revised version; SPQ2F (Study Process Questionnaire 2 Factor: Deep and Surface with two subscales: Motivation and Strategy) was developed in 2001 and assess the study approaches using 20 items only.

Learning Environment: The learning environment, within the context of Student Approaches to Learning is characterized by situational factors such as learning task, assessment, content, activities, discipline, teaching method, time on task and course structure. .

Learning Context: Part of the learning environment and may include teaching methods and strategies such as class discussions, group work and assessment processes

Chapter 16
Pervasive Computing and Ambient Intelligence Development:
An Educational Perspective

Vladimír Bureš
University of Hradec Kralove, Czech Republic

Pavel Čech
University of Hradec Kralove, Czech Republic

ABSTRACT

Ambient Intelligence (AmI) as an environment, where pervasive computing methods, tools, or products are taking place, is a concept envisioning information society in the future. AmI can be investigated from several points of view, whereas a technological perspective is the one most frequently presented. However, as the fragments of AmI vision are becoming reality, the educational perspective is of growing importance. Managerial workplace may be considered as a typical environment where pervasive, or ubiquitous, computing and AmI are being currently introduced. Hence, the proper education of future managers or IT specialists should aim at students' ability to define requirements for the structure and behaviour of AmI from different viewpoints and from final users' perspective namely. The problem is that AmI is a system with high level of complexity due to the need to unite many related aspects from different problem domains. Therefore, relevant tools and methods should be taught so that students can comprehend such a complexity. A brief description of the situation in the selected Czech university and results based on particular tools and methodological approaches are depicted in the following chapter.

INTRODUCTION

Information and communication technologies (ICT) represent the key facilitator of many changes in contemporary business environment. Information and communication technologies enable for communication cost reduction or ensure information to be at the right place in the right time for precise decision-making process. Information and communication technologies make possible to have the best of both worlds – the economic and scale efficiencies of large organizations, and the human benefits of

DOI: 10.4018/978-1-61520-741-1.ch016

small ones: freedom, motivation, creativity, and flexibility (Malone, 2004). The development in the area of ICT has been significantly supported by the progress that was achieved in the field of pervasive computing. The pervasive computing is a trend towards increasingly ubiquitous connected computing devices in the environment. Therefore, another name for this movement is ubiquitous computing (Singh, 2008).

Several companies are implementing the ubiquitous computing to support their needs in various forms such as short-range wireless systems for vehicle monitoring, sensor networks for complex systems management, and context aware devices for ad hoc networking (Braley, 2005). In this sense, Ambient Intelligence (AmI) can be perceived as an environment where pervasive computing methods, approaches, tools, or products are taking place. According to van Houten (2006), AmI refers to future digital environments that are sensitive and responsive to people. Apparently, managerial workplace is a typical environment, where pervasive computing is being more or less successfully introduced.

The vision is that intelligent devices will surround us while travelling, working or doing leisure time activities. These devices and their local networks will provide us with different services that will support our particular operations. For designing and creating appropriate architecture of this intelligent environment, which will match the given requirements, it is necessary to acquire a qualitative description of future stakeholders' needs. As stated above, the everyday workplace of managers is one of the significant application areas of AmI. Faculty of Informatics and Management University of Hradec Kralove (FIM UHK) in the Czech Republic educates either future managers or IT specialists. Its students represent prospective managers or employees providing essential technological support to an organizational management. Therefore, they should be able to impose requirements for the structure and behaviour of AmI from the point of view of final users.

Moreover, they should be able to participate in the development of solutions that form AmI.

The *problem* is that although the concept of AmI has a strong technological orientation, there are also social, psychological, ethical or political dimensions that have to be taken into account. These are briefly described in the following paragraphs. The successful application of AmI requires entwining technological, managerial and other aspects into a complex system (i.e. to consider AmI as a "soft" system in the systems approach terminology). One needs appropriate tools or techniques to be able to comprehend such complexity and people in general, and managers in particular, usually do not possess the needed skills or tools. The main objectives of this chapter is to briefly describe AmI perspectives, and outline the research at FIM UHK that was conducted while investigating the educational perspective of AmI. This chapter is based on research results presented in (Bureš, 2006) and (Bureš, 2007).

UBIQUITOUS COMPUTING AND AMBIENT INTELLIGENCE BACKGROUND

The concept of the ubiquitous computing was firstly introduced by Weiser (1991) who states: "The most profound technologies are those that disappear. They weave themselves into the fabric of everyday life until they are indistinguishable from it". As stated by van 't Hooft (2007), Weiser envisioned computers embedded in artefacts that surround us – walls, chairs, clothing, or light switches; in anything and everything – and are connected to each other and the world through different types of connections. Usually, the ubiquitous computing is compared to two examples from the past which have become ubiquitous – printing and electricity (or more specifically related networked "devices", i.e. electric devices of daily usage or book and newspapers). According to Weiser (1993), the ubiquitous computing environment allows the user an access to technology at all times while the technology remains unobtrusive to the user. Practical applications of the pervasive/ubiquitous computing efforts led to idea of AmI concept that promotes pervasive, distributed technology, not intrusive, but always present (Remagnino, 2005).

AmI is a relatively new concept envisioning information society in future. Four major aspects of AmI are of crucial importance - user friendliness, effectiveness, distributed support and interactivity. AmI is primarily based on the integration of ICT into the environment so that from the point of view of the user it is absolutely non-essential with what technologies s/he is interacting; with how many applications s/he is being in contact; how the applications are related and how the applications cooperate. In fact, the user might not be even aware that he/she is interacting with technology or applications at all (Mikulecký, 2007). That is why AmI supports the shift of computing from desktop computers to various intelligent devices integrated in every day life of users. It is obvious that the technology has to have the same function for a user as a cane for blind people in AmI environment – blind people perceive and feel their canes as an integral part of their body, not a tool that can be used in case of necessity. Unfortunately, the term "integral" is sometimes misinterpreted. As described above, the integral part means something that is almost invisible since it works in the background without users' interventions. Therefore, all digital technologies and their products can not be considered as parts of the ubiquitous computing. For instance, taking a camera for shooting and sending pictures via email is not a good example of the ubiquitous computing in education as described in (van 't Hooft, 2007). Common availability of a technology does not necessarily mean that this technology is pervasive or ubiquitous.

As already pointed out, there is a closed relationship between the ubiquitous computing and AmI concepts. Vasilakos and Pedrycz (2006) stated that AmI vision required an intensive and carefully planned integration of many different and highly advanced technologies. These technologies may include energy-efficient, high-performance computing platforms; powerful media processing hardware and software, advanced user-interface designs, or multi-agent technologies (Mikulecký, 1998). Hence, AmI consists of several networks as shown in Figure 1. AmI requires the use of distributed sensors and actuators to create a pervasive technological layer, which is able to interact transparently with a user. The interaction can be performed either passively by observing and trying to interpret what the user actions and intentions are, but also actively, by learning the preferences of the user and adapting the system parameters to improve the quality of life and work of the occupant (Remagnino, 2005).

According to van Houten (2006), the AmI vision can be applied to very diverse application environments, varying from homes, offices, or cars to homes for the elderly and hospitals. It refers to a wide range of human emotional and intellectual needs, from comfort, pleasure, and entertainment to safety, security, and health. The AmI scenarios can serve as examples of such environments. They are included in the ISTAG report (Ducatel, 2001) that introduces four scenarios of the future development of a current information society. In other words, authors tried to outline the possible development of AmI in a daily life and work around 2010. Although it is obvious nowadays that described scenarios can take place in more distant future, the vision of AmI is a very attractive starting point for future research. Research areas can include intelligence agents, knowledge technologies, mobile communications, portable devices or systems integration. Besides technological issues, these scenarios offer insights in which the social and political aspects of AmI will be very important for its development (Ducatel, 2001):

Figure 1. Ambient Intelligence networks (adapted from (Vasilakos, 2006))

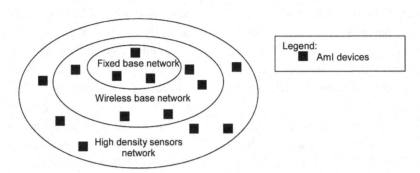

- AmI should facilitate a human contact.
- AmI should be orientated towards community and cultural enhancement.
- AmI should help to build knowledge and skills for work, better quality of work, citizenship and consumer choice.
- AmI should inspire trust and confidence.
- AmI should be consistent with a long term sustainability – personal, societal and environmental and with life-long learning. In essence, the challenge is to create an AmI landscape made up of "convivial technologies" that are easy to live with.
- AmI should be controllable by ordinary people – i.e. the "off-switch" should be within its reach: these technologies could very easily acquire an aspect of "them controlling us". The experts involved in constructing the scenarios therefore underlined the essential need that people are given the lead in a way that systems, services and interfaces are implemented.

Created scenarios are "Maria – personal ambient communicator", "Dimitrios – connecting people and expressing identities", "Carmen – traffic optimisation" and "Annette and Solomon – social learning by connecting people and creating a community memory". The basic differences among all four scenarios can be seen in Figure 2.

Four quadrants represent four alternative development paths of AmI that scenarios' authors offer to consider. There is a brief description of the required changes, basic barriers of realization and lead markets where solutions can be implemented (Ducatel, 2001):

- Maria is a scenario where the technological and socioeconomic changes are based on the existing approaches. No large changes in behaviour are assumed. The key barriers appear to be the establishment of interoperating hierarchies of agents. The lead markets for AmI here are business sector demands, which tend to be more efficiency orientated and less price-sensitive.
- Dimitrios scenario offers an alternative mode of the use of personalised ambience. The emphasis is on the play and social interaction rather than "efficiency". Lead markets for AmI may emerge first amongst "alternative or youth cultures." Changes in behaviour relate mainly to the willingness to reveal (or disguise) personality on-line. Price could be a barrier to a breakthrough to a mass market.
- Carmen scenario implies major infrastructural developments (i.e. highly developed networks of inter-operating sensor systems and dynamic database management systems). These also represent the basic barriers to realization. Scenario makes significant assumptions about changes in public behaviour such as accepting ride shares and traffic management systems.

Figure 2. Goals and actors of AmI scenarios (adapted Ducatel et al., 2001)

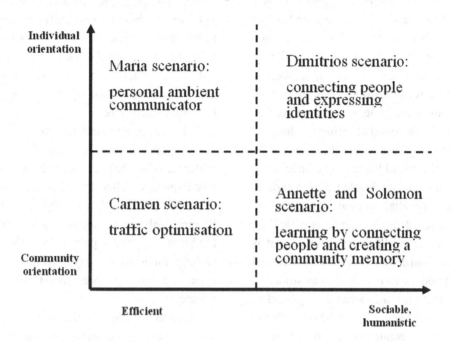

• Annette and Solomon scenario is the furthest out in terms of time, because it has high requirements both on technological and socio-economic changes. It implies significant technical developments such as a high "emotional bandwidth" for a shared presence and visualisation technologies, or breakthroughs in computer supported pedagogic techniques. In addition, the scenario presents a challenging social vision of AmI in the service of a fostering community life through the shared interests.

HOLISTIC APPROACH TO AMBIENT INTELLIGENCE

Ambient Intelligence Perspectives

The picture of the pervasive computing and AmI described in previous paragraphs emphasizes first of all the technological dimension of AmI where communication perspective, process-

ing perspective, or software perspective can be investigated. In fact, AmI is a complex system which can not be explored and understood by particular purpose simplifications. Perspectives other than the technological one were identified in previous researches. For instance, edited book (Mikulecký, 2009) offers several points of view on AmI, in which social, psychological, ethical, or political perspectives can be derived. Other perspectives such as legislative, health, financial, or educational ones may be added. The content of these perspectives is obvious from their titles. For instance, while the health perspective deals with issues such as ergonomics or electromagnetic pollution (Liu, 2000), the legislative perspective investigates how law systems in particular countries can support or prevent AmI development (e.g. the existence of strict privacy laws on video data and information), or personal information security issues. In addition, the psychological perspective deals with individual barriers that prevent successful implementation of new technologies. It also focuses on development, conceptualization, and implementation of theories and models of user actions related to decisions to accept and adopt new technology (e.g. the technology acceptance model (Davis, 1989), or the decomposed theory of planned behaviour (Taylor, 1995)), as well as challenges connected with the technology-human interface development. The social perspective investigates social factors that influence the possibilities of technology usage. These factors can be represented by the social barriers to a successful implementation of new technologies or by social "pressure" that potential receiver can perceive, i.e. the influence of social contexts (Blechar, 2005). The last but not least perspective that is presented onwards in this chapter is the educational perspective. It addresses issues such as students' and teachers' attitudes and behaviour related to the technology implementation in the educational process, the role of technology in education, or technological literacy and skills.

This more complex point of view on AmI leads to Figure 3 where other significant networks (the more general concept of systems is used) and related elements in the form of particular stakeholders, or other elements (e.g. laws or politics) are incorporated. Two significant points have to be emphasized here.

Firstly, this representation of AmI perspectives is necessarily incomplete since it is not possible to depict all related perspectives in a two-dimensional picture. Therefore, Figure 3 shows only those perspectives that appropriately represent a hierarchical system decomposition known from the hierarchy theory presented in (Weiss, 1971). Other perspectives that go through and across the hierarchy are only represented by the educational perspective.

Secondly, although the elements in form of AmI devices and participants (users or network operators) are stressed, relations are those that

Figure 3. Selected Ambient Intelligence perspectives

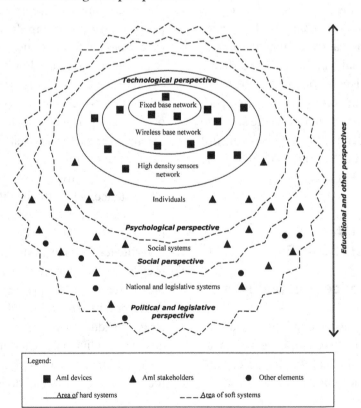

make AmI concept so promising and power-ful (albeit relations were omitted due to figure transparency). In accordance with the theory of systems the organization of particular elements, not elements themselves, is the crucial system attribute. While technological, psychological, social, legislative, or political perspectives described in Figure 3 contain relations among elements at the same level, other perspectives as health, ethical, financial, or educational perspectives go across this system and connect elements at different levels. The relations create complexity that is characteristic for the socio-technical systems. Therefore, this view on AmI assumes the movement from hard to soft systems approaches.

Ambient Intelligence and Education at FIM UHK

Systems thinking proved to be a convenient tool for AmI analysis and development in previous research (Bureš, 2006). FIM UHK offers subjects in which students of particular study programmes obtain skills and competences of mastering complexity in terms of systems thinking (ST), systems approach (SA), and object modelling (OM). In the subjects Theory of Systems I and II (TESY1 and TESY2) students get acquainted with basic principles of system thinking that is used in subsequent specialized subjects, and related system sciences and theories. While TESY1 and TESY2 are more conceptual in content, the subject Introduction to Object Modelling (IOMO) is more application oriented. It focuses on the application of ST in OM and the framework of software development process. This demonstrates how managers can contribute to the development of AmI.

When applying AmI to the business management, it is not possible to neglect achievements of respected authors in this field. Most of the educational activities are based on the distinguished work of an American mentor and consultant Peter Senge, who elaborates the concept of learning organization. ST plays a significant role in Peter Senge's work (Senge, 1990). The above mentioned subjects teach students the following concepts of a successful enterprise (Smith, 2001):

1. *Personal mastery*. According to Senge, personal mastery is the discipline of continually clarifying and deepening our personal vision, of focusing our energies, of developing patience, and of seeing reality objectively. It goes beyond competence and skills although it involves them. It goes beyond a spiritual opening although it involves the spiritual growth. Mastery is seen as a special kind of proficiency. It is not about dominance, but rather about calling. Vision is vocation rather than simply just a good idea. Therefore, the emphasis is placed on independence, critical thinking and continuum of a study in the whole study program from the beginning.

2. *Mental models*. Senge asserts that the discipline of mental models starts with turning the mirror inward; learning to unearth our internal pictures of the world, to bring them to the surface and hold them rigorously to scrutiny. It also includes the ability to carry on "learningful" conversations that balance inquiry and advocacy where people expose their own thinking effectively and make that thinking open to the influence of others. That is why students should be able to recognize in their thinking and other activities their own biases and non-functional routines. They should be able to avoid them and change their mental models. The concept of "double loop learning", in comparison to "single loop learning", is supported. For example, students are taught systems archetypes and their application in business practice.

3. *Building shared vision*. Senge says that when there is a genuine vision (as opposed to the all-to-familiar 'vision statement'), people excel and learn not because they are told to, but because they want to. But many leaders have personal visions that never get

translated into shared visions that galvanize an organization… What has been lacking is a discipline for translating vision into shared vision - not a "cookbook" but a set of principles and guiding practices. Both subjects aim to increase students' ability to explicitly express their thoughts and ideas.

4. *Team learning.* The discipline of team learning starts with a "dialogue", the capacity of members of a team to suspend assumptions and enter into a genuine "thinking together". To the Greeks dia-logos meant a free-flowing if meaning through a group, allowing the group to discover insights not attainable individually… [It] also involves learning how to recognize the patterns of interaction in teams that undermine learning. Currently, the success of an individual is based on his/her willingness and ability to work as a team member. For this reason, the educational process in both subject supports teamwork. It calls for trust, communication ability (to hear what others say), and willingness to share information.

5. *Systems thinking.* ST is the conceptual cornerstone, the fifth discipline, of Senge's approach. Disability to see interconnections in relations' dynamics leads to many deep-going problems. Systems and object thinking are mostly a new phenomena and approaches that are difficult to perceive and learn. Both subjects are therefore supported by different tools and techniques.

The IOMO subject then builds on the knowledge acquired in TESY1 and TESY2. One of the main goals of IOMO is to teach students object oriented thinking that can be harnessed for solving complex problems not only in software development. In the object oriented modelling the complexity is reduced by splitting the whole complex system into collaborating self sustained subsystems - objects. Object oriented thinking

and modelling can be used to capture complex environments consisting of mutually interlinked parts in which the cooperation is a critical factor determining properties and behaviour of the whole. Thus, we can scrutinize objects as well as environment, in which the objects exist, through the lens of the system thinking. In this manner one of the basic principles of the system thinking – the hierarchical principle - is applied in practice. If also the principle of wholeness is applied, students can achieve a broader view of AmI (e.g. they can discern the relations and intersections of AmI with social, ethical, and other aspects). IOMO then serves to display such complex system on a model. The process of modelling is in IOMO based on the best practices formulated as a methodology for describing reality and real objects and translating the real objects into their software representations. The methodology defines the basic rules, principles, roles and responsibilities that guide the actions during the process of modelling. The often used methodology in the field of software system development is the Unified Processed (UP) approach. The notation used for modelling is based on the de facto standard – UML specification. In IOMO students learn how to apply the principles given in UP on real world situations and how to describe and display the models by using the UML notation.

From the AmI point of view, all introduced methods and approaches lead to students' ability to acquire both procedural knowledge about AmI (i.e. knowing how to use technology) and conceptual knowledge about AmI (i.e. knowing about technology). The described endeavour is supported by many tools that were selected for either improvement of educational process or finding out whether this process is efficient or not. The respective research was conducted at FIM UHK. Its main hypothesis was connected to the fact that current students represent future managers. Therefore, the defined research hypothesis asserted that *appropriate education in terms of proper tools can improve the ability of stakeholders to impose requirements and contribute to the development of AmI.*

Research Methods and Data

Virtual Learning Environment Support

The biggest problem related to a learning process that students have often difficulties in freeing themselves from accustomed stereotypical ways of thinking which they use in their everyday life. This problem leads to students' inability to complete learning activities and tasks and also to the misconception of the reason why those two subjects are in the study programme. Such situation is in the direct contradiction with the ability to understand, describe and work with the concept of AmI. ST and object oriented thinking require a radical change of their mental models, i.e. the way they perceive and think about the surrounding world. This fundamental change can be accomplished by employing and/or intensifying the so-called double loop learning. This problem is identified as the most common one and thus, the one requiring most of the attention when providing students with support during their learning. That is why the subjects are supported by two e-courses. These e-courses offer students additional tools for quicker and easier elimination of the highlighted problem.

Therefore, the main stress when using the e-courses in the virtual learning environment was on the tools that enable implementation of the complete cycle of transformation of tacit and explicit knowledge, i.e. internalization, combination, externalization and socialization, also known as SECI model (Nonaka, 1995). According to Chatti (2007), these processes can be supported by many tools (see Figure 4). The retrospective analysis of the tools usage showed that utilization of provided tools was not balanced (see figures 5 and 6). Students use mostly tools for internalization (File), and externalization or combination

(Assignments and Assessments). The tools that belong into the socialization category are discussion, email, black board or chat. These tools are used only sporadically. The reason is again rooted in students' learned approach to their study acquired at secondary schools. This way is usually deeply fixed in their mental models. Therefore, the first change of mental models has to be related to learning habits and only then it is possible to continue with other desirable changes in terms of ST and OM development.

Questionnaire

An additional supportive questionnaire-based research was also conducted. Its aim was to find out, first, if students have any idea about ST and OM principles, and second, where these approaches are utilizable from the students' point of view, i.e. if ST and OM are naturally perceived as tools for AmI comprehension. The questionnaire was created by following a standard process of its elaboration, i.e. phases as questions content formulation, answers format formulation, scales setting or pre-test of a questionnaire were conducted. The process of data acquisition was divided into two main stages. In the first stage data were obtained from newly enrolled students. In the second stage data were collected from the students who had already passed the subjects. Consequently, these two groups were compared.

The analysis of data involves the sample of 98 respondents and shows interesting results. One of these results is, for example, the fact that students do not have any idea what ST or systems theory are about. And when they try to guess, they usually think that systems theory is related only to informatics or computer science. Other results show the consistency of respondents' answers. 90% of students think that ST and SA are utilizable in informatics and only 20% of them think that ST and SA can be used in a systemic science such as ecology, or management. These results confirm the problem connected with the "hard"

Figure 4. SECI model and utilizable tools (adapted from Chatti, 2007)

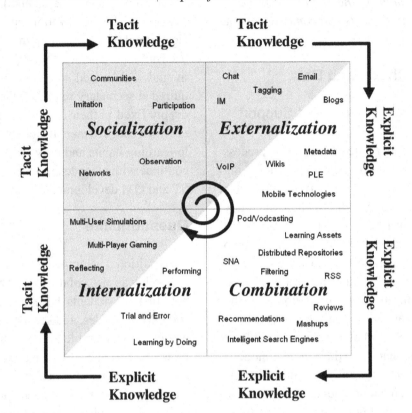

approach described in the previous paragraphs of this chapter. Students' awareness of the ST and systems theory is also influenced by the type of the secondary school they come from. Graduates from technically oriented school have better idea about ST and systems theory, while graduates from economic schools show the worse readiness to adopt this new way of thinking (while only approximately 10% of students from economic schools think that ST and SA are utilizable in problem solving, system analysis or system design, the corresponding amount of students from the technically oriented schools is 30%).

Results and Future Work

The described holistic approach to AmI and the research that was done came with interesting results revealing new questions for which answers still need to be found. "How the absence of the process of socialization in the virtual learning environment can be overcome?" might serve as an example. The significance of this question lies in the fact that the enclosure of the cycle in the SECI model is the basic prerequisite for the students' ability to comprehend complex systems such as AmI. Nevertheless, the ability to understand the AmI requirements and limitations of the holistic way is the first step which represents one of the assumptions of its development. As Figure 3 indicates, there are plenty of other factors that have to be taken into consideration. For instance, the AmI vision can become reality only if other perspectives representing the framework of its existence (e.g. the legislative one) enable the barrier-free implementation of the advanced pervasive technology.

In addition, the next significant aspect of the holistic view on AmI is that the identified perspectives even though they are part of one integral

Figure 6. Tool usage in the subject IOMO

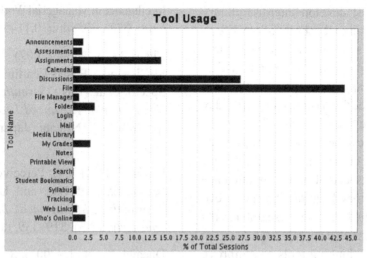

Figure 5. Tool usage in the subject TESY2

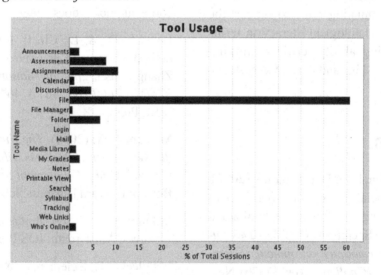

whole bring effects of their development in different time periods. For instance, the educational perspective of AmI works with the long-term effects on the contrary to the technological one. While assembly of a network and confirmation of its functionality can be performed quite quickly, the final impacts and un/successfulness of all efforts in the educational perspective will be obvious in a relatively distant future although the outcomes can be seen continuously and partial results are achieved in a short-term period.

CONCLUSION

Peter Senge (1990) asserts that we learn best from our experience, but we never directly experience the consequences of many of our most important decisions. AmI is connected with many decisions that are not related only to technological issues and challenges. Therefore, final impacts of these decisions have their own social, ethical and many other dimensions. As stated by Remagnino and colleagues (2005), in order to ensure progress of AmI we can not simply and blindly rely on technology, we must develop interdisciplinary methods encompassing all aspects of our life to develop intelligent solutions, user centric, able to understand us and our lifestyle and activities. Hence, the holistic approach to AmI is the only way how to introduce this vision to our everyday working and private lives.

This tricky task can be supported by systems thinking, which can ensure the holistic and complex approach to all aspects of ambient intelligence development. Here, the educational perspective of AmI has to be applied since the research results support the hypothesis that appropriate education in terms of systems thinking tools can improve the ability of stakeholder to impose requirements and contribute to the development of AmI. In this way, systems thinking can also support the development of technological literacy in terms of problem-solving ability, critical thinking skills, or computer skills and content knowledge (Schenker, 2007).

REFERENCES

Blechar, J., Knutsen, L., & Damsgaard, J. (2005). Reflexivity, the Social Factor, and m-Service Domestication: Linking the Human, Technological and Contextual . In Soerensen, C. (Eds.), *Designing Ubiquitous Information Environments: Socio-Technical Issues and Challenges* (pp. 57–70). New York: Springer. doi:10.1007/0-387-28918-6_7

Braley, D. (2005). Ubiquitous Computing in Practice . In Soerensen, C. (Eds.), *Designing Ubiquitous Information Environments: Socio-Technical Issues and Challenges* (pp. 365–367). New York: Springer. doi:10.1007/0-387-28918-6_31

Bureš, V. (2006). Systems Thinking as a Basis for Ambient Intelligence. *ACM SIGCSE Bulletin*, *38*(3), 318. doi:10.1145/1140123.1140224

Bureš, V., & Čech, P. (2007). Complexity of Ambient Intelligence in Managerial Work. *ACM SIGCSE Bulletin*, *39*(3), 325. doi:10.1145/1269900.1268892

Chatti, M. A., et al. (2007). The Web 2.0 Driven SECI Model Based Learning Process. In J. M. Spector et al, (Eds.), *Seventh IEEE International Conference on Advanced Learning Technologies* (pp.780-782). Niigata, Japan: IEEE Computer Society.

Davis, F. D. (1989). Perceived Usefulness, Perceived Ease of Use, and User Acceptance of Information. *Management Information Systems Quarterly*, *13*(3), 319–339. doi:10.2307/249008

Ducatel, K., et al. (2001). *Scenarios for Ambient Intelligence in 2010: Final report*. Seville, Spain: ISTAG. Retrieved February 2, 2009, from ftp://ftp.cordis.lu/pub/ist/docs/istagscenarios2010.pdf

Liu, Ch. D., & Li, Ch. B. (2000). Electromagnetic pollution and its control. In Z. Feng, & Y. Zhang (Eds.), *2nd International Conference on ICMMT 2000* (pp. 461 - 464). Beijing, China: IEEE Press.

Malone, T. W. (2004). *The Future of Work: How the New Order of Business will Shape Your Organization, Your Management Style, and Your Life*. Boston: Harvard Business School Press.

Mikulecký, P. (2009). *Ambient Intelligence Perspectives*. Amsterdam: IOS Press.

Mikulecký, P., Kelemen, J., & Ponce, D. (1998). A Multiagent Intelligent Control System. In P. Kopacek, & I. Rudas (Eds.), *2nd International Conference on Intelligent Engineering Systems* (pp. 91-93). Wien, Austria: IEEE.

Mikulecký, P., Olševičová, K., & Ponce, D. (2007). Ambient Intelligence - Monitoring and Supervision of New Type . In Kleve, P., de Mulder, R. V., & van Noortwijk, C. (Eds.), *First international seminar of the Legal Framework for the Information Society (LEFIS) on Monitoring, Supervision and IT* (pp. 115–134). Zaragoza, Spain: Zaragoza University Press.

Mukhejree, S. (Eds.). (2006). *AmIware: Hardware Technology Drivers of Ambient Intelligence*. Dordrecht: Springer. doi:10.1007/1-4020-4198-5

Nonaka, I., & Takeuchi, H. (1995). *The Knowledge Creating Company*. New York: Oxford University Press.

Remagnino, P. (2005). Ambient Intelligence: A Gentle Introduction. In Remagnino, P., Foresti, G. L., & Ellis, T. (Eds.), *Ambient Intelligence: a Novel Paradigm* (pp. 1–14). New York: Springer.

Remagnino, P., Foresti, G. L., & Ellis, T. (Eds.). (2005). *Ambient Intelligence: a Novel Paradigm*. New York: Springer.

Schenker, J. (2007). Researching Ubiquity: Ways to Capture It All . In van 't Hooft, M., & Swan, K. (Eds.), *Ubiquitous Computing in Education* (pp. 167–186). Mahwah, NJ: Lawrence Erlbaum Associates.

Senge, P. M. (1990). *The Fifth Discipline: The Art and Practice of the Learning Organisation*. New York: Doubleday.

Singh, R. (2008). Exploring Pervasive/Ubiquitous Computing Vision, Technologies, Applications and Challenges. In V. Godara (Ed.), *1st International Congress on Pervasive Computing and Management* (pp. 1-20). Sydney: Sydney College of Management.

Smith, M. K. (2001). Peter Senge and the Learning Organization. *Infed: the Informal Education Homepage*. Retrieved February 2, 2009 from http://www.infed.org/thinkers/senge.htm

Soerensen, C. (Eds.). (2005). *Designing Ubiquitous Information Environments: Socio-Technical Issues and Challenges*. New York: Springer. doi:10.1007/0-387-28918-6

Taylor, S., & Todd, P. A. (1995). Understanding Information Technology Use: A Test of Competing models. *Information Systems Research*, 6(2), 144–176. doi:10.1287/isre.6.2.144

van Houten, H. (2006). The Physical Basis of Ambient Intelligence. In S. Mukhejree et al. (Eds.), AmIware: Hardware Technology Drivers of Ambient Intelligence (pp. 9-28). Dordrecht: Springer. van 't Hooft, M., & Swan, K. (Eds.). (2007). Ubiquitous Computing in Education. Mahwah, NJ: Lawrence Erlbaum Associates.

van t' Hooft, et al. (2007). What is Ubiquitous Computing? In M. van 't Hooft & K. Swan (Eds.), *Ubiquitous Computing in Education* (pp. 3-18). Mahwah, NJ: Lawrence Erlbaum Associates.

Vasilakos, A., & Pedrycz, W. (Eds.). (2006). *Ambient Intelligence, Wireless Networking and Ubiquitous Computing*. Boston: Artech House.

Weiser, M. (1991). The computer for the 21st century. *Scientific American*, 265(3), 94–104.

Weiser, M. (1993). Some computer science issues in ubiquitous computing. *Communications of the ACM*, 36(7), 75–84. doi:10.1145/159544.159617

Weiss, P. A. (Ed.). (1971). *Hierarchically Organized Systems in Theory and Practice*. New York: Hafner.

ADDITIONAL READING

Aarts, E., et al. (Eds.). 2008. Ambient Intelligence. *Proceedings of the European Conference AmI 2008*, Nuremberg, Germany, pp. 361. Heidelberg: Springer-Verlag.

Aarts, E., & Encarnação, J. L. (Eds.). (2008). *True Visions: The Emergence of Ambient Intelligence*. Heidelberg: Springer-Verlag.

Basten, T., Geilen, M., & de Groot, H. (Eds.). (2003). *Ambient Intelligence: Impact on Embedded System Design*. Dordrecht: Kluwer Academic Publishers.

Cai, Y. (Ed.). (2005). *Ambient Intelligence for Scientific Discovery: Foundations, Theories, and Systems*. Heidelberg: Springer-Verlag.

Cook, D.J. (2009). Multi-agent smart environments. *Journal of Ambient Intelligence and Smart Environments,* (2009). 51–55.

Fishkin, K. P., et al. (Eds.). (2006). *Pervasive Computing. 4th International Conference PERVASIVE 2006*, Dublin, Ireland, pp. 402. Heidelberg: Springer-Verlag.

Godara, V. (Ed.). (2008). *Risk Assessment and Management in Pervasive Computing: Operational, Legal, Ethical, and Financial Perspectives*. Hershey, PA: Information Science Reference.

Greenfield, A. (2006). *Everyware: The Dawning Age of Ubiquitous Computing*. Berkeley, CA: New Riders Publishing.

Indulska, J., et al. (2008). Pervasive Computing. *Proceedings of the 6th International Conference PERVASIVE 2008*, Sydney, Australia, pp. 315. Heidelberg: Springer-Verlag.

Ishida, T., & Hattori, H. (2009). Participatory Technologies for Designing Ambient Intelligence Systems. *Journal of Ambient Intelligence and Smart Environments*, *1*, 43–49.

Krämer, B. J., & Halang, W. A. (Eds.). (2007). *Contributions to Ubiquitous Computing*. Heidelberg: Springer-Verlag.

Loke, S. (2006). *Context-Aware Pervasive Systems: Architectures for a New Breed of Applications*. Boca Raton, FL: Auerbach Publications.

Maña, A., & Lotz, V. (Eds.). (2006). *Developing Ambient Intelligence*. Paris: Springer-Verlag.

Merk, L. (2001). *Pervasive Computing Handbook*. Heidelberg: Springer-Verlag.

Mühlhäuser, M., & Gurevych, I. (2008). *Handbook of Research on Ubiquitous Computing Technology for Real Time Enterprises*. Hershey, PA: Information Science Reference.

Roussos, G. (Ed.). (2005). *Ubiquitous and Pervasive Commerce: New Frontiers for Electronic Business*. London: Springer-Verlag.

Sawyer, R. K. (2005). *Social Emergence: Societies as Complex Systems*. Cambridge: Cambridge University Press.

Sebe, N. (2009). Multimodal Interfaces: Challenges and Perspectives. *Journal of Ambient Intelligence and Smart Environments*, *1*, 23–30.

Steventon, A., & Wright, S. (Eds.). (2005). *Intelligent Spaces: The Application of Pervasive ICT*. London: Springer-Verlag.

Sullivan, J. W., & Tyler, S. W. (Eds.). (1991). *Intelligent User Interfaces*. New York: ACM.

Uchyigit, G., & Ma, M. Y. (Eds.). (2008). *Personalization Techniques and Recommender Systems*. Singapore: World Scientific Publishing Company.

Verhaegh, W., Aarts, E., & Korst, J. (Eds.). (2006). *Intelligent Algorithms in Ambient and Biomedical Computing*. Dordrecht: Springer-Verlag. doi:10.1007/1-4020-4995-1

Weber, W., Rabaey, J. M., & Aarts, E. (Eds.). (2005). *Ambient Intelligence*. Heidelberg: Springer-Verlag. doi:10.1007/b138670

KEY TERMS AND DEFINITIONS

Pervasive Computing: Pervasive Computing is a computing technology that pervades the users' environment by making use of seamless connectivity of multiple independent information devices embedded in the environment of the users.

Ubiquitous Computing: Ubiquitous computing is wired, wireless and ad-hoc networking that exploit highly portable or else numerous, very-low-cost computing devices.

Ambient Intelligence: Ambient Intelligence represents a vision of the future where people are surrounded by electronic artefacts and environments, sensitive and responsive.

Systems Thinking: Practice of thinking that takes a holistic view of complex events or phenomenon, seemingly caused by myriad of isolated, independent, and usually unpredictable factors or forces. ST views all events and phenomenon as 'wholes' interacting according to systems principles.

Systems Theory: A theory designed to study unified whole and self-organizing systems. Systems theory is based upon the idea that the whole is different from the sum of the individual parts. It stresses the interdependent and interactional nature of the relationships that exist among all components of a system.

Object Modeling: Object modelling is a specific approach to representation of systems included in the reality. In the object oriented modelling the complexity is reduced by splitting the whole complex system into collaborating self sustained subsystems - objects.

Virtual Learning Environment: A virtual learning environment is a software system designed to support teaching and learning in an educational setting. It is used to manage the delivery of online learning materials and assessment and it includes curriculum mapping and monitoring of the learner's progress.

Information and Communication Technology: Information and Communications Technology is an umbrella term that includes all technologies for the manipulation and communication of information, i.e. it is the catch-all phrase used to describe a range of technologies for gathering, storing, retrieving, processing, analysing and transmitting information.

Chapter 17

Re–Engineering Higher Education:
The Seamless Knowledge Management System for the University

K.V. Bhanu Murthy
Delhi School of Economics, India

ABSTRACT

The University System is confronted with a changed environment which necessitates re-engineering of higher education. The new framework is that of a new Pedagogic System that is to be embedded in the Knowledge Management System, in seamless manner, through pervasive computing. This paper argues that the University system is under great pressure from industry (society) to deliver such finished products (graduates) from its system so as to be directly absorbed into industry and that too at a mass scale and in a short period of time. The objective is to propose a complete change in the philosophy and methods and outline the re-engineering by which this can be done, in a seamless manner, through these strand of re-engineering: 1. e-learning and blended learning; 2. pervasive computing; 3. distance and open learning; as well as 4. an outcomes approach to pedagogy.

INTRODUCTION

The University System is confronted with a changed environment which necessitates re-engineering of higher education. The new framework is that of a new Pedagogic System that is embedded in the Knowledge Management System that is at the core of the re-engineering of higher education. The purpose of this paper is to understand the gap between the needs of society and the capability of the University system. In the process we study and identify the shortcomings of the traditional learning system and discover the potential of the e–learning system to transform the learning experience of the student. The aim is to discover the tools, techniques and method of e–learning that can contribute to the new e-learning/blended learning experience that is capable of drawing out the best in a student and more importantly make her ready for being absorbed by industry. Most of all the objective is to propose a complete change in the philosophy and methods in the University System and outline the

DOI: 10.4018/978-1-61520-741-1.ch017

re-engineering by which this can be done. All this needs to be done in a pervasive environment and in a seamless manner so that the learner naturally takes to learning from the environment. The focus should be on making the learner independent and this has to be achieved through targeting the expected learning outcomes.

PLAN OF THE STUDY

The opening Section 1 gives the general background and debates in the area of Knowledge Management. In Section 2 we discuss the expectations of society from the University system. Section 3 lays out the concepts of the Knowledge Management System (KMS) in the University. Section 4 exposes the traditional pedagogic system in the University and discusses the strengths and weaknesses of the traditional learning system. Section 5 highlights the same of the e-learning/blended learning system and shows the various modes of learning. Section 6 develops the theme of re-engineering of higher education and the relevance of e–learning as a tool and more for transformation and re-engineering of the University System. In the process it highlights the need for formalizing the KMS and the new Pedagogic System. The next section is on 'Seamless KMS - externalizing and internalizing pedagogy'. Section 8 is about 'Future trends - Pervasive computing and re-engineering higher education'. The last Section summarizes the conclusions.

BACKGROUND

The motivation of this paper lies in trying to understand the new role of the University and evolving a strategy to re-engineer the University System. For abiding by this premise the necessary condition is to agree that there is a need for change. The debate on what the role of the University is rightfully belongs to the domain of applied philosophy. But to propose re-engineering of such a fundamental and old institution (not a company) we really need to have a deep enough insight that can only arise from philosophy. The debate about the role of the University is as old as the institution itself[1].

Earlier the debate was about the fundamental role of the University. The question usually was about the choice between the University's role in furthering basic research versus its role in innovation meant for industry[2]. Bhanu Murthy (1995) has argued about the nexus between 'skills, technology and basic science' and has shown how the University can play a role in providing 'manpower development' for industry. Florida (1999), on the other hand, argues that we would be undermining the value of research universities if we regard them simply as sources of technology.

In more recent times the whole context of the knowledge economy has come up. There is shift in the debate now and the focus is on the relationship between the University and the challenges that the knowledge economy poses to the University system. The new emphasis is clearly on re-engineering:

"Although the knowledge economy should be good news for higher education, universities now confront a variety of technical, legal, and cultural forces that threaten to relegate us to the periphery. Avoiding that fate will require us to redefine the university on a scale not seen since the emergence of the research university". (James Hilton, 2004, p.1).

It is still strongly believed that the University system is slow to adapt.

"University systems can be categorized on a spectrum of strikingly non-adaptive (succumbing to an entrenched bureaucracy that inhibits change) to the more flexible systems that can absorb and reconstitute potentially threatening ideas…" (Charles Henry, 2008, p.1).

In what follows we have tried to re-think on all these aspects of the debate and build-up a framework that helps make us formulate the evolution of a new role for the University.

EXPECTATION FROM THE UNIVERSITY SYSTEM

Charles Henry reminds us that universities are comprised of many traditional, formal organizational models and that each is usually construed as distinct, with a recognizable set of expectations and behaviors. (Henry, 2008). The underlying concern in this paper is about the expectations of society from the University. In applied philosophy, the fundamental basis of the existence of an institution is based on the whether it is playing the role expected of it or not. If this basis is not recognized it would lead to the irrelevance of the institution. We may debate the role and have different opinions about it but we cannot afford to forget this basic premise.

The University system is poised at such a juncture that, on the one hand, it is steeped in the traditional system and on the other hand, society's need is changing rapidly, both quantitatively and qualitatively. Therefore, the situation is that the University system has developed and perhaps perfected traditional pedagogy but the outcomes of the system are unable to satisfy the felt needs of society. If the modernization of the system does not take place at the juncture at which it is required there would be an expectation gap that would exponentially widen because the expectation is grows exponentially and the traditional system has reached a plateau.

Industry, even up to the distant future would he need large volumes of trained graduates. They are unable to meet the bill of training that is required on-the-job. This slows down the process of catching-up with the burgeoning demand that industry faces. Along with industry grows the development of society's needs. Therefore,

this trend extends to other sectors as well as the NGO sector, the research organizations (market – research, financial research as well as social research) and auxiliary and ancillary services. While the University system produces graduates it dose not equip them with appropriate skills that are desired by industry as well as other sectors.

The important thing is to not allow a narrowing down the connotation of 'skill'. In the traditional system 'skill' is associated with hands-on jobs. Therefore, there was a segregation of 'vocational' or 'technical', training, which was interpreted narrowly as working with the hands, from knowledge based training that the University system imparted. Today, 'skill' needs to be interpreted differently. The simple reason that increasingly even those occupations that were 'skill- based' and where they were expected to work with their hands have been transformed. There is a shift in their needs. Knowledge is increasingly being embedded into the systems that are supporting, if not driving industry. The need is, therefore, to sharpen the methods of 'thinking', so that the embedded knowledge can be effectively and quickly harnessed for carrying out tasks. The needs of training are therefore, not so much for repetitively physical activity or 'hands–on' experience, which in any case cannot be simulated in the University, outside industry, but for training the mind so as to develop training 'skills' in thinking and acting.

The required skill set is the following:

- Basic knowledge of the relevant area, including allied subjects.
- The ability to quickly gather and internalize knowledge.
- The ability to perceive and understand situations that need knowledgeable response.
- The ability to evolve appropriate and effective responses to deal with such situations.

This kind of skill development is not in the domain of polytechnics. It is either possible on the job or through the University system. Polytechnics work with minimal knowledge and concentrate 'skill – development' of the earlier kind. Since industry is unable to deliver the University which has a social obligation to society has to deliver, on the desired lines.

Traditionally, the term 'vocational' has been defined as:

"That which prepares learners for careers that are based in manual or practical activities, traditionally non-academic and directly related to a specific trade, occupation or vocation, hence the term, in which the learner participates. It is sometimes referred to as technical education, as the learner directly develops expertise in a particular group of techniques or technology". (Buzzell, 1987, p.10).

Vocational education, therefore, needs to be re-interpreted. It is no longer skill enhancing in the traditional sense. It provides a vital link between the University system and industry. It is a role that devolves upon the University system and is a value–addition to the existing knowledge-based education.

Such a role does not take away from the basic objective of the University to create knowledge and to do research in basic sciences and social science. This knowledge shall ultimately be incorporated into the knowledge base facilitates or drives industry. But the University has an added objective of providing such training that makes the products of the University System, acceptable to industry. This is a social obligation that the University system bears towards the society. The immediate society is the community of students. The somewhat distant society is the industry. If industry is not capable of bringing about the necessary change and if the University system sticks to its old role, then there would be an impasse.

The three dimensions of this process are

- To create courses that are 'industry-oriented'.
- To transform teaching methods so as to enable 'new' skill development.
- To produce at a mass scale graduates who possess such qualifications, have done such vocational courses and have been shaped by modern methods so as to imbibe and internalize such 'new' skills.

This brings out the expectations from the University system. The desirable response of the University system is to re-vamp its system of education. In fact there is a controversy about very relevance of knowledge management. (T.D. Wilson, 2002, p.1) is the biggest critic of knowledge management. He states,

".. 'knowledge management' is an umbrella term for a variety of organizational activities, none of which are concerned with the management of knowledge. Those activities that are not concerned with the management of information are concerned with the management of work practices, in the expectation that changes in such areas as communication practice will enable information sharing."

An apt rebuttal comes from Prusak (1999, p.1), who says that;

"Some skeptics may argue that consultants developed knowledge management to replace declining revenues from the waning re-engineering movement. Others may feel that knowledge management is just a "rebadging" of earlier information and data management methods. Perhaps the majority of skeptics take the position—not an unnatural one—that every so-called new approach is, in reality, either old or wrong."

The main challenge of re-engineering is, therefore, to develop a 'new' knowledge management system (KMS) for the University. This raises the question of what is the traditional system of knowledge and teaching, in the university and by contrast what the 'new' one would be.

KNOWLEDGE MANAGEMENT SYSTEM IN THE UNIVERSITY

There exists an implicit structure of a traditional KMS in the University. This needs to be overhauled so as to make the University system relevant for industry (society). Knowledge is gained either by experience, learning and perception or through association and reasoning. The term knowledge is also used to mean the confident understanding of a subject, potentially with the ability to use it for a specific purpose.

Knowledge Management refers to a range of practices used by organisations to identify, create, represent, and distribute knowledge for reuse, awareness, and learning across the organisations. Knowledge Management programs are typically tied to organisational objectives and are intended to lead to the achievement of specific outcomes, such as shared intelligence, improved performance, competitive advantage, or higher levels of innovation.

Another approach to KM states that 'KM is: 'Knowing what you know and profit from it' and 'Making obsolete what you know before others obsolete it." This point towards a philosophy of combining domain knowledge with dynamism, and a grasp of the future.

The unreliability of memory limits the certainty of knowledge about the past, while unpredictability of events yet to occur limits the certainty of knowledge about the future. One of the definitions of KM says that knowledge management is management of Change, Uncertainty, and Complexity. We shall be seeing how the University system is, at present, facing such a situation.

All of the above has been stated and developed in the context of companies. How does this translate in terms of the University?

The keywords that can be filtered from the above are:

- 'philosophy';
- 'organisational objectives';
- 'knowledge for reuse';
- 'learning organisation';
- 'specific outcomes';
- 'domain knowledge';
- 'grasp of the future'; and
- 'management of Change, Uncertainty, and Complexity'

The main criticism of the University system is that it does not respond fast enough. It is not forward looking. The philosophy needs to be revamped to so as to rejuvenate the purpose and role of the University. The objectives need to be redefined with respect to the new context to – 'grasp of the future'. The 'organizational objectives' need to be reconciled with societal objectives.

The speed of knowledge generation and distribution is so tremendous that there is every possibility of sizeable losses. Therefore, 'reuse' of knowledge implies two things. One, disembodiment of knowledge, which means that knowledge can no longer internalized and remain so within the teachers' minds but needs to be 'externalized' and stored. This needs a KMS. Two, it means storage, retrieval and dissemination of 'domain knowledge'. There can be no denying that the University faces and future that is full of 'Change, Uncertainty, and Complexity'. The main job of the University is creation, accumulation and dissemination of knowledge. It is therefore, obvious that the University deserves a KMS.

The first thing to be emphasized is that the knowledge system spans across schooling, the University and the job or vocation. Like any system it has certain elements and certain process taken along with the methods. As we transcend from an era of information scarcity to information glut, there is need for re-focusing on human sense-making processes underlying decisions, choices, and performance. In this new paradigm for increasingly uncertain and complex environments, dynamically evolving performance outcomes are the key drivers of how 'smart minds' use 'smart technologies' to leverage opportunities and challenges.

Transformation of KMS

Knowledge transfer (one aspect of Knowledge Management) has always existed in one form or another. Examples include on-the-job peer discussions, formal apprenticeship, corporate libraries, professional training, and mentoring programs. However, since the late twentieth century, additional technology has been applied to this task, such as knowledge bases, expert systems, and knowledge repositories. Knowledge Management System attempt to manage the process of creation or identification, accumulation, and application of knowledge or intellectual capital across an organisation.

Knowledge Management, therefore, attempts to bring under one system a set of practices, various strands of thought and practice relating to: intellectual capital. And aims at integrating the knowledge worker in the knowledge economy through the idea of the learning organization.

In the case of the University the learning organization is the Pedagogic System. While Knowledge Management is closely related to the Pedagogic System it may be distinguished from the Pedagogic System whose focus on the management of specific knowledge assets and development and cultivation of the channels through which knowledge flows. The KMS on the other hand includes both the stock and the flow of knowledge.

What Is A System?

A system is a complete whole that operationalize any phenomenon. Knowledge is in the domain of philosophy so long as it not operationalized. Once it is operationalized it becomes an engine for management of the phenomenon or institution. Therefore, the KMS is responsible for the creation, acquisition and dissemination of knowledge. Therefore, the KMS is responsible for the creation, acquisition and dissemination of Knowledge in The University and from the University to the rest of society.

In general system consists of:

- Elements;
- Processes;
- Internal and External environment;
- Relationships; and
- Methods.

The elements and process are connected to each other and with the environment through the relationships. These taken along with the methods that operationalize knowledge and the processes, is known as the KMS. Relationships and methods are responsible for the mechanics of the system and in the process do transform the system itself.

In Figure 1 below we have shown a schema of the knowledge management system for the University. The knowledge base and research is linked to the Industry (and society in general). The pass-outs (products) of the University are absorbed by Industry. The dotted line between the University and Industry is porous. This implies a constant interaction and flow. The dotted line between Pedagogy and the taught shows that there is very little self-learning.

The elements are integrated. The processes are dynamic with feedback effects. These would transform themselves and transform the system in the process.

Figure 1. Knowledge Management System In The University

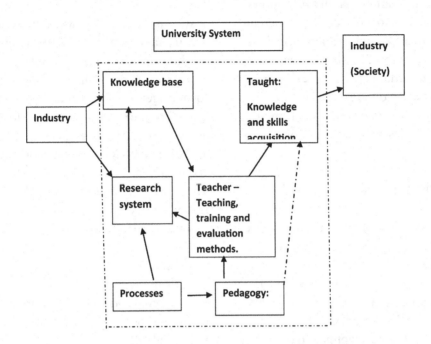

TRADITIONAL PEDAGOGIC SYSTEM

Then there are open systems and closed systems. A closed system lacks the potential for policy implications and interventions because there is no interaction with the exterior or the external environment of the system.

A closed System in like a perpetual machine which, once it is in motion is unrelated to any other influence. The open system on the other hand has the potential for change. It can be a tool for policy change. The traditional role of the University has been like a closed system. In the case of the KMS the external environment is the society. It has remained insulated to the needs of industry (society). The dotted line in Figure 2 is like a semi-permeable membrane between the University and industry (society). This restricts the possibility of policy interventions and change.

There are physical or natural system and social system. A thermostat is a physical system for temperature control, which is a physical state.

An eco-system is a natural system that sustains life around it. A generic system could also have its instances. In this sense, the traditional pedagogic system; and the e–learning system are both instances[3] of a sub-systems of the KMS.

The Pedagogic System

Firstly, there is a need to conceptualize the pedagogic system. Secondly, we need to distinguish between the traditional and e-learning systems. And, finally, we need to look at both critically in the light of the expectations of society from the University system.

The traditional pedagogic system consists of four elements:

- Teacher
- Student
- Teaching methods
- Evaluation methods

Figure 2. Traditional Pedagogic System (Knowledge augmenting)

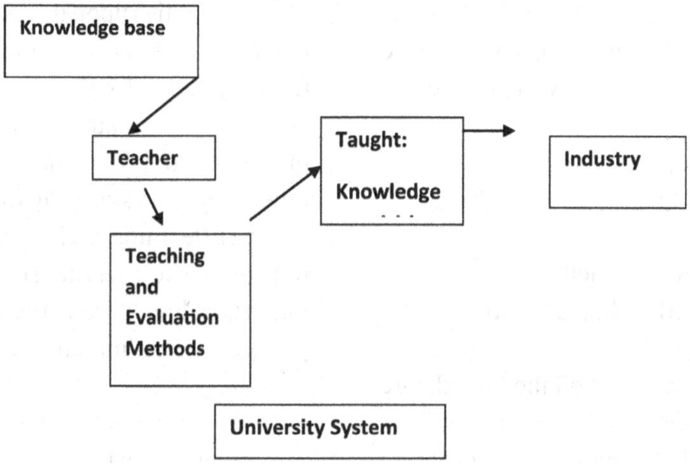

The teacher draws from the Knowledge base which includes the traditional teaching resources like text books and imparts Knowledge to student. The methods include an evaluation method which is done with a view to evaluate the knowledge competency of the student.

The three shortcomings of the traditional pedagogic system are:

1. It is not skill augmenting but its is only knowledge augmenting;
2. There is virtually no self–evaluation and feed back into the system that might enable a constant improvement in the system; and
3. It cannot function without the intervention of the teacher.

In addition, if the traditional system becomes insulated and cut off from the needs of industry and society, in general, it would perpetuate knowledge that is not of great relevance to society. Also it would not the able to adapt to the needs of industry (society).

In short, it would be a closed system and the student that it turns out would not be accepted and absorbed by industry (society). This has been reflected in two ways one, that there is a disjoint between the University and the society.

This is shows as a dotted line between the two, in Figure 2. And, two that it would lead to situation where the students (graduates) would not be seen as a 'human resource', by industry (society). They would at the best be seen as raw material that needs the necessary training to the able to convert them into a human resource, relevant to industry (society).

Table 1 above lays out the skill requirements of industry. The University is better equipped to impart the first two skills. The training can be completed by industry for the third type of skill. This too can be done by collaborating with industry[4]. This can be linked to the new organizational structure that is flatter. There are fewer levels in the hierarchy. This necessitates greater independence on the part of new entrants into industry. The new pedagogy has to take care of this.

Table 1. Skill Development for Industry (Society)

• **Cognitive skills.** => Critical analysis and synthesis. • **Key skills.** => Learning, communication, information literacy. • **Practical and professional skills.** => Field work, lab skills and professional requirements.

THE E-LEARNING SYSTEM

The e-learning system is more complex and more advanced. It consists of the following elements:

- Knowledge base;
- E–resources;
- Teacher;
- Teaching and training method; and
- Student – as a skilled human resource.

The e–resources are based on the knowledge base and cannot be separated from it. But they go beyond the knowledge base and incorporate teaching-training methods. The teacher's role is no longer direct. Her role is to augment the e–resource. The e-resources are now responsible for training, teaching and evaluation. The e–learning system enables training such that a student can develop skills as are required by industry. This is the main advantage of e-learning. In addition the other major advantage is that it enables a better distance learning platform. It also enables better self–learning and self-evaluation. Therefore, the re-engineering that is being proposed is to develop three modes of delivery. Thus, e-learning system transforms the teacher's role5. It becomes more creative. Rather than teaching and learning by the rote it enables a student to become skilled and independent. The distance learning enables the higher education to become capable of delivering mass-based solutions.

There are two main planks of e-learning - Modes of e-learning and the E-learning environ-ment. Blended learning is relatively inexpensive because it relies upon the extisting real resources, namely, teachers and infrastructure. It is particularly suited for developing countries. But the change is not so autonomous or quick. Between this mode and E-intensive mode there are two other modes as stated in Table 2.

The E-learning environment has been explained in Table 3. The e-learning environment is the most important break from the traditional system of pedagogy. The immense advantages are:

- It improves the intellectual reach tremendously.
- It is capable of igniting interest.
- It gives the necessary flexibility to teacher and taught.
- It makes study unpressured.
- It reduces drudgery.
- It taps visual learning skills.
- It may improve retention.
- It encourages structured learning.
- It may enable modular learning.

Of course many of these things can be found in the traditional methods as well. But the difference is that not all teachers would have the same level of personal qualities and skills to be able to bring about these effects. Especially, differentials in the learning experience of students can be minimized with the help of E-content development. The effort would go into developing the system initially and then addressing the problems as they come, in an incremental manner.

Table 2. E-learning Modes (In ascending order of cost)

Blended learning – this combines face to face teaching with e-learning **E-enhanced** –baseline e-services i.e., digital resources, a course website or eDesktop, computer conferencing or study online. **E-focused** -Online ICT is a required element of teaching support; some online teaching and student support for all students. **E-intensive** - all, or most, teaching and student support is delivered online.

Table 3. E-Learning Environment

• E-learning databases • Electronic access to resources • Search Engines and Metasearch Engines • Computer aided instruction • Computer mediated conferencing • E-learning journey (first contact, information/guidance, registration, course materials, tuition and support, assessment, degree ceremony)

RE-ENGINEERING OF HIGHER EDUCATION

A general definition of re-engineering is, "the application of technology and management science to the modification of existing systems, organizations, processes, and products in order to make them more effective, efficient, and responsive"[6]. According to Michael Hammer and James Champy re-engineering is to "examine the goals of an organization and to redesign work and business processes from the ground up rather than simply automate existing tasks and functions".

It is indicative of radical change. However, neither of these definitions emphasizes a change in philosophy and methods. A radical change in philosophy is envisaged - A change in the purpose and role of The University in society. The change in methods is aimed at through 'An Outcomes Approach' to pedagogy[7].

Adults have become a rapidly growing part of the student population at colleges and universities nationwide. However, methods and practices designed for a traditional age population do not necessarily serve an adult learner well. Apart from distance learning that has been outlined below this is another major reason to think in terms of re-engineering of higher education. (Voorhees and Lingenfelter (2003).

In this context, it is important to distinguish between a 'process' and 'method'.

"Method is a way of doing something, especially a systematic way; implies an orderly logical arrangement (usually in steps)."
"A series of operations performed is a process.[8]"

Therefore, 'method' includes procedural steps, that is, it includes a process within itself. In our context it means that the outcomes approach to pedagogy is a 'method' and 'teaching-learning' is a 'process' embedded in the method. This distinction is important because in the ordinary course

the term Business Process Re-engineering (BPR) is used. It does not distinguish between process and method. BPR may suffice for describing 're-engineering' as is ordinarily understood but in the given context it does not.

An alternative definition of method that fits the bill is:

"The procedures and techniques characteristic of a particular discipline or field of knowledge."

Method is now being used in an overall sense to mean the following:

- Outcomes Approach
- Content Development
- Modes of Delivery
- Learning Environment

The shift in philosophy refers to the recognition of the new external environment and a change towards a greater responsiveness to needs of society and industry[9].

While we automatically think of students as learners, teachers are learners as well. This may be particularly true for learning technologies. Most faculty received their academic training in a pre-Internet world and may have had no formal exposure to learning principles and practices. Since technology, pedagogy, and our disciplines change, faculty shall remain lifelong learners. In this sense it is essential to induct teachers into content development for e-learning[10]. The process of introducing e-learning systems should hence involve the training of faculty from existing institutions to adapt themselves so that they may further train other faculty in continuing the process of establishing e-learning systems.

Teaching does not necessarily result in learning. Students differ in learning strategies, abilities, motivation and personal circumstances. What is desired is to achieve successful learning. Part of the answer is to identify the barriers to student success, which may range from the time a class meets to the way material is presented. There could be designs to enhance successful learning, such as flexible learning, blended learning, online access to programs and resources, and self-assessment tools. The fundamental questions are 'What should higher education mean in the 21st century? And, how should the University to meet future needs?' What is being proposed here is a learning outcomes approach to education and the use of blended learning.

The emphasis in defining learning outcomes is on laying out what the teacher expects from a student at the end of the learning process. This is not the same as the objectives which refer to what the teacher wants to teach. The learning outcomes are from the point of view of the students. These would depend on the level of the student, their past knowledge, and need.

The outcomes can be classified as:

- Knowledge
- Values
- Skills
- Understanding

While it may be difficult to include all outcomes in each module but it is necessary to specify outcomes in accordance with this classification. For instance, knowledge as a learning outcome that needs to be specified as - list, define or identify. Understanding relates to terms like - differentiate, discuss and associate. Skills are related to action verbs like – calculate, demonstrate and classify. Similarly, values relate to – assess, rank or compare.

Teaching does not necessarily result in learning. Students differ in learning strategies, abilities, motivation and personal circumstances. What is desired is to achieve successful learning. Part of the answer is to identify the barriers to student success, which may range from the time a class meets to the way material is presented. There could be designs to enhance successful learn-

ing, such as flexible learning, blended learning, online access to programs and resources, and self-assessment tools. The fundamental questions are 'What should higher education mean in the 21st century? And, how should the University to meet future needs?' What is being proposed here is a learning outcomes approach to education and the use of blended learning.

Peer group review is an ongoing, continuous process done amongst each other by brainstorming. The most important thing is external review which is outlined below.

Content Validity

It also known as logical validity and refers to the extent to which a text represents all facets of a given concept. The external reviewer who is an expert on the subject shall evaluate the content (subject matter). It involves assessment of level of the content, the breadth and clarity of the content and finally, the validity of the language since language signifies meaning.

Face Validity

Face validity is testing by a non-expert, who could be a student or a lay person, who verifies that at the look of it the content is intelligible, attractive and acceptable. Here the main criterion is simplicity.

Table 4. E- Content Development

• Defining learning outcomes
• Defining stages of learning
· Writing Lessons/Chapters[xi]
• Stream lining style and content
· Brainstorming over meaning (import)[xii]
• Peer group review
• External review
○ Content Validity
○ Face Validity
○ Pedagogic Validity

Pedagogic Validity

Pedagogic validity is an innovation by this author. Here we mean that the e-content is validated from the point of view of the model reflected in Figure 4. It implies that it its implementation of the e-content expresses internal consistency amongst the three dimensions, namely, learning outcomes, learning-teaching process, as embedded in the e-content, and the level and appropriateness of assessment of learning outcomes. If the learning outcomes only indicate knowledge and values the learner cannot be tested for skills and under-standing. Similarly, depending on the depth of the knowledge it may or may not be possible for a student to make comparisons. So it may not be expected that the student can draw out the 'value' aspect. The course may not be designed to teach certain skills. So it may be unjustified to expect students to display such skills.

SEAMLESS KMS - EXTERNALIZING AND INTERNALIZING PEDAGOGY

In net, it may be said that the central idea behind the new pedagogic system is that the teaching learning process must be, at once be externalized and internalized. It has to be internalized in the sense that it becomes a part of the consciousness of the learner and does not remain as a system that is disjointed from the consciousness, as is the case with the existing pedagogic system. In the existing system pedagogy is limited to the confines of the classroom and examinations halls. The learning environment is at present internal to these structures and systems. Therefore, there is a need to externalize the pedagogic system. On the other hand, the KMS has to blend into the general environment of the learner so that the learner learns, applies, internalizes by naturally picking up things. For this the ultimate step is to internalize the pedagogic process and methods into the environment. This however would be possible only through the medium of pervasive computing. It would help in embedding learning into the environment. It is in this sense that the crux of the philosophy of re-engineering higher education is to institute a seamless KMS that blends into the general environment of learning. At once, it would achieve internalization and externalization of the KMS.

Here it must be noted that the concept of blended learning has been vastly expanded. Conventionally blended learning only refers to a blend of face-to-face with e-learning. On the

Figure 4. Pedagogy in the new Outcomes Approach

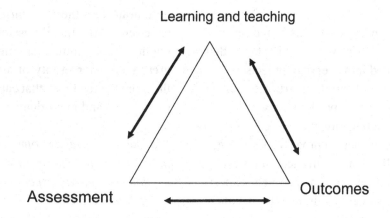

other hand we have included in the definition of blended learning the blending of the learning process and methods into the environment and through the environment into the consciousness of the learner.

FUTURE TRENDS - PERVASIVE COMPUTING AND RE-ENGINEERING HIGHER EDUCATION

Pervasive computing is starting to find a place for itself in industrial use, outside the consumer realm. Everyday industrial devices and objects like industrial robots are gaining intelligence through embedded networking chips that enable them to analyze all sorts of data. Different industries have, off late, been taking advantage of the idea of creating networks of devices that are connected to corporate computing systems that handle functions such as maintenance or inventory. What is proposed here is the need to do the same with higher education.

The mission of the pervasive computing initiative is to see how information technology can be diffused into everyday objects and settings, and to see how this can lead to new ways of supporting and enhancing people's lives that go above and beyond what is possible with the computer today.

Specifically, the initiative focuses on three-interlinked objectives:

- Create information artifacts based on new software and hardware architectures that are integrated into everyday objects.
- Look at how collections of artifacts can act together, so as to produce new behavior and new functionality.
- Investigate the new approaches for designing for collections of artifacts in everyday settings and ensure that people's experience in these new environments is coherent and engaging.

Lots of projects regarding the use of pervasive computing in e-learning have been developed. Some of them examine the exploitation of common devices such as projectors, microphones and cameras in order to record educational sessions in real time and to allow students to follow the educational process from a distance, trying to integrate the traditional activities within a classroom with the tele-education ones (Abowd, 1999), (Shi, 2003).

As pervasive computing is incrementally integrated with all facets of everyday life, it is reasonable to expect influences on educational activities as well. Numerous efforts within projects were made to create environments that capture as much of the university classroom experience as possible by automating the production of online lecture notes with electronic whiteboards and other gadgets and tools such as, embedded microphones and cameras.

"The ability of the computer to act, for example, as a tireless 'individual tutor' or to provide access to an unlimited wealth of resources and information are familiar scenarios and are continually used as justification for expenditure on IT both in the classroom and at home." (Selwyn, 2002, p.428).

Learning is circumscribed the limitations of the mode between the student and the content to be mastered. For example, the more the colors, the motion and feel, the more enriching is the learning experience. And this is possible only if the bandwidth of a communications medium is wider. The greater the interactivity of a medium, the more the more the feedback that can be communicated to motivate and individualize learning.

"In the next decade, our society may change from its present extensive use of technology as a mediator of human experience to a reliance on technology-permeated experience as a primary form of personal consciousness. In response, our

paradigm for distance learning must evolve so that we can replicate the workplaces and communities of the future in schools today. This will aid students in filtering and interpreting the complex, pervasive informational environment that sophisticated media are creating in society." (Dede, 1991, p.146).

In has however, been warned that "policies should be developed so that the benefits of these innovations for distance learning are realized as rapidly as possible, but we must ensure that these powerful new media do not shape the instructional message in unwanted ways."

Learning technology alone does not necessarily advance learning; well-integrated learning methods and practices often do. With learning principles and practices in mind, technology is to be used in service of learning. New technologies may advance learning; even traditional technologies, when implemented with pedagogically sound methods and practices, can result in significant learning gains. This is the basis of "blended learning".

Games, simulations, and virtual worlds provide educators with an opportunity to engage learners in an immersive and interactive environment that requires knowledge, decision making, and information management skills. However, the use of immersive learning environments can be controversial; their association with play and fun is often considered non-educational. Even so, games, simulations, and virtual worlds are gaining increased cultural acceptance. Research suggests that these environments can play a significant role in facilitating learning through engagement, group participation, immediate feedback, and providing real-world contexts. (Oblinger, 2006).

"Three concerns were firstly issued for pervasive computing: (i) low cost and low-power computers with equally convenient displays; (ii) software for pervasive applications and (iii) networks that act as platforms of intercommunication among all." (Konstantinidis, 2007, p.292).

Communication and collaboration of the heterogeneous and different environments that interfere in pervasive computing has been also a major issue when demanding ubiquity, invisibility, interconnectivity and co-operation between pervasive devices, as well as, memory affiliation.

"The importance of computer-based learning is growing at all levels of education. The move to a learning society needs changes in personal attitudes and learning infrastructure. Web based learning generally is seen as the chance to innovative learning process. The direction is that learning can take place anywhere, at the moment when it is needed. The focus on individualizing learning process based on time, place, duration, and learning style is on the rise. Pervasive computing, with its focus on users and their tasks rather than on computing devices and technology, provides an attractive vision for the future of web based learning." (Rarnadoss, B. and S.R. Balasundaram, 2004, p.1).

This clearly points out towards the need for an outcomes approach to pedagogy.

Some possible scenarios:

Student weblogs could allow students to keep track of their thinking over time, to pose issues, to receive comments by others. Students could link to web sites that were helpful to them, to points made by other students that clarified things. She could keep certain sections private; others open for public discussion, others to discussion by students only. Teacher weblogs could allow teachers to keep track of their own ideas over time. Certain sections could be open to students, others to teachers, and some to both.

Researchers would find a treasure trove of things to study in weblogs and online discussions. They wouldn't have to physically enter classrooms and disrupt ongoing discussions. Researcher weblogs would let researchers document the evolution of their research over time and to share their thoughts with others.

Students and teachers alike could communicate through their mobile phones and other devices as and when an idea clicks. Students could have a database of correct and wrong responses that they gave to an assignment. They could also contribute to the dialogue of knowledge base building by cross-verifying their learning with reality, at their homes or workplaces.

Using portable computing devices (such as laptops, tablet PCs, PDAs, and smart phones) with wireless networks enables mobility and mobile learning, allowing teaching and learning to extend to spaces beyond the traditional classroom. Within the classroom, mobile learning gives instructors and learners increased flexibility and new opportunities for interaction. Mobile technologies support learning experiences that are collaborative, accessible, and integrated with the world beyond the classroom.

Some of these ideas might already be implemented in part in certain contexts. What the present paper emphasizes is that a much more fundamental dialogue, thinking, evolution of initiatives and most of all an acceptance of the above framework is needed so that the philosophy and methods of the University are re-engineered through a visualizing and implementing a new KMS.

And, all this and more can be done silently, surely and seamlessly.

Strands of Re-Engineering

The four strands of re-engineering higher education so as to align it to the needs of society are the following:

- e-learning/ blended learning;
- pervasive computing;
- distance / open learning; and
- an outcomes approach to pedagogy.

E-learning is cost intensive. It hence needs to be broad-based. This implies distance or open learning because the numbers are much larger. Traditionally the Pedagogic System was based on an objectives approach. The outcomes approach makes the KMS target oriented. The outcomes approach is based on the learning outcomes and not the teaching objectives. The emphasis is on the learner than the teacher. It has been said that for each teaching approach there are ten learning approaches. This lends greater variety and can personalize the pedagogic process. This is what enables it to become capable of developing individual skills. In the industry there are two factors which make such KM system work better. Firstly, the motivation level upon joining a job is much greater. Secondly, on the job there is a peer group that makes the learning process much better and

Figure 3. E-learning system (Personalized and Skill augmenting)

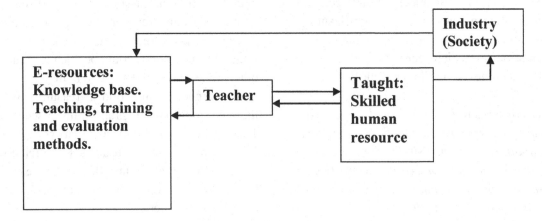

faster. The University system, particularly the new Pedagogic System needs to adapt itself to be able to carry out this process re-engineering. The KMS in its new for by incorporating the above element would be capable of meeting the challenges that it faces from society.

Once this happens the University System becomes more relevant for society. This is depicted in the Figure 3 by the boundary of the pedagogic system becoming co-terminus with that of the University system.

CONCLUSION

The University System is confronted with a changed environment which necessitates re-engineering of higher education. The new framework is that of a new Pedagogic System that is to be embedded in the Knowledge Management System, in seamless manner, through pervasive computing. This paper argues that the University system is under great pressure from industry (society) to deliver such finished products (graduates) from its system so as to be directly absorbed into industry and that too at a mass scale and in a short period of time. The objective is to propose a complete change in the philosophy and methods and outline the re-engineering by which this can be done, in a seamless manner, through these strand of re-engineering:

1. e-learning and blended learning;
2. pervasive computing;
3. distance and open learning; as well as
4. an outcomes approach to pedagogy.

The new KMS has to blend into the general environment of the learner so that the learner learns, applies, internalizes by naturally picking up things. For this the ultimate step is to internalize the pedagogic process and methods into the environment. This however would be possible only through the medium of pervasive computing.

Some of these ideas might already be implemented in part in certain contexts. What the present paper emphasizes is that a much more fundamental dialogue, thinking, evolution of initiatives and most of all an acceptance of the above framework is needed so that the philosophy and methods of the University are re-engineered through a visualizing and implementing a new KMS.

REFERENCES

Abowd, G., D. (1999). Classroom 2000: An experiment with the instrumentation of a living educational environment. *IBM Systems Journal*, *38*(4), 508–530.

Bhanu Murthy, K. V. (1995). *Manpower development - Skills, technology and basic science. Paper in Delhi University Seminar on Role of the university in manpower development for industry* (pp. 47–50). New Delhi: Aakriti.

Buzzell, C.H. (1987). Let Our Image Reflect Our Pride. *Vocational Education Journal, 62*(8) November-December.

Florida, R. (1999). *Industrializing Knowledge: University-Industry Linkages in Japan and the United States*. Cambridge, MA: MIT Press.

Hammer, M., & James, C. (1993). *Re-engineering the Corporation*. New York: Harper Business.

Henry, C. (2008). Can Universities Dream of Electric Sheepskin? *Systemic Transformations in Higher Education Organizational Models, 11*(1), Winter.

Hilton, J. (2004). *Role of the University in Knowledge Economy*. Presentation at SAC Conference. Retrieved from http://connect.educause.edu/Library/Abstract/TheRoleoftheUniversityint/43 102?time=1223297362

Konstantinidis, S. T., & Bamidis, P. D. (2007). *E-Learning Environments in Medical Education: How Pervasive Computing Can Influence the Educational Process.* Sofia, Bulgaria: BCI.

Newman, J. H. (1852). *The Idea of a University Defined and Illustrated: I* (Ker, I. T., Ed.). Oxford: Clarendon Press.

Oblinger, D. (2006). *Simulations, Games, and Learning.* ELI White Paper. ELI3004. Retrieved from http://connect.educause.edu/

Pelikan, J. (1992). *The Idea of the University: A Reexamination.* New Haven, CT: Yale University Press.

Prusak, L. (2001). Where did knowledge management come from? *IBM Systems Journal, 40*(4), 1002–1007.

Rarnadoss, B. & Balasundaram, S. R. (2004). Aspects of pervasive computing for web based learning. *International conference on information technology, Hyderabad, 3356,* 419-425.

Selwyn, N. (2002). Learning to Love the Micro: The Discursive Construction of 'Educational' Computing in the UK, 1979-89. *British Journal of Sociology of Education, 23*(3), 427–443. doi:10.1080/0142569022000015454

Shi, Y., & Xie, W. (2003). The smart classroom: merging technologies for seamless tele-education. *Pervasive Computing, IEEE, 2*(2), 47–55. doi:10.1109/MPRV.2003.1203753

Voorhees, R. A., & Lingenfelter, P. E. (2003). *Adult Learners and State Policy.* Chicago: SHEEO and CAEL.

ADDITIONAL READING

Annetta, L. (2006). Serious Games: Incorporating Video games in the Classroom . *EDUCAUSE Quarterly, 29*(3).

Bennett, F. (1999) Education and the future, *Educational Technology & Society,* 2, 1. Retrieved from http://ifets.ieee.org/ periodical/vol 1_99/fbennett_short_article.htm

Bromley, H. (1997). The social chicken and the technological egg: educational computing and the technology/ society divide . *Educational Theory, 47*(1), 51–65. doi:10.1111/j.1741-5446.1997.00051.x

Brown, J. S. (2006) New Learning Environments in the 21st Century: Exploring the Edge, Forum Futures (Forum for the Future of Higher Education).2006. Cambridge, MA.

Chickering, A. W. and Steven C. E. (1996). Implementing the Seven Principles: Technology as Lever, *AAHE Bulletin,* October, 3–6.

Cohen, D., & Prusak, L. (2001). *In Good Company: How Social Capital Makes Organizations Work.* Boston, MA: Harvard Business School Press.

DeVaney, C. (1998). Will educators ever unmask that determiner, technology? *Educational Policy, 125,* 568–585. doi:10.1177/0895904898012005006

Foreman, J. (2004). Game-Based Learning: How to Delight and Instruct in the 21st Century . *EDUCAUSE Review, 39*(5), 51–66.

Gardner, H. (1983). *Frames of mind: The theory of Multiple Intelligences.* New York: Basic Books.

Hawkridge, D. (1983). *New Information Technology in Education.* London: Croom Helm.

Hugh, G. P. (1968). The Strategy Sense of 'Methodology' . *Philosophy of Science, 35*(3), 248–257. doi:10.1086/288212

Kulik, J. A., Kulik, C. L. C., & Cohen, P. A. (1980). Effectiveness of computer-based college teaching: A meta-analysis of findings. *Review of Educational Research, 50,* 525–544.

National Research Council. (1999). *How People Learn: Brain, Mind, Experience, and School, John D. Bransford* (Ann, L. B., & Rodney, R. C., Eds.). Washington, D.C.: National Academies Press.

Olson, D. R. (1985). Computers as tools of the intellect. *Educational Researcher, 14*(5), 5–70. doi:10.2307/1174200

Olson, D. R., & Bruner, J. (1974). Learning through experience and learning through media . In Olson, D. (Ed.), *Media and symbols: The forms of expression, communication, and education*. Chicago: University of Chicago Press.

Pascarella, E. T., & Patrick, T. T. (2005). How College Affects Students: *Vol. 2. A Third Decade of Research*. San Francisco: Jossey-Bass.

Reed, L. (2000). Domesticating the personal computer: the mainstreaming of a new technology and the cultural management of a widespread technophobia . *Critical Studies in Media Communication, 17*(2), 159–185. doi:10.1080/15295030009388388

Richard, V. E. (2006). Digital Game-Based Learning: It's Not Just the Digital Natives Who Are Restless . *EDUCAUSE Review, 41*(2), 17–30.

Salomon, G., & Howard, G. (1986). The Computer as Educator: Lessons from Television Research . *Educational Researcher, 15*(1), 13–19.

Selwyn, N. (1999). Why the computer is not dominating schools: a failure of policy or a failure of practice . *Cambridge Journal of Education, 29*(1), 77–91. doi:10.1080/0305764990290106

Spurlin, J. E. (2006). *Technology and Learning: Defining What You Want to Assess*, ELI White Paper, July.

U.S. Congress - Office of Technology Assessment (1989). Linking for Learning: A New Course for Education. Washington, DC: 157.

Wagner, E. D. (2005). Enabling Mobile Learning . *EDUCAUSE Review, 40*(3), 40–53.

KEY TERMS AND DEFINITIONS

Pedagogic System: Teacher-Taught process, method of teaching.

E–Learning: Electronic learning, learning through the medium of Internet or Web.

Seamless: Perfectly consistent, having no rough edges.

Learning Outcomes: Expected result of learning process.

Blended Learning: Combining face to face teaching with e-learning.

Vocational Education: Careers that are based in manual or practical activities.

E-Resources (Electronic Resources): Databases, e-journals and books, web links.

Method: A way of doing something (usually involving steps).

Process: A series of operations performed

Pedagogic Validity: Internal consistency amongst the three dimensions, namely, learning outcomes, learning-teaching process and evaluation.

E-Content Development: Creation of study material and learning environment in electronic format.

ENDNOTES

[1]   Jaroslav Pelikan's, The Idea of the University: A Reexamination (1992) is a thoughtful, philosophical work of an eminent scholar who engages in dialogue with John Henry Newman's famous lecture series, The Idea of a University Defined and Illustrated (1852).

[2]   Bhanu Murthy (1995).

3   An instance is a replica set in a certain context.

4   I have designed one such course in collaboration with a leading bank in my University.

5   In fact the recent approach is to develop blended learning systems that combine face-to-face teaching with e-learning.

6   Sci-Tech Dictionary.

7   See Figure 4.

8   Dictionary.

9   Here industry includes agriculture and services.

10   This has been the core of the experiment that has been carried out at my initiate in my University.

Chapter 18

Virtual Vidyalaya:
An Integration of Pervasive Computing and E-Learning

Ashutosh Kasera
Rai Business School, Delhi, India

Piyush Ranjan
Rai Business School, Delhi, India

ABSTRACT

Pervasive computing is an evolving environment for the next generation providing with Information & Communication Technology everywhere, for everyone, at all times. e-learning is a phenomenon which is catching up the fire fiercely not only in corporate training world but also in the different sections of society. Pervasive computing is still in the evolving stage and opens a great naïve market yet unexplored. This chapter studies the features of Pervasive Computing which can take e-learning to the greater heights opening a new horizon for its growth and development. It also tries to analyze the factors that can contribute to the success of e-learning not only in making it reach the corporate training world but also in the rural areas of the world making a dream of education to all a reality in the environment of Pervasive Computing. It also studies and tries to find out the scope of e-learning in the light of Pervasive Computing.

INTRODUCTION

In the last couple of years, Pervasive Computing, sometimes also known as ubiquitous computing has been evolving as a new-brand computing phenomenon attracting a number of researchers to this area. Pervasive Computing is the result of computer technology advancing at exponential speeds, a trend toward all man-made and some natural products having hardware and software. The key feature behind developing this new computing phenomenon is the evolution of concepts and its applications, finding out the adaptable means of interaction between the humans and the embedded machines. Pervasive Computing goes beyond the realm of personal computers. It is the idea that almost any device, from clothing to tools, to appliances to cars, to homes to the human body to coffee

DOI: 10.4018/978-1-61520-741-1.ch018

mug, can be embedded within chips to connect the device to an infinite network of other devices. It is about completely changing the definitions of the computers and the way it is seen and perceived in the current scenario. The basic objectives behind developing such systems are to make the computers penetrate deep in the lives of human beings making it Pervasive not only in name but in real sense as well. Similarly, just like air and water are Pervasive for human life, the objective is to make computing the same to human lives. It is also about the interactions between humans and machines and making them user-friendly to such a great extent that it gets merged in the daily lives of all the human beings. The goal of Pervasive Computing, which combines current network technologies with wireless computing, voice recognition, internet capability and artificial intelligence, is to create an environment where the connectivity of devices is embedded in such a way that the connectivity is unobtrusive and always available. The purpose of Pervasive Computing is to make computers easy to use just as our pen, paper or spoon and fork. e-learning describes the use of 'tools' such as computers, the Internet and in general, Information and Communication Technology (ICT), to provide learning or education in one or more subject areas. In the words of Pittinsky (2003, p. 206), "Among technologies missing are tools that support the varied subjects and teaching styles that comprise the full constellation of instruction that exists."

'Vidyalaya' is a word taken from the vocabulary of hindi language meaning "A School" or "An Institution" or "A Temple of Knowledge". Virtual specifies the presence without any physical existence. It gives an implication of its existence without being physically present as in the traditional approach as in the different parts of the world. In this paper, a study has been done to create a 'Virtual Vidyalaya' i.e. "A Virtual Temple of Knowledge" with the application of Pervasive Computing in the field of e-learning. This paper tries to find out, if Pervasive Computing Systems

can be applied in the process of learning and the ways in which it can benefit the learners from the different sections of the society to avail the benefits derived from this emerging wave of e-learning with an integration of Pervasive Computing.

BACKGROUND

Eight billion embedded microprocessors are produced each year. This number is expected to rise dramatically over the next decade, making electronic devices ever more Pervasive. These devices will range from a few millimeters in size as in small sensors to several meters as in displays and surfaces. They may be interconnected via wired and wireless technologies into broader and efficient networks. Pervasive Computing Systems (PCS) and services may lead to a greater degree of user knowledge of, or control over, the surrounding environment, whether at home, or in an office or car. They may also show a form of 'intelligence'. For instance, a 'smart' electrical appliance could detect its own impending failure and notify its owner as well as a maintenance company, to arrange for a repair.

'Hole in the Wall' as it is well known and named by Dr. Sugata Mitra (2006), Chief Scientist at NIIT is a revolutionary experiment going on which started with the slums in Kalkaji, New Delhi. On 26th January, 1999, his team carved a 'hole in the wall' that separated the NIIT premises from the adjoining slum in Kalkaji, New Delhi. A freely accessible computer was put for use through this hole. The installation of this computer drew the attention amongst the children of slum dwellers. Without any prior experience and education these children learnt to use the computer on their own. Based on this experiment the following hypothesis was drawn by Dr. Sugata Mitra:

The acquisition of basic computing skills by any set of children can be achieved through incidental learning provided the learners are given access to a suitable computing facility, with entertaining and motivating content and some minimal (human) guidance.

This experiment opens up a new window for a universe of opportunities in e-learning ready to be explored. It gives a vision of the different aspects of e-learning still untouched by a huge mass ranging from the slums of developed cities to the rural areas left behind in the growth process of the developing and under-developed countries at large.

Another experiment done at Hopkins University, revealed that young children aged between 36 and 42 months, can learn better 'if they figure it out themselves' (Reuters, 2006).

The famous 21 prepositions as laid down by Sloman (2001, p. xii - xiv) lays down a foundation for the evolving market of e-learning in the arena of corporate training. Time has proven that the largest audience for online education is working adults who need to hold down full-time jobs while advancing their education. Gurwell(2003) has rightly stated that Online education could be Internet's biggest growth area. In his own words – "The biggest growth in the Internet, and the area that will prove to be one of the biggest agents of change, will be in e-learning," said Cisco's chief executive officer, John Chambers.

The first wave of computing technologies started with the era of Mainframe computers, where one computer was shared by many people through their individual computers. The next wave was of personal computers where one person used to share one computer generally known as desktop. The third wave is currently sweeping us with Pervasive Computing where one person is having many embedded computers in the environment making the technology to work in the background.

Embedded microprocessors are the hidden chips that control everything from cell phones and microwave ovens to jumbo jets and antilock brakes. It is these embedded microprocessors that are preparing the ground for the evolution of Pervasive Computing in the form of a revolution.

Processors for PCs, workstations and servers get all the attention, but embedded microprocessors make the world go round. It is estimated that the average U.S. household has about 60 embedded microprocessors.

MAIN FOCUS

Emerging Market

There is a mismatch between an Institution perception of the use of technology by learners and the actual use. In the words of Conole(2006, p. 63) "Students expect good quality material, which is interactive and engaging; however there is a mismatch between this expectation and what the majority of students are being given in their institutions." This makes one to think about the choices that a learner wants and needs, giving way to new markets for the expansion of e-learning. Pervasive Computing is opening the market for e-learning in two different areas ready to fulfill the needs of different groups of users.

The two areas, which are clearly different from each other in terms of their needs and requirements, have been identified during the study. The analysis of these areas during the study gives an overview described briefly in the following words-

Primary Education: With the lack of infrastructure and human resources in the countries like India, the grand dream of government to have 'Education for all' seems to be a dream only. Some other means of transforming this dream to reality needs to be sought after. With the evolution of Pervasive Computing and e-learning, the scenario seems to be changing. It is showing a ray of light in this dark cave. An integration of Pervasive Computing along with e-learning can spread its wings to reach to the remote corners of the world providing the basic education to each and every citizen. A whole new world of basic education is open to be explored giving such a huge market opportunity.

Professional Education: In such a dynamic and fast changing world, there is a continuous need of knowledge up-gradation to keep up with the current trends by the professionals all over the world. The professionals have their limitations in terms of time and cost. They are always looking for small cost-effective capsule modules as per their needs of training. The application of Pervasive Computing in imparting these modules opens up a huge market that can quench the thirst of information and knowledge at the professional level as well.

It is quite important to note that the above mentioned markets are completely different from each other. The needs, the assumptions, the market, the people, the content and the methods are completely different. Even the demography of the beneficiaries is completely different. Thus, a generalized model cannot be designed which can cater to the needs of both the beneficiaries. Looking into the assumptions and requirements, two different models are needed to make Pervasive Computing really work in providing e-learning solutions to the masses at large.

Next in the line comes the categorization of users as per their needs and requirement. With such a big population, the needs are different. In order to cater to this big market, a proper categorization should be created. Even in Primary as well as Professional Education, we have the subgroups of people. Separate approach is required for each group. Again, a single model cannot cater to the needs of the people in these subsections. During the study, an analysis based on the learning requirements of the users gives us a broad categorization listed as below-

Rural Segment: Rural segment is characterized by a poorer infrastructure, less finances, lower levels of literacy, lower accessibility and higher cost of Internet access and limited understanding and appreciation of the potential of e-learning. e-learning can never replace a traditional education system, but it can act as a tool to help and enhance the process of learning based on the unique circumstances of the environment in which it is implemented.

Underprivileged Segment: As depicted in the experiment carried out by Dr. Sugata Mitra "Hole-in-the-Wall" is waiting for the initiatives to be taken by the government or industry or a merger of two for the investment in the education of the poor young children who have no alternatives to join the mainstream of the education system for a formal education. The developing countries like India have not enough resources to invest in the traditional system installing the required infrastructure and manpower for establishing schools and to arrange for the needed teachers. It sounds very enthusiastic to drive the wave of Pervasive Computing carrying e-learning to cater to the needs of this segment.

Corporate Segment: The World of Corporate is big and proposes a huge market yet to be captured. With the rapid changes in terms of technology and processes in today's dynamic world, there is a huge need for the training of professionals from different specializations of working domain. Another challenge is the geographical location. The best of the talents are out of the reach of the prospective learners from all over the country. The time and the efforts are quite limited on the trainer part that acts as a boom for the spread of e-learning modules specifically designed for this segment of the Industry. The success of e-learning holds back on its effective and efficient implementation. There can be no better carrier as Pervasive Computing to bring in this change for the corporate.

Dropped-out Segment: Pervasive computing is the biggest boon for the population who has been cut-off from the formal mode of education system. The reasons are innumerable: Family responsibilities, lack of finance, some tragedy in the family and many more. Even if they decide to get back into the mainstream, it is very difficult for them to become the part of the system once again. They might not be comfortable because of the age differences amongst the learners, not having the freedom of time to attend the course on a regular basis or being hesitant to join the mainstream. The motivation to join the mainstream can come, if it is provided on their own terms with due consideration of their limitations. Pervasive Computing offers the motivation, the flexibility, the freedom and an interesting approach that can surely lure them to become the part of the system.

Pervasive Computing Devices for E-Learning

Pervasive Computing involves three converging areas of ICT namely Pervasive Computing Devices, Pervasive Computing Connectivity and Users Interface. Each one of it has a very important role to play in an effective and efficient implementation of e-learning using Pervasive Computing. An analysis of the different alternatives available under each head was done during this study. As each of it is going to play an important but a different role integrating e-learning with Pervasive Computing, a short description of it needs to be understood first.

Pervasive Computing Devices: Pervasive Computing devices are available in various forms and sizes; from handheld units looking like cellular phones to near-invisible devices set into 'everyday' objects like clothing, furniture etc. These will all be able to communicate with each other and act 'intelligently'. Such devices can be separated into three categories:

Sensors: These are the input devices that detect environmental changes, user behaviors, human commands etc;

Processors: These are the electronic systems that interpret and analyze input-data;

Actuators: These are the output devices that respond to processed information by altering the environment via electronic or mechanical means. For example, air temperature control is often done with actuators. However the term can also refer to devices which deliver information, rather than altering the environment physically.

Pervasive Computing Connectivity: Pervasive Computing systems heavily rely on the inter-connection of independent electronic devices into wider networks. This can be achieved via both wired such as Broadband and cables; and wireless networking technologies such as Wi-Fi or Bluetooth, with the devices themselves being capable of assessing the most effective form of connectivity in any given scenario. The effective development of Pervasive Computing Systems depends on their degree of interoperability, as well as on the convergence of standards for wired and wireless technologies.

Users Interfaces: Since Pervasive Computing is changing everything, so the user interfaces cannot be left behind. These interfaces need to be different from what is available today on desktop PCs or laptops. There will be a range of devices generally with small screens and alternative input options. The user interface should be according to the devices and keeping in view the ease of use which can not put an extra burden on learning to interact with the machines. Users Interfaces are a major cause for success or failure of a complete system and utmost care needs to be taken while designing user interfaces for e-learning.

Why Pervasive Computing for E-Learning?

Location Flexibility: Pervasive Computing makes the learner interact and inter-connect with a number of devices from the rest of the world irrespective of the geographical location. This opens up the doors of the world providing with the best practices available for learning and practice.

Content Flexibility: Pervasive Computing also supports and promotes the content independence. The learners have the flexibility to accept the modules that are needed, skipping those which are of no relevance to them. Designers can work at a broader outline standardizing the code and segregating the interface to be plugged in as per the local requirements of the learners. This reduces the efforts to be applied along with making the content independent in nature widening its scope of reach.

Time Flexibility: Time flexibility is one of the major advantages of Pervasive Computing applications. Anyone can access the contents whenever they want. They are not required to access the contents at the pre-defined time frame as in the traditional education system approach which makes it a bit unfeasible for the users with their time limitations. Pervasive Computing Systems gives a freedom to access the contents at the users' own comfort with the utilization of their time in the best possible ways making it more acceptable.

Digitization of Teaching and Learning Process: The complete process of different activities gets facilitated with Pervasive Computing. It integrates the e-learning minimizing the challenges of scarce resources inviting more and more participation from the population. With a growing market of e-learning, teaching process is getting enhanced with the application of Pervasive Computing technologies resulting in an automated teaching process replacing the traditional education system.

Informal training: Pervasive Computing in e-learning supports and promotes opening up a new and effective channel of informal training. Informal training caters to a larger section of society in digital world liberating the population from the bondages restricting them to take part in the learning process due to social or cultural beliefs.

Robust: Pervasive Computing in e-learning in the present context has made its impact for being robust in use and a low maintenance cost and effort due to the massive advancement in technology.

Interesting: The application of Pervasive Computing in e-learning draws lots of attention from the all the sections of society. Human nature is of high curiosity and people get interested to explore the new technology alluring them for a new enthralling learning process. Computers increase learners' enjoyment and thereby making it easier to teach them.

Fuel for Pervasive Computing: The driving force in the form of fuel is needed for any technology to work creating a huge demand for a source of energy for power supply. Without the presence of the power supply no technology whether ICT, Pervasive Computing, e-learning or any other can make an impact or its application anywhere in the world. These Pervasive Computing devices run on the minimum power available that adds up to its advantage.

RECOMMENDATIONS

As a part of this study, different alternatives and means available for the implementation of Pervasive Computing for e-learning have been studied and analyzed deeply. Based on the analysis and the study, some recommendations have been given in the following section for a successful, effective and efficient implementation of this system:

Regional language: Pervasive Computing is changing the quality of life in urban areas but the use of it is very limited in rural areas. The absence of regional language is amongst one of the major causes behind this digital divide between the urban and rural areas. Most of the applications are developed with the user Interface designed in English language and unfamiliarity with this language is one of the biggest factors contributing to this problem. In rural areas, where the majority of the population is English-illiterate, Pervasive Computing has to speak a language the locals understand. This is where user-interface localization steps in and a need for the introduction of local language interface in Pervasive Computing for e-learning implementation is needed.

Multiple Languages: The ability of Pervasive Computing Systems to support instructions in multiple-languages is another usability deciding the reach and impact of Pervasive Computing for e-learning. Population in general finds it disheartening on its lack of ability to support multiple languages. Humans learn better when learning materials are presented in their respective languages. (Wagner, D. and Kozma, R., 2003, p. 15) says "ICT investments would involve not only the development of the hardware, software, and network infrastructure, but also the development of language-appropriate and culturally relevant content software." This aspect poses enormous challenges in a country, which has a host of different languages like India.

Pervasive Computing systems targeting semi-literate or illiterate users must present the information in the language of the target learners. It may be costly to translate the information into a number of languages, but it makes educational and usability sense. At the 2001 census, the number of raw returns of mother tongues has totaled 6,661. There are 216 languages with more than 10,000 native speakers in India. 22 languages are recognized as official languages. In India, there are 1,652 languages and dialects in total.

Multimedia Content: It was found during this study that despite being the cheapest, Radio is the least preferred of the education technologies. One of the main reasons for the low interest in radio is the radio's lack of visual information. In this respect, television and computer offer better alternatives. Presenting information in multiple modes increases the probability of learning. In the words of (Mayer R., 2001, p. 103) "the attractiveness of flexibility may increase the probability that students will take multimedia courses if they have choices". To this aspect can be added the presentation information in multiple modes i.e. text, speech and audio. (Goetze and Strothotte 2001, p. 2) note that interactively presenting pictures corresponding to words in a text may improve reading skills of adult learners. Compared to television and radio, computers are better equipped for this task.

Information for semi-literate and illiterate users should be presented using multiple media.

Where necessary, interaction should be used to enhance the integration of the multiple media. Fortunately, availability and cost of technology with Pervasive Computing no longer stands in the way of achieving such systems.

Cultural and Traditional Differences: Cultural differences directly influence decision-making when it comes to the ambitious target of globalization for many commercial software and online applications (Marcus, 1993, p. 100-109; Marcus & Gould, 2000, p. 32-46). Cultural preferences have become one of the most significant subjects and focuses of technology development, as it slowly turns away from issues of usability to issues of fulfilling users' cultural and social needs (Bourges-Waldegg & Scrivener, 1998, p. 287-309). In the next stage of pervasive computing development, it can be expected that the most essential concern will be to comprehend the needs of users all around the world, with regard to differences in language, customs, and behavior.

Filtering Inappropriate Content: Controversial or offensive content is deemed to be controversial or offensive according to individual, community, or culturally based standards. In some cases, this type of content may be considered to be harmful to children. Offensive content includes such things as legal pornography; violence; alcohol and tobacco advertising aimed at minors; and other content that may be considered to be objectionable on social, religious, cultural, or other grounds. Facilitating e-learning through the application of Pervasive Computing opens a number of unauthorized channels vulnerable to the new and curious generation, making regulation and content filtering an important aspect behind the policy of making online contents accessible to the public at large.

Model for E-Learning with the Facilitation of Pervasive Computing

Most of the traditional learning is based on the broadcast model that needs to be transformed to the peer-to-peer model. Today, learning is centered on the interests of the learner and their interests can only be aroused by doing rather than receiving. Pervasive Computing and Internet collectively becomes the interface connecting the students to the rest of the world.

In traditional education system, a human teacher was the media to disseminate information, which has been replaced partially by Google making it one of the best e-learning applications in digital world. The learners used to refer to their teachers for their need of information and knowledge. Today, the learners are referring to the Google for their basic needs of information and then referring to the teacher as a facilitator helping them in their learning process. In this digital world, learners structure their own learning to gather knowledge along life's way, to harvest and organize knowledge compromising what they know to give place to what is yet an unknown world.

The learner who can exercise their choices in subjects, materials and learning styles owns the process of learning in this digital world. They use blogs, wikis, folksonomies, RSS, podcast etc. whatever tools and devices are available to choose from always scanning for more enriched multimedia explosions. For example, the use of blogs acts like opening classroom walls motivating the learners with real world writing experiences. These make knowledge as a process that is actively constructed making the learners responsible for their own learning. It makes learning interactive and experimental. This is one of the major reasons making games as an effective and a very efficient tool for enhancing the process of learning.

There can be no better option than Pervasive Computing in the hands and environment of the learners opening up new horizons in the field of learning and teaching. Different models are needed to cater the different categories of users as mentioned earlier. A single model which can work for everyone cannot be feasible in practice. This opens new research areas still to be explored

on such dedicated and specialized models for the integration of Pervasive Computing into e-learning.

FUTURE TRENDS

There are many visions for the future development of Pervasive Computing System devices. Several research groups are endeavoring to produce networks of devices that could be small as a mole of sand. The idea is that each one would function independently, with its own power supply, and could also communicate wirelessly with the others. These could be distributed throughout the environment to form dense, but almost invisible, Pervasive Computing networks, thus eliminating the need for overt devices. At the other extreme, augmented reality would involve overlaying the real world with digital information. This approach emphasizes the use of mobile technologies, geographical positioning systems and internet-linked databases to distribute information via personal digital companions. Such devices could come in many forms like -

Children might have them integrated into school bags, whereas adults might use devices more closely resembling personal digital assistants (PDAs). Ultimately a spectrum of devices may become available. These will range from miniaturized (potentially embedded in surrounding objects) to a variety of mobile (including handheld and wearable) devices. While these could exist as standalone systems, it is likely that many will be interlinked to form more comprehensive systems.

CONCLUSION

Pervasive Computing has been in development for almost 20 years but still remains some way from becoming a fully operational reality. Some core technologies have already emerged, although the development of battery technologies and user interfaces pose particular challenges. It may be another 5-10 years before complete Pervasive Computing Systems become widely available. This depends on market forces, industry, public perceptions and the effects of any policy or regulatory frameworks.

e-learning facilitation using Pervasive Computing can be a reality only by the adaptation of such devices by the population at large in a cost-effective method and the change in the learning environment not only from the Individual perspective but also from the Institutional perspective. Instead of viewing learning as a distribution process, it needs a change in its basic concept making it an interactive process. Learners will be not only at the receiving end but at the giving end as well. They are not going to act just as a consumer of information but there roles are changing as the producer of information as well. Researchers and Practitioners from both the fields need to join and sit together for the integration of the technology and the educational pedagogy to design a system which can fulfill the requirements of the learners.

REFERENCES

Bourges-Waldegg, P., & Scrivener, S. A. R. (1998). Meaning, the central issue in cross-cultural HCI design. *Interacting with Computers*, *9*(3). doi:10.1016/S0953-5438(97)00032-5

Conole., et al. (2006). *JISC LXP: Student experiences of technologies*. Final report. Retrieved February 21, 2009 from http://www.jisc.ac.uk/media/documents/programmes/elearningpedagogy/lxpprojectfinalreportdec06.pdf

Goetze, M., & Strothotte, T. (2001), An Approach to Help Functionally Illiterate People with Graphical Reading Aids. In *Proc. of the International Symposium on Smart Graphics.*

Gurwell, L. (2003). *Online education could be Internet's biggest growth area*. Retrieved February 19, 2009 from http://findarticles.com/p/articles/mi_qn4190/is_20030411/ai_n10044548

Marcus, A. (1993). Human communication issues in advanced UIs. *Communications of the ACM*, *36*(4). doi:10.1145/255950.153670

Marcus, A., & Gould, E. W. (2000). Cross-currents: Cultural dimensions and global Web user-interface design. *Interaction*, *7*(4). doi:10.1145/345190.345238

Mayer, R. (2001). *Multimedia Learning*. Cambridge, UK: Cambridge Press.

Mitra, S. (2006). Hole-in-the-Wall Lighting the spark of Learning. *Beginnings*. Retrieved February 19, 2009 from http://www.hole-in-the-wall.com/Beginnings.html

Pittinsky, M. (2003). *The Wired Tower: Perspectives on the Impact of the Internet on Higher Education*. Upper Saddle River, NJ: Prentice Hall.

Reuters. (2006). *Kids learn better if they figure it out themselves: study*. Retrieved February 20, 2009 from http://www.reuters.com/article/gc08/idUSL0862420070308

Sloman, M. (2001). *The E-learning Revolution: From Propositions to Reality*. London: CIPD Publishing.

Wagner, D., & Kozma, R. (2003). *New Technologies for Literacy and Adult Education: A Global Perspective*. International Literacy Institute, National Center for adult literacy, University of Pennsylvania. Retrieved February 20, 2009 from http://www.literacy.org/products/wagner_kozma.pdf

ADDITIONAL READING

Adam, G. (2006). *Everyware: The Dawning Age of Ubiquitous Computing*. New Riders.

Andrea, E. (2007). *Globalized e-learning cultural challenges, Idea Group Inc*. IGI.

Beetham Helen & Sharpe Rhona. (2007). *Rethinking Pedagogy for a Digital Age: Designing and Delivering E-learning*. Routledge.

Birchall David & Woolfall Damian. (2003). *Corporate e-learning: Delivering business benefits*. Grist Ltd.

Bowles Marcus, S. (2004). *Relearning to E-learn: Strategies for Electronic Learning and Knowledge*. Melbourne University Publishing.

Bruck, P. A., Andrea, B., Zeger, K., & Ansgar, Z. (2005). *E-content: Technologies and Perspectives for the European Market*. Springer.

Caladine, R. (2008). *Enhancing E-Learning with Media-Rich Content and Interactions, Idea Group Inc*. IGI.

Carliner Saul & Shank Patti. (2008). The E-Learning Handbook: Past Promises, Present Challenges, John Wiley and Sons, 2008

Charles, W. (2003). *DeFillippi Bob*. Educating Managers with Tomorrow's Technologies, Information Age Publishing.

Erik, D., Ralf, K., & Martin, W. (Eds.). (2007). Creating New Learning Experiences on a Global Scale, EC-TEL 2007, Crete, Greece, P.A.: Springer

Joseph, F., Reggie, K., & Lee, W. F. (Eds.). (2008). Hybrid Learning and Education: First International Conference, Ichl Hong Kong, China, P A: Springer

Karen, M. (2002). *Blending E-Learning: The Power Is in the Mix*. American Society for Training and Development.

Kehal Harbhajan, S., & Singh Varindear, P. (2004). *Digital economy: impacts, influences and challenges, Idea Group Inc*. IGI.

Littlejohn Allison & Pegler Chris. (2007). *Preparing for Blended E-learning: Understanding Blended and Online Learning*. Routledge.

Picciano Anthony, G., & Sloan Alfred, P. (2007). *Blended Learning: Research Perspectives Foundation*. Sloan Center for OnLine Education, Sloan Consortium, Sloan-C.

Piskurich George, M. (2003). *Preparing Learners for E-Learning*. John Wiley and Sons.

Piskurich George, M. (Ed.). (2003). *The AMA Handbook of E-learning: Effective Design, Implementation, and Technology Solutions, AMACIM Div American Management Association Pope Christine & Phillips Jack J., (2001). Implementing E-Learning Solutions, American Society for Training and Development Tai Luther, (2007). Corporate e-learning: an inside view of IBM's solutions*. Oxford University Press US.

Varuna, G. (2008). *Handbook of Research on Assessment and Management in Pervasive Computing: Operational, Legal, Ethical and Financial Perspectives, Idea Group Inc*. IGI.

KEY TERMS AND DEFINITIONS

Bluetooth: Bluetooth is a wireless protocol for exchanging data over short distances from fixed and mobile devices, creating personal area networks (PANs).

Broadband: Pertaining to or denoting a type of high-speed data transmission in which the bandwidth is shared by more than one simultaneous signal.

Computing: To determine or calculate by the means of a computer.

Folksonomies: A type of classification system for online content, created by an individual user who tags information with freely chosen keywords and also the cooperation of a group of people to create such a classification system

ICT: Information and Communications Technology

Microprocessor: Central Processing Unit of computer contained on an integrated-circuit chip.

PDA: Abbr. for Personal Digital Assistant which is a lightweight, hand-held, usually pen-based computer used as a personal organizer.

Pervasive: To become diffused through every part of its containment.

RSS: Any of various XML file formats suitable for disseminating real-time information via subscription on the Internet which has become a popular technology for bloggers and podcasters to distribute their content.

Podcast: A Web-based audio broadcast via an RSS feed, accessed by subscription over the Internet.

Vidyalaya: An institution sacred like a place of worship for imparting knowledge.

Wi fi: is a trademark of the Wi-Fi Alliance, founded in 1999 as Wireless Internet Compatibility Alliance (WICA), based on the IEEE 802.11 standards (also called Wireless LAN (WLAN) and Wi-Fi). This certification warrants interoperability between different wireless devices.

Chapter 19
Developing Learning Communities:
Improving Interactivity of an Online Class

Pawan Jain
Fort Hays State University, USA

Smita Jain
University of Wyoming, USA

ABSTRACT

This study concerns the design and development of online instruction and specifically targets interaction and communication between online learners. Facilitating appropriate and meaningful interactions in designing instruction is a major goal for anyone developing an online class. The guiding question of the study was: how do the instructional design elements and discipline area impact the quantity of learner-learner interactions? The data for this study came from the online courses offered at one of the major Rocky Mountain University. The research subjects and courses were taken from the College of Education, College of Business, College of Arts and Sciences and College of Health Sciences. Forty graduate online classes, 10 from each college, were analyzed. The findings of this study suggest that the interactivity in an online class depends on group size, grade weight for discussion, use of web 2.0 technologies and multimedia and the discipline it belongs to.

INTRODUCTION

For hundreds of thousands of years, people lived in hunting and gathering economy until humans made the transition to an agricultural economy. The agricultural society continued until about

200 years ago, when the Western world ushered in the Industrial Revolution. A few decades ago, the industrial economy began to give way to the present day information-based society (Dagget, 1998). The advent of the computer and the Internet were instrumental in changing society to a global, knowledge-based economy or to what is known today as the information age (Crossman, 1997).

DOI: 10.4018/978-1-61520-741-1.ch019

This shift in society has had an insurmountable impact on institutions of higher education. Today higher education is reaching beyond the walls of the traditional classroom by providing alternative methods of educational delivery through the use of the Internet and the World Wide Web. This type of distance education delivery is referred to as online learning.

Facilitating appropriate and meaningful interactions in designing instruction is a major goal for anyone developing a course, especially an online course. Although not supported by a specific research study, Kearsley (1998) claims that the "single most important element of successful online education is interaction among participants." He further states that it is "the instructor's role as a facilitator to ensure that a high-level of interaction occurs in an online course" (p. 3).

The concept of interaction has received considerable attention in the literature related to distance Internet-based learning (Hill, Wiley, Nelson & Han, 2004). Daniel and Marquis's (1988) challenged the educators to "get the mixture right" between independence (student-content interaction) and interaction (mainly student-teacher interaction). In the 21st century we are still challenged to get the mixture right (Anderson, 2003). Appropriate mixtures will result in increased learning and exciting new educational opportunities; inappropriate mixes will be expensive, exclusive and exigent. Our responsibility as experienced educators remain-to insure that the modes of interaction that we practice and prescribe maximize the attainment of all legitimate educational objectives and support and increase motivation for deep and meaningful learning (Anderson, 2003).

In this study the researcher assumes that the opinion of Kearsley (1998), "single most important element of successful online education is interaction among learners" (p. 3) holds and wants to understand the role the various instructional design elements and differences in discipline plays in impacting the overall interaction among learners.

Hence, the guiding question of the study is: do the instructional design elements and the discipline area impact the overall interaction among learners as defined by the number of learner-learner interactions?

BACKGROUND

As access to the Internet and World Wide Web has continued to grow, Web-based learning has continued to expand. With approximately half of the households in the United States (or 150 million people connected to the Internet), an estimated 2 million students are taking post-secondary courses that are fully delivered online (Galt Global Review, 2001). Millions of other students at all educational levels (primary, secondary, post-secondary, continuing education) participate online in hybrid, mixed mode, and Web-enhanced face-to-face courses (Picciano, 2002).

Interaction has been recognized as one of the most important components of learning experiences both in conventional education and distance education (Vygotsky, 1978; Holmberg, 1983; Moore, 1993). Gunawardena and Zittle (1997) revealed that social presence contributed more that 60% of learner satisfaction with computer conferencing courses. A common element for learning in a typical classroom environment is the social and communicative interactions between student and teacher, and student and student (Stubbs, 1976). The ability to ask a question, to share an opinion with a fellow student, or to disagree with the point of view in a reading assignment are all fundamental learning activities (Picciano, 2002). In online education, it is particularly important to provide an environment in which meaningful interaction can occur (Collins & Berge, 1996).

There is a scarcity of research on the importance of interaction in education especially in online education. There have been a few studies and opinion papers on the relationship of interaction to learning (Picciano, 2002). Many observers and researchers have supported the concept interactions among learners are important elements in the design of a Web-based course (Fulford & Zhang, 1993; Kearsley, 1995; Klesius, Homan & Thompson, 1997; Kumari, 2001; Picciano, 1998; 2001; Sherry, 1996; Smith, 1996; Zirkin & Sumler, 1995). Both students and faculty typically report increased satisfaction in online courses depending on the quantity of interactions (Dziuban & Moskal, 2001; Gunawardena & Zittle, 1997; Hartman & Truman-Davis, 2001; Kanuka & Anderson, 1998; Shea, Fredericksen, Pickett, Pelz, & Swan, 2001).

Previous research has indicated a strong, positive relationship exists between student perceptions of their interaction in the course and their perceptions of the quality and quantity of their learning (Dziuban & Moskal, 2001; Shea et al., 2001). Interactions among learners and positive contributions to students' learning are directly related (Laurillard, 1993; Moore, 1993; Ramsden, 1992). Michael Beaudoin (2001) examined the relationship between student interaction and learning. In the study, he divided an online class into three groups (high interaction, moderate interaction, and low interaction). He finds that the high interaction students achieved the highest performance. Adelskold *et al.* (1999) suggested collaborative interaction among learners could have greater effects on learning in a problem solving situation than other types of interaction.

Rust (2006) in her study, found that there is a significantly positive relationship between the number of postings per person and the student retention rate. She also concluded that a significantly positive relationship exists between the students' perceptions of the interaction and their final grade. Picciano (2002) showed, using correlation analysis, that perceived interaction and the actual interaction were significantly positively correlated.

Taiwei (2006) used structural equation modeling to show that learner-learner interaction plays an important role in student motivation. Students who were engaged in learner-learner interaction were more motivated than those who were not engaged in learner-learner interaction. Karayan and Crowe (1997) used surveys to examine students' perceptions of electronic discussion groups. Their research was designed to discover whether or not student behaviors changed as a result of participation in an electronic discussion group. They believed that the convenience of interaction, the provision for different kinds of learners, and the opportunity to "think through writing" would be evidenced in changes in student behaviors (p. 70).

According to Berge (1997), online class size is an area that is scarcely researched that may have significant affect on students learning and interaction. A research study by Jiang & Ting (2000) found that grades for discussion and requirements for discussion were significantly and positively correlated to students' perceived learning. Bouton and Garth (1983) stated that learning is a group process: the learner actively constructs knowledge by formulating ideas into words, and these ideas/concepts are built upon through reaction and responses of others (Harasim, 1990, p. 43). A unique feature of online education is its capability to support this interactive group process. As Internet-based education programs expand, educators are being challenged to go beyond delivering information to remote learners to building community among them (Bruffee, 1993; Dede, 1990, 1996; Harasim, Hiltz, Teles & Turoff, 1995; Kaye, 1995; Renniger & Shumar, 2000). Several researchers have found that the social aspects of the online learning environment are very important (Meyer, 2000).

MAIN FOCUS OF THE CHAPTER

John Dewey (1916) noted that "Every expansive era in the history of mankind has coincided with operation of factors which have tended to eliminate distance between peoples and classes previously hemmed off from one another" (Dewey, 1916, p.100). Distance educators also follow this tradition of using the technologically "expansive" of eras to remove the distances from distance education.

The field of distance education has a very long history, however significant to this study, is the brief history of online learning and the need to expand the research base that exists specific to online pedagogy. The majority of research has focused on the continuous debate of comparing online course with traditional courses (Strachota, 2003). The majority of such research has arrived at the conclusion that both the environment of the face-to-face course as well as online course are considered to be equally as effective (Johnson, Aragon, Shalik & Palma-Rivas, 2000; Phipps & Merisotis, 1999; Saba, 2000).

Of concern to the practice of online learning is the scarcity of research studying the impact of effective design of instruction on appropriate and meaningful interactions. There is no single "best way" to improvise these interactions. "Each institution, discipline, region, and user group will develop unique cultural practices and expectations related to their need for and use of interaction. Too much of our practice in distance education is not evidence based and our actions and instructional designs are often grounded on untested assumptions about the value of the modes of interaction (or lack thereof). Thus, research that focuses on interaction in all its forms is critically important" (Anderson, 2003). The guiding question of the study is: do the instructional design elements and the discipline area impact the overall interaction among learners as defined by the number of learner-learner interactions?

SAMPLE

The data for this study came from the graduate online courses offered at the University of Wyoming during the fall of 2007. Ten classes each, from the College of Education, College of Business, and College of Arts and Sciences and 9 classes from the College of Health Sciences, were analyzed. Hence, the analysis was conducted on a total of 39 online classes.

PROCEDURE

Data were collected on the actual number of student postings to the formal instructional discussion board. The site that provided the archived data for the study is recognized as being one that offered a large number of online courses each semester. The research courses were taken from the College of Education, College of Business, College of Arts and Sciences and College of Health Sciences. The postings to be counted included all comments or questions made to the formal instructional discussion board by the learner addressing other learner(s). These learner-learner postings were then sub-classified as Planning, Contributing, Reflecting, Social Interaction and Parroting, based on the rules developed by the researcher (Table 1). Actual number of student postings made to the formal instructional discussion board by the learner addressing other learner(s) was counted for three different weeks during the semester- week 3; week 8 & week 14, for each of the 39 online classes included in the study. So, the total number of the observation for this study was 117. To control for the variability in class size, this count of the number of learner postings per week was normalized by dividing by the class size and was the dependent variable for this study. By analyzing the Course syllabus and structure, data on exact grade weight assigned to the discussion, use of chat sessions, class size and group size statistics were recorded.

Rules for Sub-Categorizing the Learner-Learner Interaction

On the basis components of collaborative behavior described by Johnson & Johnson (1996), Curtis & Lawson (2001) developed a list to describe the various activities in an online course and based on that list, the researcher developed the following set of rules to categorize student postings into four sub-categories- Learner-Learner interactions, Learner- Course management system (CMS) interactions, Social Interactions and Parroting

ANALYSIS

Data were organized in SPSS 15.0 statistical software for analysis. Descriptive statistics were utilized to summarize, organize and simplify the data (Gravetter, & Wallnau, 1996). Means and standard deviations of the sample were determined to tell us about the distribution of the variables included.

To control for the variability in class size, the dependent variables (overall interactions per week) was normalized by dividing by the size of the class. Bivariate Correlation analysis was used to find the relationship between the dependent variable and the interval and ordinal independent variables- group size and grade weight for discussion and a t-test was employed to understand the differences due to the use of chat sessions. One-way Analysis of Variance was used to find the relationship between the dependent variable and the nominal independent variable, discipline. Follow-up tests were conducted to analyze the pairwise differences among the means and Scheffe's post hoc comparison test was employed for this purpose

Multiple regression analyses were used to identify the individual contribution of each of the independent variable included in the study. A change in R^2 test was employed to test if the independent variable made a unique contribution in predicting the dependent variable. Equation of the following form was estimated:

$$Y_i = \alpha + \beta_1 X_{1i} + \beta_2 X_{2i} + \beta_3 X_{3i} + \beta_4 X_{4i} + \varepsilon_i \qquad (1)$$

Where,

Y_i: Number of Learner-learner interactions per week normalized by class size.
X_1: Use of chat session
X_2: Group size
X_3: Grade weight for discussion
X_4: Discipline
α: Intercept
β_j: Regression coefficients
ε_i: Residual

Overall Interaction and Learning

This study is based on the assumption that the more the interaction, the greater is the learning. To test this assumption the researcher used average grade for classes included in the study as a proxy for learning. This is not the best measure of learning, but it does serve as a beginning point and a concrete measure of learning application. The result of the bivariate correlational analysis showed that the average grade was significantly positively correlated with the overall interactions per student per week, rho $= 0.32$, p < 0.01(Figure 1). One of the reasons for a smaller correlation coefficient might be that the grade is not the only or the best indicator of learning. The student's final grade is the undiscussed average (Biggs, 1999).

The above analysis tested the assumptions of this study. Hence, more interaction results in better learning, which also supports the opinions and researches by various authors in the literature (Dziuban & Moskal, 2001; Gunawardena & Zittle, 1997; Hartman & Truman-Davis, 2001; Kanuka & Anderson, 1998; Shea, Fredericksen, Pickett, Pelz, & Swan, 2001).

Table 1. Rules for Sub-categorizing the Learner-Learner Interaction

ActivityLearner-Learner Interactions	DescriptionGroup skills: a generic code applied to expressions that encourage group activity and cohesiveness	ExampleI know that [names] have given you good advice, but I think it's worth knowing that you need patience.
	Organizing work: Planning group work; setting shared tasks and deadlines.	I just want to set a time-line for myself. Is everyone OK with that?
	Initiating activities: Setting up activities such as chat sessions to discuss the progress and organization of group work.	I would like to chat on the blackboard. What about this Friday at 7.30pm SA time?
	Monitoring group effort: Comments about the group's processes and achievements.	I believe the overall contribution and collaboration of working as a group requires an increase within itself as part of our learning.
	Help seeking: Seeking assistance from others.	Does anyone know how to read the chart on pg. 12 of the text..?
	Feedback seeking: Seeking feedback to a position advanced.	What do you think about answering the question that…has put forward?
	Help giving: Responding to questions and requests from others.	To read the chart, look at the Appendix A of the text..
	Feedback giving: Providing feedback on proposals from others.	I agree with you and I believe… …….. Good point…
	Exchanging resources and information to assist other group members.	"With the implementation of an internet service … there has been a major shift in the communication function in business."
	Sharing knowledge: Sharing existing knowledge and information with others.	I think we also need to give thought to the following. 1. The issues of quality/efficiency in teaching and learning…
	Challenging others: Challenging the contributions of other members and seeking to engage in debate.	I agree but I wondered about the applicability of the argument: "The individuals or other units in a system …" (Rogers, p. 295). The example used in the book to support is a valid argument but I am unconvinced ….
	Explaining or elaborating: Supporting one's own position (possibly following a challenge).	Chery, you have a good point about generalizations but I think the cell phone is a little harder to see why the less fortunate may need it more than the wealthy. I think it has a lot to do with the marketing of the product……..
Learner – CMS interaction	Help seeking: Seeking assistance from others about the use of technology.	Does anyone know how to edit/add/append data on the student pages?
	Feedback seeking: Seeking feedback to a position advanced.	What do you think about tutorial on how to …..in an online class?
	Help giving: Responding to questions and requests from others about the use of technology.	To access the chat room, click on virtual chat in the blackboard; chat screen will come up; click on enter…
	Feedback giving: Providing feedback on proposals from others about the use of technology.	I like your idea of a generic booklet and everyone contributing aspects of interesting internet services…
	Reflecting on medium: Comments about the effectiveness of the medium in supporting group activities.	The email for the discussion group seems to work OK for me. You know it has gone through because you actually receive your email back almost straight away if it has worked.
Social Interaction	Social interaction: Conversation about social matters those are unrelated to the group task. This activity helps to 'break the ice'.	Regarding chat - my weekend is pretty hectic – I have my family flying in from Greece … so the Greek festivities will be in full swing.

continued on following page

Table 1. continued

Parroting	Repeat or mimic (another's words, etc) unthinkingly, one line agreement/disagreement statements	I agree with you Me too…

Adapted from Curtis & Lawson (2001)

Figure 1. Scatter plot showing the relationship between the average grade and overall interaction

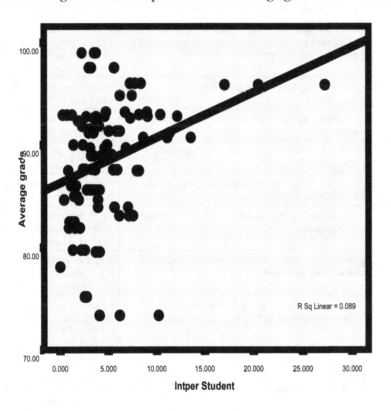

RESULTS

Correlational Analysis

Table 2 presents the Pearson's product moment correlation coefficients between the 4 variables included in the study. The result of the correlational analysis showed that 2 out of 3 independent variables (Grade weight and Group size) were significantly correlated with the independent variable, interactions per student per week.

The reader should be cautious while interpreting the magnitude of the correlation coefficient as most of the variables had skewed distributions due to the presence of outliers, which would reduce the magnitude of correlation coefficient (Lomax, 2007, p. 188). So, most of the coefficients shown in Table 2 are under-estimate of actual size of the correlation.

Regression Analysis

After testing the underlying assumptions, the researcher conducted the multiple regression analysis. The linear combination of independent variables was significantly related to overall interactions among learners, $F(4, 112) = 6.83$, $p < 0.01$. The coefficient of determination (R^2) was

Table 2. Correlation matrix showing the bivariate relationships among the variables included in the study

		1	2	3	4
1	Intper Student	1.00			
2	Grade Weight	0.19*	1.00		
3	Group Size	-0.35*	0.06	1.00	
4	Chat session	0.10	0.23	0.04	1.00

* Significant at 0.05 level

Table 3. Summary of regression analysis for understanding the individual unique contributions of the independent variables in predicting the overall interactions per student per week (N = 117)

Excluded variable	Change in SE	Change in R²	F-statistic	Df (n,d)	p-value	VIF
Discipline	0.18	0.10	4.96	(3,110)	0.003	1.84
Group Size	0.10	0.05	6.77	(1,110)	0.011	1.28
Grade Weight	0.01	0.01	1.64	(1,110)	0.20	1.31
Chat Session	0.01	0.01	0.56	(1,110)	0.457	1.12

0.27, indicating that approximately 27% of the variance of the overall interactions in the sample can be accounted for by the linear combination of the independent variables included in the study. The results of the regression analysis showed that discipline and group size were significant predictors of the dependent variable at 5% level of significance, while the use of chat session and grade weight were not significant in predicting the overall interactions per student per week.

To further support the above results and to find the individual contribution of each predictor variable, the researcher used multivariate regression analysis to conduct a change in R square test. The result of this analysis is presented in Table 3.

Overall Interaction and Group Size

The size of groups is an important element of the success of the online learning process (Learning Team Handbook, 2003). A unique feature of online education is its capability to support the interactive group process (Gusky, 1997). This study found a significantly negative relationship between the overall interaction and group size (tables 1 & 2).

Hence, the overall interaction among students was higher when the group size was small which supports the fact that smaller virtual learning groups build synergistic learning efforts among students in online courses (Scarnati, 2001).

Overall Interaction and Grade Weight for Discussion

Online courses included in this study incorporate a threaded discussion element in their courses with a varying grade weight assigned to it. This study found a weak positively significant correlation between the overall interaction and the grade weight (table 1). But a more powerful regression analysis failed to find any significant unique contribution made by this variable in explaining the variation in the dependent variable (Table 3). Hence, the grade weight assigned to the discussions was not a significant predictor of the overall interactions among students. This result contradicts the views of Jiang & Ting (2000) who found a significant positive correlation among discussion grade weight and students' perceived learning.

Table 4. Summary statistics for overall interaction per student per week for the different disciplines

College	Mean	SD
A & S	3.42	2.03
Business	2.81	1.35
Education	5.71	2.77
Health Science	7.36	6.16

Overall Interaction and Differences in Disciplines

In this study the researcher selected sample courses from 4 different disciplines. Ten courses each from Colleges of Business, Arts & Sciences and Education and 9 courses from College of Health Sciences were included. The results showed that the Health Sciences courses had a higher overall interaction per student per week then the other disciplines but the differences in interaction between Education courses and Health sciences courses was not significant (Table 4). The researcher did not find any literature that researched this variable in the past.

Overall Interaction and use of Chat Sessions

This study failed to find any significant relationship between use of chat sessions and overall interactions (tables 1 & 2), which is in direct contrast to the views of Rohfeld & Hiemstra (1995), who concluded that chat sessions are important to build a friendly and social environment which fosters learning.

CONCLUSION

This study began by asking "do the instructional design elements and the discipline area impact the

Figure 2. Distribution of the overall interaction per student per week for the four disciplines

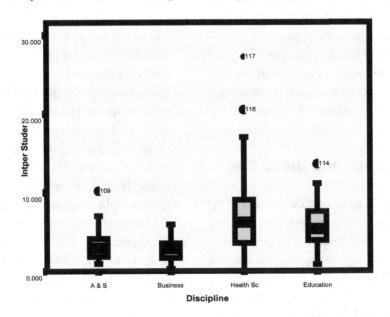

overall interaction among learners as defined by the number of learner-learner interactions?" The following conclusions can be drawn on the basis of analysis done:

- Design Elements:
  1. There is a statistically significant negative relationship between group size and overall interaction. The smaller is the group size, the higher is the overall interaction.
  2. There is no statistically significant relationship between the grade weight for threaded discussions and the overall interaction.
  3. There is no statistically significant relationship between use of chat sessions and overall interaction, i.e. the interactivity in an online class does not depend on the use of chat sessions.
- Discipline:
  4. The differences in discipline made a unique contribution in predicting the overall interactions, i.e. the interactivity in an online class depends on the discipline it belongs to.

The results of this study can prove to be very important in designing effective and interactive online courses. To improve the interaction in an online class, students must be divided into smaller groups. The results of regression analysis showed that differences in discipline made a unique contribution in predicting the overall interactions and was the most important predictor of overall interaction. This result suggests that the interactivity in an online class depends on the discipline it belongs to and hence, future research must focus on impact of instructional design elements on overall interactions within a discipline.

FUTURE RESEARCH

1. Similar studies can be conducted using a more representative sample of online courses particularly from different institutions.
2. The researcher limited this study to interactions in online classroom but it can be extended to a face to face class as well.
3. This study was limited to graduate level classes but future research can be extended to undergraduate classes as well.
4. A longitudinal study should be conducted to understand the impact of technological advancement over time on overall interaction in an online class.
5. The researcher considered four different predictor variables but a future study may include more variables that can influence the interactivity of an online class.
6. A future study may be conducted on similar lines using non-parametric estimation techniques.

REFERENCES

Adelskold, G., Alklett, K., Axelsson, R., & Blomgren, G. (1999). Problem-based distance learning of energy issues via computer network . *Distance Education, 20*(1), 129–143. doi:10.1080/0158791990200110

Anderson, T. (2003). *Modes of interaction in distance education: Recent developments and research questions. Handbook of distance education.* Hoboken, NJ: Lawrence Erlbaum Associates, Inc.

Beaudoin, M. (2001). *Learning or lurking? Tracking the 'invisible' online student.* Paper delivered at the 7th Sloan-C International Conference on Asynchronous Learning Networks.

Berge, Z. L. (1997). Computer conferencing and the on-line classroom. *International Journal of Educational Telecommunications, 3*(1).

Biggs, J. B. (1999). Teaching for Quality Learning at University: Assessing for learning quality. Buckingham, UK: Society for research into higher education (SRHE) and Open University Press.

Bouton, C., & Garth, R. Y. (1983). *Learning in groups. New directions in teaching and learning, (No. 14)*. San Francisco: Jossey-Bass.

Bruffee, K. A. (1993). *Collaborative learning: Higher education, interdependence, and the authority of knowledge*. Baltimore: John Hopkins University Press.

Collins, M., & Berge, Z. (1996). *Facilitating interaction in computer mediated online courses*. Paper presented at the FSI/AECT Distance education conference, Tallassee, FL.

Crossman, D. M. (1997). The evolution of World Wide Web as an emerging instructional technology tool . In Khan, B. H. (Ed.), *Web-based instruction* (pp. 19–23). Englewood Cliffs, NJ: Educational Technology Publications.

Curtis, D. D., & Lawson, M. J. (2001). Exploring Collaborative Online Learning. *Journal of Asynchronous Learning Networks, 5*(1), 21–34.

Dagget, W. R. (1998). Technology in education: Striving for excellence and equity. *League for innovation in community college: Leadership abstract, 11*(2), 1-2.

Daniel, J. Marquis, C. (1988). Interaction and independence: Getting the mix right. *Distance education: International perspectives*.

Dede, C. (1996). The evolution of distance education: Emerging technologies and distributed learning. *American Journal of Distance Education, 10*(2), 4–36. doi:10.1080/08923649609526919

Dede, C. J. (1990). The evolution of distance learning: Technology-mediated interactive learning. *Journal of Research on Computers in Education, 22*, 247–264.

Dewey, J. (1916). *Democracy and Education*. New York: Macmillan.

Dziuban, C., & Moskal, P. (2001). *Emerging research issues in distributed learning*. Paper delivered at the 7th Sloan-C International Conference on Asynchronous Learning Networks, Orlando, FL.

Fulford, C. P., & Zhang, S. (1993). Perceptions of interaction: The critical predictor in distance education. *American Journal of Distance Education, 7*(3), 8–21. doi:10.1080/08923649309526830

Galt Global Review. (December 2001). *Education news: Virtual classrooms booming*. Retrieved from http://www.galtglobalreview.com/education/virtual_classrooms.html

Gravetter, F. J., & Wallnau, L. B. (1996). *Statistics for the behavioral science*. Minneapolis, MN: West Publishing Company.

Gunawardena, C. N., & Zittle, F. J. (1997). Social presence as a predictor of satisfaction within a computer-mediated conferencing environment. *American Journal of Distance Education, 11*(3), 8–26. doi:10.1080/08923649709526970

Gusky, T. (1997). *Implementing master learning*. New York: Wadsworth Publishing Company.

Harasim, L. (1990). Online education: An environment for collaboration and intellectual amplification . In Harasim, L. (Ed.), *Online education: Perspectives on a new environment* (pp. 39–64). New York: Praeger.

Harasim, L., Hiltz, S., Tales, L., & Turoff, M. (1995). *Learning networks: A field guide to teaching and learning online*. Cambridge, MA: MIT Press.

Hartman, J. L., & Truman-Davis, B. (2001). Factors related to the satisfaction of faculty teaching online courses at the University of Central Florida. In J. Bourne & J. Moore, (Eds), *Online Education: Proceedings of the 2000 Sloan Summer Workshop on Asynchronous Learning Networks*, (Vol. 2, Sloan-C series). Needham, MA: Sloan-C Press.

Hill, J. R., Wiley, D., Nelson, L. M., & Han, S. (2004). Exploring research on internet-based learning: From infrastructure to interactions . In *Handbook of research on educational communications and technology*. London: Lawrence Erlbaum Associates, Publishers.

Holmberg, B. (1983). Guided didactic conversation in distance education . In Sewart, D., Keegan, D., & Holmberg, B. (Eds.), *Distance education: international perspectives*. London: Routledge.

Jiang, M. & Ting, E. (2000). A Study of Factors Influencing Students' Perceived Learning in a Web-Based Course Environment. *International Journal of Educational telecommunication, 6*(4), 317-338.

Johnson, D. W., & Johnson, R. T. (1996). Cooperation and the use of technology . In Jonassen, D. H. (Ed.), *Handbook of research for educational communications and technology* (pp. 1017–1044). New York: Simon and Schuster Macmillan.

Johnson, S. D., Aragon, S. R., Shaik, N., & Palma-Rivas, N. (2000). Comparative analysis of learner satisfaction and learning outcomes in online and face-to-face learning environments. *Journal of Interactive Learning Research, 11*(1), 29–49.

Kanuka, H., & Anderson, T. (1998). Online social interchange, discord, and knowledge construction. *Journal of Distance Education, 13*(1), 57–74.

Karayan, S.S., & Crowe, J.A. (1997). Student perceptions of electronic discussion groups. *The Journal, 24*(9).

Kaye, A. (1995). Computer supported collaborative learning . In Heap, N., Thomas, R., Einon, G., Mason, R., & MacKay, H. (Eds.), *Information Technology and Society* (pp. 192–210). London: Sage.

Kearsley, G. (1995). The nature and value of interaction in distance education. *Distance Education Symposium 3: Instruction*. University Park, PA: American Center for the Study of Distance Education.

Kearsley, G. (1998). *A guide to online education*. Retrieved from http://home.sprynet.com/~gkearsley/online.htm

Klesius, J., Homan, S., & Thompson, T. (1997). Distance education compared to traditional instruction: The students' view. *International Journal of Instructional Media, 24*(3), 207–220.

Kumari, D. S. (2001). Connecting graduate students to virtual guests through asynchronous discussions: analysis of an experience. *Journal of Asynchronous Learning Networks, 5*(2). Retrieved from http://www.aln.org/alnweb/journal/Vol5_issue2/Kumari/Kumari.htm

Laurillard, D. (1993). *Rethinking university teaching: a framework for the effective use of educational technology*. London: Routledge.

(2003). *Learning team handbook*. Phoenix, AZ: University of Phoenix.

Lomax, R. G. (2007). *An Introduction to Statistical Concepts for Education and the Behavioral Sciences* (2nd ed.). Mahwah, NJ: Lawrence Erlbaum.

Meyer, J. D. (2000, November). *Quality of life in the school of the global village*. Paper presented at the Teaching Online in Higher Education 2000 virtual conference. Retrieved from http://as1.ipfw.edu/2000tohe/papers/meyer.htm

Moore, M. (1993). Three types of interaction. In Harry, K., John, M., & Keegan, D. (Eds.), *Distance education: new perspectives*. London: Routledge.

Moore, M., & Kearsley, G. (1996). *Distance education: A system view*. Belmont, CA: Wadsworth Publishing Company.

Phipps, R. A., Wellman, J. V., & Merisotis, J. P. (1998). *Assuring quality in distance learning: A report prepared for the Council for Higher Education Accreditation*. Washington, DC: The Institute for Higher Education Policy.

Picciano, A. G. (1998). Developing an asynchronous course model at a large, urban university. *Journal of Asynchronous Learning Networks, 2*(1). Retrieved from http://www.aln.org/alnweb/journal/vol2_issue1/picciano.htm.

Picciano, A. G. (2001). *Distance Learning: Making Connections across Virtual Space and Time*. Upper Saddle River, NJ: Prentice-Hall.

Picciano, A. G. (2002). Beyond student perceptions: Issues of interaction, presence, and performance in an online course. *Journal of Asynchronous Learning Networks, 6*(1).

Ramsden, P. (1992). *Learning to teach in higher education*. London: Routledge.

Renniger, A., & Shumar, W. (2000). *Building virtual communities: Learning and change in cyberspace*. Cambridge, UK: Cambridge University Press.

Rohfeld, R. W., & Hiemstra, R. (1995). Moderating discussion in the electronic classroom. In Z.L. Berge, & M.P. Collins (Eds.), Computer mediated communication and the online classroom Volume III: Distance learning, (pp. 91-104). Cresskill, NJ: Hampton Press.

Rust, D. Z. (2006). *Examining interaction in online courses in relation to student performance and course retention*. EdD dissertation, Tennessee State University.

Saba, F. (2000). Research in distance education: A status report. *International Review of Research in Open and Distance Learning, 1*(1), 1–9.

Scarnati, J. (2001). On becoming a team player. *Team Performance Management, 7*(1,2), 5.

Shea, P., Fredericksen, E., Pickett, A., Pelz, W., & Swan, K. (2001). Measures of learning effectiveness in the SUNY Learning Network. In J. Bourne & J. Moore (Eds.), *Online Education: Proceedings of the 2000 Sloan Summer Workshop on Asynchronous Learning Networks*, (Vol. 2, *Sloan-C series*). Needham, MA: Sloan-C Press.

Sherry, L. (1996). Issues in distance learning. *International Journal of Distance Education, 1*(4), 337–365.

Smith, C. K. (1996*). Convenience vs. connection: Commuter students' views on distance learning.* Paper presented at the Annual Forum of the Association for Institutional Research, Albuquerque, NM, (ERIC Document Reproduction Service No. ED 397 725).

Strachota, E. M. (2003). Student satisfaction in an online course: An analysis of the impact of learner-content, learner-instructor, learner-learner and learner-technology interaction, Doctoral dissertation, The University of Wisconsin-Milwaukee, Milwaukee, WI. *Dissertation Abstracts International, 64*(08), 2746.

Stubbs, M. (1976). *Language, Schools, and Classrooms*. London: Methuen.

Taiwei, O. (2006). *Learning online: The effects of interaction levels on student self-efficacy, task value, learning strategies, and achievement*. PhD, Dissertation, University of Northern Colorado.

Vygotsky, L. S. (1978). *Mind in society: the development of higher psychological processes.* Cambridge, MA: Harvard University.

Zirkin, B., & Sumler, D. (1995). Interactive or non-interactive? That is the question! An annotated bibliography. *Journal of Distance Education, 10*(1), 95–112.

ADDITIONAL READING

Alexander, M. W., Perreault, H., Zhao, J. J., & Waldman, L. (2009). Comparing AACSB Faculty and Student Online Learning Experiences: Changes between 2000 and 2006. *The Journal of Educators Online, 6*(1).

Anderson, T. (2009). *The Theory and Practice of Online Learning.* Athabasca University Press, 2009

Bielman, V., Putney, L., & Strudler, N. (2000). *Constructing community in a postsecondary virtual classroom.* Paper presented at the annual meeting of the American Educational Research Association, New Orleans, LA

Buzzetto-More, N. A. (2007). Principles of Effective Online Teaching. *Informing Science,* 2007.

Charalambos, V., & Stock, M. M. (1999). Factors influencing interactions in an online course. *American Journal of Distance Education, 13*(3), 22–36. doi:10.1080/08923649909527033

Christopher, M. M., Thomas, J. A., & Tallent-Runnels, M. K. (2004). Raising the bar: Encouraging high level thinking in online discussion forums. *Roeper Review, 26*(3), 166–171. doi:10.1080/02783190409554262

Cook, K.C. & Grant-Davie, K. (2005). *Online Education: Global Questions, Local Answers.* Baywood Publication, 2005.

Fite, S.D. (2003). *Influences on Learner-Learner Interaction in Online Classes.* Texas A & M University, 2003.

Hiltz, S. R., & Goldman, R. (2005). Learning Together Online. Routledge, 2005.

Jennings, S. E., & Bayless, M. L. (2003). Online vs. traditional instruction: A comparison of student success. *Delta Pi Epsilon Journal, 45,* 183–190.

Keefe, T. J. (2003). Using technology to enhance a course: The importance of interaction. *EDUCAUSE Quarterly, 1,* 24–34.

Limniou, M., Papadopoulos, N., & Whitehead, C. (2008). Integration of simulation into pre-laboratory chemical course: Computer cluster versus WebCT. *Computers & Education, 52*(1), 45–52. doi:10.1016/j.compedu.2008.06.006

Lytras, M.D. Ordonez de Pablos, P. (2009). *Social Web Evolution: Integrating Semantic Applications and Web 2.0 Technologies.* Idea Group Inc (IGI), 2009.

Palloff, R. M., & Pratt, K. (2007). Building online communities: Effective strategies for the Virtual Classroom. John Wiley and Sons, 2007

Rovai, A. P., & Jordan, H. M. (2004). Blended Learning and Sense of Community: A comparative analysis with traditional and fully online graduate courses. *International Review of Research in Open and Distance Learning, 5*(2).

Salmon, G. (2004). E-moderating: the key to teaching and learning online. Routledge, 2004

Swan, K. (2002). Building communities in online courses: the importance of interaction. *Education Communication and Information, 2*(1), 23–49. doi:10.1080/1463631022000005016

Swan, K. (2004). Relationships Between Interactions and Learning In Online Environments. *The Sloan Consortium.* Retrieved on March 16, 2009, from http://www.sloan-c.org/publications/books/interactions.pdf

Tallent-Runnels, M. K., Thomas, J. A., Lan, W. Y., Cooper, S., Ahern, T. C., Shaw, S. M., & Liu, X. (2006). Teaching courses online: A review of the research. *Review of Educational Research, 76*(1), 93–135. doi:10.3102/00346543076001093

KEY TERMS AND DEFINITIONS

Distance Education: in this dissertation refers to "online delivery of education to remote locations, using either or both synchronous and asynchronous delivery of course content" (Distance Education at Postsecondary Education instructions: 1997-1998). In this research project, Distance Education does not include correspondence or broad-cast based education.

Face-to-Face Learning: Refers to teaching and learning that occurs when both teachers and students are confined within a single room.

Traditional Courses: Refers to the courses essentially taught in a face-to-face classroom environment but may use some web-based technology to support the course content.

Learner-Learner Interaction: Refers to the human interaction consisting of two-way communication between one learner and other learners (Moore & Kearsley, 1996).

Learner-Instructor Interaction: Refers to the human interaction consisting of communication between the learner and the instructor (Moore & Kearsley, 1996).

Instructional Design Elements: Refer to the components of a course that facilitate learning. For the purpose of this study 3 different instructional design elements will be considered: Group size, grade weight assigned to threaded discussions, and use of chat sessions.

Compilation of References

Abdulrazak, B., Helal, A., Jansen, E., King, J., & Yang, H. (2005). *A Programming Model for Pervasive Spaces.* Submitted to the 3rd International Conference on Service Oriented Computing, Amsterdam, The Netherlands, December 12-15.

Abe, S. (2005). Support Vector Machines for Pattern Classification. Kobe, Japan: Springer.

Aberson, C. L., Berger, D. E., Healy, R., Kyle, D. J., & Romero, V. L. (2000). Evaluation of an Interactive Tutorial for Teaching the Central Limit Theorem . *Teaching of Psychology, 27,* 289–291. doi:10.1207/S15328023TOP2704_08

Abowd, G., D. (1999). Classroom 2000: An experiment with the instrumentation of a living educational environment. *IBM Systems Journal, 38*(4), 508–530.

Abraham, J., & Ramanatha, K. S. *(2008). Estimation of Communication Overhead during Pair-wise Key Establishment in Wireless Sensor Networks. In* 16th IEEE International Conference on Networks, *New Delhi, India.*

Abudlrazak, B., El-Zabadani, H., Helal, A., & Jansen, E. (2005). Self-Sensing Spaces: Smart Plugs for Smart Environments. In *Proceedings of the third International Conference on Smart homes and health Telematic (ICOST),* Sherbrooke, Québec, Canada.

Acs, G., Buttyan, L., & Vajda, I. (2006). Provably secure on-demand source routing in mobile ad hoc networks. *IEEE Transactions on Mobile Computing, 5*(11), 1533–1546. Retrieved from http://ieeexplore.ieee.org/stamp/stamp.jsp?tp=&arnumber=1704818&isnumber=35972. doi:10.1109/TMC.2006.170

Adelskold, G., Alklett, K., Axelsson, R., & Blomgren, G. (1999). Problem-based distance learning of energy issues via computer network . *Distance Education, 20*(1), 129–143. doi:10.1080/0158791990200110

Ahire, S. L., & Dreyfus, P. (2000). The impact of design management and process management on quality: an empirical investigation. *Journal of Operations Management, 18,* 549–575. doi:10.1016/S0272-6963(00)00029-2

Akyldiz, F., Su, W., Sankarasubramaniam, Y., & Cayirci, E. (2002). Wireless Sensor Networks: A Survey. *International Journal of Computer and Telecommunications Networking, 38*(4), 393–422.

Alahuhta, P., Beigl, M., Gellersen, H., Holmquist, L., Mattern, F., & Schiele, B. (2001, September). Smart-Its Friends: A Technique for Users to Easily Establish Connections between Smart Artifacts. In *Proc. of UBICOMP 2001,* Atlanta, GA.

Ali, M., Aref, W., Bose, R., Elmagarmid, A., Helal, A., Kamel, I., & Mokbel, M. (2005). NILE-PDT: A Phenomenon Detection and Tracking Framework for Data Stream Management Systems. In *Proceedings of the Very Large Databases Conference (VLDB),* Trondheim, Norway.

Alvesson, M., & Skoldbergg, K. (2000). *Reflexive Methodology: New Vistas for Qualitative Research.* London: Sage Publication.

Amores, J., Sebe, N., & Radeva, P. (2006). Boosting the Distance Estimation Application to the K-Nearest Neighbor Classifier. *Pattern Recognition Letters, 27*(3), 201–209. doi:10.1016/j.patrec.2005.08.019

Amsden, A. H. (2007). *Escape from Empire: the Developing World's Journey Through Heaven and Hell.* Cambridge, MA: The MIT Press.

Anderson, J. (2000). A Deployment System for Pervasive Computing. In *Proceedings of International Conference on Software Maintenance, ICSM'00,* San Jose, CA.

Anderson, T. (2003). *Modes of interaction in distance education: Recent developments and research questions. Handbook of distance education.* Hoboken, NJ: Lawrence Erlbaum Associates, Inc.

Anderson, T., Borriello, G., Esler, M., & Hightower, J. (1999). Next Century Challenges: Data-Centric Networking for Invisible Computing (The Portolano Project at the University of Washington). In the proceedings of Mobicom 99, Seattle, Washington.

Argyroudis, P. G., & O'Mahony, D. (2005). Secure Routing for Mobile Ad Hoc Nteworks. *IEEE Communications Survey and Tutorials, 2*(3), 2–21. doi:10.1109/COMST.2005.1610547

Ariyaeeinia, A., Sotudeh, R., & Xu, J. (2005). User Voice Identification On FPGA. In Perspectives in Pervasive Computing. London: IEE.

Ashby, N., & Miller, S. (Eds.). (1970). *Principles Of Modern Physics.* New York: Holden-Day, Inc.

Bailey, C., & Freeman, M. (2005). Designing an ubiquitous computing development kit. In Perspectives in Pervasive Computing. London: IEE.

Bailey, C., Meng, H., & Pears, N. E. (2005). FPGA Based Video Processing System for Ubiquitous Applications. In Perspectives in Pervasive Computing. London: IEE.

Balakrishnan, K., Deng, J., & Varshney, P. K. (2005, March). Twoack: preventing selfishness in mobile ad hoc networks. In *The IEEE Wireless Communications and Networking Conference(WCNC'05),* (pp. 2137– 2142), New Orleans, LA. Retrieved from http://ieeexplore.ieee.org/stamp/stamp.jsp?arnumber=01424848

Banavar, G., et al. (2000). Challenges: An Application Model for Pervasive Computing. In *Proceedings 6th Annual International Conference on Mobile Computing and Networking (MobiCom 2000),* August, Boston.

Banks, M., Olsen, A., & Pearson, D. (2007). *Global Student Mobility – An Australian Perspective Five Years On. IDP Australia.* New York: Prentice Hall.

Barbier, F. (2002). Composability for Software Components- An Approach Based on the Whole Part Theory. In *Eighth IEEE International Conference on Engineering of Complex Computer Systems (ICECCS 02),* December 2 - 4, (pp. 101), Greenbelt, MD.

Basu, K., Das, S., & De, P. (2004). An Ubiquitous Architectural Framework and Protocol for Object Tracking using RFID Tags. In *Proceedings of ACM Mobi Quitous Networking Conference,* Boston.

Beaudoin, M. (2001). *Learning or lurking? Tracking the 'invisible' online student.* Paper delivered at the 7th Sloan-C International Conference on Asynchronous Learning Networks.

Becker, C., Handte, G., Schiele, G., & Rothermal, K. (2004). PCOM: A Component System for Pervasive Computing. In *Proceedings of the 2nd IEEE International Conference on Pervasive Computing and Communication, PreCom04,* March 14-17, Orlando, FL.

Beigl, M., Gellersen, H., & Schmidt, A. (2001). Media-Cups: Experience with Design and Use of Computer-Augmented Everyday Artifacts. *Computer Networks . Special Issue on Pervasive Computing, 35*(4), 401–409.

Beranek, L. L. (Ed.). (1996). *Acoustics.* New York, USA: Acoustical Society Of America.

Berge, Z. L. (1997). Computer conferencing and the on-line classroom. *International Journal of Educational Telecommunications, 3*(1).

Betz, F. (1993). *Managing Technology Competing Through New Ventures, Innovation and Corporate Research.* Upper Saddle River, NJ: Prentice Hall.

Beuscart, R., Renard, J.-M., Delerue, D., & Souf, A. (1999). Telecommunication in Healthcare for a Better Coordination between Hospitals and GP's: Routine

Application of the "ISAR- Telematics" Project. *IEEE Transactions on Information Technology in Biomedicine, 3*(2), 101–108. doi:10.1109/4233.767085

Bhanu Murthy, K. V. (1995). *Manpower development - Skills, technology and basic science. Paper in Delhi University Seminar on Role of the university in manpower development for industry* (pp. 47–50). New Delhi: Aakriti.

Bhatnagar, S. (2004). *E-governmnent: From Vision to Implementation*. New Delhi: Sage Publications India Pte Ltd.

Biggs, J. B. (1987). *Student approaches to learning and studying*. Camberwell, Australia: Australian Council for Educational Research.

Biggs, J. B. (2003). Teaching for quality learning at university, (2nd ed.). Milton Keynes, UK: SRHE and Open University Press.

Biggs, J.B., Kember, D, & Leung, D, Y, P. (2001). The revised two-factor Study Process Questionnaire: R-SPQ-2F. *The British Journal of Educational Psychology, 71*, 133–149. doi:10.1348/000709901158433

Bijwaard, G. E., Janssen, M. C. W., & Maasland, E. (2008). Early mover advantages: an empirical analysis of European mobile phone markets. *Telecommunications Policy, 32*(3-4), 246–261. doi:10.1016/j.telpol.2007.08.006

Birkinshaw, J., & Piramal, G. (Eds.). (2005). *Sumantra Ghoshal on Management: A Force for Good*. Harlow, UK: FT Prentice Hall.

Blake, C. L., & Merz, C. J. (1998). *UCI Repository of Machine Learning Databases*. Univ. California, Dept. Inform. Computer Science, Irvine, CA. [Online]. From http://www.ics.uci.edu/~mlearn/ML-Repository.html

Blaß, E. O., & Zitterbart, M. (2006). An Efficient Key Establishment Scheme for Secure Aggregating Sensor Networks. In *ACM Symposium on Information, Computer and Communications Security*, Taiwan, (pp. 303-320).

Blechar, J., Knutsen, L., & Damsgaard, J. (2005). Reflexivity, the Social Factor, and m-Service Domestication: Linking the Human, Technological and Contextual . In

Soerensen, C. (Eds.), *Designing Ubiquitous Information Environments: Socio-Technical Issues and Challenges* (pp. 57–70). New York: Springer. doi:10.1007/0-387-28918-6_7

Bloom, B. (1970). Space/Time Trade-Offs in Hash Coding with Allowable Errors. *Communications of the ACM, 13*, 422–426. doi:10.1145/362686.362692

Bluetooth SIG Security Expert Group. *Bluetooth Security white paper*. (2002). Retrieved 2002, from http://grouper. ieee.org/groups/1451/5/Comparison %20of%20PHY/ Bluetooth_24Security_Paper.pdf

Bluetooth, S. I. G. *Specification of the Bluetooth System*. (2004). Retrieved November 2004, from http://www.bluetooth.org/

Bonatti, P., & Samarati, P. (2000). Regulating Service Access and Information Release on the Web. In *Proc. Seventh ACM Conf. Computer and Comm. Security (CCS '00)*.

Borriello, G., Farkas, K.I., Pering, T. &Want, R. (2002). Disappearing hardware. *Pervasive Computing, 1*(1).

Bourges-Waldegg, P., & Scrivener, S. A. R. (1998). Meaning, the central issue in cross-cultural HCI design. *Interacting with Computers, 9*(3). doi:10.1016/S0953-5438(97)00032-5

Bouton, C., & Garth, R. Y. (1983). *Learning in groups. New directions in teaching and learning, (No. 14)*. San Francisco: Jossey-Bass.

Braley, D. (2005). Ubiquitous Computing in Practice . In Soerensen, C. (Eds.), *Designing Ubiquitous Information Environments: Socio-Technical Issues and Challenges* (pp. 365–367). New York: Springer. doi:10.1007/0-387-28918-6_31

Bresin, R., Fernström, M., & Rocchesso, D. (2003, April). Sounding Objects. *IEEE MultiMedia, 10*(2), 42–52. doi:10.1109/MMUL.2003.1195160

Brown, J., & Weiser, M. (1997). Beyond Calculation: The Next Fifty Years of Computing. New York: Springer-Verlag.

Bruffee, K. A. (1993). *Collaborative learning: Higher education, interdependence, and the authority of knowledge*. Baltimore: John Hopkins University Press.

Brumitt, B., Krumm, J., Meyers, B., & Shafer, S. (2000). Ubiquitous Computing & The Role of Geometry. IEEE Personal Communications.

Buchegger, S., & Boudec, J. L. (2002). Nodes Bearing Grudges: Towards Routing Security, Fairness and Robustness in Mobile Ad Hoc Networks. In *Proceedings of Tenth Euromicro Workshop on Parallel, Distributed and Network based Processing* (pp. 403-410), Canary Islands, Spain. Washington, DC: IEEE Computer Society.

Bunnell, T. (2006). *Malaysia, Modernity and the Multimedia Super Corridor*. London: RoutledgeCurzon.

Bureš, V. (2006). Systems Thinking as a Basis for Ambient Intelligence. *ACM SIGCSE Bulletin, 38*(3), 318. doi:10.1145/1140123.1140224

Bureš, V., & Čech, P. (2007). Complexity of Ambient Intelligence in Managerial Work. *ACM SIGCSE Bulletin, 39*(3), 325. doi:10.1145/1269900.1268892

Burges, C. J. C. (1998). A tutorial on support vector machines for pattern recognition. *Data Mining and Knowledge Discovery, 2*(2), 121–167. doi:10.1023/A:1009715923555

Buzzell, C.H. (1987). Let Our Image Reflect Our Pride. *Vocational Education Journal, 62*(8) November-December.

Campbell, C., Maglio, P., Matlock, T., Smith, B., & Zhai, S. (2000). In *Proceedings of The third International Conference on Multimodal Interfaces*, Beijing, China (LNCS Vol. 1948, pp. 1-7). Berlin: Springer.

Camtepe, S. A., & Yener, B. (2005). *Key Distribution Mechanisms for Wireless Sensor Networks: a Survey. TR-05-07*. Department of Computer Science, Rensselaer Polytechnic Institute.

Caulson, C. A., & Jeffrey, A. (Eds.). (1977). *Waves: A mathematical approach to the common types of Wave motion*. London: Longman.

Chakraborty., et al. (2002). A Reactive Service Composition Architecture for Pervasive Computing Environment. In C. G. Omidyar, (Ed.), *Proceedings of the IFTP Tc6/Wg 6.8 Working Conference on Personal Wireless Communications* (October 23-25), *IFIP Conference Proceedings,* (vol. 234, pp. 53-62). Deventer, The Netherlands: Kluwer B.V.

Chan, H., & Perrig, A. (2003). Security and Privacy in Sensor Networks. *IEEE Computer, 36*(10), 103–105.

Chatti, M. A., et al. (2007). The Web 2.0 Driven SECI Model Based Learning Process. In J. M. Spector et al, (Eds.), *Seventh IEEE International Conference on Advanced Learning Technologies* (pp.780-782). Niigata, Japan: IEEE Computer Society.

Chaudhuri, A., Flamm, K., & Horrigan, J. (2005). An analysis of the determinants of internet access. *Telecommunications Policy, 29*, 731–755. doi:10.1016/j.telpol.2005.07.001

Chen, Y., & Wang, A. J. (2002). Learning with kernels. Cambridge, MA: MIT Press.

Clemmer, T. P. (1995). The role of medical informatics in telemedicine. *Journal of Medical Systems, 19*, 47–58. doi:10.1007/BF02257190

Coffield, F., Moseley, D., Hall, E., & Ecclestone, K. (2004). Should we be using learning styles? What research has to say to practice? Report published by the Learning and Skills Research Centre, UK.

Cohen, P., & Oviatt, S. (2000). Multimodal interfaces that process what comes naturally. *Communications of the ACM, 43*(3), 45–53. doi:10.1145/330534.330538

Collins, G. W. (Ed.). (2003). Fundamental Numerical Methods and Data Analysis.

Collins, M., & Berge, Z. (1996). *Facilitating interaction in computer mediated online courses*. Paper presented at the FSI/AECT Distance education conference, Tallassee, FL.

Conole., et al. (2006). *JISC LXP: Student experiences of technologies*. Final report. Retrieved February 21, 2009 from http://www.jisc.ac.uk/media/documents/

programmes/elearningpedagogy/lxpprojectfinalreport-dec06.pdf

Corts, C., & Vapnik, V. N. (1995). Support Vector Networks . *Machine Learning, 20*, 273–297.

Corts, C., & Vapnik, V. N. (1995). The Nature of Statistical Learning Theory. Berlin: Springer.

Councill, W. T., & Heineman, G. T. (Eds.). (2001). *Component Based Software Engineering: Putting the Pieces Together*. Reading, MA: Addison Wesley.

Covey, S. R. (1999). *The 7 Habits of Highly effective People*. New York: Pocket Books.

CPOL. *High-Performance Policy Evaluation*. (2005). Presented at the 12th ACM conference on Computer and communications security.

Crossbow. (2003). Smarter Sensors in Silicon.

Crossman, D. M. (1997). The evolution of World Wide Web as an emerging instructional technology tool . In Khan, B. H. (Ed.), *Web-based instruction* (pp. 19–23). Englewood Cliffs, NJ: Educational Technology Publications.

Crowell, B. (Ed.). (2005). *Vibrations And Waves*. Fullerton, CA: Light And Matter.

Cruz-Neira, C., Sandin, D. J., DeFanti, T. A., Kenyon, R. V., & Hart, J. C. (1992). The CAVE Automatic Virtual Environment. *Communications of the ACM, 35*(2), 64–72. doi:10.1145/129888.129892

Curtis, D. D., & Lawson, M. J. (2001). Exploring Collaborative Online Learning. *Journal of Asynchronous Learning Networks, 5*(1), 21–34.

Czerwinski, S., Zhao, B. Y., Hodes, T., Joseph, A., & Katz, R. (1999). *An Architecture for a Secure Service Discovery Service*. Proc. MobiCom.

Dagget, W. R. (1998). Technology in education: Striving for excellence and equity. *League for innovation in community college: Leadership abstract, 11*(2), 1-2.

Dahill, B., Levine, B. N., Royer, E., & Shields, A. C. (2002). A secure routing protocol for ad hoc networks.

Technical Report UMass Tech Report (pp. 02-32), University of Massachusetts, Amherst, MA.

Dalglish, C., & Newton, C. (2002). Relationship between firm survival and innovation: an introduction to the literature. *Innovation: Management . Policy & Practice, 4*(2-3), 209–214.

Daniel, J. Marquis, C. (1988). Interaction and independence: Getting the mix right. *Distance education: International perspectives*.

Das, S., Kumar, M., & Shirazi, B. (2003, April). Pervasively Secure Infrastructures (PSI) through Communitys Computing. In *Proc of the Texas Workshop on Security of Information Systems*, College Station, USA, (pp. 5-10).

Davenport, R., Helal, S., Mann, W., Russo, J., & Sukojo, A. (2004). SmartWave Intelligent Meal Preparation System to Help Older People Live Independently. In *Proceedings of the Second International Conference on Smart homes and health Telematic (ICOST2004)*, Singapore.

Davis, F. D. (1986). *A technology acceptance model for empirically testing new end-user information systems: theory and results*. Doctoral dissertation, MIT Sloan School of Management, Cambridge, MA.

Davis, F. D. (1989). Perceived usefulness, perceived ease of use, and user acceptance of information technology. *Management Information Systems Quarterly, 13*, 319–339. doi:10.2307/249008

Davis, K., Heitmann, L., Kollatschny, S., & Lessard, C. (1996). Challenges Facing Technology Assessment in Modern Health Care. *IEEE Engineering in Medicine and Biology, 15*(5), 55–59. doi:10.1109/51.537058

de Bruin, H., & van Vliet, H. (2002). The Future of component-Based Development is Generation, not Retrieval. In *proceedings of ECBS'02, Workshop on CBSE – Composing Systems from Components*. Lund, Sweden, April 8-11.

Dede, C. (1996). The evolution of distance education: Emerging technologies and distributed learning. *American Journal of Distance Education, 10*(2), 4–36. doi:10.1080/08923649609526919

Deng, H., Li, W., & Agarwal, D. P. (2002). Routing Security in Wireless ad hoc Networks. *IEEE Communications Magazine, 40*(10), 70–75. doi:10.1109/MCOM.2002.1039859

Deng, H., Li, W., & Agrawal, D. P. (2002). Routing Security in Wireless Ad Hoc Network. *IEEE Communications Magzine, 40*(10). Retrieved from http://ieeexplore.ieee.org/stamp/stamp.jsp?tp=&arnumber=1039859&isnumber=22296

Dewey, J. (1916). *Democracy and Education.* New York: Macmillan.

Dictionary of Psychology. (2nd ed.).(2006). neurolinguistic programming. New York: Oxford University Press, USA.

Dilts, R., & Erickson Klein, R. (2006). Neuro-linguistic Programming . In *The Milton H. Erickson Foundation: Newsletter, Summer, 26(2)*. Historical.

Dimitriou, T., & Krontiris, I. *(2005). A Localized, Distributed Protocol for Secure Information Exchange in Sensor Networks. In* 5th IEEE International Workshop on Algorithms for Wireless, Mobile Ad Hoc and Sensor Networks, *(pp. 1 – 8).*

Doclos, F., Estublier, J., & Morat, P. (2002). Describing and Using Non Functional Aspects in Component Based Applications. In *Proceedings of the 1st international conference on Aspect Oriented Software Development,* Enschede, The Netherlands, April 22-26.

Dolan, R. J., & Simon, H. (1996). *Power Pricing: How Managing Price Transforms the Bottom Line.* New York: The Free Press.

Ducatel, K., et al. (2001). *Scenarios for Ambient Intelligence in 2010: Final report.* Seville, Spain: ISTAG. Retrieved February 2, 2009, from ftp://ftp.cordis.lu/pub/ist/docs/istagscenarios2010.pdf

Dunkels, A., Voigt, T., & Alonso, J. (2004). Making TCP/IP viable for wireless sensor networks. In *Proceedings of the European Workshop on Wireless Sensor Networks,* (pp. 364–379).

Dziuban, C., & Moskal, P. (2001). *Emerging research issues in distributed learning.* Paper delivered at the 7th

Sloan-C International Conference on Asynchronous Learning Networks, Orlando, FL.

Ellison, C. (2002). Home Network Security. *Intel Technolog, 6,* 37–48.

Ellison, C. (2003). *UPnP Security Ceremonies.*V1.0, Intel Co. Retrieved October 2003.

Elzabadani, H., Helal, A., Jansen, E., Kaddourah, Y., King, J. & Mann, W. (2005). Gator Tech Smart House: A Programmable Pervasive Space. *IEEE Computer magazine,* 64-74.

El-Zabadani, H., Helal, A., Mann, W., & Schmaltz, M. (2006). *PerVision: An integrated Pervasive Computing/Computer Vision Approach to Tracking Objects in a Self-Sensing Space.* Submitted to the 4th IEEE International Conference on Pervasive Computing and Communications (PerCom), Pisa, Italy.

Enders, S. J., Pharm, D., Enders, J. M., & Holstad, S. G. (2002). Drug-Information Software for Palm Operating System Personal Digital Assistants: Breadth, Clinical Dependability and Ease of Use. *Pharmacotherapy, 22*(8), 1036–1040. doi:10.1592/phco.22.12.1036.33601

Endres, C., & Butz, A. (2005). A Survey of Software Infrastructure and Frameworks for Ubiquitous Computing. *Mobile Information Systems Journal, 1*(1).

Enns, H. R. (Ed.). (2005). *Computer Algebra Recipes for Mathematical Physics.* Boston: Birkhauser.

Entwistle, N. (1989). Approaches to studying and course perceptions: the case of the disappearing relationship. *Studies in Higher Education, 14*(2), 155–156. doi:10.1080/03075078912331377466

Esler, M., et al. (1999). Next Century Challenges: Data Centric Networking for Invisible Computing. In *Proceedings of 5th Annual International Conference on Mobile Computing and Networking, Mobicom99,* August 15-19, Seattle, WA.

Estrin, D., Govindan, R., Heidemann, J. S., & Kumar, S. *(1999). Next Century Challenges: Scalable Coordination in Sensor Networks. In* Proceedings of International

Conference on Mobile Computing and Networking, *Seattle, WA, (pp. 263 – 270).*

Eustice, K. (1999). A Universal Information Appliance. *IBM Systems Journal, 38*(4).

Fall, K., & Varadhan, K. (1997). *Ns Notes and Documentation.* Technical Report, UC Berkeley, LBL USC/ISI and Xerox PARC.

Fatah, S. A., Fraser, D. S., Jones, T., Kindberg, T., Kostakos, V., O'Neill, E., & Penn, A. (2006). Design Tools for Pervasive Computing in Urban Environment. In *proceedings 8th International Conference on Design & Decision Support Systems in Architecture and Urban Planning,* Eindhoven, The Netherlands, Springer.

Firk, K. F. (Ed.). (2000). *Essential Physics Part-1.* CT: Guilford.

Fischer, S., Stewart, T., Mehta, S., Wax, R., & Lapinsky, S. (2003). Handheld computing in medicine. *Journal of the American Medical Informatics Association, 10*(2), 139–149. doi:10.1197/jamia.M1180

Flamm, K., & Chaudhuri, A. (2007). An analysis of the determinants of broadband access. *Telecommunications Policy, 31*(6-7), 312–326. doi:10.1016/j.telpol.2007.05.006

Fletcher, R. (1987). Practical Methods of Optimization, (2nd ed.). New York: John Wiley & Sons, Inc.

Flexible Sensors Make Robot Skin. (n.d.). Retrieved August 10, 2008, from http://radio.weblogs.com/0105910/2004/09/22.html

Flissi, A., Gransant, C., & Merle, P. (2005). A Component Based Software Infrastructure for Ubiquitous Computing. In *Proceedings of 4th International Symposium on Parallel and Distributed Computing,* Lille, France, July 04-06.

Florida, R. (1999). *Industrializing Knowledge: University-Industry Linkages in Japan and the United States.* Cambridge, MA: MIT Press.

Fornell, C. (1992). A national customer satisfaction barometer: the Swedish experience. *Journal of Marketing, 55*(1), 1–21.

Frederickson, H. G. (1999). The repositioning of American public administration. *Political Science and Politics, 32*(4), 701–711. doi:10.2307/420159

Freund, Y. (1997). A decision-theoretic generalization of online learning and an application to boosting. *Journal of Computer and System Sciences, 55,* 119–139. doi:10.1006/jcss.1997.1504

Freund, Y., & Schapire, R. E. (1999). A short introduction to boosting. *Journal of Japanese Society for Artificial Intelligence, 14*(5), 771–780.

Fulford, C. P., & Zhang, S. (1993). Perceptions of interaction: The critical predictor in distance education. *American Journal of Distance Education, 7*(3), 8–21. doi:10.1080/08923649309526830

Funk, J. L. (2009). The emerging value network in the mobile phone industry: The case of Japan and its implications for the rest of the world. *Telecommunications Policy.* Available online.

Galt Global Review. (December 2001). *Education news: Virtual classrooms booming.* Retrieved from http://www.galtglobalreview.com/education/virtual_classrooms.html

Garlan, D., & Schmerl, B. (2001). Component Based Software Engineering for Pervasive Computing Environment. In *Workshop on Component Based Software Engineering: Component Certification and System Prediction,* (held during ICSE'01), Toronto, Canada, May.

Garlan, D., & Sousa, J. (2002). Aura: an Architectural Framework for User Mobility. In Ubiquitous Computing Environments. In *the Proceedings of the 3rd Working IEEE/IFIP Conference on Software Architecture,* (pp. 29-43).

Gay, D., Levis, P., von Behren, R., Welsh, M., Brewer, E., & Culler, D. (2003). *The NesC Language: A Holistic Approach to Networked Embedded Systems* (pp. 1–11). Proceedings of Programming Language Design and Implementation.

Gefen, D., Karahanna, E., & Straub, D. W. (2003). Trust and TAM in online shopping: An integrated model. *Management Information Systems Quarterly, 27*(1), 51–90.

Ghosh, A. (2008 May 12). Neuro-linguistic programming is the newest fad in BPOs. *The Economic Times. Communicate2.* (n.d). Retrieved July 30, 2008, from http://www.communicate2.com

Giddens, A. (1984). *The Constitution of Society: Outline of the Theory of Structuration.* Cambridge, UK: Polity Press.

Gifford, S. (2005). Experiences with Location Sensing Systems. Presented at the *2005 NSF CISE/CNS Pervasive Computing Infrastructure Experience Workshop,* at the University of Michigan.

Gifford, S., & Sharma, S. (2005). Using RFID to Evaluate Evacuation Behavior Models. Presented at the *2005 North American Fuzzy Information Processing Society conference.*

Giraldo, C., Helal, A., Kaddoura, Y., Lee, C., Mann, W., & Zabbadani, H. (2003). Smart Phone Based Cognitive Assistant. In *Proceedings of the The 2nd International Workshop on Ubiquitous Computing for Pervasive Healthcare Applications,* Seattle, WA.

Giraldo, C., Helal, S., & Mann, W. (2002). mPCA - A Mobile Patient Care-Giving Assistant for Alzheimer Patients. In *First International Workshop on Ubiquitous Computing for Cognitive Aids (UbiCog'02), in conjunction with The Fourth International Conference on Ubiquitous Computing (UbiComp'02),* Göteborg, Sweden.

Giraldo, C., Helal, S., Kaddourah, Y., Lee, C., Mann, W., Ran, L., & Winkler, B. (2003). Enabling Location-Aware Pervasive Computing Applications for the Elderly. In *Proceedings of the First IEEE Pervasive Computing Conference,* Fort Worth, TX.

Goetze, M., & Strothotte, T. (2001), An Approach to Help Functionally Illiterate People with Graphical Reading Aids. In *Proc. of the International Symposium on Smart Graphics.*

Goldberg, D. E. (2005). *Genetic Algorithms in Search, Optimization, and Machine Learning.* Delhi, India: Pearson.

Gravetter, F. J., & Wallnau, L. B. (1996). *Statistics for the behavioral science.* Minneapolis, MN: West Publishing Company.

Gray, J. (2001). Using Software Component Generators to Construct a Meta-Weaver Framework. In *Proceedings of the 23rd international conference on Software Engineering,* Toronto, Ontario, Canada, May 12-19, Washington, DC, (pp. 789-790).

Grinder, J. (n.d). Retrieved July 28, 2008, from http://en.wikipedia.org/ wiki/John Grinder

Gronbaek, K., Mogensen, P., & Orbaek, P. (2001). Interaction techniques for spatial organization of digital and Physical materials – The Topos Approach. In *the Proceedings of First Danish Human- Computer Interaction Research Symposium,* (pp. 51-52).

Gunasekaran, V., & Harmantzis, F. (2007). Emerging wireless technologies for developing countries. *Journal of Technology in Society, 29*(1).

Gunasekaran, V., & Harmantzis, F. (2008). Towards a Wi-Fi ecosystem: technology integration and emerging service models. *Telecommunications Policy, 32,* 163–181. doi:10.1016/j.telpol.2008.01.002

Gunawardena, C. N., & Zittle, F. J. (1997). Social presence as a predictor of satisfaction within a computer-mediated conferencing environment. *American Journal of Distance Education, 11*(3), 8–26. doi:10.1080/08923649709526970

Gurwell, L. (2003). *Online education could be Internet's biggest growth area.* Retrieved February 19, 2009 from http://findarticles.com/p/articles/mi_qn4190/is_20030411/ai_n10044548

Gusky, T. (1997). *Implementing master learning.* New York: Wadsworth Publishing Company.

Gutschoven, B., & Verlinde, P. (2000), Multi-modal identity verification using support vector machines (SVM). In *Proc. 3rd Int. Conf. Information Fusion,* (vol. 2, pp. 3-8).

Hacioglu, K., & Ward, W. (2003). Question Classification with Support Vector Machines and Error Correcting Codes. In the *Proceedings of HLT-NACCL 2003, Edmonton, Alberta, Canada,* (pp. 28-30).

Hammer, M., & James, C. (1993). *Re-engineering the Corporation.* New York: Harper Business.

Harasim, L. (1990). Online education: An environment for collaboration and intellectual amplification . In Harasim, L. (Ed.), *Online education: Perspectives on a new environment* (pp. 39–64). New York: Praeger.

Harasim, L., Hiltz, S., Tales, L., & Turoff, M. (1995). *Learning networks: A field guide to teaching and learning online.* Cambridge, MA: MIT Press.

Hartman, J. L., & Truman-Davis, B. (2001). Factors related to the satisfaction of faculty teaching online courses at the University of Central Florida. In J. Bourne & J. Moore, (Eds), *Online Education: Proceedings of the 2000 Sloan Summer Workshop on Asynchronous Learning Networks,* (Vol. 2, Sloan-C series). Needham, MA: Sloan-C Press.

Haykin, S. (1999). *9. Self-organizing maps. Neural Networks - A comprehensive foundation* (2nd ed.). Upper Saddle River, NJ: Prentice-Hall.

Hazen, T. J., & Park, A. (2002). ASR dependent techniques for speaker identification. In *Proc. of ICSLP,* Denver, CO, (pp. 1337– 1340).

Hearn, G., & Rooney, D. (2002). The Future Role of Government in Knowledge-based Economies. *Foresight, 4*(6), 23–33. doi:10.1108/14636680210453461

Heeks, R., & Stanforth, C. (2007). Understanding e-Government Project Trajectories from an Actor-Network Perspective. *European Journal of Information Systems, 16*(2), 165–177. doi:10.1057/palgrave.ejis.3000676

Heines, J. M. (2000). Evaluating the effect of a course web site on student performance. *Journal of Computing in Higher Education, 12,* 57–83. doi:10.1007/BF03032714

Helal, A. (2005). Programming Pervasive Spaces. *IEEE Pervasive Computing magazine, 4*(1).

Helal, A., Kaddourah, Y., & King, J. (July 2005). Cost-Precision Tradeoffs in Unencumbered Floor-Based

Indoor Location Tracking. In *Proceedings of the third International Conference On Smart homes and health Telematic (ICOST),* Sherbrooke, Québec, Canada.

Henricksen, K., & Indulska, J. (2004). A Software Engineering Framework for Context Aware Pervasive Computing. In *Proceedings of the 2ⁿᵈ IEEE International Conference on Pervasive Computing and Communication, PreCom04,* March 14-17, Orlando, FL.

Henricksen, K., Indulska, J., & Rakotonirainy, A. (2001). Infrastructure for Pervasive Computing: Challenges . In Bauknecht, K., Brauer, W., & Muck, T. (Eds.), *Informatic 2001* (pp. 214–222). Vienna, Austria.

Henry, C. (2008). Can Universities Dream of Electric Sheepskin? *Systemic Transformations in Higher Education Organizational Models, 11*(1), Winter.

Hill, J. R., Wiley, D., Nelson, L. M., & Han, S. (2004). Exploring research on internet-based learning: From infrastructure to interactions . In *Handbook of research on educational communications and technology.* London: Lawrence Erlbaum Associates, Publishers.

Hill, J., Szewczyk, R., Woo, A., Hollar, S., Culler, D., & Pister, K. (2000). System Architecture Directions for Network Sensors. In *Proceedings of International Conference on Architectural Support for Programming Languages and Operating Systems,* Cambridge, (pp. 93 – 104).

Hilton, J. (2004). *Role of the University in Knowledge Economy.* Presentation at SAC Conference. Retrieved from http://connect.educause.edu/Library/Abstract/TheRoleoftheUniversityint/43102?time=1223297362

Holak, S. L., & Lehmann, D. R. (1990). Purchase intentions and the dimensions of innovation: an exploratory model. *Journal of Product Innovation Management, 7,* 59–73. doi:10.1016/0737-6782(90)90032-A

Holmberg, B. (1983). Guided didactic conversation in distance education . In Sewart, D., Keegan, D., & Holmberg, B. (Eds.), *Distance education: international perspectives.* London: Routledge.

Hu, Y. C., & Perrig, A. (2004). A Survey of Secure Wireless Ad Hoc Routing. *IEEE Security and Privacy Magazine*, *2*(3), 28–39. doi:10.1109/MSP.2004.1

Hu, Y. C., & Perrig, A. (2004). A Survey of Secure Wireless Ad Hoc Routing. *IEEE Security and Privacy Magazine, 2*(3), 28-39. Retrieved from http://ieeexplore. ieee.org/stamp/stamp.jsp?arnumber=01306970

Hu, Y.-C., Perrig, A., & Johnson, D. B. (2005). Ariadne: A secure on-demand routing protocol for ad hoc networks. [Retrieved from]. *Wireless Networks*, *11*(1-2), 21–38. doi:10.1007/s11276-004-4744-y

Huang, P. B. Jiajun, Chen, Chun, Qiu, Guang (2007). An Effective Feature-Weighting Model for Question Classification. In *Proceedings of the 2007 International Conference on Computational Intelligence and Security*, (pp. 32-36).

IDA (Infocomm Development Authority). (2007). *Singapore's vibrant telecoms market*. The China Telecom (Singapore) Inauguration Ceremony on 31 January 2007, Singapore. Retrieved September 2008, from http://www. ida.gov.sg/News%20and%20Events/20060814181223. aspx?getPagetype=21

Ioannis, E., Maria, K., Markaki, E., & Vasilakos, A. V. (2000). A Hybrid Genetic Approach for Channel Reuse in Multiple Access Telecommunication Networks. *IEEE Journal on Selected Areas in Communications*, *18*(2), 234–243. doi:10.1109/49.824804

Ishchenko, D., Kinne, C. P., Mork, B. A., Quest, R. P., Wang, X., & Yerrabelli, A. D. (2005). *Power Line Carrier Communications Systems Modeling*. Presented at the International Conference on Power Systems Transients (IPST'05) in Montreal, Canada on June 19-23, Paper No. IPST05 – 247.

Jackson, P. (2003). Ten Challenges for introducing Web-supported learning to overseas students in the social sciences . *Active Learning in Higher Education*, *4*(1), 87–106. doi:10.1177/1469787403004001007

Jacucci, E., Hanseth, O., & Lyytinen, K. (2006). Taking complexity seriously in IS research. *Information Technology & People*, *19*(1), 5–11. doi:10.1108/09593840610649943

Jang, S. L., Dai, S. C., & Sung, S. (2005). The pattern and externality effect of diffusion of mobile telecommunications: the case of the OECD and Taiwan. *Information Economics and Policy*, *17*(2), 133–148. doi:10.1016/j. infoecopol.2004.05.001

Jayasooriya, T. G., & Manandhar, S. (2005). Networking In A Smart Home - Providing Lightweight Networking Services for Heterogeneous Devices. In Perspectives in Pervasive Computing. London: IEE.

Jiang, M. & Ting, E. (2000). A Study of Factors Influencing Students' Perceived Learning in a Web-Based Course Environment. *International Journal of Educational telecommunication, 6*(4), 317-338.

Joachims, T. (1998). Text categorization with support vector machines: Learning with many relevant features. In Proc. of the European Conf. on Machine Learning. Berlin: Springer.

Joachims, T., Cristianini, N., & Shawe Taylor, J. (2001). Composite Kernels for Hypertext categorization. In proc. of Int'l Conf. on Machine Learning.

Johnson, D. B., & Maltz, D. A. (1996). Dynamic Source Routing in Ad hoc Wireless Networks. In T. Imielinski & H. Korth (1st Ed.) Mobile Computing (pp. 153-181). Amsterdam: Kluwer Academic Publishers.

Johnson, D. W., & Johnson, R. T. (1996). Cooperation and the use of technology . In Jonassen, D. H. (Ed.), *Handbook of research for educational communications and technology* (pp. 1017–1044). New York: Simon and Schuster Macmillan.

Johnson, S. D., Aragon, S. R., Shaik, N., & Palma-Rivas, N. (2000). Comparative analysis of learner satisfaction and learning outcomes in online and face-to-face learning environments. *Journal of Interactive Learning Research*, *11*(1), 29–49.

Jones, M. (1997). Structuration theory. In W. J. Currie, & R. D. Galliers (Eds.), Re-thinking Management Information Systems, (pp. 103-135). Oxford, UK: Oxford.

Jones, M., Orlikowski, W., & Munir, K. (2004). Structuration Theory and Information Systems: A Critical Reappraisal . In Mingers, J., & Willcocks, L. (Eds.), *Social Theory and Philosophy for Information Systems* (pp. 297–328). Chichester, UK: John Wiley & Sons.

Kalantzis, M., & Cope, B. (2000). Towards an inclusive and international education . In King, R., Hill, D., & Hemmings, B. (Eds.), *University Diversity*. Wagga Wagga, Australia: Keon Publications.

Kalasapur, S., & Shirazi, B. A. (2007). Dynamic Service Composition in Pervasive Computing. *IEEE Transactions on Parallel and Distributed Systems, 18*(7), 907–918. doi:10.1109/TPDS.2007.1039

Kanuka, H., & Anderson, T. (1998). Online social interchange, discord, and knowledge construction. *Journal of Distance Education, 13*(1), 57–74.

Karayan, S. S., & Crowe, J. A. (1997). Student perceptions of electronic discussion groups. *The Journal, 24*(9).

Karlof, C., & Vagner, D. (2003). *Secure routing in wireless sensor networks: attacks and countermeasures. In 1st IEEE int'l workshop on sensor network protocols and applications.*

Kaye, A. (1995). Computer supported collaborative learning . In Heap, N., Thomas, R., Einon, G., Mason, R., & MacKay, H. (Eds.), *Information Technology and Society* (pp. 192–210). London: Sage.

Kearsley, G. (1995). The nature and value of interaction in distance education. *Distance Education Symposium 3: Instruction*. University Park, PA: American Center for the Study of Distance Education.

Kearsley, G. (1998). *A guide to online education*. Retrieved from http://home.sprynet.com/~gkearsley/online.htm

Keefe, J. W. (1979). Learning Style: an Overview . In Keefe, J. W. (Ed.), *Student Learning Styles: Diagnosing and Prescribing Programs*. Reston, VA: NAASP.

Khanbary, L. M. O., & Vidyarthi, D. P. (2008). A GA Based Fault-Tolerant Model for Channel Allocation in Mobile Computing. *IEEE Transactions on Vehicular Technology, 57*(3), 1823–1833. doi:10.1109/TVT.2007.907311

Khanbary, L. M. O., & Vidyarthi, D. P. (2008). Mobility Management Model for Healthcare Services. In *Proceedings of the International Conference on High Performance Computing, Networking and Communication Systems* (pp.47-53), Orlando, FL.

Kiczales, G. lamping, J., Mendhekar, A., Maeda, C., Lopes, C., Loingtier, J. M., & Trwin, J. (1997, June). Aspect Oriented Programming. In *Proceedings of ECOOP '97*, (LNCS 1246). Berlin: Springer-Verlag.

Kieburtz, R. B., et al. (1996). A Software Engineering Experiment In Software Component Generation. In *Proceedings of the 18th international conference on Software Engineering*, Berlin, March 25-29.

Kittler, J., & Hojjatoleslami, A. A. (1998). Weighted combination of classifiers employing shared and distinct representations. In *IEEE Proc. Computer Vision and Pattern Recognition*, (pp 924-929). Retrieved from http://www.idiap.ch/~norman/fusion

Klesius, J., Homan, S., & Thompson, T. (1997). Distance education compared to traditional instruction: The students' view. *International Journal of Instructional Media, 24*(3), 207–220.

Knerr, S., Personnaz, L., & Dreyfus, G. (1990). Single-layer learning revisited: A stepwise procedure for building and training a neural network. Neurocomputing: algorithms, architectures and applications. Berlin: Springer.

Knight, K., & Rich, E. (1991) Artificial Intelligence (2 ed.), (pp. 24). New York: McGraw-Hill.

Kohonen, T. (1982). Self-organized formation of topologically correct feature maps. In Biological Cybernetics, (pp. 43-69).

Konstantinidis, S. T., & Bamidis, P. D. (2007). *E-Learning Environments in Medical Education: How Pervasive Computing Can Influence the Educational Process.* Sofia, Bulgaria: BCI.

Krzywinski, M. (2003). Port Knocking: Network Authentication across Closed Ports. *SysAdmin Magazine, 12*, 12–17.

Kulkarni, D., & Tripathi, A. (2008). Context Aware Role Based Access Control in Pervasive Computing Systems. In *Proceedings of the 13th ACM Symposium on Access Control Models and Technologies*, Ester Park, CO, June 11-13.

Kumari, D. S. (2001). Connecting graduate students to virtual guests through asynchronous discussions: analysis of an experience. *Journal of Asynchronous Learning Networks*, *5*(2). Retrieved from http://www.aln.org/alnweb/journal/Vol5_issue2/Kumari/Kumari.htm.

Lapinsky, A., Weshler, J., Mehta, S., Varkul, M., Hallett, D., & Stewart, T. (2001). Handheld computers in critical care. *Critical Care (London, England)*, *5*(4), 227–231. doi:10.1186/cc1028

Laurillard, D. (1993). *Rethinking university teaching: a framework for the effective use of educational technology*. London: Routledge.

Lee, S. (2007, October). *The determinants of the global broadband deployment: an empirical study*. Paper presented at the Pacific Telecommunications Councils 2008 Conference, Washington, DC. Retrieved from www.ptc.org/ptc08/participants/speakers/papers/Sangwon-Lee_FullPaper.pdf

Leigh, J. & DeFanti, T. (1997). CAVERN: A Distributed Architecture for Supporting Scalable Persistence And Interoperability in Collaborative Virtual Environments. *Journal of Virtual Reality Research, Development and Applications, 2*(2.1).

Leigh, J., Johnson, A., DeFanti, T., et al. (1999). A Review of Tele-Immersive Applications in the CAVE Research Network. In IEEE VR '99, Houston TX.

Leigh, J., Rajlich, P., Stein, R., Johnson, A. E., & DeFanti, T. A. (1998). A Tool for Rapid Tele-Immersive Visualization. In *IEEE Visualizaton '98*. Research Triangle Park, NC: LIMBO/VTK.

Levis, P., Lee, N., Welsh, M., & Culler, D. *(2003). TOSSIM: Accurate and Scalable Simulation of Entire TinyOS Applications. In* Proceedings of ACM Conference on Embedded Networked Sensor Systems, *(pp. 26 – 137)*.

Levitt, D. S., & Dubner, J. S. (2005). *Freakonomics: A Rogue Economist Explores the Hidden Side of Everything*. New York: HarperCollins.

Li, X., & Roth, D. (2002). Learning Question Classifiers. In COLING'02.

Lin, J. M. (2006). *Industrial spatial distribution phenomena of technological innovation diffusion — a case study of IC industry in Taiwan*. Unpublished master dissertation, National Chung Kung University, Taiwan. Retrieved November 12, 2008, from http://0-etdncku.lib.ncku.edu.tw.lib1.npue.edu.tw/ETD-db/ETD-search/view_etd?URN=etd-0725106-013137

Liu, Ch. D., & Li, Ch. B. (2000). Electromagnetic pollution and its control. In Z. Feng, & Y. Zhang (Eds.), *2nd International Conference on ICMMT 2000* (pp. 461-464). Beijing, China: IEEE Press.

Lomax, R. G. (2007). *An Introduction to Statistical Concepts for Education and the Behavioral Sciences* (2nd ed.). Mahwah, NJ: Lawrence Erlbaum.

Loos, C. (2002). E-Health with Mobile Grids: The Akogrimo Heart Monitoring and Emergency Scenario. *Akogrimo consortium, Information society*. Retrieved from http://www.Akogrimo.org/ download/White_Papers_and_Publications.

López-Rubio, E., Ortiz-de-Lazcano-Lobato, M., Muñoz-Pérez, J. J., & Gómez-Ruiz, A. J. (2004). Principal Components Analysis Competitive Learning. *Neural Computation*, *16*(11), 2459–2481. doi:10.1162/0899766041941880

Mahapatra, S. S., Roy, K., Banerjee, S., & Vidyarthi, D. P. (2006). Improved Genetic Algorithm for Channel Allocation with Channel Borrowing in Mobile Computing. *IEEE Transactions on Mobile Computing*, *5*(7), 884–892. doi:10.1109/TMC.2006.99

Makishima, M. (Ed.). (2002). *Human Resource Development in the Information Age: The Cases of Singapore and Malaysia. ASEDP 61, Institute of Developing Economies*. Chiba, Japan: Japan External Trade Organization.

Malone, T. W. (2004). *The Future of Work: How the New Order of Business will Shape Your Organization, Your Management Style, and Your Life*. Boston: Harvard Business School Press.

March, J. G., & Olsen, J. P. (1984). The new institutionalism: organizational factors in political life. *The American Political Science Review, 78*(3), 734–749. doi:10.2307/1961840

Marcus, A. (1993). Human communication issues in advanced UIs. *Communications of the ACM, 36*(4). doi:10.1145/255950.153670

Marcus, A., & Gould, E. W. (2000). Crosscurrents: Cultural dimensions and global Web user-interface design. *Interaction, 7*(4). doi:10.1145/345190.345238

Marglin, S. A. (2008). *The Dismal Science: How Thinking Like an Economist Undermines Community*. Cambridge, MA: Harvard University Press.

Mark, W. (1999). Turning pervasive computing into mediated spaces. Armonk, NY: IBM. Jalote, P. (Ed.), (2004). Software Engineering. Mumbai.

Market Intelligence Center. (2006). *The Taiwanese WiMax industry. Statistics report*. Taipei, Taiwan: Institute for Information Industry.

Marshall, J. (2007). Smartphones are the PCs of developing world. *New Scientist, 195*(2615), 24–25. doi:10.1016/S0262-4079(07)61964-2

Marti, S., Giuli, T. J., Lai, K., & Baker, M. (2000). Mitigating Routing Misbehavior in Mobile Ad Hoc Networks. In *Proceedings of 6ᵗʰ ACM/IEEE International conf. on Mobile Computing and Networking* (pp. 255–265), Boston. New York: ACM Press.

Martin, E. (2006). Survey Questionnaire Construction. *Survey Methodology*, 13.

Marton, F., & Säljö, R. (1976). On qualitative differences in learning: Outcome and Process. *The British Journal of Educational Psychology, 46*, 4–11.

Marton, F., & Säljö, R. (1997). Approaches to learning. In Marton, F., Hounsell, D., & Entwistle, N. (Eds.), *The experience of learning: Implications for teaching and studying in higher education*.

Mason, R., & Weller, M. (2000). Factors Affecting Students Satisfaction on a Web Course. *Australian Journal of Educational Technology, 16*(2), 173–200.

Masujima, M. (Ed.). (2005). Applied Mathematical Methods in Theoretical Physics. Weinheim, Germany: WILEY-VCH Verlag GmbH & Co. KGaA

Masuyama, S., & Vandenbrink, D. (2003). (Eds.). Towards a Knowledge-based Economy: East Asia's Changing Industrial Geography. Singapore, Nomura Research Institute, Tokyo and Institute of Southeast Asian Studies.

Mayer, R. (2001). *Multimedia Learning*. Cambridge, UK: Cambridge Press.

Mc Keachie, S. J. (1995). Learning styles can become learning strategies. *The National Teaching and Learning Forum, 4*(6), 1–2.

McClean, S. M., F., & Millard, P. (2006). Using Markov Models to assess the Performance of a Health and Community Care System. In *Proceedings of the 19th IEEE Symposium on Computer-Based Medical Systems*, (pp.777-782).

McColl, E. (2001). Design and use of questionnaires: a review of best practice applicable to surveys of health service staff and patients. *Health Technology Assessment, 5*(31).

McCowan, I., et al. (n.d.) *Towards Computer Understanding of Human Interactions, 8*. Retrieved August 10, 2008, from http://www.idiap.ch/~mccowan/publications/mccowan-eusai.pdf

McGregor, M. A., & Holman, J. (2004). Communication technology at the Federal Communications Commission: E-government in the public interest? *Government Information Quarterly, 21*(3), 268–283. doi:10.1016/j.giq.2004.04.005

McGuire, P. (2005). The Cyborg Astrobiologist: Scouting Red Beds for Uncommon Features with Geological Significance. *International Journal of Astrobiology, 4*(2). doi:10.1017/S1473550405002533

Mei-Ju, S., et al. (2005). Application of Wireless Network in a Medical Emergency Service Network. In *IEEE Proceedings of 7th International Workshop on Enterprise Networking and Computing in Healthcare Industry, 23-25 Jun*, (pp.45-50).

Meyer, J. D. (2000, November). *Quality of life in the school of the global village*. Paper presented at the Teaching Online in Higher Education 2000 virtual conference. Retrieved from http://as1.ipfw.edu/2000tohe/papers/meyer.htm

Michiardi, P., & Molva, R. (2002). CORE: A collaborative reputation mechanism to enforce node cooperation in mobile ad hoc networks. In *Proceedings of Sixth IFIP conference on Security Communications and Multimedia*, (pp. 107-121), Portoroz, Slovenia. Amsterdam: Kluwer Publisher.

Middlehurst, R. & Woodfied, S. (2003). *The role of transnationals, private and for profit provision in meeting global demand for tertiary eduction: mapping, regulation and impact*, Centre for Policy and Change in Tertiary Education, University of Surrey, Report commissioned by the Commonwealth of Learning and UNESCO.

Mikulecký, P. (2009). *Ambient Intelligence Perspectives*. Amsterdam: IOS Press.

Mikulecký, P., Kelemen, J., & Ponce, D. (1998). A Multiagent Intelligent Control System. In P. Kopacek, & I. Rudas (Eds.), *2nd International Conference on Intelligent Engineering Systems* (pp. 91-93). Wien, Austria: IEEE.

Mikulecký, P., Olševičová, K., & Ponce, D. (2007). Ambient Intelligence - Monitoring and Supervision of New Type . In Kleve, P., de Mulder, R. V., & van Noortwijk, C. (Eds.), *First international seminar of the Legal Framework for the Information Society (LEFIS) on Monitoring, Supervision and IT* (pp. 115–134). Zaragoza, Spain: Zaragoza University Press.

Mingers, J., & Willcocks, L. (Eds.). (2004). *Social Theory and Philosophy for Information System*. Chichester, UK: John Wiley & Sons.

Mishra, A., Nadkarni, K., & Patcha, A. (2004, February). Intrusion detection in wireless ad hoc networks. *IEEE Wireless Communications, 11*(1), 48–60. Retrieved from http://ieeexplore.ieee.org/stamp/stamp.jsp?tp=&arnumber=1269717&isnumber=28409

Mitchell, M. (1999). *An Introduction to Genetic Algorithms*. London: MIT Press.

Mitra, S. (2006). Hole-in-the-Wall Lighting the spark of Learning. *Beginnings*. Retrieved February 19, 2009 from http://www.hole-in-the-wall.com/Beginnings.html

Monroe, K. B., & Lee, A. (1999). Remembering versus knowing: issues in buyers' processing of price information. *Journal of the Academy of Marketing Science, 27*(1), 207–225. doi:10.1177/0092070399272006

Moore, G. A. (2005). *Dealing with Darwin: How Great Companies Innovate at Every Phase of Their Evolution*. New York: Portfolio.

Moore, G. C., & Benbasat, I. (1991). Development of an instrument to measure the perception of adopting an information technology innovation. *Information Systems Research, 2*(3), 192–222. doi:10.1287/isre.2.3.192

Moore, M. (1993). Three types of interaction . In Harry, K., John, M., & Keegan, D. (Eds.), *Distance education: new perspectives*. London: Routledge.

Moore, M., & Kearsley, G. (1996). *Distance education: A system view*. Belmont, CA: Wadsworth Publishing Company.

Mori, S., Suen, C. Y., & Yamamota, K. (1992). Historical review of OCR research and development. *IEEE Proc., 80*, 1029–1058. doi:10.1109/5.156468

Moudgil, M. (2008 November 11) Tapping into your full potential. *The Mail Today*, (pp 27).

Mukhejree, S. (Eds.). (2006). *AmIware: Hardware Technology Drivers of Ambient Intelligence*. Dordrecht: Springer. doi:10.1007/1-4020-4198-5

Mukherji, A. (2008, April). Retrieved from http://timesofindia.indiatimes.com/articleshow/2915234.cms.

Mukkamala, S., Janoski, G., & Sung, A. H. (2002). Intrusion Detection using neural networks and support vector machines. In IEEE Proc. of Int'l Joint Conf. on Neural Networks, (pp. 1702-07).

Muller, P. O., & Stich, C. M. & Zeidler, C. (2001). Component Based Embedded Systems. In I. Crnkovic & M. Larson, (Ed.), Building Reliable Component Based Software Systems, (pp. 303-324). Boston: Artech House.

Newman, J. H. (1852). *The Idea of a University Defined and Illustrated: I* (Ker, I. T., Ed.). Oxford: Clarendon Press.

Nicholson, B., & Sahay, S. (2001). Some political and cultural issues in the globalization of software development: case experience from Britain and India. *Information and Organization*, (11): 25–43. doi:10.1016/S0959-8022(00)00008-4

Nonaka, I., & Takeuchi, H. (1995). *The Knowledge Creating Company*. New York: Oxford University Press.

Norman, D. (1998). *The invisible computer: why good products can fail, the personal computer is so complex, and information appliances are the solution*. Cambridge, MA: MIT Press.

Oblinger, D. (2006). *Simulations, Games, and Learning*. ELI White Paper. ELI3004. Retrieved from http://connect.educause.edu/

Olshavsky, R. W., Aylesworth, A. B., & Kempf, D. S. (1995). The price-choice relationship: A contingent processing approach. *Journal of Business Research*, *33*(3), 207–218. doi:10.1016/0148-2963(94)00070-U

Olson, E. M. (1995). Organizing for effective new product development: the moderating role of product innovativeness. *Journal of Marketing*, *59*, 48–62. doi:10.2307/1252014

Orlikowski, W. J. (1992). The Duality of Technology: Rethinking the Concept of Technology in Organizations. *Organization Science*, *3*(3), 398–427. doi:10.1287/orsc.3.3.398

Orlikowski, W. J. (2000). Using Technology and Constituting Structures: a Practice Lens for Studying Technology in Organizations. *Organization Science*, *11*(4), 404–428. doi:10.1287/orsc.11.4.404.14600

Orlikowski, W., & Barley, S. R. (2001). Technology and institutions: what can research on information technology and research on organizations learn from each other? *Management Information Systems Quarterly*, *25*(2), 245–265. doi:10.2307/3250927

Panfilis, S. D., & Berre, A. J. (2004). Open issues and concerns on Component Based Software Engineering. In *Proceedings of 'Ninth International Workshop on Component Oriented Programming (WCOP 2004)'*, 14-18 June, Oslo, Norway.

Park, K., Cho, Y. J., Krishnaprasad, N., Scharver, C., Lewis, M., Leigh, J., & Johnson, A. (2000). CAVERNsoft G2: a Toolkit for High Performance Tele-Immersive Collaboration. In *ACM 7th Annual Symposium on Virtual Reality Software & Technology (VRST)*, Seoul, Korea.

Patrick, M. (n.d.). *How to Build a Computerized Android Robot Head*. Retrieved August 10, 2008, from www.howtoandroid.com/HowToBuildRobotHead.html

Paul McKenna will make you thin. (n.d.). Retrieved July 30, 2008, from http://www.skyone.co.uk/mckenna

Pavlovski, C., Kim, H., & Wood, D. (2004). Ubiquitous Mobility in Clinical Healthcare. *IEEE Proceedings of the IDEAS Workshop on Medical Information Systems: The Digital Hospital, 1-3 Sept.* (pp.147 – 153).

PECOS. (n.d.). PECOS Project Website. Retrieved from http://www.pecos-project.org

Pelikan, J. (1992). *The Idea of the University: A Reexamination*. New Haven, CT: Yale University Press.

Perkins, C.E., Royer, E. & Das, S.R. (2003). *Ad hoc On Demand Distance vector (AODV)*. RFC 3561.

Phipps, A.G. (2001). Empirical Applications of Structuration Theory. *Geografiska Annaler, 83 B*(4).

Phipps, R. A., Wellman, J. V., & Merisotis, J. P. (1998). *Assuring quality in distance learning: A report prepared for the Council for Higher Education Accreditation*. Washington, DC: The Institute for Higher Education Policy.

Picciano, A. G. (1998). Developing an asynchronous course model at a large, urban university. *Journal of Asynchronous Learning Networks*, *2*(1). Retrieved from http://www.aln.org/alnweb/journal/vol2_issue1/picciano.htm.

Picciano, A. G. (2001). *Distance Learning: Making Connections across Virtual Space and Time.* Upper Saddle River, NJ: Prentice-Hall.

Picciano, A. G. (2002). Beyond student perceptions: Issues of interaction, presence, and performance in an online course. *Journal of Asynchronous Learning Networks, 6*(1).

Pierson, J. (2005). Domesticalon at work in small businesses . In Berker, T., Hartmann, M., Punie, Y., & Ward, K. (Eds.), *Domestication of media and technology* (pp. 205–226). Berkshire, UK: Open University Press.

Pierson, J., Jacobs, A., Dreessen, K., & De Marez, L. (2008). Exploring & designing wireless city applications by way of archetype user research within a living lab. *Observatorio Journal, 5*, 99–118.

Pittinsky, M. (2003). *The Wired Tower: Perspectives on the Impact of the Internet on Higher Education.* Upper Saddle River, NJ: Prentice Hall.

Pohle, T., Knees, P., Schedl, M., Pampalk, E., & Widmer, G. (2007). Reinventing the Wheel: A Novel Approach to Music Player Interfaces. *IEEE Transactions on Multimedia, 9*(3). doi:10.1109/TMM.2006.887991

Porter, M. E. (2001). Strategy and the Internet. *Harvard Business Review, 79*(3), 62–79.

Pozzebon, M. (2004). The Influence of a Structurationist View on Strategic Management Research. *Journal of Management Studies, 41*(2), 247–272. doi:10.1111/j.1467-6486.2004.00431.x

Pozzebon, M., & Pinsonneault, A. (2005). Challenges in Conducting Empirical Work Using Structuration Theory: Learning from IT Research. *Organization Studies, 26*(9), 1353–1376. doi:10.1177/0170840605054621

Pressman, R. (2001). *Software Engineering: A practitioner approach* (6th ed., pp. 847–857). New York: McGraw Hill.

Pressman, R. (Ed.). (2005). *Software Engineering –A Practitioner's Approach.* Mumbai: McGraw Hill Publications.

Principe, J. C., Euliano, N. R., & Lefebvre, W. C. (1999). *Neural and Adaptive Systems: Fundamentals through Simulations.*

Prusak, L. (2001). Where did knowledge management come from? *IBM Systems Journal, 40*(4), 1002–1007.

Rajendra, V., & Su, B. X. (2007). Secure Routing Techniques to Mitigate Insider Attacks in Wireless Ad Hoc Networks. *IEEE proceedings.* Retrieved from http://www.cs.utsa.edu/faculty/boppana/papers/Whns07-preprint.pdf

Ramani, K. V. (2004). IT Enabled Applications in Government Hospitals in India: Illustrations of telemedicine, e-governance, and BPR. In *IEEE Proceedings of the 37th International Conference on System Sciences, 5-8 Jan,* (pp.8), Hawaii.

Ramasamy, B., Chakrabarty, A., & Cheah, M. (2004). Malaysia's leap into the future: an evaluation of the multimedia super corridor. *Technovation, 24*, 871–883. doi:10.1016/S0166-4972(03)00049-X

Ramaswamy, S., Fu, H., Sreekantaradhya, M., Dixon, J., & Nygard, K. (2003). Prevention of Cooperative Black Hole Attack in Wireless Ad Hoc Networks. *International Conference on Wireless Networks (ICWN' 03),* Las Vegas, NV. Retrieved from http://www.cs.ndsu.nodak.edu/~nygard/research/BlackHoleMANET.pdf

Ramburuth, P., & McCormick, J. (2001). Learning Diversity in Higher Education: A comparative study of Asian international and Australian Students. *Higher Education, 42*, 333–350. doi:10.1023/A:1017982716482

Ramsden, P. (1992). *Learning to teach in higher education.* London: Routledge.

Ramsden, P. (2003). *Learning to Teach in Higher Education* (2nd ed.). London: RoutledgeFalmer.

Rao, A. R., & Monroe, K. B. (1989). The effect of price, brand name, and store name on buyers' perceptions of product quality: an integrative review. *Journal of Marine Research, 26,* 351–357. doi:10.2307/3172907

Rarnadoss, B. & Balasundaram, S. R. (2004). Aspects of pervasive computing for web based learning. *International conference on information technology, Hyderabad, 3356,* 419-425.

Rauber, A., Pampalk, E., & Merkl, D. (2002). Using Psycho-Acoustic Models and Self-Organizing Maps to Create a Hierarchical Structure of Music by Sound Similarity. In *Proc. Int. Conf. Music Information Retrieval (ISMIR),* Paris, France, (pp. 71–80).

Raymond, D. (2007). *Waves.* Retrieved Jan 17, 2009 from http://physics.nmt.edu/~raymond/classes/ph13xbook/node5.html

Reeves, C. A., & Bednar, D. A. (1994). Defining quality: alternatives and implications. *Academy of Management Review, 19*(3), 435–440. doi:10.2307/258934

Remagnino, P. (2005). Ambient Intelligence: A Gentle Introduction . In Remagnino, P., Foresti, G. L., & Ellis, T. (Eds.), *Ambient Intelligence: a Novel Paradigm* (pp. 1–14). New York: Springer.

Remagnino, P., Foresti, G. L., & Ellis, T. (Eds.). (2005). *Ambient Intelligence: a Novel Paradigm.* New York: Springer.

Renniger, A., & Shumar, W. (2000). *Building virtual communities: Learning and change in cyberspace.* Cambridge, UK: Cambridge University Press.

Retrieved from http://ieeexplore.ieee.org/stamp/stamp.jsp?arnumber=01181388

Retrieved from http://ieeexplore.ieee.org/stamp/stamp.jsp?tp=&arnumber=1203362&isnumber=27104

Reuters. (2006). *Kids learn better if they figure it out themselves: study.* Retrieved February 20, 2009 from http://www.reuters.com/article/gc08/idUSL0862420070308

Rhodes, B. J. (1997). The wearable remembrance agent: a system for augmented memory. In *Proc. of First International Symposium on Wearable Computers (ISWC '97),* (pp.123).

Richardson, J. T. E. (1990). Reliability and replicability of the approaches to studying questionnaire. *Studies in Higher Education, 15*(2), 155. doi:10.1080/03075079012331377481

Rifkin, R., & Klautau, A. (2004). In Defense of One-Vs.-All Classification. *Journal of Machine Learning, 5,* 101–141.

Riley, K., & Hobson, M. (Eds.). (2002). *Mathematical methods for physics and engineering.* Cambridge, UK: Cambridge University Press.

Rivest, R. L. (1995). The RC5 Encryption Algorithm. In *Proceedings of 2nd Workshop on Fast Software Encryption,* (LNCS 809, pp. 86 – 96). Berlin: Springer-Verlag.

Robbins, A. (1986). *Unlimited power: the new science of personal achievement.* New York: Simon & Schuster.

Robertson, G., & Turk, M. (2000). Perceptual user interfaces. *Communications of the ACM, 43*(3), 33–34.

Rodríguez, M. D., Favela, J., Martínez, E. A., & Muñoz, M. A. (2004). Location-Aware Access to Hospital Information and Services. *IEEE Transactions on Information Technology in Biomedicine, 8*(4), 448–455. doi:10.1109/TITB.2004.837887

Rogers, E. M. (1962). *Diffusion of Innovation* (3rd ed.). New York: Free Press.

Rohfeld, R. W., & Hiemstra, R. (1995). Moderating discussion in the electronic classroom. In Z.L. Berge, & M.P. Collins (Eds.), Computer mediated communication and the online classroom Volume III: Distance learning, (pp. 91-104). Cresskill, NJ: Hampton Press.

Rosenberg, D. (2002). *Cloning Silicon Valley: The Next Generation High-Tech Hotspots.* London: Reuters.

Royer, E. M., & Toh, C. K. (1999). A Review of Current Routing Protocols for Ad Hoc Mobile Wireless Networks. *IEEE Personal Communication, 6*(2), 46-55.

Rust, D. Z. (2006). *Examining interaction in online courses in relation to student performance and course retention.* EdD dissertation, Tennessee State University.

Saba, F. (2000). Research in distance education: A status report. *International Review of Research in Open and Distance Learning, 1*(1), 1–9.

Saperstein, J., & Rouach, D. (2002). *Creating Regional Wealth in the Innovation Economy: Models, Perspectives, and Best Practices*. Upper Saddle River, NJ: Financial Times Prentice Hall.

Satyanarayanan, M. (2001). Pervasive Computing: Issues and Challenges. *IEEE Personal Communications, 8*(4), 10–17. doi:10.1109/98.943998

Satyanarayanan, M. (2001). Pervasive Computing: Vision and Challenges. IEEE Personal Communications.

Saunders, G., & Klemming, F. (2003). Integrating technology into traditional learning environment: Reasons for and risks of success. *Active Learning in Higher Education, 4*(1), 74–86. doi:10.1177/1469787403004001006

Scarnati, J. (2001). On becoming a team player. *Team Performance Management, 7*(1,2), 5.

Schaorghofer, N. (Ed.). (2005). *The Third Branch Of Physics: Essays On Scientific Computing*. Author.

Schenker, J. (2007). Researching Ubiquity: Ways to Capture It All . In van 't Hooft, M., & Swan, K. (Eds.), *Ubiquitous Computing in Education* (pp. 167–186). Mahwah, NJ: Lawrence Erlbaum Associates.

Schiefele, J., Dörr, K., Olbert, M., & Kubbat, W. (1999). Stereoscopic Projection Screens and Virtual Cockpit Simulation for Pilot Training. In *Proceedings of the 3rd Annual Immersive Projection Technologies Workshop*, (pp. 211-222).

Schmidt, A., Spiekermann, S., Gershman, A. & Michahelles, F. (2006). Real World Challenges for Pervasive Computing. *IEEE Pervasive Computing, 5*(3), 91-93, C3.

Schmidt, M. (1996). Identifying speaker with support vector networks. In Interface '96 Proc., Sydney.

Scholkopf, B., & smola, A. J. (2002). *Learning with kernels*. Cambridge, MA: MIT Press.

Selwyn, N. (2002). Learning to Love the Micro: The Discursive Construction of 'Educational' Computing in the UK, 1979-89. *British Journal of Sociology of Education, 23*(3), 427–443. doi:10.1080/0142569022000015454

Senge, P. M. (1990). *The Fifth Discipline: The Art and Practice of the Learning Organisation*. New York: Doubleday.

Seno, A. A. (2003). A Wide-Open Valley but Not Much Silicon. *Newsweek: The International Magazine*, 90-93.

Serway & Jewett (Ed.). (2003). *Physics for Scientists and Engineers*. College Text.

Shea, P., Fredericksen, E., Pickett, A., Pelz, W., & Swan, K. (2001). Measures of learning effectiveness in the SUNY Learning Network. In J. Bourne & J. Moore (Eds.), *Online Education: Proceedings of the 2000 Sloan Summer Workshop on Asynchronous Learning Networks*, (Vol. 2, Sloan-C series). Needham, MA: Sloan-C Press.

Sherry, L. (1996). Issues in distance learning. *International Journal of Distance Education, 1*(4), 337–365.

Shi, Y., & Xie, W. (2003). The smart classroom: merging technologies for seamless tele-education. *Pervasive Computing, IEEE, 2*(2), 47–55. doi:10.1109/MPRV.2003.1203753

Siegwart, R. (2008, June 26). *Design and Realization of an Ear for Robot*, (p. 1). Retrieved August 10, 2008, from http://www.asl.ethz.ch/education/proj_apps/gifs/doku29.pdf

Singh, G., Serra, L., Png, W., Wong, A., & Ng, H. Brick-Net. (1999). Sharing Object Behaviors on the Net. In IEEE VRAIS '95, Research Triangle Park, NC, March 11-15, (pp. 19-25).

Singh, R. & Singh, A.K. (2008). Transcending from Virtual Reality into TELE-IMMERSIVE Technologies and Applications – A Perspective. *ACM Ubiquity, 9*(23).

Singh, R. (2008). Exploring Pervasive/Ubiquitous Computing Vision, Technologies, Applications and Challenges. In V. Godara (Ed.), *1st International Congress* on *Pervasive Computing and Management* (pp. 1-20). Sydney: Sydney College of Management.

Sloman, M. (2001). *The E-learning Revolution: From Propositions to Reality.* London: CIPD Publishing.

Smith, C. K. (1996*). Convenience vs. connection: Commuter students' views on distance learning.* Paper presented at the Annual Forum of the Association for Institutional Research, Albuquerque, NM, (ERIC Document Reproduction Service No. ED 397 725).

Smith, J. (2002). Learning Styles: Fashion Fad or Lever for Change? The Application of Learning Style Theory to Inclusive Curriculum Delivery. *Innovations in Education and Teaching International, 39*(1), 63–70. doi:10.1080/13558000110102913

Smith, M. K. (2001). Peter Senge and the Learning Organization. *Infed: the Informal Education Homepage.* Retrieved February 2, 2009 from http://www.infed.org/thinkers/senge.htm

Smits, M., & Pijl, G. (1999). Developments in Hospital Management and Information Systems. In *IEEE Proceedings of the 32nd International Conference on System Sciences, 5-8 Jan,* 9, Hawaii.

Soerensen, C. (Eds.). (2005). *Designing Ubiquitous Information Environments: Socio-Technical Issues and Challenges.* New York: Springer. doi:10.1007/0-387-28918-6

Stahl, B. C. (2008). *Information Systems: Critical Perspectives.* New York: Routledge.

Stallings, W. (2005). Cryptography and Network Security, Principles and Practice (4th, Ed.). Upper Saddle River, NJ: Pearson Education.

Stavness, I., Gluck, J., Vilhan, L., & Fels, S. (2005). The music table: A map-based ubiquitous system for social interaction with a digital music collection. In *Int. Conf. on Entertainment Computing (ICEC05).*

Stevens, W. R. (1994). *TCP/IP Illustrated (Vol. 1).* Reading, MA: Addison Wesley.

Stillman, L. J. H. (2006). *Understandings of Technology in Community-Based Organisations: A Structurational Analysis.* Unpublished doctoral dissertation, Faculty of Information Technology, Monash University, Australia.

Stolworthy, Y. & Suszka-Hildebrandt, S. (2001). Mobile Information Technology at the Point-of-Care. *Medscape Nurses, 3*(1).

Stones, R. (2005). *Structuration Theory.* New York: Palgrave MacMillan.

Strachota, E. M. (2003). Student satisfaction in an online course: An analysis of the impact of learner-content, learner-instructor, learner-learner and learner-technology interaction, Doctoral dissertation, The University of Wisconsin-Milwaukee, Milwaukee, WI. *Dissertation Abstracts International, 64*(08), 2746.

Stubbs, M. (1976). *Language, Schools, and Classrooms.* London: Methuen.

Szyperski, C. (1999). *Component Software- Beyond Object Oriented Programming.* Reading, MA: Addison-Wesley.

Taiwei, O. (2006). *Learning online: The effects of interaction levels on student self-efficacy, task value, learning strategies, and achievement.* PhD, Dissertation, University of Northern Colorado.

Tapscott, D. (2001). Rethinking Strategy in a Networked World. *Strategy + Business,* 24.

Tapscott, D., & Williams, A. D. (2006). *Wikinomics: How Mass Collaboration Changes Everything.* New York: Penguin Group.

Tarantola, A. (Ed.). (2005). *Elements for Physics: Quantities.* Qualities, and Intrinsic Theories.

Tawney, B. (2005). Analyzing the Patient Load on the Hospitals in a Metropolitan Area. In *IEEE Proceedings of Systems and Information Engineering Design Symposium, 29 April,* (pp. 215-221).

Taylor, S., & Todd, P. A. (1995). Understanding Information Technology Use: A Test of Competing models. *In-*

formation Systems Research, 6(2), 144–176. doi:10.1287/isre.6.2.144

Tian, Q., Xie, Q., Yu, J., Sebe, N., & Huang, T. S. (2004). Towards an Improved Error Metric. In *Proc. IEEE Int'l Conf. Image Processing*.

Trigwell, K. H., & Prosser, M. (1996). Perceptions of the learning environment and approaches to learning university science at the topic level. In *HERDSA Conference*, Melbourne.

Tripathi, A. K., Ratneshwer & Gupta, M. (2008). Some Observations on Software Processes for CBSE. *Software Process Improvement and Practice, 13*(5), 411–419. doi:10.1002/spip.356

Tripathi, A. K., Sarker, B. K., Kumar, N., & Vidyarthi, D. P. (2000). A GA Based Multiple Task Allocation Considering Load. *International Journal of High Speed Computing, 11*(4).

Tripathi, A. K., Vidyarthi, D. P., & Mantri, A. N. (2006). A Genetic Task Allocation Algorithm for Distributed Computing System Incorporating Problem Specific Knowledge. *International Journal of High Speed Computing, 8*(4), 363–370. doi:10.1142/S0129053396000203

van Houten, H. (2006). The Physical Basis of Ambient Intelligence. In S. Mukhejree et al. (Eds.), AmIware: Hardware Technology Drivers of Ambient Intelligence (pp. 9-28). Dordrecht: Springer. van 't Hooft, M., & Swan, K. (Eds.). (2007). Ubiquitous Computing in Education. Mahwah, NJ: Lawrence Erlbaum Associates.

van t' Hooft, et al. (2007). What is Ubiquitous Computing? In M. van 't Hooft & K. Swan (Eds.), *Ubiquitous Computing in Education* (pp. 3-18). Mahwah, NJ: Lawrence Erlbaum Associates.

Vars, A., & Versino, C. (1992). *Clustering of socio-economic data with Kohonen maps*. Neural Network World.

Vasilakos, A., & Pedrycz, W. (Eds.). (2006). *Ambient Intelligence, Wireless Networking and Ubiquitous Computing*. Boston: Artech House.

Venkatesh, V., Morris, M. G., Davis, G. B., & Davis, F. D. (2003). User acceptance of information technology: Toward a unified view. *Management Information Systems Quarterly, 27*(3), 425–478.

Veryzer, R. W. Jr. (1998). Key factors affecting customer evaluation of discontinuous. *Journal of Product Innovation Management, 15*, 136–150. doi:10.1016/S0737-6782(97)00075-1

Vesanto, J., & Alhoniemi, E. (2005). Clustering of the Self-Organizing Map. *IEEE Transactions on Neural Networks, 11*(3), 586–602. doi:10.1109/72.846731

Vidyarthi, D. P., Tripathi, A. K., & Mantri, A. N. (1997). Task Partitioning Using Genetic Algorithm. *International Conference in Cognitive Systems*, India, New Delhi.

Vidyarthi, D. P., Tripathi, A. K., Sarker, B. K., & Rani, K. (2003). Comparative Study of Two GA based Task Allocation Models in Distributed Computing System. *Fourth International Conference on Parallel and Distributed Computing, Applications and Technologies*, China, Chengdu.

Voorhees, R. A., & Lingenfelter, P. E. (2003). *Adult Learners and State Policy*. Chicago: SHEEO and CAEL.

Vygotsky, L. S. (1978). *Mind in society: the development of higher psychological processes*. Cambridge, MA: Harvard University.

Wagner, D., & Kozma, R. (2003). *New Technologies for Literacy and Adult Education: A Global Perspective*. International Literacy Institute, National Center for adult literacy, University of Pennsylvania. Retrieved February 20, 2009 from http://www.literacy.org/products/wagner_kozma.pdf

Wallace, M., Fertig, M., & Schneller, E. (2007). *Managing Change in the Public Services*. Maldan, MA: Blackwell Publishing.

Walsham, G. (2001). *Making a World of Difference: IT in A Global Context*. Chichester, UK: John Wiley & Sons.

Walsham, G. (2005). Learning about being critical. *Information Systems Journal, 15*, 111–117. doi:10.1111/j.1365-2575.2004.00189.x

Wang, J. L. (2005). Two-stage channel assignment scheme in wireless networks. *International Journal of Communication Systems, 18*(6), 571–584. doi:10.1002/dac.718

Want, Z. & Garlan, D. (2000). *Task-Driven Computing.* Technical Report, CMU-CS-00-154, School of Computer Science, Carnegie Mellon University, May.

Weiser, M. (1991). The computer for the 21st century. *Scientific American, 265*(3), 94–104.

Weiser, M. (1991). The Computer for the 21st Century. Scientific American, (pp. 94-104). Reprinted in IEEE Pervasive Computing, March 2002, (pp. 19-25).

Weiser, M. (1993). Some computer science issues in ubiquitous computing. *Communications of the ACM, 36*(7), 75–84. doi:10.1145/159544.159617

Weiser, M. (1993). Some Computer Science Issues in Ubiquitous Computing. *Communications of the ACM, 36*(7). doi:10.1145/159544.159617

Weiss, P. A. (Ed.). (1971). *Hierarchically Organized Systems in Theory and Practice.* New York: Hafner.

Weston, J., & Watkins, C. (1999). *Multi-class Support Vector Machines.* Paper presented at M. Verleysen, (Ed.), the Proc. ESANN99, Brussels, Belgium.

Williams, P. (2002). The learning web: The development, implementation and evaluation of internet-based undergraduate materials for the teaching of key skills. *Active Learning in Higher Education, 3*(1), 40–53. doi:10.1177/1469787402003001004

Winsborough, W. H., & Li, N. (2002). Towards Practical Automated Trust Negotiation. In *Proc. Third Int'l Workshop Policies for Distributed Systems and Networks (POLICY '02).*

Winslett, M., Yu, T., Seamons, K. E., Hess, A., Jacobson, J., & Jarvis, R. (2002). Negotiating Trust on the Web. *IEEE Internet Computing,* 30–37. doi:10.1109/MIC.2002.1067734

Wixom, B. H., & Todd, P. A. (2005). A theoretical integration of user satisfaction and technology acceptance. *Information Systems Research, 16*(1), 85–102. doi:10.1287/isre.1050.0042

Wood, A. D., & Stankovic, J. A. (2002). Denial of service in sensor networks. *IEEE Computer, 35*(10), 54-62. Retrieved from http://ieeexplore.ieee.org/stamp/stamp.jsp?arnumber=01039518

Wulff. (1996). *Design of Hospital Organizations.* Doctoral dissertation, Eindhoven Technical University.

www.upnp.org/download/standardizeddcps/UPnPSecurity Ceremonies_1_0secure.pdf. (2003, October).

Cybernetics. (n.d). Retrieved August 10, 2008, from http://en.wikipedia.org/ wiki/Cybernetics

Electronic Visualization Laboratory (EVL). (n.d.). *The CAVE Virtual reality system.* Retrieved May 31, 2008, from http://www.evl.uic.edu/pape/CAVE/oldCAVE/CAVE.overview.html

Taipei City Council. (2007). *Taipei City WIFLY plan.* Retrieved June 10, 2008, from http://www.tupc.taipei.gov.tw

Xiao, Y., Krishna Rayi, V., Sun, B., Du, X., Hu, F., & Galloway, M. (2007). A Survey of Key Management Schemes in Wireless Sensor Networks. *IEEE Computer Communications, 30*(11), 2314–2341. doi:10.1016/j.comcom.2007.04.009

Yang, H., Luo, H., Ye, F., Lu, S., & Zhang, L. (2004). Security in mobile ad hoc networks: challenges and solutions. *IEEE Wireless Communications, 11*(1), 38–47. Retrieved from http://ieeexplore.ieee.org/stamp/stamp.jsp?tp=&arnumber=1269716&isnumber=28409

Yu, J. Amores, Sebe, N., & Tian, Q. (2006). Toward Robust Distance Metric analysis for Similarity Estimation. In IEEE Proc. Int'l Conf. of Computer Vision and Pattern Recognition.

Yu, T., & Winslett, M. (2003). A Unified Scheme for Resource Protection in Automated Trust Negotiation. In *Proc. IEEE Symp. Security and Privacy.*

Yu, Z., & Guan, Y. *(2005). A Key Pre-distribution Scheme Using Deployment Knowledge for Wireless Sensor Networks. In* Proceedings of 4th ACM/IEEE International Conference on Information Processing in Sensor Networks, *(Poster Article No. 35).*

Zapata, M. G. (2001). Secure ad hoc on-demand distance vector (SAODV) routing. In *IETF Internet Draft*. Retrieved from http://tools.ietf.org/id/draft-guerrero-manet-saodv-06.txt

Zhang, L. F. (2000). University students' Learning approaches in three cultures: An investigation of Biggs 3P model. *The Journal of Psychology, 134*(1), 37–55. doi:10.1080/00223980009600847

Zhang, X., & Li, Y. (1993). Self-organizing map as a new method for clustering and data analysis. In *Proceedings of International Joint Conference on Neural Networks (IJCNN'93)*.

Zheng, Y., Cao, J., Chan, A. T. S., & Chan, K. C. C. (2007). Sensors and Wireless Sensor Networks for Pervasive Computing Applications. *Journal of Ubiquitous Computing and Intelligence, 1*(1), 17–34. doi:10.1166/juci.2007.003

Zhu, F., Mutka, M., & Ni, L. (2005). Service Discovery in Pervasive Computing Environments. *IEEE Pervasive Computing / IEEE Computer Society [and] IEEE Communications Society, 4*, 81–90. doi:10.1109/MPRV.2005.87

Zhu, F., Mutka, M., & Ni, L. (2006). A Private, Secure and User-Centric Information Exposure Model for Service Discovery Protocols. *IEEE Transactions on Mobile Computing, 5*, 418–429. doi:10.1109/TMC.2006.1599409

Zirkin, B., & Sumler, D. (1995). Interactive or non-interactive? That is the question! An annotated bibliography. *Journal of Distance Education, 10*(1), 95–112.

Zomaya, A. Y., & Wright, M. (2002). Observation on Using Genetic Algorithms for Channel Allocation in Mobile Computing. *IEEE Transactions on Parallel and Distributed Systems, 13*(9), 948–962. doi:10.1109/TPDS.2002.1036068

About the Contributors

Varuna Godara is the CEO of Sydney College of Management, Australia and SAP Australia certified consultant. Dr. Godara is the chair of International Congress on Pervasive Computing and Management. Previously, she worked as Director of Marketing at SCBIT and was a permanent faculty in Department of Business Systems, School of Management in University of Western Sydney, Australia from July 2003 to September 2008. Dr. Godara received her Bachelor degree in Computer Science in 1997, MBA in 1999, Maters in Computer Applications, and PhD in 2003. Her research interests are mainly in ERP, Pervasive business, E-business management, e-governance and innovation in business. She has authored a book in 2008, has contributed chapters in refereed books, papers in many refereed journals and presented research work in reputed conferences. She has also published popular articles and poems in various books and magazines. She was awarded with Roll of Honour two times by Kurukshetra University, India and was awarded once by National Library of Poetry, US.

* * *

Ramesh Kumar Agrawal received M. Tech. degree in computer application from Indian Institute of Technology, Delhi. He has done his Ph.D. in computational physics from Delhi University. Presently, he is working as an Associate professor in School of Computer and Systems Sciences, Jawaharlal Nehru University, New Delhi. His current areas of research are classification, feature extraction and selection for pattern recognition problems in domains of image processing, security and bioinformatics.

Rodney Arambewela is a full-time staff member in the Faculty of Business and Law. Before working at Deakin University, he was employed as an International Business Development Manager at Telstra and as Trade Commissioner for Sri Lanka. He has over 20 years of international marketing experience and has worked in the UK, Europe, the Middle East and Asia and the Pacific. His research interests include International Education, Teaching and Learning, Customer Satisfaction, International Marketing, Services Marketing and Brand Management.

Manju Bala is a student of Ph.D. in School of Computer and Systems Sciences, Jawaharlal Nehru University, New Delhi. she received B. E. in Computer Science and Engineering from Maharishi Dayanand University and M. Tech. degree in Computer Science from IASE Deemed University, Rajasthan. Her current area of research is pattern recognition.

Vladimír Bureš, Ph.D., (*1977) is an assistant professor at the Faculty of Informatics and Management at the University of Hradec Kralove, Czech Republic. He cooperates with both the Department of Economics and Management and the Department of Information Technologies. He is the author of several books and papers published in conference proceedings and journals. He has been involved in several development and research projects. In his research activities he is focused on knowledge economy and knowledge management, theory of systems, e-learning and t-learning.

Pavel Čech, Ph.D., (*1976) is an assistant professor at the Department of Information Technologies, Faculty of Informatics and Management, University of Hradec Kralove, Czech Republic. In his research activities he deals with object modelling, programming, information and knowledge technologies, e-learning and t-learning. He has been working on more then 10 different projects (e.g. Hypergeo project funded by the 5th EU Framework IST Programme, ELU – Enhanced Learning Unlimited project funded by the 6th EU Framework IST Programme, VitalMind project funded by the 7th EU Framework IST Programme, or realization of information servers for tourism, ecology, security and quality).

Ankur Choubey, is presently studying Bachelor of Engineering 3rd year in Computer Sciences and Engineering from Institute of Technology and Management, Gurgaon, one of the topmost private colleges in Delhi-NCR, India. He did his schooling from Bhartiya Vidya Bhavan, New Delhi, India with a good academic record. Apart from his usual curriculum he has also received a one-month training on web development technology ASP.NET. Other technical skills include those of Java and C/C++. He has been actively trying to write some articles and papers to be submitted in international as well as national journals and magazines, including the college magazines within a few months. In addition to that he has received a BEC VANATAGE certification.

Joydip Dhar, is currently an assistant professor at IIITM, Gwalior, India. He holds a MSc. in Mathematics and a Ph. D in "Mathematical Modeling" from Indian Institute of Technology, Kanpur, India. Dr. Dhar has over 11 years of teaching experience, during which he has authored and co-authored more than 35 papers in various reputed International conferences and Journals. He is a former member of American Mathematical Society and a life time member of Indian Mathematical Society and Indian Society of Technical Education. He has guided and mentored several M Tech. and Ph. D. thesis in various research disciplines. In his free time, he seeks to spend most of his time with his family and holds a passion for Indian classical Music, Driving and Cricket.

Jitesh Dundas is currently working as a Research Associate at Edencore Technologies (www.edencore.net). He currently stays in Mumbai, India. Mr. Jitesh Dundas did his Masters in Computer Applications (M.C.A.) from Pune University in July 2007. He has worked as a Software Engineer with Kotak Mahindra Bank, KPIT Cummins. He has over 2 years of work experience in software development and research. He has written 3 research papers which are published in international conferences and journals. His areas of research areas include Computer Science, Cell and Molecular Biology and Bioinformatics. He is a member of societies like CSI, ACM and AICSIT. Mr. Dundas can be reached at jbdundas@gmail.com (Phone No: +91-9860925706).

S. Durga received the B.Tech degree in Information Technology from Madurai Kamraj University, Tamilnadu, the ME degree in Network s and Internet Engineering from Karunya University. She is currently a Assistant professor in the Department of Information Technology, Karunya University, Tamilnadu, India. Her current research interests include mobile computing, internetworking and security, and pervasive computing.

Manyata Goyal is currently a student of M Tech. at IIITM, Gwalior, India. Miss Manyata did her schooling from the town of Bina, in Madhya Pradesh. A bright student throughout her schooling, Miss Manyata has won several school level competitions. After coming to IIITM, Miss Manyata has heavily contributed in organization and management of various events and activities held at college and intra-college level. She is also a student member of ACM, CSI and IETE. She has active interests in programming and is a co-member of team, representing Indian in ACM world finals 2009, Sweden. Miss Manyata is passionate about learning new technologies and taking novel and difficult challenges. Her primary area of interest is Soft Computing techniques. In her spare time, she loves to read and play guitar.

Ratneshwer Gupta is a lecturer in Department of Computer Science (MMV), Banaras Hindu University, Varanasi (India). He is pursuing his PhD (verge to submission) from Department of Computer Engineering, Institute of Technology, Banaras Hindu University (India) under supervision of Dr. Anil K. Tripathi. His research area is Component Based Software Engineering. He is working on software processes, interdependence and composability issues of Component Based Software Engineering. He has four years of teaching experience and has 3 papers in international journals and 7 papers in international/national conference proceedings. He was awarded National Doctoral Fellowship by All India Council for Technical Education, New Delhi (India) and Junior Research Fellowship by University Grant Commission, India.

Shilp Gupta is currently a student of M Tech. at IIITM, Gwalior, India. Mr. Gupta did his schooling from Dehradoon, a town established at the foothills of Himalayas in upper northern regions of India. From a fairly young age, Mr. Gupta showed active interests in programming, and continued to win several school level programming contests. After coming to IIITM, Mr. Gupta continued his passion for programming and participated and got selected in several reputed programming contests organized by Google and ACM. His biggest achievement was to win the ACM Asia Regional this year, to head his team to ACM world finals 2009 at Sweden. He also has research interests primarily in the field of Artificial Neural Networks and Soft Computing Techniques. In his spare time, Mr. Gupta loves to watch Movies and listening to rock music.

Pawan Jain is working as an instructional designer at Fort Hays State University and received his PhD from University of Wyoming.

Smita Jain is working at Fort Hays State University and helping with the India expansion project. She received her MS degree in Instructional Technology.

Ashutosh Kasera is working as an Associate Professor at Rai Business School, New Delhi, India. His areas of interests are varied, including Computer Architecture, Computer Networks, Distributed DBMS, Data Structure, Design and Analysis of Algorithms, Software Engineering to name a few. Some of his major areas of research are Sustainable Development of ICT, ICT in rural segment and various aspects of e-learning. He has presented a number of research papers in various National and International conferences of repute along with a few of his publications in books. He is also working as a consultant in the field of applications of ICT and has been visiting, delivering lectures in his areas of expertise to a number of Institutes of repute.

Lutfi Mohammed Omer Khanbary Received the B.E.E. degree in 1995 from Aden University, Aden, Yemen, and the M.Tech. degree in 2006 from Jawaharlal Nehru University (JNU), New Delhi, India, where he is currently working toward the Ph.D. degree in computer science with the School of Computer and Systems Sciences, JNU, on study leave from the Department of Computer Science and Engineering, Aden University.His research interests include mobile computing, network management, and genetic algorithms.

K.V. Bhanu Murthy is Professor Department of Commerce, South Campus and Delhi School of Economics, Delhi University. He is a Ph.D. in Economics from Department of Economics, Delhi School of Economics, in the area of Industrialization Strategy. His recent contributions are in the areas of econometrics, environmental economics, agricultural market efficiency, international business social responsibility and business ethics. He has received several awards including best paper awards and best economics expert award. He has more than 30 papers in international journals and conferences. He has done two international and one national project.

Ravi Prakash Pandey has completed his graduation in Science from Saket College Faizabad, India. He achieved the post graduate degree in Management from Dr. R. M.L. Avadh University, Faizabad, India and in Computer Application from IGNOU, India. He started his teaching career in engineering education from DR. RML Avadh University, Faizabad, India. He is working as a Senior Lecturer in the Institute of Engineering and Technology, Dr. R. M.L. Avadh University, Faizabad, India. He has more than 10 years of experience to teach the undergraduate and postgraduate classes. He has published more than 20 research papers in national and international journal/conference in the area of management, wireless sensor network, mobile ad hoc network, and image processing. He has delivered numerous invited and plenary conference presentations and seminars in International and national conferences in India. He has delivered many invited talks in India. His research area includes International Business Management, wireless sensor network, mobile ad hoc network, and image processing. He has guided more than100 students for their projects on Java, C, C++.

Sunita Prasad is currently working as a Sr. Lecturer in Centre for Development of Advanced Computing (CDAC), NOIDA, India under M/O Information Technology, Govt. of India. She received her M.Tech (IT) from Guru Gobind Singh Indrapratha University in 2006. Her research interest lie in the field of wireless networking especially ad hoc networks routing optimization and security. She is a life member of Institution of Electronics and Telecommunication Engineering (IETE) and published many papers in National and International conferences.

Piyush Ranjan is working as an Associate Professor in the area of Information Technology at Rai Business School, New Delhi. He is a man of high caliber and expertise in Web- based programming and Database management. His interest of teaching includes MIS, Web Programming, Database Management System and Network Administration. He is also an IT consultant and has been a visiting faculty member in a number of Management Institutes of repute. His current research area includes Environmental Impact of Microprocessor technology, Sustainable Development of Computer Technology, ICT for remote Indian villages & e- learning. He has presented a number of research papers at various National & International Conferences.

Sanjeev Sharma is a Reader and Head of the School of Information Technology, Rajiv Gandhi Prodyogiki Vishwavidyalaya, Bhopal, M.P. (Bhopal), India. He started his teaching career in engineering education from Vidisha District, India. He has more than 12 years of experience to teach the undergraduate and postgraduate classes. He has published more than 39 research papers in national and international journal/conference in the area of wireless sensor network, mobile Computing and Data Mining. He has delivered numerous invited and plenary conference presentations and seminars in International and national conferences in India. He has delivered many invited talks in India. His research area includes wireless sensor network, mobile Computing and Data Mining. He has guided more than 53 students for their M. Tech. dissertations. He has no. of projects funded by U.G.C. or A.I.C.T.E., India. He is member of various committees in India.

Raj Shree has completed her graduation in Science from Bareilly College, Bareilly, India. She achieved the post graduate degree in Computer Technology & Application from Rajiv Gandhi Prodyogiki Vishwavidyalaya, Bhopal, India. She started her teaching career in engineering education from Sahu Ram Swaroop Mahila Mahavidya, Bareilly, India. She also served M.J.P Rohilkhand University, Bareilly. She has more than 5.8 years of experience to teach the undergraduate and postgraduate classes. Ms. Raj Shree is a Lecturer in the Department of Information Technology, SIST, Baba Saheb Bhimrao Ambedkar University, Lucknow. Her field of research includes various fields of Wireless Ad Hoc Networks, Sensor Networks, Mobile Computing, Routing Security. She has published around 15 papers in various national and international journals/conferences including IEEE explorer also. She topped in her post graduation from RGTU, Bhopal. She has delivered numerous conference presentations and seminars in the International and national conferences in India.

Vivek Shukla has completed his graduation in Science from Bareilly College Bareilly, India. He achieved the post graduate degree in Physics from Bareilly College, Bareilly, India, Computer Application from Dr. R. M.L. Avadh University, Faizabad . He started his teaching career in Science education from Bareilly College, Bareilly, India. He also served Sanjivi College of Engineering and Technology, Baharaich as a Lecturer. Now He is pursuing his M. Tech. degree in Computer Technology & Application from Rajiv Gandhi Prodyogiki Vishwavidyalaya, Bhopal, India. He has more than 7 years of experience to teach the undergraduate and postgraduate classes. He has published more than 15 research papers in national and international journal/conference in the area of wireless sensor network, mobile ad hoc network. He has delivered no. of conference presentations and seminars in International and national conferences in India. His research area includes wireless sensor network, mobile ad hoc network.

Ramesh Singh is working as a Senior Scientist at National Informatics Centre, New Delhi, India. He is heading "Systems Software Division", at NIC, New Delhi. Prior to joining NIC, He worked as a Scientist in DRDO. He has worked extensively in the O.S, Database Management Systems and other System Software's. He also heads National Digital Preservation Initiative at National Informatics Centre. He has studied at IIT, Kahragpur and at IIT Delhi. He holds a M.Tech degree in Computer Applications from IIT Delhi. He actively participates in academia in and around New Delhi. He is a visiting faculty at IIT New Delhi, and teaches Computer Graphics at Undergraduate Level. He is also a visiting faculty at Delhi College of Engineering, New Delhi and teaches Human Computer Interface (HCI) and Distributed Computing at the M.Tech Level in the institute. His Present research interests are in the field of Mobile

Computing, Ubiquitous and Pervasive Computing and Human Computer Interface respectively. He has to his credit more than twenty five International research papers and five book chapters.

Abhishek Vaid is currently a student of M Tech. at IIITM, Gwalior, India. Mr. Vaid did his schooling from Delhi, and too admission at IIITM, through an all Indian Examination – AIEEE in 2004. During his Higher Education, Mr. Vaid has worked on several projects both in technical and Managerial domain. His current research interests are primarily in Software Engineering, Data Mining, Personality Assessment Techniques, Multi-Objective Optimizations Techniques and Soft Computing Techniques. Mr. Vaid holds author to more than 4 papers during his B. Tech and M. Tech. and seeks to pursue a Ph. D. in future. In his spare time, he loves listening to Music and browsing lucrative buying deals online.

Deo Prakash Vidyarthi Received the Master degree in computer applications from M. M. M. Engineering College, Gorakhpur, India, in 1991 and the Ph.D. in computer science from Jabalpur University, Jabalpur, India (work done at Banaras Hindu University, Varanasi, India) in 2002. He taught undergraduate and postgraduate students at the Department of Computer Science, Banaras Hindu University, for over 12 years. He is currently an Associate Professor with the School of Computer and Systems Sciences, Jawaharlal Nehru University, New Delhi, India. His research interests include parallel and distributed system, grid computing, and mobile computing.

Index